How to Plan, Develop, and Implement
LOTUS NOTES
in Your Organization

MIKE FALKNER

Wiley Computer Publishing

John Wiley & Sons, Inc.

New York • Chichester • Brisbane • Toronto • Singapore

Publisher: Katherine Schowalter
Editor: Theresa Hudson
Managing Editor: Micheline Frederick
Text Design & Composition: North Market Street Graphics, Selena Chronister

This text is printed on acid-free paper.

This publication is designed to provide accurate and authoritative information in regard to the subject matter covered. It is sold with the understanding that the publisher is not engaged in rendering legal, accounting, or other professional service. If legal advice or other expert assistance is required, the services of a competent professional person should be sought.

John Wiley & Sons, Inc. is an accredited member of the IBM Independent Vendor League.

Library of Congress Cataloging-in-Publication Data:
Falkner, Michael.
    How to plan, develop, and implement Lotus Notes in your
  organization / Michael Falkner.
          p.   cm.
    Includes index.
    ISBN 0-471-12570-9 (pbk./CD-ROM : alk. paper)
    1. Lotus Notes for Windows.   2. Business—Computer programs.
  3. Database management—Computer programs.   4. Electronic mail
  systems.   I. Title.
  HF5548.4.L692F35   1996
  650'.0285'46—dc20   95-50548
                                                          CIP

Printed in the United States of America
10 9 8 7 6 5 4

Dedicated to Dan for strengthening my personal vision, to Bill for taking our vision for Notes and implementing it beyond my imagination, and to Jon for his support and confidence that his Dad could really finish this book.

C O N T E N T S

Chapter 6   Presenting the Vision for Notes   125

Chapter 7   Implementing Notes   145

Chapter 8   Developing Applications in Notes   185

Chapter 9   50 Ways to Use Notes   **217**

INTRODUCTION

Most of us justified the purchase of our personal computer by listing our numerous requirements for word processing, spreadsheets, and data management. If the decision was still nip and tuck, we threw in the need to hook up to the company minicomputer or to an on-line service such as CompuServe. In no time, our world was well-structured for us—we cranked out document or spreadsheets, printed over the network, and saved the files on a server somewhere.

Despite periodic visits to a software store to stay current on the latest software, very few of us had heard much about a package called Lotus Notes. Then, one day, the corporate zealot stopped by with a laptop to show us "the future." Soon, the IS department was mandating Lotus Notes as the new electronic mail package. All of a sudden, everyone was talking about it, databases were popping up all over the network, and we were growing increasingly curious about this new phenomenon. Soon, whether you sought it out or it found you, Lotus Notes was changing the way you and your colleagues exchanged information. With Notes, companies were eliminating paperwork and delivering a wealth of knowledge to employees and trading partners. Employees were building ad hoc systems to solve simple business needs without a programming staff. Everybody wanted their information in Notes!

When I first experienced Notes as a member of an internal information systems group, I had a lot of questions with few sources for answers. Sure, the manuals told me how to build databases, write programs, and send mail. What I really needed, however, was a source of information that could explain what Notes was; the kind of impact of Notes would have on our company; what kind of resources, time, and money we would need to take care of it; and how we could best use the product to change our company for the better. The purpose of this book is to become one source of information on Lotus Notes and a guidebook for all the issues that surround it. We'll explore the product and the components that make it up. We'll look at the way Notes will change your company and what it takes to make it a success. We'll investigate the culture that surrounds Notes and we'll look at 50 sample applications that may spark your own imagination for a Notes solution to your own challenges.

How To Use This Book

How to Plan, Develop, and Implement Lotus Notes in Your Organization covers a broad spectrum of topics, starting with an overview of Notes and its long history, working through the discovery, planning, and implementation stages of bringing Notes in your organization, and ending with a look to the future of Notes. It makes no assumptions about your level of Notes knowledge. Instead, it strives to guide you from wherever you are to a fuller understanding of Notes and what it can do for you.

As you read this book, picture yourself in a meeting room with a consultant who has been hired to tell you all that you want to know about Notes. He or she can explain the history, tell you war stories about implementing or programming Notes, and philosophize about the future of Notes. He or she can demonstrate the product, show you a few databases, and even build a quick database for you. The consultant is here to serve you, and you can pick and choose what you want to learn.

Your new paper consultant, *How to Plan, Develop, and Implement Lotus Notes in Your Organization,* is also designed to help you choose what you want to learn. Although each chapter builds on a base of knowledge that expands with the next, the book is also designed to allow you to move quickly to the chapters that cover your area of interest. For example, if you have not experienced Notes, the early chapters will help you understand where it came from and what features the product has. More experienced users may want to move quickly to the chapters on planning, implementing, or developing for Notes. The following synopsis is provided to help you use the book more effectively:

Chapter 1: *What Is Notes?*	Describes the Lotus Notes product, the history of its development, its market position, and why you should choose it for your company.
Chapter 2: *The Components of Lotus Notes*	Describes the feature and capabilities of Lotus Notes and the terms used to describe it.

Chapter 3: *How Notes Will Change You and Your Company*

Discusses the evolution of workgroup computing and the changes that will occur in the user community and information systems groups as Notes arrives on the scene.

Chapter 4: *Assimilating Notes*

Explores the five phase of acceptance when bringing Notes into an organization, and examines both the user and Notes provider perspective.

Chapter 5: *The Best and Worst Ways to Use Notes*

Examines the tasks for which Notes is well suited and those tasks for which Notes is not a good candidate.

Chapter 6: *Presenting the Vision for Notes*

Builds a case for implementing Notes through the development of a proposal to top management.

Chapter 7: *Implementing Notes*

Walks you through the planning and implementation of Notes into your organization.

Chapter 8: *Developing Applications in Notes*

Describes the infrastructure required to support Notes development, and discusses the development and maintenance process.

Chapter 9: *50 Ways to Use Notes*

Details the purpose and content of 50 Notes databases provided on the CD-ROM that accompanies this book.

Chapter 10: *Developing a Notes Application*

Walks you through the complete development cycle of a Notes database.

Chapter 11: *The Morning After*

Describes a day in the life of ABC Company after Notes is installed and the 50 databases are deployed into the user community.

Chapter 12: *The Culture Surrounding Lotus Notes*

Describes the organizations that support Lotus Notes and the services that they provide.

Chapter 13: *Notes Add-Ons and Third-Party Products*

Covers many of the third-party products available to enhance Lotus Notes and applications built with it.

Chapter 14: *The Lotus Notes Future*

Discusses the viability of Notes in the marketplace and what Notes might look like in the future.

Appendix A: *A Summary of Notes 4.0 Features*

Provides an overview of the new features available in Lotus Notes version 4.0.

Appendix B: *Loading and Using the Software*

Provides detailed instructions on how to install the software on the accompanying CD-ROM.

About the Author

MIKE FALKNER has been a developer, user support and network manager, Bix Six Consultant, IS manager, and an author, columnist, and contributing editor for *PC Computing*. He has also written over 100 articles for trade publications including *PC Magazine, Computer Shopper,* and *Windows Sources.* He currently works for an accounting software firm where he headed the team that implemented Notes into the organization.

He welcomes all comments about *How to Plan, Develop, and Implement Lotus Notes in Your Organization* and may be reached at 0003314955 @mcimail.com.

How to Plan, Develop, and Implement
LOTUS NOTES
in Your Organization

What Is Notes?

Notes, Notes, Notes! All everyone talks about is Notes!

Sound familiar? Lotus Notes is taking corporate America by storm as computer users, information systems departments, and managers discover the power it brings to their desktop. For years, computer users have been looking for an effective way to share information with their co-workers, vendors, and customers. They want a product that can become the repository of the knowledge for their company and can facilitate access to that information. They want the databases to understand their business rules and forward information to them when they need to know it.

Lotus Notes does all of this and more. Take a look at a typical Notes installation today and you'll find users obtaining electronic approvals for purchase requisitions, invoices, vacations, and expense reports. You'll see customers and resellers tapping databases containing technical specifications, procedures, and marketing information that is updated on a daily basis. Every user's electronic mailbox automatically forwards messages, reminders, action items, and links to other key information to their desktop.

But, the magnitude of its capabilities often makes Notes a difficult product to explain. Ask five people to describe Notes and they'll give you five different answers because Notes fills a different need for each one of them. Even Lotus sometimes has trouble describing Notes, as evidenced by this definition given in a Lotus marketing presentation: "Notes is a graphical, client-server application development and deployment platform, enabling a whole new class of applications."

In a very simple sentence, Notes stores information, displays it, and moves it throughout your organization. It helps typical office users store information for others to share, and it helps them find and view the information quickly. For the person who creates systems for the company, Notes provides a programming environment that supports rapid development of solutions to business problems. Remote users can view or download information with a few mouse clicks. The research analyst can arrive in the morning and find that Notes has polled several databases and retrieved the latest information during the night.

So far, we've talked in general terms about Notes and it's time to really get into what the package is all about. If we analyze the components of Notes, we'll find that it is all of the following:

- ◆ a database
- ◆ a word processor
- ◆ a remote communications package
- ◆ a client-server application
- ◆ a replicator
- ◆ an electronic mail system
- ◆ a desktop assistant
- ◆ a development environment

Obviously, there is a lot to know about Notes and, as you begin to understand it, you'll be able to see how the pieces work together to build a powerful information engine. Let's take a closer look into each of these components and begin our exploration of Notes.

Notes Is a Database

First and foremost, Notes is a database for storing text, numbers, pictures, and even files from applications like Microsoft Word or Lotus 1-2-3. You enter the information into formatted screens called forms, as shown in Figure 1.1.

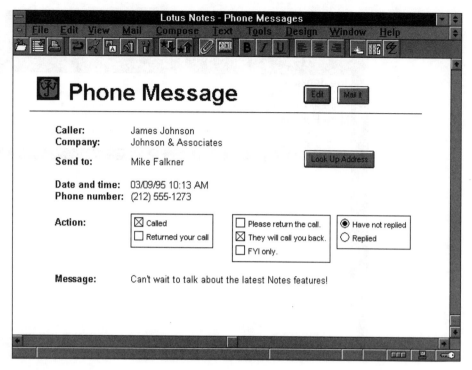

FIGURE 1.1 A Notes form.

All the information stored in a single form is called a document. You can display a summary of your documents in report-like screens called views, as shown in Figure 1.2. You can sort the information, search on it, filter it, print it, and even create links to other documents in the database.

I know, you're wondering why not just buy a good database like Lotus Approach or Microsoft Access that does the same stuff. They have great graphical tools for developing some pretty sophisticated screens and very attractive reports. Microsoft Access includes a programming language and Lotus Approach even accesses Notes databases. In fact, both Approach and Access can run circles around Notes—if you just want to develop a traditional database application.

But with a traditional database, it's up to you to find the database on the network and pull out the information you need. The database resides on a server somewhere, and you can only access the information when you are connected to the network. Someone in the IS department or a consultant usually customizes the screens and reports for you unless you are a programmer with rights to change the database design. When changes are made, everyone has to live with them.

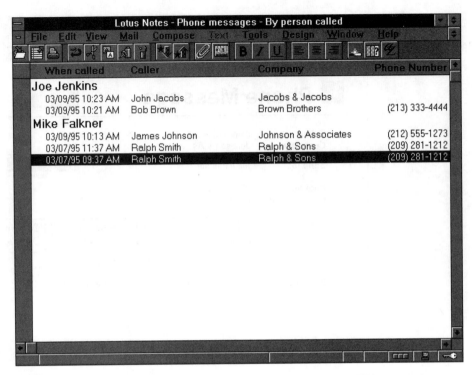

FIGURE 1.2   A Notes view.

Notes has some of the characteristics of a traditional database and it is often used much like one. However, many people create systems in Notes that move the information to the places where they need it, when they need it, and without huge development costs. Notes databases have electronic mail built into them so documents can be mailed to other databases. Several copies of the same database can reside on servers throughout the network, on servers in other buildings or states, and on a local PC, and Notes worries about how the data is synchronized. Users can customize the way they look at their data without changing the database for others.

Notes Is a Word Processor

Any Notes form can contain one or more fields called Rich Text fields that can accept large volumes of text information. As you add information to one of these fields, Notes acts like a word processor, using a rudimentary ruler to control tabs, paragraph indents, word wraps, and margins, as shown in the message section of Figure 1.3.

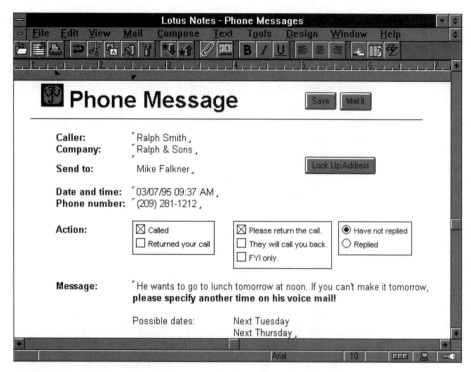

FIGURE 1.3 Notes as a word processor.

Notes supports fonts and attributes such as bold, underline, and italics, and it can create simple tables. When users want to store an excerpt from a word processing document, they can simply use Cut to move the excerpt to the clipboard and Paste to place it in Notes.

Admittedly, the Notes word processing features are not as sophisticated as a Microsoft Word or WordPerfect; they exist so you can create documents that can be displayed and printed with the look you'd expect from a Windows document. Most users will agree that Notes can be frustrating to work with at times (just try building a Notes table quickly) and that it is not the best at importing formatted text from other packages. Still, it is still a powerful enough tool to format documents nicely and print them in a publishable form.

Notes Is a Remote Communications Package

When you call a server from your remote PC, Notes accepts the connection and regards you as a local network connection. With Notes, you can browse through databases and add information as if you were sitting next to the server. Sure, it can cost a bundle in phone charges if you do it every day, but if you need to access some information right away, you don't have to leave the comfort of Notes to get to it.

As more of your business contacts begin to use Notes, they may request a server-to-server connection between your server and theirs. Notes can be set up to automatically call any other Notes server at almost any interval. Without your intervention, one Notes server can call another Notes server, exchange information and electronic mail, and then hang up and call the next server in its list of possible connections. Research services like the Gartner Group now offer their newsletters and information via Notes so you can download it electronically instead of waiting for it in your inbox.

Notes Is a Client-Server Application

On a traditional network, a local workstation (or client) simply attaches to a server and creates drive letters like F: or G: to represent the disk space on the server. Any time you perform an operation like sorting a database on the server, the local PC is used to process the sort, and both the PC and the server transfer millions of bytes over the network during the process.

Notes uses the client-server architecture to improve performance and minimize network traffic. In the client-server model, the software on the client machine connects to an application running on the server that, in turn, controls the databases. To perform a sort for a view in the Notes client-server environment, the Notes client sends a command to the Notes server to perform the sort at the server. The Notes server processes the request and returns only the items required to display the view. If the connection to the server is lost, Notes will notify you of the error but still remain logically connected to the database. When the connection is reestablished, Notes can continue to work in the database in most cases as if the connection was never lost.

Notes Is a Replicator

By now, you've probably heard the word "replicate" bandied about by those already initiated into the Notes fraternity. Replication means that Notes can automatically synchronize the data in multiple copies of the same database. It is one of the most powerful features of Notes, allowing you to place copies of the same database wherever they are needed. Notes keeps track of the relationships between the original database and replicas (or copies) of that database and updates the replicas as often as you determine.

Notes remembers every time you add or change information in a database. If there is another copy of the database on the network somewhere, Notes will automatically update both your database and the copy; it's as if you were both entering information into the same database. Notes will replicate the database based on a schedule that the Notes administrator sets up, and, if the database resides outside the network on another Notes server, your server can be programmed to call the other server via modem and automatically replicate its information.

Figure 1.4 is an example of the power of Notes replication. The training department updates the training schedules in the morning. Users in the marketing department upstairs sign up for a class at 9:30 and remote users in Dallas do the same at 8:30. During the day, Notes will update each server with the new schedules and the people who have signed up for classes.

This feature is a boon to people on the road who want more than just electronic mail capabilities from the home office. Any database that resides on a server can also reside on a local PC. When the PC calls the home server, it can synchronize any local databases with their counterparts on that server. Although Notes also allows you to stay connected to a server as if you were on the local network, replication simply brings the information you need to your local PC so you can use it when and where you need it.

Notes Is an Electronic Mail System

Along with replication, mail is the Notes feature that helps you move information effortlessly throughout the network. Actions taken in a data entry form can automatically generate messages to the people who need to know that something has changed. You can mail any document in the database to any Notes user simply by selecting a Mail command from a menu.

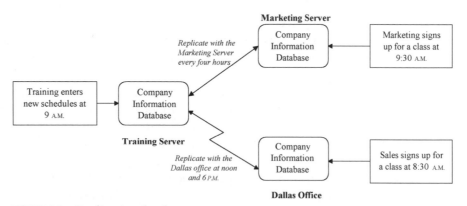

FIGURE 1.4 Replicating databases.

Your electronic mailbox is a Notes database like all the other databases in Notes, which means you can completely customize it to match your needs. The menu option to send mail is always active on your Notes menu bar, so, if you decide to send a message while you are in another database, you can simply access the Mail menu, create and send the message, and then return to the screen you were working on.

Best of all, *any database* can become a mailbox. Any form can be programmed to send the document that you are creating via electronic mail to a database. If you want all timecards to go to the home office, for example, you can distribute a custom form to everyone who accepts the timecard information and mail it to the timecard database, wherever it may be. In this way, users don't need to access the timecard database to enter timecard information.

Notes Is a Desktop Assistant

Notes uses folders and icons to help you organize your databases and recognize what they are. When you open a database for the first time or simply add a database to your desktop, Notes places an icon on your desktop that represents the database. The icon identifies the database name, its location on the network, and the number of documents that you have not yet read. Double-click on the icon and Notes opens the database (see Figure 1.5).

In version 3.0 of Notes, the desktop has six folders that help you to organize your databases. Once Notes has achieved widespread use throughout your company, there will be plenty of database icons to fill the folder, so it's helpful to organize the icons as you add them. Each tab on the folder contains the name of the folder, and you can move databases between folders as your needs change.

Version 4.0 enhances the usefulness of the desktop screen by allowing more tabs, consolidating menus, and supporting one icon to represent many replicas of one database.

Following the Lotus SmartSuite standard (a standard established for their suite of office automation application called SmartSuite), Notes has a customizable toolbar that can enhance any application that you develop. Toolbar icons can be customized with scripts to automate your most common tasks like composing a mail message or loading your favorite database. Notes also comes with predefined icons for tasks such as attaching files and changing fonts; you can also cycle through different sets of toolbars using the toolbar button at the bottom of the screen.

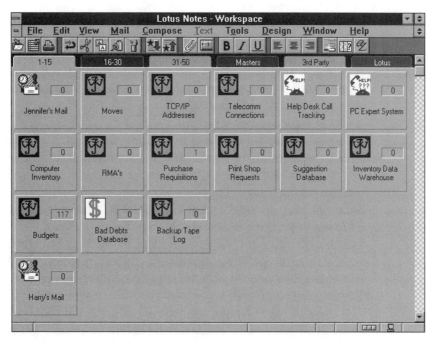

FIGURE 1.5   The version 3.0 desktop.

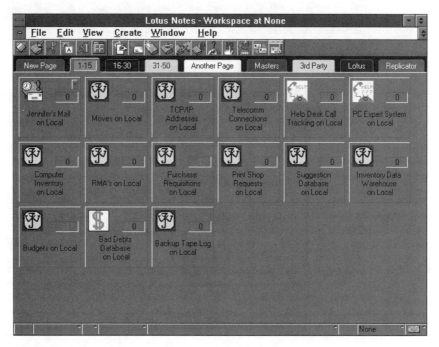

FIGURE 1.6   The version 4.0 desktop.

Notes Is a Development Environment

Notes comes with a good set of tools to develop the forms and views you need to add and manage the information in your database. Lotus ships the product with starter databases, called templates, that can be used as a foundation for your own databases. These databases already have forms and views set up that are copied into your new database. With templates, you can create a working database in a couple of minutes. If you prefer, you can modify the template or just create your own database from scratch.

Any field or button in a Notes form can be enhanced by using the Notes script language. These scripts are a combination of spreadsheet-like functions such as **@IF** and **@ISNUMBER,** and commands that emulate the features on the Notes menu bar such as File Save. Figure 1.7 shows an example of using the script language to build a Save button. For more sophisticated users, Notes 4.0 now includes LotusScript, a BASIC-like language that allows even greater control of your forms and views than the Notes macro language.

The success of Notes has also created a demand for more sophisticated hooks from Notes into other databases. In response, Lotus has created a

FIGURE 1.7   Creating a Save button.

C language interface to Notes called the Notes API (Applications Programming Interface) that allows you to develop programs that tap the same routines that Lotus uses to execute Notes functions. With another development tool, Notes ViP, you can create Notes applications using object-oriented tools to access a variety of databases. Third-party packages such as Info-Pump enhance Notes development by allowing you to move information between SQL databases and Notes.

The History of Notes

This brief overview of Notes demonstrates how versatile and broad the capabilities of the product really are. This breadth is the result of years of vision, planning, and development that started over 10 years ago. Let's take a quick look at the roots of Notes to help you understand how it became what it is today.

Notes is the brainchild of Ray Ozzie, president of Iris Associates, the company that developed Notes. Ozzie wanted to build a software product that would make it easier for computer users to work together, a concept that has become popularized as groupware. In the early 1980s, Ozzie had started work on Notes when Lotus Development founder Mitch Kapor convinced him to join Lotus to develop a new, integrated product called Symphony that combined spreadsheet, word processing, graphics, communications, and database features into one package.

When Symphony was released, it enjoyed moderate success despite the general resistance to an all-in-one package. Lotus then funded Ozzie to continue his work on Notes; from that deal, Iris Associates was born in 1984. Lotus purchased the source code for Notes in 1988, and by late 1989, Lotus Notes was finally introduced to the world. Lotus was and continues to be responsible for the sales, marketing, and support of Notes while Iris Associates develops and enhances the product, receiving development fees and royalties on each copy sold.

Only in the last two years has Notes become prominent in the marketplace. When Notes was first announced, the term groupware was fairly new and there wasn't much on the market that fit into the category. Lotus targeted large corporations, selling 200 user licenses directly to corporations to the tune of $62,500. Although the product impressed people with the power of its replication feature, it often disappointed them when they tried to use the interface.

Steady improvements in the product and ongoing marketing efforts continued to generate demand as corporations began to realize the power of Notes. By version 3.0, Lotus had made significant enhancements to the product, enough to set off a surge of growth as most major corporations added Notes to their list of technologies to consider.

But though Notes 3.0 continued to be popular, the approximate $300 per-user street price was still a barrier to prospects who might be able to use Notes but who didn't need it or want to pay for the development environment. Many users just wanted a run-time version so they could access databases and use the forms developed by the home office. To reach this market, Lotus introduced a $99 version of Notes in early 1994 called Notes Express. Unfortunately, Notes Express was not the product that everyone wanted. Instead of a slimmed-down product that acts like Notes, Lotus created a much more limited product that only allowed access to databases that were created using five templates. Information managers and users found it difficult to justify buying a product that couldn't share the databases that they had already developed. Notes Express was soundly trounced in the trade rags and failed to garner widespread popularity.

By 1994, Notes was generating a significant share of Lotus' revenues, and Lotus was paying Iris Associates large royalty payments on the sales of Notes licenses. Lotus had sold almost 1 million copies of Notes and, with renewed marketing efforts to grab market share before Microsoft released its groupware software, Lotus was expecting an even larger increase in Notes sales. In May 1994, Lotus acquired Iris Associates and made it a wholly owned subsidiary, a move attributed to a need to eliminate the growing royalty payments and protect its investment in Notes.

It didn't take long for Lotus to recover from the Notes Express episode. The company announced at Lotusphere 95 Lotus Notes Desktop, the $155 run-time version that was the product that everyone wanted. Notes Desktop does not allow users to modify an application, but it will run any application developed in the full version of Notes. The product is a boon for large sites that cringed at the cost of full deployment knowing that only a handful of users would really develop anything in Notes.

The Future of Notes

As Notes grew in popularity, Lotus realized that its direct sales approach could not effectively service the surging demand for the product. In 1993, it switched marketing gears and moved to the reseller channel to sell Notes. Lotus created several opportunities for resellers in Notes sales and consulting activities through its Business Partners program. For as little as $495, a Business Solution Partner can buy Notes (and other products) and become eligible to resell it to customers. Active value added resellers (VARs) can sign up for the Premium Business Partner program and receive more benefits from Lotus by selling a minimum number of Notes licenses.

The reseller strategy has been very successful for Lotus. There are over 5,000 Notes partners and a burgeoning number of Notes consultants throughout the United States. Lotus aggressively markets Notes through ad campaigns and direct mailers to customers and potential leads. Companies that sign up for support automatically receive a database with the names of all the Lotus partners shown in views sorted by product offered, type of Business Partner, state, and other items.

Following the successful certification model espoused by Novell for years, Lotus also created the Lotus Notes Certification Program to help end users identify qualified Notes consultants and vendors. Partners can become Lotus Notes Certified (LNC) Specialists and Lotus Notes Certified Instructors and advertise the accreditation to bring in more business. If a partner belongs to the Lotus developer programs, they must have one and possibly two LNCs on the payroll to continue in the program.

Lotus is also building the market appeal of Notes by encouraging other vendors to integrate their products with it. Accounting software vendors, such as Great Plains Software, have created integration modules that allow their software to communicate with Notes. When you enter an invoice, for example, the accounting software can be programmed to send a mail message to Notes to the person who needs to approve it. The recipient clicks on the approval button in Notes and a message is sent back to the accounting software to fill in the approval box with the appropriate information.

The idea of integration appeals to most software vendors because few of them have the resources and cash to build a sophisticated workflow engine like Notes into their software. For example, flowchart software vendor AllClear now uses Notes as a repository for the flowcharts that its clients develop so that users can find the correct chart easily and quickly. Many companies are also discovering that Notes can be a valuable way to communicate with their customers and suppliers. In addition, because the cost of buying enough hardware and phone lines to support the thousands of potential connections can be prohibitive, Lotus teamed up with companies like CompuServe and AT&T to offer access to Notes services without the big cash outlay.

These vendors have placed Notes servers in almost every major metropolitan area so you can reach almost any customer or vendor that you want. It's up to your server to call and download your databases regularly. From then on, based on a schedule that you agree on, the AT&T servers replicate the information throughout its network. You pay for replication services, access time, and any other services that you use—a bargain compared to ramping up for hundreds or thousands of vendors calling your server.

With these services in place, you can see that Notes could evolve into a tool for small business or even home use. Imagine your favorite mail order vendor with a database of its products available online in your local area. You could download the latest catalogue, look for items that suit your fancy, and order them using a form in Notes. The vendor could send you one electronic mail message confirming your order and another to tell you that it's been shipped.

Small businesses have many of the same administrative problems as large businesses but usually can't afford a full-time Notes person on staff. But thanks to the large number of Notes resellers and consultants, Lotus has created an infrastructure for its product that enables it to support these small businesses. Consultants that used to just sell accounting software now offer Notes consulting and support as well. As a part of its service offering, AT&T sells help desk support for any Notes user on its network.

Lotus announces new alliances and even grander plans for Notes on almost a monthly basis. Chapter 14 goes into more details about other new Notes technologies and alliances. Many of the items may even be available by the time this book is published, and, with a barrage of new announcements always in the queue, that chapter may never be complete.

The recent buyout of Lotus by IBM Corporation also signals a whole new set of possibilities for Lotus Notes. Over the years, Lotus has spent a lot of money and energy to give Notes the commanding market lead it has today. But faced with less-than-stellar profit figures, Lotus needs to expend even more resources to firmly establish Notes as the workgroup standard and stave off its completion. IBM offers a large bankroll and extensive marketing channels that can solidify Notes' leadership in the industry.

The Competition

Notes has been so successful because it really has no competition that can match all of its features and functions. Microsoft realized several years ago that Notes gives Lotus an entrée into most corporations and a huge opportunity to sell its other products. Microsoft has successfully gained market share for many of their workgroup products such as Microsoft Office but until recently it hadn't been able to field anything comparable to Notes. Then, Microsoft Exchange was released.

Exchange is a new messaging and workgroup engine that Microsoft hopes will unseat Notes as the workgroup leader. Like Notes, in Exchange you can create forms and views as well as replicate information between servers. Microsoft's standard programming language, Visual Basic, is also included with Exchange, and the product runs on popular client platforms such as Windows, Unix, and Macintosh.

Exchange concentrates much more heavily on mail and predefined workgroup applications. It stores information as messages in folders, as compared to Notes which stores it in a database as a document. Notes ships with some predefined applications including a call-tracking system and rudimentary mail, but most workgroup applications development must be purchased or developed internally. Exchange, on the other hand, comes heavily laden with workgroup tools for group scheduling, electronic forms, and electronic mail.

While Microsoft's entry into the workgroup environment gives Lotus some competition, Exchange still doesn't offer the flexibility of the Notes databases, forms, and views. Notes applications appear to be much more intuitive, and the market is full of third-party applications that tap into them. Exchange was built to service mail, scheduling, and forms. Notes was built for developing sophisticated database applications.

For several years, Novell's GroupWise software (formerly called Word-Perfect Office) has come close to creating the kind of workflow environment that Notes offers. The product has electronic mail, forms routing (via InForms), to-do's, calendaring, and meeting scheduling, and it supports forums where users can add messages and responses. Further, the software can be loaded on DOS, Windows, Macintosh, and Unix clients.

Like Exchange, GroupWise focuses on the core of the workgroup applications—calendars, schedules, and mail. Novell has opened up GroupWise by creating an architecture called the Collaborative Computing Environment (CCE) that allows developers to integrate different groupware front ends or components into it. In effect, Novell is offering GroupWise as a solution while making it easy for other companies or internal staff to simply use parts of it while substituting products that make a better fit. In fact, Notes can exchange with GroupWise without interface software.

As you consider Exchange and GroupWise as Notes competitors, you will realize that these two industry giants are not heading down the same path as Lotus. Microsoft and Novell have built sophisticated mail servers that move messages throughout an organization and give you some flexibility in how you view them. With Notes, in contrast, you can create a database that stands alone as a system, or you can build a database that spawns messages to users and mails information to other databases. The focus is on the power of the database, not the electronic mail engine; therefore, with Notes, you do have to customize your mail database to add items like a to-do list, and you must create a database to have a discussion forum.

Notes succeeds in taking on the big guns in addition to competing with other electronic mail packages including Lotus' own cc:Mail. Notes ships with the mail function built into it. Version 3.x doesn't have all the bells and whistles of a package like cc:Mail, but most users don't need a high-powered mail package to send the kind of messages they write. Besides, version 4.0 solved the problem by modifying the Notes mail system to allow you to use cc:Mail for Windows as your default Notes mail application instead of a Notes database.

What makes Notes mail different from other mail systems is that it, too, is a database. It not only sends mail but can also be programmed to perform other tasks. You can compose a message from within any database and program it to route messages automatically with the push of a button. People seriously considering Notes will want to think about dropping their current electronic mail package to benefit from these features and to eliminate the costs of supporting the other mail system.

The popularity of groupware has also spawned entry-level products like Collabra Share that have groupware features without a development language. Share users can post messages in forums, categorize the topics, and view the contents of the forum in a three-part window that is similar to the new Notes 4.0 look. The recent purchase of Collabra by Netscape makes it attractive to active Internet users who want basic groupware functionality without building their own internal network for accessing information.

Notes has also made serious inroads into the market for PC-based text retrieval systems, a segment owned by a very small group of software vendors. One of the leaders, Folio Corporation, owns a large share of the DOS and Windows markets and is still a popular solution for people who manage bulletin boards and want to provide their customers access to information. Folio announced its plans to bridge its Views software to Notes so its users can benefit from Folio's superior search capabilities while allowing them to have the data available in Notes. Folio created Folio Filter to allow users to cut, paste, and save Notes information to a Folio database. It's Apply Query feature helps users access Views from Notes and search both Notes and Views databases. To complete the bridge, Folio added a DocLinks module to create hot links between Notes and Views databases.

In larger companies, document management is big business and Notes is a good candidate for siphoning some of the demand away from these vendors. Document management systems allow users to store documents in an electronic library and control changes and updates to those documents. These systems often have features that route documents to the appropriate editors and approvers and track and store versions of a document. Their library functions allow you to find documents quickly, check them out for changes, or even merge several documents.

With some creative development efforts, Notes can replace some of these functions and capture more customers. As with most of the Notes quasi-competitors, however, many of the document management firms are integrating with Notes to enhance their products and maintain their position with their users. Packages such as the Saros Document Manager and PC DOCS are still much better suited to the massive number of documents that must be stored and they often use a powerful database back end such as Sybase, Oracle, or Microsoft SQL Server as the document repository.

Notes and the Internet

The popularity of the Internet has added a new twist to the way companies are thinking about sharing information. Before the popularity of the World Wide Web (WWW), there were very few sources of information that were accessible and easy to use on the Internet. As soon as Web browsers like Netscape became readily available and cheap, there was an incredible growth in the number of Web servers and sites that publish information and manage discussions over the Internet.

Some companies are now leaning toward the Internet as an alternative to using Notes servers. After all, an Internet connection and Web browser site license are fairly inexpensive (and sometimes free) compared to the cost of building a Notes infrastructure. Web server software allows you to graphically view layers of menus that lead to screens of information and downloadable files. You can participate in discussion forums and complete forms and submit them.

As Web server software improves, it may eliminate the need for some companies to use Notes. With Collabra Share and Netscape, for example, there is no need for Notes if all you want to do is manage discussion databases. But if you look at the power of the Notes database, the Internet is a long way away from truly managing information in a workgroup environment. Notes still gives you the ability to build custom applications that process the forms, route messages automatically, and even connect to fax servers and telephone switches. In Notes, data replication to other servers and the local desktop is much more sophisticated and more useful than a simple download. The Notes server-to-server communications capabilities automate the transfer of information to local and remote users, often eliminating the need for some users to connect to the home server.

Instead of looking at Notes and the Internet as competition, many companies are considering them as synergistic products. Notes can be used internally to build and manage databases of information and disperse it to active Notes users who regularly contact the server. Using Lotus'

InterNotes, a company can automatically publish information on its Web server directly from a Notes database. Less active or casual users can look up information via the Internet, and database administrators have to monitor only one database.

Why Choose Notes?

Obviously, there aren't a lot of packages out there that match the feature set of Lotus Notes. But none of us really likes to pick a product just because we don't have another choice. Therefore, let's review the many good business reasons why you might want to choose Notes:

- ♦ Notes is a high priority to Lotus, and it is always moving forward.
- ♦ Numerous vendors are integrating with Notes.
- ♦ Notes is a mature, 10-year-old product.
- ♦ There are hundreds of Notes consultants available to help users.
- ♦ Hundreds of Notes applications already exist.
- ♦ Technical and nontechnical people can develop applications quickly.
- ♦ IBM.

Notes is a high priority for Lotus, and Iris Associates has continually improved it. Sales of the Lotus flagship product 1-2-3 and its other offerings have not maintained their historic growth and appear to be losing ground to competitors. Conversely, Notes is showing rapid growth and has spawned large, revenue-generating support and consulting groups. Lotus added Notes to SmartSuite, and it continues to more tightly integrate Notes and its other products.

As mentioned, many vendors are integrating their products with Notes. To build an effective internal information system, companies need to find products that can integrate so that information can move everywhere it's needed. If Notes becomes the information hub, and accounting vendors integrate with it, then a company has more opportunities to select the best accounting package and find one that will support the flow of information via Notes.

Notes is also a mature product that has been in development for over 10 years. To be sure, Notes has had its share of bugs in every version, and it isn't bulletproof yet. Nevertheless, Lotus has built a dependable product with a robust feature set that only a product at version 4.0 could have. Notes is already available for Windows, Windows NT, Macintosh, Sun, and other Unix platforms, and it is forming alliances regularly.

There are hundreds of Notes consultants chomping at the bit to come into your office and implement Notes. Many of them have five or more years experience with Notes. They also have databases and templates that can save you a lot of time in developing your internal systems. General computer consultants worth their salt also know that they need to understand Notes and be able to explain it to their clients because the topic will invariably come up when they discuss business solutions.

Numerous Notes applications have already been developed, which means you don't have to factor in a lengthy development cycle to get started with Notes. Lotus ships Notes with templates for support calls, discussions, purchase requisitions, and more. And each new version comes with a few more databases, so some applications can be brought online without a lot of effort.

Both technical and nontechnical users can develop systems quickly in Notes. Instead of waiting through development cycles or a programmer to free up, users can create interim systems that can get the job done and improve their business processes immediately. When programming resources are available, they can quickly build a prototype system and put a solution in place without a huge effort.

Best of all, you can't ignore the IBM factor. The influx of IBM talent and funds will ensure that Notes will grow and improve. IBM historically provides excellent customer support, and it views Notes as an important piece of its overall workgroup strategy. The phrase "you can't go wrong buying IBM" may not *always* be true, but it doesn't hurt to have a multibillion dollar company behind a product.

The Risks in Choosing Notes

Every decision that a company makes involves risk, and choosing Notes is no different. A company-wide implementation of any product can't be taken lightly, and the decision should be carefully weighed before moving forward. Some of the many risks in choosing Notes include:

◆ The cost.
◆ Difficult to justify another product because of sunk costs.
◆ Lack of acceptance by the users.
◆ Requires an internal guru or outside consultant.

The cost of bringing Notes into a company is probably foremost in everyone's mind, and certainly it is one of the biggest risks. If you want Notes to be effective, you need to put it on every desktop in your company sooner or later. Sure, you can use it in small workgroups and still see some benefits, but the big savings in time and efficiency come when everyone has

Notes and they can all access the same information, the same forms, and the same reports. That also means spending the money, investing in training, upgrading hardware, and buying servers.

A small pilot program can introduce Notes into your organization for a relatively small cost and give all interested parties a chance to see it in action. You'll still have to buy a server, upgrade any 386 PCs and possibly some low-end 486s, and buy a Notes license for each user. The price tag for a 10-user pilot adds up to about $15,000 to $20,000 but, compared to wasting tens of thousands of dollars in licenses and hardware after a failed effort, the investment is small and relatively safe.

Once you've invested in Notes, it will be almost impossible to justify a switch to another product. You'll have spent a lot of money in hardware and a lot of time in training and software development. If another product like Microsoft Exchange looks appealing, a switch will require a significantly higher cost benefit to offset the investment that you've already made in Notes.

One of your biggest risks is lack of acceptance by the people who will be using Notes. Many of the benefits derived from Notes come when everyone has it and uses it. The early adopters of Notes are often zealots, and they can sometimes alienate potential users by pushing it too hard. Conversely, managers who *won't* use it set an example for their staff and can delay the implementation of Notes projects. In short, Notes has to be a company-wide effort backed by all management levels before it can succeed in a big way.

If you can't afford to have a Notes guru on staff, you're going to need outside consultants and developers to help you get up to speed. Notes consulting is one of the hottest new markets for consultants and there are a few marginal ones that may offer an attractive rate to help you get started. But, without the proper research and reference checking, you could end up with an unqualified Notes consultant who will steer you toward inadequate hardware and implement a Notes topology that may delay the implementation of Notes projects. A word to the wise: Take the time to find a qualified consultant.

Making a Commitment to Notes

By now, you've probably built up both some excitement and some trepidation about Notes. Committing to using Notes in your workgroup or business is a big step, and the decision shouldn't be made without considering everything that you read. However, you don't have to break the bank or brainwash everyone to get started.

The best way to try Notes is to select a pilot project that can show significant returns for the amount of time and money that is going to be spent to get it started. Everyone has one or two problem areas in his or her work setting or business that could be solved with better information, improved workflow, and the elimination of paperwork. If users see that they will profit by using Notes, they will readily accept it.

Enlist the help of the company's information systems group or hire a reputable consultant who can establish a stable Notes environment that you can depend on. Notes requires maintenance, and you'll have your hands full dealing with new applications, training, fine-tuning, and learning the Notes environment. Hire a knowledgeable person or group to keep the server running, back up your information, and organize the data on the server. Even the best application will fail if the server is always down and users can't get to their Notes databases.

Even after the pilot succeeds and before you wax eloquent about its success, ask yourself if you really want to go for the whole enchilada and put Notes in more places. Notes will spread like wildfire once people see it in action. Be prepared for questions such as: "When do I get Notes?" and "How come Marketing got Notes before we did?" In other words, once you go public with Notes, you've already committed to putting it everywhere in the company.

2

The Components of Lotus Notes

There are plenty of books on the market that describe how to use Notes, and we don't intend to rehash that information here. The purpose of this chapter is to dig deeper into the discussions started in Chapter 1 and to give you an overview of the Notes components so you can "speak the language" when discussing Notes. If you are somewhat familiar with Notes, this chapter can refresh your knowledge or fill in some gaps. At the end of this chapter, there is also a brief history of how Notes improved through the years.

Although most Lotus Notes components remained the same between version 3.x and version 4.0, many of the menu choices at the top of the screen changed. The text that follows makes reference to the version 3.x menus in the examples. You can easily come up with the equivalent Notes 4.0 selection by using the Release 3.0 Menu Finder in the Notes 4.0 Help menu. Once you complete this chapter, you may want to immediately review Appendix A to better understand how the enhancements in version 4.0 have affected each Notes component.

The Notes Desktop

The Notes desktop provides a simple interface that helps users find and access the databases that they need. The icons on the desktop represent databases, and, when you double-click on an icon, Notes opens the database so that you can review the information. You can use the Window menu to pop back to the desktop, open other databases, and then move back and forth between them (see Figure 2.1). When you exit a database, Notes returns you to the desktop.

The icons are placed on the desktop by using the File Open Database menu as shown in Figure 2.2. Notes displays the Notes servers that are available along with a common sense description of the database instead of a techy file name. A click on the Add Icon button places the icon in the folder that you have selected. The desktop can also show you on which server the database resides and how many documents have changed since you last read its contents. Once the databases are open, users can use the customizable toolbar and the menus to modify forms and views and automatically locate unread documents.

The Notes desktop menu remains the same for all applications when you open a database. Of course, some of the menu choices may change or be un-

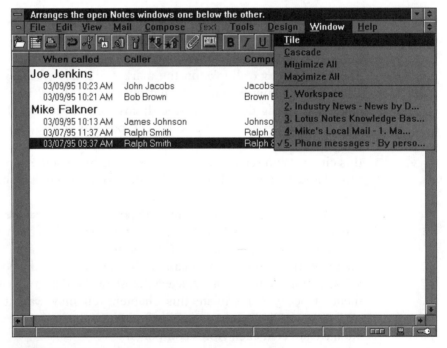

FIGURE 2.1   Moving between Notes windows.

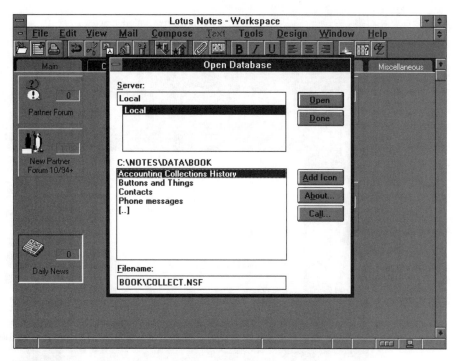

FIGURE 2.2   Locating a Notes database.

available at times. But you can always create a mail message, find the macro menu, and compose a new document in the same way for every database.

The Notes desktop also provides users with information about databases so that they can manage the ones that they create (see Figure 2.3). Through the File menu, a user can find out how large the file is, who's been accessing it, and who has rights to read and write information to it. The database manager can control how much of the database is replicated to other copies of the database and the users can create replicas of the databases to their local PCs.

The desktop is also the control panel for remote communications with the Notes servers. Using the Tools menu, remote users can initiate a call to the server and replicate whatever databases they have highlighted on the desktop. After replication, the desktop reports how many documents have not been read so that users can easily scan through the database for changes.

Like any other desktop application, users will want to customize their Notes desktop to their way of doing things. However, it doesn't hurt to set up some guidelines to help them organize their desktop to take better advantage of it. For example, one tab should be set aside to display icons for all the databases that are stored on their local PC. With the Notes replication feature, several copies of a database may exist on different servers and on a

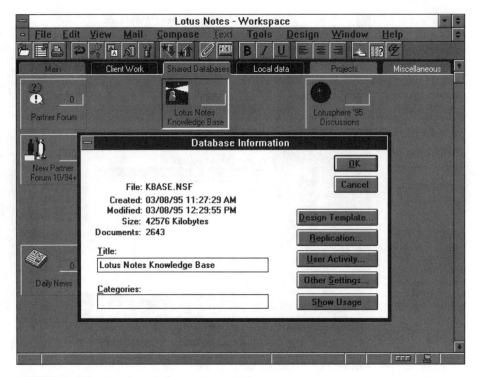

FIGURE 2.3   The Database Information window.

local PC. The icon for all of the copies is the same, and users may think that they have updated a server when, in reality, they have only changed a local copy. If they don't replicate with the server for a couple of days, neither will their changes. A Local tab would remind them that the databases in it are local copies that must be replicated to the server for a change to happen. (See Appendix A for a cool 4.0 feature that also solves this problem!)

The desktop also has a valuable toolbar that can be standardized for the entire company. Toolbar icons like Cut and Paste are pretty standard, but users should also have File Attach, Text Fonts, Navigate Next, Expand All, and Collapse All to help them with mail and discussion databases. Developers can create icons for the toolbar that make it easier to use Notes applications; therefore, some space on the toolbar should be reserved for future expansion. If the developers are creative, they may even want to build an entire toolbar just for a series of related Notes applications.

You can also use the desktop icons to help users understand how a database fits into the bigger picture. For example, human resources icons may have a common theme, say a green or yellow background with HR in the upper corner, with different words or pictures to indicate what the database includes. Or the icon for each company knowledgebase could contain a certain kind of book, with different colors representing the various departments or function groups. Just by looking at the icon, the users can more easily remember the purpose and content of the database.

There are six full-screen windows on the Notes desktop, each brought forward one at a time by selecting one of six tabs at the top of the screen. The icons that represent the databases are fairly large, take up a fixed amount of space, and are aligned to an invisible grid. Version 4.0 of Notes added a seventh tab, the Replicator, to assist users with replication.

Notes allows you to have several databases and many views and forms open within a database at one time. However, version 3.x limits you to nine open at any one time. Nine may seem like a lot of windows until you have your mail database open and find yourself following a trail of doclinks and fielding a phone call that requires a quick lookup in another database.

The Notes 3.x desktop handles multiple windows and, once you have the databases, forms, and views open, you can tile or cascade them on the screen. Unfortunately, Notes is an information-intensive application and tiled windows don't leave much screen left over for looking at the information. Realistically, usually you will open a database, select a view, open a form, go back to the view, open another form, and so on.

The Notes developers recognized many of the shortcomings of the Notes 3.x desktop and added some welcome changes in Notes 4.0. The new desktop screen has two windows, one showing a list of view and design elements available in the database and the other displaying the same type of view that was shown for a Notes 3.x database. A third window can be shown by dragging the border at the bottom of the screen toward the top of the screen (see Figure 2.4). When you select a view from the list in the left window, Notes updates the right window to show all of the documents that are available in that view. When you select one of those documents, Notes opens it and displays its contents in the window at the bottom of the screen.

This new approach is a significant improvement because it streamlines the desktop and eliminates a lot of menu selecting and window swapping once you open a database. The new desktop is an efficient browser that previews documents for you as you select them. Before this change, if you weren't sure where you could find a document, you could spend several minutes just opening and closing documents to see if you had the correct one.

The Notes Database

The Notes database is the repository for documents, forms, views, and macros for a specific project or subject area, and it isn't limited to holding only one kind of document, say an invoice or a mail message. Instead, you

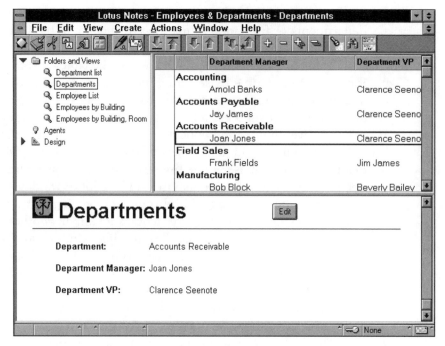

FIGURE 2.4   Notes version 4.0 desktop screen for displaying databases.

can store any number of documents in almost any kind of format in a database. To illustrate this concept, let's say that you are in charge of a laboratory. You have defined the procedures for the experiments that you want to perform, and you purchased the equipment. You also created the experiments, performed them, and logged the results of the tests as they occurred. You would like to save all this information in a Notes database to help you manage the lab activities.

The database can contain any or all of this information. You can create data entry forms to capture all of the information that you want to store. You might create views that show only the procedure documents, the purchase orders, or the equipment sorted by serial number. Other views could detail the tests to be performed and the results of the tests. Even though the information is almost completely different for every view, it can all reside in the same database.

Notes databases normally reside on a Notes server. They have both a technical name and a descriptive name that Notes uses when a directory of databases is requested. One word of caution: There is nothing in Notes that prevents you from using the same descriptive name for two databases so it's important to funnel all new database additions through an administrator who can catch duplicates.

The descriptive name of the database can only be 32 characters, and since only 25 of those characters will fit on an icon, it's helpful to have some standards here as well. For example, let's assume that you have several departments and you want users to be able to differentiate which databases belong to which department. You could store databases in a directory called MKTG or ENG and it would help users find the files. However, this directory name does not display in the text on the desktop icon, forcing the user to use a menu choice to discover where the database is stored. Instead, it might be helpful to agree on a three- or four-letter mnemonic, like Mktg, to begin the description or, if you can be frugal with the rest of the name, just use Marketing to start it off. The rest of the name can be descriptive enough to indicate to users what the database contains and still fit on the icon. For example, Mktg-Status Reports is much more descriptive than Status Reports and would eliminate confusion on a user's desktop.

Once a database is created, the Notes administrator assigns access rights to everyone using the database based on each person's needs. The administrator can also create a list of names and assign the list rights so that he or she merely has to add a person's name to the list to give him or her those rights. In Figure 2.5, notice that the list contains a user name (John Smith) and several group names (Admin, All).

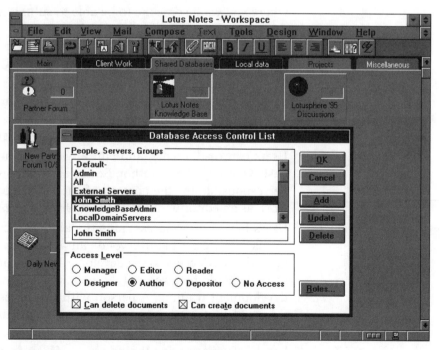

FIGURE 2.5 Database Access Control window.

Figure 2.5 also illustrates the different levels of access that can be assigned to a user. Let's take a look at the levels of access so you can see how you might take advantage of them in an application.

No Access   Users cannot do anything with this database. The default access for databases created on a local computer is Designer, and, if a user replicates it to a Notes server, everyone will have almost unlimited access to it (see the discussion of Designer access that follows). The administrator should, at a minimum, set the default access to the database to No Access. A policy should be instituted stating that all new databases be placed on a server by a Notes administrator who reviewed the access control so that users don't inadvertently receive more access than they should have.

Reader   Users can read any document in the database but they can't change or delete documents. This is the best level for users of general information databases and probably the most common access level.

Depositor   Users can create documents but they can't read any of them. Once a document is saved, they can't ever look at it or any other documents. Depositor access is good for surveys or tests where you want someone to be able to submit a form but not retract or change anything once it's complete.

Author   Users can read any documents in the database, create a document, and make changes to the documents that they created. This is where workgroup computing becomes powerful because a manager can ask the people with Author access to create and store documents in the same database without fear that someone without authority will change them.

Editor   Users can read, create, and edit any documents in the database. One step above Author, Editor access allows someone to be responsible for the content of the entire database and to work as an editor with the authors of the documents.

Designer   Users have Editor access, plus the ability to create and edit forms and views that everyone can access. This access level gives the user access to the developer features of Notes; therefore, it should be given only to people who have some Notes development training. A person with this access can build a thing of beauty or completely mess up the database.

Manager   Users at this access level hold the fate of the database in their hands. They can wipe the database off the face of the earth, give everyone unlimited rights to it, and do anything they please with it. This level is usually reserved for the Notes administrator and the owner of the database.

Let's use the lab example to demonstrate how access rights can be used. Let's assume you run the lab and are responsible for the lab database, and therefore have Manager access. You hire two college interns to perform the tests and give them Author access so that they can enter the test results. You didn't choose Depositor access since your supervisors often ask the interns to expand on their findings and update the documents. You next give your supervisors Editor access so they can add their comments to every test in the database. You have one supervisor capable of enhancing the forms and views so you give him or her Designer access to the database.

Forms

Forms are the data entry screens for Notes. They are used to create documents in a Notes database; once a document is created, the form becomes a template to display, from which you edit the contents of the document. A database can contain any number of forms, and you can even use different forms to view the same document.

You don't have to be a developer or even a power user to create a useful Notes form. You may need a developer to help you tap some of the more powerful features of forms like database lookups, but, if you understand the basic elements of Notes forms, you can create one fairly quickly. As other users develop their databases, you can borrow their designs and save even more time. The 50 databases included with this book are an excellent source of designs to help you build your own databases!

The starting point for creating a form is the screen layout. Notes forms are almost completely unstructured so you have a lot of freedom in how you lay them out. You can place pictures and text anywhere on the form, and the form can expand past the size of one screen. Both the text on the form and the fields that hold information can be assigned attributes such as bold, italic, colors, fonts, and font sizes. Notice in Figure 2.6 that the form has a logo in the upper left-hand corner, a large and descriptive screen title, and the text lined up evenly down the page.

The flexibility of a Notes form can also pose design problems, however. Since any proportionally spaced font can be used anywhere on the form, it's possible that text on different lines won't quite line up and look aesthetically pleasing. To counter this problem, a developer should use the Notes ruler to create tabs and align the text on them.

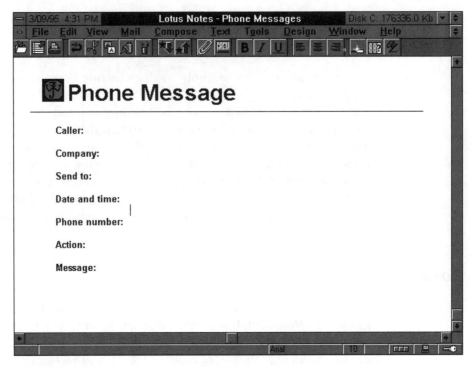

FIGURE 2.6 Designing a form and placing text and pictures.

Once the text is placed on the form, it's time to add the fields to it. The fields define the kind of information that will be entered, how it will be tested for validity, and how it will be modified and formatted before it is saved as a part of the document. Each field can be unique to the form or it can be shared with other forms so that any changes to its characteristics affect all the forms that use it (see Figure 2.7).

As noted, there are nine data types that you can use in a form. These field types define the look and characteristics of the field and shouldn't be changed once the database has been built. These types are:

Text This field can hold thousands of characters of any kind. The text can include carriage returns but it cannot be formatted with characteristics like bold and underline.

Numbers This field accepts any positive or negative numeric value with or without decimals.

Time This field holds a date, a time, or both. Notes stores the value in a way that allows a developer to add and subtract fields to compute the number of days or time elapsed between the two.

FIGURE 2.7   Defining a field.

Keywords	This field definition contains a list of values called keywords that are available for selection by the user. The values can be stored by the developer in the form or derived from a lookup function that interrogates a view in the same database or another database. The field can also be set up to allow more than one item to be selected, and it can be displayed as a check box, radio button, or simple text.
Rich Text	This field can hold almost unlimited text, pictures, embedded objects, and file attachments. The text can be formatted with fonts and character attributes like bold and italic. The information is not available for display in a view.
Names	This is a text field with additional capability to recognize the contents of the field as a Notes user name. Name fields are commonly used to store the intended recipients of mail messages that will be sent from the database.
Author Names	This field is used to provide document-level security. If an author name field exists and the current user is not in the

field, the user will not have author access to the document even if he or she has author access to the database.

Reader Names Like author names, this field is used to provide document-level security. If a reader name field exists and the current user is not in the field, the user will not have reader access to the document even if he or she has reader access or higher to the database.

Sections These fields allow a developer to change the access rights of a section of a form to help control its use. Every field that follows the section field can be accessed only by the users specified in the section definition. In version 4.0, sections are no longer field types. Instead, sections are established using menu selections.

The default field type for a new field is Editable, which means that values can be entered into the field and edited by the user. In some cases, however, you may want a field that calculates a value based on other values. Notes accommodates this by allowing you to mark the field as Computed and to add a formula that will compute the value for it.

One disadvantage of all of the fields is that there is no way to limit the length of the field. In traditional development environments, a developer can usually define a field as a 10-character text field or a number field of seven digits and two decimal places. With Notes, users can just keep typing as many characters as they want in the field. Developers can add a validation test that stops the user from moving to another field until the length is shorter but they can't stop them from entering whatever they want before the test.

The unstructured nature of Notes fields also poses some problems in the design of the form. Since a field has no realistic length limit, information entered into a field could spill into the text on the same line and next to it. Instead of scrolling the field or stopping the entry, Notes simply forces the text to keep moving to the right and even onto the next line if necessary, as shown on the Send to line in Figure 2.8.

In effect, it is impossible to guarantee that all items on a form will appear at the same place on the screen for every document. A good developer simply keeps this in mind when the form is designed and avoids placing buttons and text next to fields that may spill over. In addition, the ruler can be used to set a hanging indent at the beginning of the field so that even though the text spills over onto the next line, it still lines up with the text above it.

Rich text fields also pose a similar problem in that you can store an almost unlimited amount of text, pictures, and file attachments in one. If

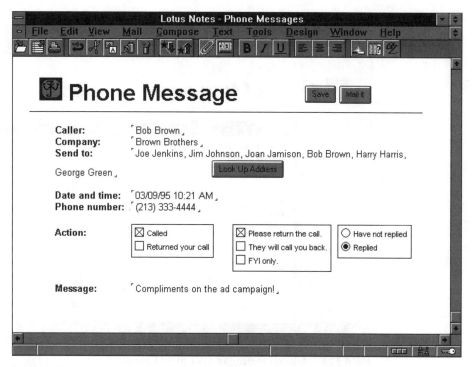

FIGURE 2.8 Unstructured means unpredictable.

you have two or three such fields, you may have to scroll down several pages to move from one field to another. In many cases, designers limit the number of rich text fields in a form, and they place them at the end of the form to minimize the disruption of the form by lengthy text.

Although it may appear that you are losing a lot of control of your form, there are still plenty of ways to add some structure to it. As you enter information into a field, Notes processes three formulas during its evaluation of the information. The first formula defines a default value that is displayed when a new document is created. The default can be a fixed value or it can be calculated based on a formula. Once information is entered into a field, Notes applies a translation formula to what was entered. With this formula, you can attempt to clean up the values that are entered with functions like **@Trim,** which removes excess spaces, or **@ProperCase,** which converts the text to proper case. Notes then applies a validation formula to the information where tests can be performed to determine if the information falls in the proper range or matches certain criteria. If the value entered fails the test, a formula can be added to display the error in a dialog box and not accept the values entered (see Figure 2.9).

FIGURE 2.9 Adding formulas to control forms.

As shown in Figure 2.9, the SendTo field defaults to Joe Smith. The default formula could also have used a view to automatically determine the person for whom they answer the phone. The translation formula converts whatever is typed to proper case. The validation formula checks if there is any text in the field, and, if not, it displays an error message.

After the fields are placed on the form and the formulas that go into them are defined, the form attributes must be set up before it is ready to accept information. The attributes window is a catch-all for the form name, colors, the type of document it creates, and several other options. Except for the document type, all of the options can usually be changed at a later time without serious consequences.

Although there are a number of attributes, let's take a look at some of the key design attributes and how you can best use them:

Name   The form name is used by Notes in the Compose menu to describe the forms that are in the database. Notes sorts the form names and displays them in alphabetic order in the Compose menu. To sort them in different order, precede the name with a letter or number (A. or 1.).

Document Type	A Notes form can create three types of documents: a document, a response, or a response to a response. A document is the most common document type, with all documents being peers to each other when displayed in a view. A response has the same attributes as a document but it must be associated with a document. Responses are often used to capture additional information, and they stay with the document even if the documents are all sorted in a view. A response to a response is the same as a response except that it is associated with a response document, not a document.
Include in Compose Menu	A form does not have to be added to the Compose menu. By not placing the name in the Compose menu, the form can only be accessed by using a button in another form.
Inherit Default Field Values	If a form is displayed and another form is selected from the Compose menu, this setting will cause Notes to bring the field values from the first form into the new document created by the menu choice. Only fields with the same name will receive the values brought in. So, if the first form has a field called CustomerName and the second form also has a field called CustomerName, the field in the second form will automatically receive the value of the field in the first form.
Automatically Refresh Fields	Notes does not automatically recalculate every formula in a form when users move from field to field. It only calculates the values for the field that a user just exited. On the other hand, if a form has 100 fields in it, users would have to wait for Notes to recalculate every one of them every time they hit the Enter key. If all the values in a form need to be updated immediately, this setting must be activated.
Read Access/ Compose Access	In addition to the access controls on the database, the access for every form can be tuned using the Read Access and Compose Access buttons. For example, a database may exist where some users want to add documents, some want to edit documents created by other users, and some only need to read documents. If the database access is set to Reader, they can't edit the documents. With Editor access, they have too

many rights. Instead, each user can be given Editor access for the entire database first and then have his or her rights limited in each of the forms with the access buttons.

Color　　Color may not seem too important but it does affect how people feel about the form. There are a lot of colors listed, but only white, light blue, and possibly yellow and green seem to make an attractive backdrop for the form's text and the information entered into it. No matter which color you use, it should appeal to the user, not send them away screaming.

Finally, after all the settings are chosen, the form is ready to use. Although you now have a working form, there are still a number of simple techniques available to improve the usability of the form and control the actions of the users who access it. Some of them require the use of the Notes macro language, and you may need a little help from a developer.

Buttons are a simple way to automate tasks in a form. A button can be placed anywhere on the form, and all it needs to do its job is a script that contains commands, @functions, and formulas that define the actions that you want to perform. The script can be a single statement, perhaps displaying a dialog box, or it can be very large, performing calculations and modifying several fields. Figure 2.10 contains a form with several buttons that automate simple tasks. The dialog box shows how to define a button that every document can use, a Save button. Without a Save button, you would normally save a document and return to the previous view by selecting File Save from the menu (or the Save icon on the toolbar) followed by a File Close Window. Instead, you can create a button called Save that has two formulas in it:

```
@Command([FileSave]);
@Command([FileCloseWindow])
```

When a user wants to save, he or she simply clicks on the button.

You can also use the Text Paragraph attributes to hide or expose different sections of your form, depending on how the user is viewing it. There is no reason to have a Save button on the screen if the user is reading a document, and no reason for an Edit button if the user is already editing it. Place the Edit button on one line and the Save button on the next. Highlight the line on the form that has the Save button on it, and set the Paragraph attribute to Hide when Reading. Highlight the Edit line and select Hide when Editing. When the user is reading the document, only the Edit button

FIGURE 2.10   Creating a Save button.

will show. When he or she pushes the Edit button and puts the document in Edit mode, only the Save button will show (see Figure 2.11).

The hiding techniques can also be used to change the look of an entire form. Let's say you have a customer name and address screen with a lot of fields, but users prefer to see a brief summary of the information when they call up the form. You can create a special area in the form with a summary of information derived from the other fields in the form. The rest of the document can be set to Hide when Reading while the new section can be set to Hide when Editing. When a user views the form, only the summary will show. If he or she edits the document, the more complex form will show.

In some applications, you want users to enter information in one form before they complete another form. By using a combination of the form attribute Include in the Compose menu and a button, you can guide users to the forms that you want them to access, in the order you want them to follow. For example, let's say that you have a database of sales contacts. You want to enter the name of the company first and then create a document for each contact with the company name in it. Every time you receive a sales lead from a contact, you want to enter the lead, attach it to the contact, and bring the company name and contact with it.

FIGURE 2.11 Hiding buttons.

To make sure all this happens correctly, you design it so that only the company form shows in the Compose menu. The form would have a button called Add Contact that would display a form for entering contacts. That form would have a button called Leads that would store the lead information. By setting the form attributes to Inherit Default Values, the company name and then the contact information would flow down to all the forms that need it.

Although the Compose menu supports only nine forms, you can add more by using tiered menus. The Compose menu is based on the form names stored in the database. By using a special format for a form name, you can instruct Notes to display part of the name as a menu choice that leads to another menu of forms. Let's say, for example, that you have a database with two forms, one for placing orders for parts and another for service orders. The menu would look like Figure 2.12, showing both forms on the menu.

The menu is fine until the database grows and you have more than nine forms. To work around the problem, you can change the form description from Enter Orders for Parts to Orders\For parts. The backslash tells Notes to use the word to the left of it, Orders, as the first menu choice and to use the words to the right, For Parts, as a selection in the second menu. You would make the same change for service orders. Figure 2.13 shows the results of the changes.

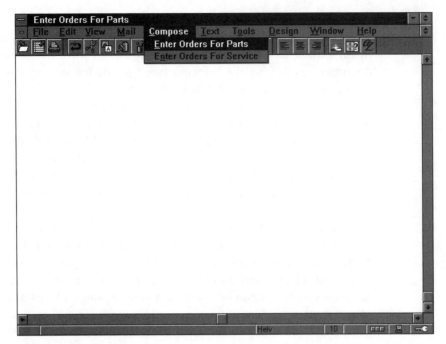

FIGURE 2.12   The Compose menu before tiers.

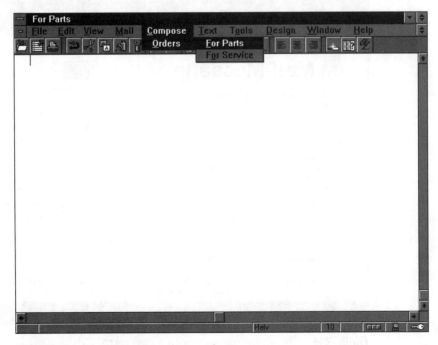

FIGURE 2.13   The Compose menu with tiers.

In all of these examples, we've used one form to display one document. However, Notes can use any form in the database to display any document in the database. Of course, the form needs to have the same fields as the document to display the information, but the feature provides some interesting flexibility in a workflow environment.

Let's assume that we use a phone message form to log phone calls and send them to the appropriate person's inbox. The person entering the phone message uses the form shown previously in Figure 2.8. When the person pushes the Mail It button, the internal form for the document is changed to the name of a form that exists in the Mail system. When it arrives at the appropriate inbox, the recipient would see the message on the form shown in Figure 2.14.

Notice that the form has an additional field for the recipient to add more information about the phone call and its outcome. The Replied radio button has been checked, indicating that the phone message has been answered. The subject was built from many of the other fields into one succinct message that can be used on a view to show the user all of his or her phone messages.

There are many other features in forms that can help you accomplish what you need to build documents in Notes. Version 4.0 brings even more

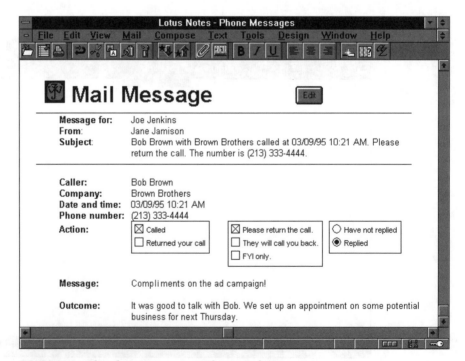

FIGURE 2.14   The phone message with a new form.

changes to forms design, and they will be discussed further in Appendix A. Now you should be able to discuss your needs with a developer, be more reasonable in what you ask for, and ask intelligent questions when a developer says what he or she can and can't do.

Views

Views provide Notes users with an on-screen summary of the documents in a database. To display a form, you must first display a view, find the document that you want, and double-click on that document to recall it. A database can have many views and each view can represent all the documents in the database or just a portion of them.

Notes doesn't really have a report writer so a view also represents the closest thing to a report that you'll find. With a little programming, you can build fairly sophisticated views of the database, so, except for the lack of a decent title at the top of the page, the views make a pretty good report. If you want fancy reports, you can use a database package like Lotus Approach that can read Notes databases and use its own reporting capabilities to generate the reports you need.

Views are a columnar representation of the information in a database, and, to create a view, you just define the columns you want to see. The column can include the contents of a field or be derived from a formula that calculates the results based on one or more fields in the database. Each column can have a title and be sized to an appropriate column width (see Figure 2.15).

The column formula allows a developer a great deal of freedom in displaying information and cleaning it up to look the way users want it to look. The formula can be as simple as a single function to convert the text to proper case (**@ProperCase(Field)**) or a complex, multiline formula to remove unwanted text. For example, the replies to messages from Notes Mail and many external mail packages add the **RE:** category to the subject. When you want to view your mail by subject, the messages with **RE:** preceding the subject are not sorted with original mail messages. To rectify the situation, the view can include a column with the following formula that eliminates **RE:**s and cleans up the view:

```
@If(@Contains(Subject; "RE:") | @Contains(Subject; "Re:");
    @Trim(@MiddleBack(Subject; ":"; 250)));
@If(@Contains(Subject; "]:");
@Trim(@MiddleBack(Subject; "]: "; 250)); @Trim(Subject)))
```

Mail systems create many different **RE:**s so the formula looks for **RE:**, Re:, or a bracketed [Re:], finds the colon or brackets, and returns up to 250 characters to the right of them.

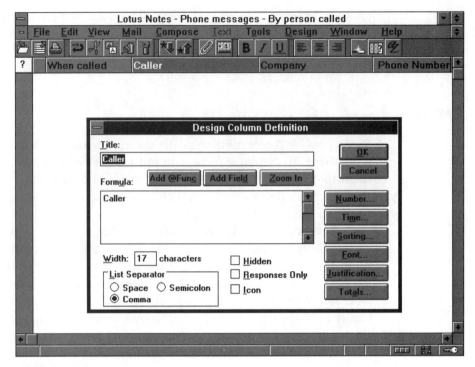

FIGURE 2.15 Designing a view.

Column formatting is fairly standard, with selections for justification (left, right), number and date formats, and fonts. You can enhance the look of the column by using a column formula to add text and spaces. In the views that are a part of the discussion template that comes with Notes, the column that displays the subject also includes the author's name. By using one column, combining the two fields, and adding parentheses around the author name, the developer eliminates a special column for the author, which the user would have to scroll to the right off the screen to view.

You have two options in Notes for sorting a column of information—sorting or categorizing. With sorting, you are simply asking Notes to sort the column in ascending or descending alphabetic order. Categorization, on the other hand, not only sorts the column but also displays the unique occurrence of values in the column on their own line. In Figure 2.16, the view is sorted by the recipient of a phone message and categorized on the same name. Notice how the name is placed on a single line and all the documents follow.

If you have a form that contains a keyword field that allows multiple values, you can create a view that lists the document under every category to which it belongs. Say, for example, that you have a database of computer

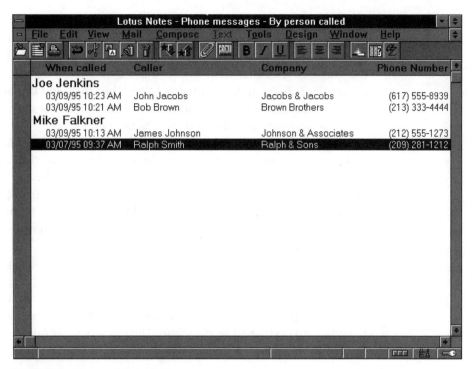

FIGURE 2.16 A categorized view.

articles with a form containing a keyword field for the types of hardware or software in the article. You add one article on Microsoft Office and assign it to three categories: spreadsheet, word processing, and electronic mail. When the view is categorized by article type, Notes will display the article under all three categories even though it only resides in the database once.

Sometimes you may want a view to display in a certain order, but a column sort won't do the trick. For example, you want to show a view of trouble calls by status with Urgent first, Important next, and Low Priority last. An ascending alphabetic sort would put Important ahead of Urgent and a descending sort would place Important after Low Priority. Instead, you can create a column that uses a formula to put them in the correct order and then hide the column. In the previous example, the column could have a formula like:

```
@if(Status="Urgent";1;@if(Status="Important";2;3))
```

The formula returns a value of 1 for urgent messages, 2 for important messages, and 3 for all others. The sorted column would arrange the statuses correctly, and, by hiding it, the unwanted numbers would not show on the view.

Although Notes also allows you to calculate and display totals, you'll find the results a little strange. Instead of displaying a group of items followed by a subtotal, Notes places the subtotals at the top of the list next to the sort category and then displays the detail items below it, as shown in Figure 2.17. It's visually confusing to say the least, and it makes reports difficult to read. To help, you can build a summary view that shows only the totals by selecting the Hide Details check box.

The final touch, after adding and formatting the columns, is to set the view attributes and selection formula. Like forms, the view name shows up alphabetically in the View menu, and the menu is limited to nine selections. To work around the limit, a view name can be tiered using a backslash to separate the menu choice from the submenu choice. The number of views in a database far exceeds the number of forms, so tiered view menus are commonplace.

Clearly, views are a powerful tool, but they come at a price. The more complex the view and its formulas, the longer it takes Notes to calculate it or refresh it before it can display the information. If the views are set to automatically refresh when a document is added, the user will have to wait for Notes to update all of the views. Developers wisely create only the views

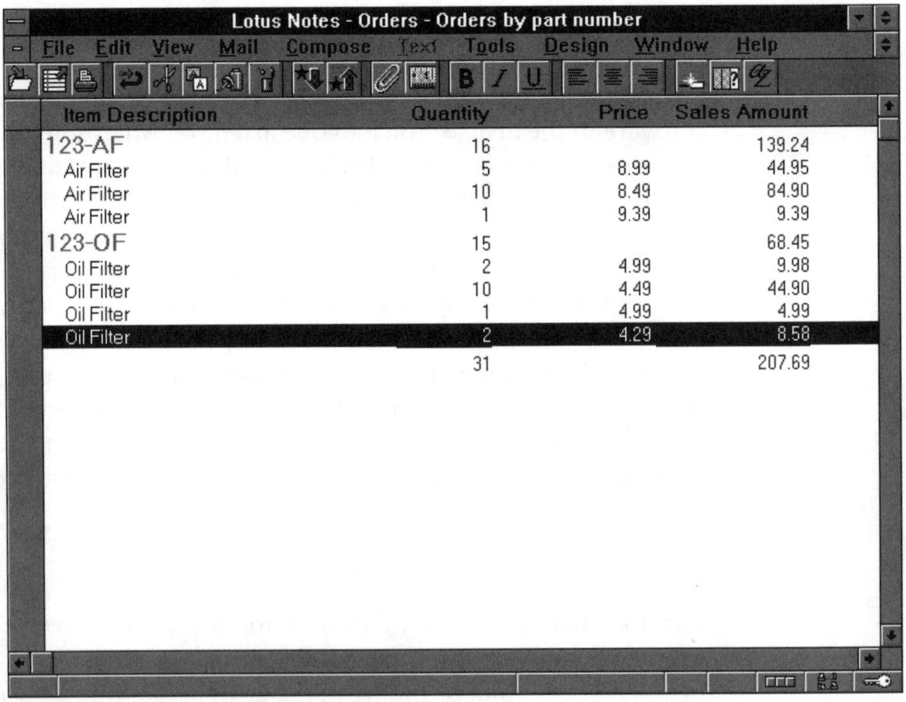
Lotus Notes - Orders - Orders by part number
File Edit View Mail Compose Text Tools Design Window Help
Item Description
Quantity
Price
Sales Amount
123-AF 16 139.24
Air Filter 5 8.99 44.95
Air Filter 10 8.49 84.90
Air Filter 1 9.39 9.39
123-OF 15 68.45
Oil Filter 2 4.99 9.98
Oil Filter 10 4.49 44.90
Oil Filter 1 4.99 4.99
Oil Filter 2 4.29 8.58
31 207.69

FIGURE 2.17 Totals in a Notes view.

that are necessary, and they prepare the users for any slowdowns before they implement the database.

Although we've covered the basics of creating views, there are many more powerful attributes that deserve attention. One of the most valuable attributes is Unread Marks, where Notes keeps track of any document that has been changed since the last time the database was opened. Instead of constantly browsing the entire database to find new information, Notes can flag unread documents by displaying a star to the left of the document in a view, as shown in Figure 2.18, and by changing the color of the display. You can even display only the documents that haven't been read to save you time when you review the database.

Color attributes have even more importance in a view than in a form. The view packs a lot of information about a document on the screen, and color often makes it much easier to find a particular document. With categories, for example, the main category could be maroon with a 12-point font, and its subcategory could be a bold blue with 10-point type. The actual lines would simply be black on a white background, which provides an excellent visual aid for locating documents.

Finally, you can limit what shows up on the view with a selection formula. This formula is a filter that is applied to every document in the data-

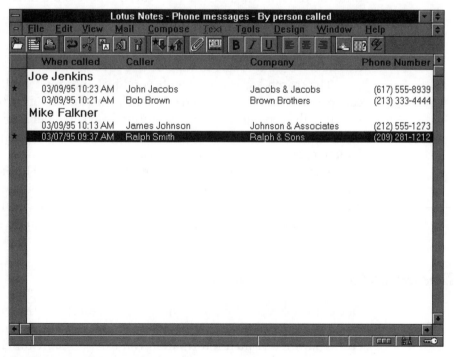

FIGURE 2.18   Unread marks in a view.

base when the view is used. It can test any field in the database, including internal Notes fields such as the form name so, even though the database has disparate kinds of information, the view can display only the items you want to see.

Views have a lot more uses than just as a tool to display a summary of documents. Whenever a developer needs to search another database to validate a field in a form, for example, he or she must create a view in that database that sorts on the field that is being validated. In most cases, no one really needs to see the view so, by adding parentheses around the view name, Notes will exclude it from the View menu.

Views also enable you to import or export information from 1-2-3 spreadsheets, structured text, and tab-delimited files. Once you display a view and select a file, Notes maps the columns of data in the file to the columns in the view, or vice versa. For imports, you also can specify which form is attached to the information, and you can instruct Notes to calculate any computed fields as the information comes into the view.

An even more powerful use of a view is the Notes full-text search, which is a way to look for words anywhere in Notes documents. A database doesn't automatically have this capability, but it's easy to add using the File menu. The cost, however, is a substantially larger database and longer save times as you add documents. The search is accessible through a search bar that appears at the top of the view, as shown in Figure 2.19. You simply type in the text that you are looking for, and Notes limits the current view to those documents that contain the text. When you open the document, the text that you want is surrounded by a red rectangle.

The search bar can go well beyond just entering text. It supports logical operators such as AND and OR to help you find combinations of text. By selecting the expanded search bar button, you can enter formulas and functions that will be applied to the text, call up a form to search using Query by Example, or save queries for later recall.

Views are the portal to all information in Notes. They are easy to create, and a good view can help users find information quickly. Users can create their own personal views of a database, and if they want to learn just enough to be productive in Notes, views is the feature to master.

Document Links (Doclinks)

One of the benefits of views is the ability to resort and filter the same information in many formats to expedite the search for information. In many cases, however, related information can exist in many different databases, and users want to be able to tie it together easily. Document links, known in

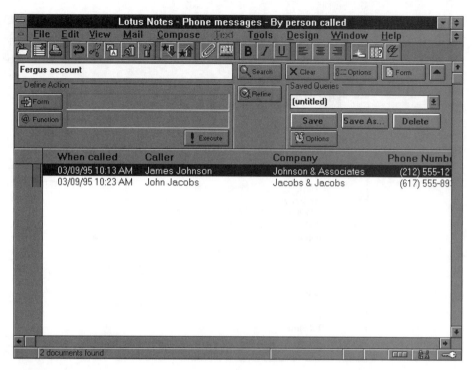

FIGURE 2.19 Performing a full-text search in a view.

Notes as doclinks, provide those connections between databases or documents in the same database.

A doclink is a pointer stored in one document that links to another document somewhere in a database. It is represented by a small icon in the shape of a page, and it can be placed in any rich text field in a document. To create a doclink, you first display a view, select a document, and choose Make DocLink from the Edit menu. You then locate the document that will hold the doclink, switch to Edit mode, and paste the doclink into a rich text field. The icon will appear along with any other text that is in the field, as shown in the message field in Figure 2.20.

With the doclink in place, it is a simple task for users to view the related document. When they double-click on the doclink, Notes displays the document represented by the doclink as if they had opened the database, found the document, and opened it. When they are finished, they close the form window and Notes returns them to the original document.

In addition to making the connection, doclinks contain information about the link, enabling you to make sure the doclink points to what you want *before* you use it. If you click and hold on the DocLink icon, Notes displays the name of the database, the view that shows the document, and the

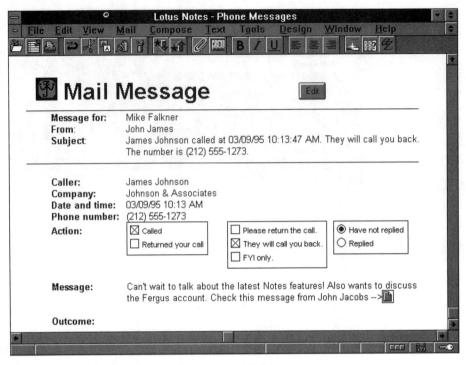

FIGURE 2.20   The DocLink icon in a rich text field.

contents of the Subject field, if it exists. Some documents may have several doclinks, and this simple description of the doclink can help you choose the correct one.

Doclinks are also intelligent about local and remote copies of a database. When a remote user replicates a database to his or her local computer, he or she gets all the doclinks as well. The user may also have replicated the database that contains the document identified by the doclink. Of course, the user wouldn't want Notes to call the server to find a linked document if it resides locally, so Notes checks the local system first to see if the database exists.

Since the Notes electronic mail system is also a database, you can also paste doclinks into your mail messages and send them to other users. Say, for example, that you are reviewing a Notes document and you find some valuable information that you would like to share with your supervisor or a fellow employee. Normally, you would copy the text, paste it into an electronic mail message, and send it to its destination. Instead, you can make a doclink, use the Mail menu to compose a document, write a quick "Joe. . . . read this!", and paste in the doclink. When the message arrives, Joe can double-click on the doclink and read the information.

Macros (Agents in Version 4.0)

Macros are scripts created with the Lotus macro language that perform tasks on one or all the documents in a database. They can be used for something as simple as changing a status in five documents to a global update to all documents to fill in new fields that you added to a form. In fact, macros are the only easy way to make mass changes to a database. The options for defining which documents to change are fairly flexible, letting you change all the documents in a database, just the documents in the active view, or those documents in a view that have been selected.

Macros are accessible from the Tools menu whenever you are displaying a view. It's difficult to control the use of a macro when it's prominently displayed in the Tools menu, so macros are often just utility routines added to make quick changes to the database or to repair problems. But the power of the macro language is such that macros can also be an important step in an application, which the user may just have to remember to run at the right time.

Macros do have some automation capabilities, which free the user from having to remember when to run them. An option can be selected that schedules a macro to run in the background on a workstation or server every hour, every day, or once a week. Consequently, instead of a user having to remember to do something like check the database for all work orders older than three days, a macro could be set up to check the database and mail a message to a supervisor when the situation is discovered.

Notes also supports mail paste macros, macros that execute every time a mail message is received by a mail-enabled database. These macros help complete the workflow cycle by allowing a developer to initiate mail messages to users in a workgroup based on the receipt of a document or on some value in it. If a supervisor wants to be notified automatically when a priority one support call comes in, for example, then the macro could immediately send him or her a message when the document hits the mailbox.

The mail paste macro also gives the developer a tool to which to attach a different form that will help users better utilize the information mailed to their database. For example, let's assume that the corporate mail databases have a form for sending a maintenance request to the Facilities group. As a user, you enter some basic information (the light bulb needs replacing in room 123) and send the message. It arrives at the Facilities database where the mail paste macro changes the form to a more detailed work order form that has room for completion dates, a description of services performed, and even a button to mark the document complete and send a notice to the originator.

Macros require some programming experience for all but the simplest task. Much like the buttons used in forms, each macro is assigned a name and then programmed with formulas, @functions, and commands that make changes to the database. The macro name then appears alphabetically in the Tools Run Macro menu. But macros don't have to be complicated to be effective. Let's say that a salesperson quit and his or her phone messages need to be assigned to another salesperson. Instead of recalling every document and changing the name to the new salesperson, you could create the macro in Figure 2.21.

Once a view was displayed by the recipient of the phone message, you could select all of the documents to be changed and run the macro to change the SendTo field to the new name. When the macro finishes, the view will refresh and show the changes.

Macros can also use an @function to prompt a user for information. A formula could be created to display a dialog box with the names of the salespeople in a pull-down list. The function could also search another database or view for their names. When the macro is run, the dialog box appears and the user can enter information that the macro can use. Unfortunately, macros do not include any kind of programming loop to reuse what was just entered. The macro is executed in its entirety for each document selected, so

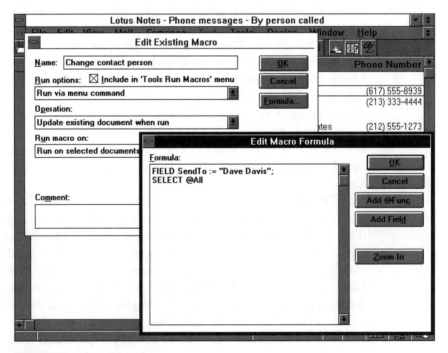

FIGURE 2.21 Creating a macro.

the dialog box would pop up for every document. There *are* simple work-arounds, but nothing user friendly.

Macros were renamed to Agents in version 4.0 and significantly enhanced to give the developer more control of what happens in the database when the agent is executed. Developers can create the equivalent of several mail paste and execute macros based on a time schedule. Many actions that formerly required a script command, such as deleting a document, can now be set up by selecting an action from a menu. Refer to a more detailed description of agents in Appendix A.

Mail Enabling

The ability to mail documents seamlessly between Notes databases is a key contributor to the success of Notes. To developers, mail enabling means that, based on just about any kind of change in a database, they can notify anyone with a connection to the corporate electronic mail system about that change. To users, it means that they can receive proactive messages that help them react more quickly and do their job better.

Mail enabling sounds like a big deal, but it doesn't take a lot of training to use it. Any document can be mailed to anyone without any programming using the Mail Forward menu choice. A user can simply open a document, select Mail Forward, and Notes will place the document in the message section of the form that they typically use to send mail.

It's not that difficult to mail enable a form either. To turn a message into a mail message all you need to use are the fields called SendTo (for the recipient) and Body (for the message). If a subject exists in the form, Notes will place it in the mail message as well. When Mail Send is selected from the Compose menu or **@Command([MailSend])** is used in a button, Notes sends the document to its new destination.

In some applications, mail enabling is almost transparent. Instead of placing the required fields on the form, the developer hides them and designs them to fill with values automatically. The SendTo field may be set up to send mail only to a certain database. The Subject field can be a combination of the user's name, the date and time that the document is created, and an excerpt from a text field. The Body field may be placed below a heading that says "Please indicate all the problems that you have experienced so we can better assist you." When the user presses a button called Submit Request, a macro automatically mails the document without the user knowing it.

If the user needs to send a document to a specific person, it's easy to access the name and address book and fill in the SendTo field correctly (see Figure 2.22). Notes has an @function, **@MailAddress,** that brings up the

FIGURE 2.22 Using the Name and Address Book.

Name and Address Book in a search window. You can switch between the system-wide address book and your local address book. As you type in the first few letters of the person's name, Notes brings up the names of the people that match what you've typed.

Mail enabling doesn't limit you to the confines of Notes databases and the Notes mail system. There are many products that can connect your Notes installation to external mail systems. Notes also has a very tight relationship with cc:Mail, Lotus' own electronic mail product, and many installations take advantage of its strong gateway products that can reach MCI Mail, the Internet, CompuServe, and many other external mail systems. In effect, your mail-enabled application can send a message to anyone connected to your Notes mail system.

Replication

In Chapter 1, you read a brief description of replication, another key contributor to the success of Notes. Replication allows Notes to synchronize copies of the same database with additions and updates made to any copy.

The synchronization can occur locally over a network or remotely over telephone lines.

Replication is very important for Notes users because it eliminates the need for a user to either copy an entire database of information every time it is updated; or to export a file of changes, transmit it to the intended user, and require the user to import and update the database manually. Users don't have to know what needs to be changed; Notes keeps track of the changes for them.

Replication is also a powerful way to disseminate information anywhere at any time without the intervention of an operator. All databases can be set up to automatically replicate at almost any interval with another server that holds a copy of the database. If your company has a couple of remote sites and a campus of buildings connected by a network, Notes can regularly connect to those sites and replicate any and all databases so that users can have local and more speedy access to the information.

Notes databases are, in most cases, not mission-critical, therefore periodic replication is more than adequate. The Notes administrator should weigh the need for updated information against the cost of transmitting it. In most cases, replication once or twice a day is more than adequate to keep everyone up to date. For more time-critical applications like electronic mail servers can be set to call many times a day or when a certain number of messages are pending. Each database can have its own replication schedule, which means that although the server may call other servers 10 times a day, databases will be replicated only at their scheduled times.

Replication isn't just a feature for remote users. In companies with several buildings or floors, network bottlenecks occur that would cause slowdowns if all the users in the entire company tried to access the same database on a single Notes server. Instead, a Notes administrator can place copies of a database on servers that are closer to the intended users and use periodic replication to keep them up to date. The users don't tie up the corporate backbone and their response times are speedier.

Lotus still has some work to do on replication to streamline it. Each time that you make a change to even one field in the document, Notes requires the entire document to be sent as a part of the replication. When you view a database for unread documents, the entire document is marked as unread even if only one character has changed. Lotus is working on a better approach, a field-level replication, that transfers only the information in the fields that changed.

If you are out in the field, replication can be a mixed blessing depending on the contents of the database and how people use it. If the database is too broad, external users will get what they need, plus a whole lot more that they don't need. Many people also store word processing documents, spreadsheets, and pictures along with the text they enter into a document. Those attachments take up a lot of space and, in turn, require a long session on the phone to download the changes to the database. There are several ways to work around the problem and help the people in the field get only what they need. One way is to keep the database streamlined so that it contains only the information that the external users need. An even better way is to add fields to the form that allow users to selectively choose what they need and what they don't need.

Notes gives you several options to help you decide what information comes to your local computer and what doesn't. In the Database Information menu, you can bring up a window (shown in Figure 2.23) where you can set parameters that control which documents are replicated. You can also enter a formula to define what information will be replicated using the same macro language found in forms and views.

The first option in the window, *Do not replicate deletions to replicas of this database,* allows you to keep your local copy cleaned up and small without wiping out information in the master copy on the server. You may also want to be able to read all of the attached documents but delete them later to save room. If another option, Remove documents saved more than xx days ago (where xx is a user-selectable number of days) is also selected,

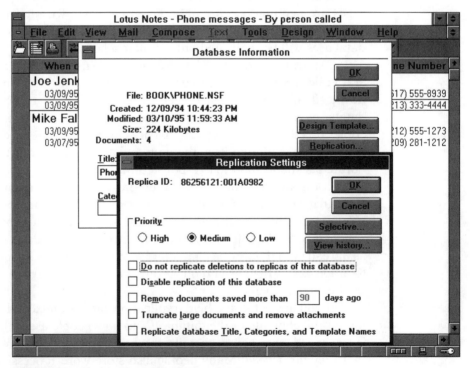

FIGURE 2.23   Options for replicating a database.

Notes will automatically clean out old documents from the database without harming the master copy.

If you just don't want attachments, the option Truncate large documents and remove attachments, will stop them from arriving. You can still look at the attachments, however, by calling the Notes server and connecting to it as if you were a local user. Before you make the call, you browse the database and find the documents that have attachments of interest to you. Then, you call the server, connect, open the master copy of the database, and view only the attachments you need. If you want a copy of an attachment, you detach it to your local computer. It will cost more in phone charges for the one session but a lot less over time than it would to replicate all attachments in a database.

In some cases, selective replication is a better alternative because you want all the documents that match a certain criteria, including all attachments as well. By pressing the Selective button in the Replication Settings window, you can enter the formula that defines those documents you want. Whenever you connect to the server, Notes evaluates each document that would replicate before it sends the information to your local computer.

A knowledgebase is a good example of the type of database that would use selective replication. Let's say that your company has three disparate product lines and a knowledgebase of information about sales, service, and support of these products. As a remote sales representative, you handle only one product line and have only a casual need to review the other two. If the database is set up correctly with a product line identifier, you can add a selection formula that replicates just information about the product line that you sell. When you need information on the other two, you call the server and access the master copy of the database.

In cases where external users like vendors and customers need to access a database, you can use selective replication to build a special version of the database, a firewall database of sorts, with only the information that they need to see. Although you could try to limit an external user's access to views and forms on the server copy of the original database to save space and maintenance, a sharp user can break that security when the database is brought down to his or her local computer.

The firewall database shown in Figure 2.24 is a selectively replicated database that resides on a server instead of on a local computer. The Notes administrator would create a selection formula that only brings informa-

FIGURE 2.24 A firewall Notes database.

tion to the database that is flagged in some field as For Internal/External Use. Any company proprietary information would not come across, and the remote external user could replicate or call and connect to the server as he or she needed.

Application Templates

When you create a new database, Notes gives you the option to start from scratch with an empty database or copy the forms, views, and macros from a database called a template. Templates represent a Notes database that has already been developed and given a special name and location so that they are available to other developers. Lotus ships a growing number of templates with the Notes product to help users understand how to develop forms, views, and macros.

The beauty of using a template is that Notes can then automatically update any database that uses that template with all the changes that a developer makes to it. To developers that means they can maintain the forms, views, and macros in a single template and be assured that all users will be apprised of those changes the next time the database is replicated. The users are spared the hassles of stopping their work to load an upgrade.

Of course, this same power can cause chaos if the developer isn't careful. Any changes that have been saved will be transferred at the next replication, and if those changes haven't been tested yet, this automatic distribution could be disastrous. Most developers avoid this problem by working on a copy of the template and then replacing the design in the template when they are finished.

Selecting a template doesn't mean that you can't customize the database that you created. It means that any changes you make may be replaced by changes made by the template developer if you happen to use the same view or form names. Once a template has been used to create a database, the connection to the template can be turned off and the database can then stand on its own. Any changes to the database, including form, views, and macros, are still replicated to all other copies of the database.

Security

Notes is an ideal platform for information sharing, but obviously, no one wants the wrong people looking at the information in their databases. Lotus takes security very seriously in Notes, as is apparent by the many levels of security for general access to Notes and databases. Over time, Notes hackers have discovered a few holes in the Notes Access controls, even finding ways to send viruses into a database using Notes Mail. Yet, Notes is still a fairly secure system as long as it is diligently monitored and passwords are changed regularly.

Notes security is independent of the operating system. You don't have access to the server operating system nor can you try to log in to the server. When you call a modem that is controlled by Notes, you must be using Notes or you'll get absolutely nowhere.

Security starts with the Notes administrator as he or she builds a Notes server. After the server is given a name and set up in the appropriate domain, Notes creates a unique certification ID that is the key to access that server. Users or servers that want to access the new server must send their unique ID file to the Notes administrator who goes through a process of certifying their ID for access to the server. If the server needs to replicate with an external server at another company, both companies need to exchange IDs before either server can replicate with the other.

Most Notes installations have multiple servers, and it would be very time-consuming to recertify every user each time a new server is added. Instead, Notes supports a system of hierarchical certificates that allows Notes administrators to certify a user or server to access all servers at or below a certain level. If users are certified using the highest certifier ID, then they have access to all servers certified with the same ID or lower, as shown in Figure 2.25.

Although certification is important, all that it really allows you to do is to see the Notes server. If you don't have access to any databases, all you can do is browse through the list of servers and databases and read the titles that are available. Of course, if someone somehow gets certified and connected, he or she can access any database that has a default access control higher than No Access.

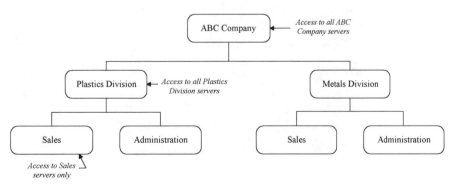

FIGURE 2.25 An example of hierarchical certificates.

Every user who is added to Notes also receives an ID file. The user ID file holds all the information regarding who you are and what certifications you have. It must also reside on the computer that you use to access Notes, which means that if you share computers with other users, you will need to place a copy of your ID on every computer.

The next level of security is the user password. Notes does not require a password when you use databases that reside on your local computer. However, Notes will request a user password on the first attempt to access a database on a Notes server. The password only allows users to *access* the servers available to the active ID so, if users don't have rights to *read* a database on a server, they essentially won't have access to it either.

Since Notes asks for the password only once, your computer is very vulnerable should you step away from your desk for a long period of time. Notes is satisfied that the person using the computer has been verified, therefore anyone can simply sit down and browse to his or her heart's content before you return. If you are concerned about security, enter a time value on the password dialog box show in Figure 2.26 to notify Notes to automatically log you out after a certain time period. Notes doesn't shut

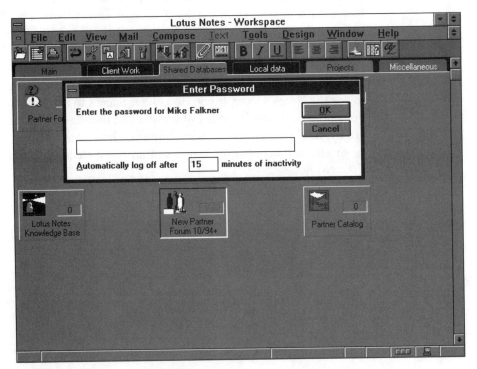

FIGURE 2.26   Setting a value to automatically log off a user.

down, but it will prompt you again for a password the next time you try to open a database on a server.

The rest of Notes security is set using the database access controls. Notes assigns a default access control to every database. The default is configurable and should be set to No Access so that the database designer can control who can access the database. However, the typical Notes default on a local computer is Designer access, which means that everyone who has access to the database can read, write, change, and delete all the documents, forms, views, macros, and settings in that database. By insisting that all databases be placed on the server by a Notes administrator, access controls can be checked and set properly in a database before other users can access it.

The database access control list simply defines which users and servers can access the database and what level of access rights they have. We covered the levels of user access in depth previously in this chapter in the discussion of forms, which explained that you can implement as much control as you need to make sure that users can only access what they need to see and change. Every database is unique, and users can have different access rights to various databases, depending on their needs.

Access lists can hold user names, server names, or a name that represents a list of users called a group. Group names simplify access control by allowing you to place a single group name in the access list instead of every user's name. The Notes administrator creates a group name in the Notes Name and Address Book and adds names to it as required. Instead of constantly changing the access control list in all the databases, you can often manage access by using a group name in the Database Access Control List, shown in Figure 2.27, and updating the group when changes are needed.

As described in the sections on views and forms, you can take security one level deeper by controlling the views and forms that a user can access. Users can be locked out of a form or view, be given read-only rights, or they can have full access to them. In effect, you could allow users into a database but limit them to one view and no forms if you needed that kind of security.

As you can see, Notes can be fairly secure if the right precautions are taken. Frankly, the biggest security weakness in the entire installation often is the Notes administrator and support team. After all, the administrator must have the master password to the certification IDs and all of the user IDs, and the support people often have manager rights to many databases. Much of Notes security hinges on certificates and cross certificates stored in the Notes Name and Address Book. If the views for those certificates are not restricted, users can simply grab a certificate and mail it to someone. Name and Address Books are often sent to remote users and, if the certificates aren't removed, it's pretty easy to bypass security on a local computer.

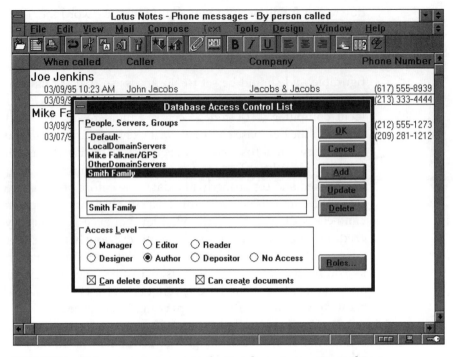

FIGURE 2.27   Using a group name in the Database Access Control List.

Ideally, administrators and the support team will be chosen for their skills and trustworthiness. Even so, the entire support team should be required to sign nondisclosure agreements to discourage curiosity and mobile certificates. That should keep security risks low.

The Evolution of Notes

Now that you've read about the Notes components, let's look at the evolutionary process that changed Notes into what it is today. When Notes was introduced in 1989, only visionaries really understood what it was capable of. It was a new concept that ran on a PC and used an OS/2 server to process information, a platform that was not necessarily the most popular choice at the time. The interface was usable, but there was plenty of room for growth.

Version 2.0 brought welcome enhancements to the look and feel of Notes. The menus were rearranged to help make the product easier to use. Tabs were added to folders so that each of them could have a name, and more color was used. Doclinks were introduced, allowing users to move easily from one document to another simply by double-clicking on the DocLink icon.

With version 3.0, Notes hit its stride with major enhancements for users, developers, and administrators. From inside a view, users could access a full-text search feature to find the occurrence of any text in the database. The index process required up to 50 percent more disk space, but the feature made Notes a good solution for text retrieval applications once relegated to specialized products. By adding selective replication, Lotus allowed remote users to copy only the information they needed from a database to their local PC instead of bringing down the entire file.

Lotus also gave Notes the look of its SmartSuite products 1-2-3, AmiPro, and Approach. Version 3.0 brought another menu realignment and further improvements to the interface. Users could now create SmartIcons, attach a macro program to them, and execute them with the click of the icon while in any database. Doclinks grew smarter, checking for the linked document on the local PC before prompting you to dial the server to find it. Lotus also made it possible to place a pop-up box on top of any item in a form and, when you clicked on it, Notes would display the information you had stored in the box.

Developers were the big winners with the 3.0 upgrade. Lotus added macro commands that allowed programmers to display a dialog box that prompted users for information when a button was pushed or a macro was executed. Lotus finally published the names of systems variables such as $REF, a variable that represents the very long and unique ID assigned to each document. With the new design synopsis, developers were finally able to print out everything they needed to know about the database, forms, views, and fields.

Commands were also added to the macro language, enabling a form to send mail messages from within a document. With the new sections feature, Notes forms were able to bring access control down to the form level; therefore, a designated section of a form could have more control than the rest of the form. Version 3.0 brought shared fields into existence so that developers could create a field once, use it in many forms, and implement a global change simply by modifying a single field.

The new version also introduced database lookups where a field in a form could search Notes databases and return values from those databases. If you had some standard forms that everyone needed to use, you could set them up so they were accessible from the Mail menu under the Custom choice.

To help organize the number of items in your Compose and View lists, Lotus introduced tiered menus in version 3.0. By placing a backslash (\) between words, Notes summarized all items with a common name to the left of the backslash in a single line to show a shorter list of selections in the menu. By selecting an arrow displayed next to the menu choice, you were presented a secondary menu created from the names listed to the right of the backslash.

For administrators, the need for NetBIOS drivers on each client machine to communicate with the server was irritating, and it often caused memory problems on PCs and Macs. In version 3.0, Lotus added IPX and Appletalk support to eliminate the requirement for the additional NetBIOS drivers. The new version also allowed administrators to register new users in batches from files instead of laboriously adding each user and certifying them one at a time. With the new remote console feature, system managers could view server statistics, see who was logged on, and change the Notes setup variables.

Version 4.0 came on the heels of the unprecedented popularity of version 3.0 and generated high hopes for the rapidly growing Notes community of users and developers. Changes were made in the interface, in the development tools that build Notes applications, and in the processes that the server can perform. The details of the 4.0 improvements are described in more detail in Appendix A.

3

How Notes Will Change You and Your Company

As evidenced by the more than 1 million copies sold, Notes has found its way into many organizations. In fact, it seems that every major corporation in the country either has Notes or is considering Notes to improve the way it does business. Even smaller companies can afford Notes, and, with all the consultants and third-party applications available, they don't even need a full-time staff to monitor it.

If you have concerns about whether Notes can handle the workgroup needs of your business or company, just read the computer press about the companies that are using Lotus Notes today. You'll find most of the Big Six accounting firms, plus such giants as AT&T, MCI, 3M, Johnson & Johnson, and plenty more that use Notes. These companies represent thousands of users and enough applications to test the power of Notes.

Sure, these are big players and they have enough money to spend on any kind of project they feel like funding. But these companies don't necessarily use Notes to solve the complicated, impossible, or mission-critical problems of their business. They buy Notes because all of these companies struggle with moving information from department to department, floor to floor, building to building, and branch to branch. They believe that Notes can help them solve these problems. All of these companies have seen huge changes throughout their organizations as a result of their implementation of Notes. Why? Because systems built with Notes are often significantly different from any of the applications they previously used. Notes provided a way to change how they traditionally stored and searched out information. Now their users can find the information they want on their desktop whenever they need it and pass it along to their peers and their managers without a hassle.

The Seeds of Change

In many cases, the changes wrought by Notes seem so dramatic because people are simply not used to having convenient access to so much information; they no longer have to remember file names and learn five different applications to get it. Local area networks started popping up in the early '80s but it took years of development, patience, and heartburn before they were dependable enough for users to rely on as the repository and conduit for the company's information. Many of the people who lived through the growth of networks survived by memorizing DOS and Netware commands and by placing file names and commands for launching applications on mountains of sticky notes in their work area. Consequently, Notes databases appear a little too easy to tap into and they are often skeptical.

When Notes was nothing more than a twinkle in Ray Ozzie's eye, local area networks were expensive and fairly limited. One of the early networks from 3Com consisted of an Altos computer as the server with a whopping 10MB hard drive and server software running on the Xenix operating system. 3Com built the network cards for the PCs, and all the users were connected via coax cable. There were no CONFIG.SYS files in DOS in those days, so the network installation actually modified the DOS system files. This pioneering server operating system was able to partition the 10MB hard disk into 320KB volumes, emulating the equivalent of a double-density, 5¼" floppy disk. When you started up your computer, you had the luxury of connecting to the pseudo-floppies and loading your information onto the network. The price tag: over $10,000 for the server, the software, and a couple of network cards.

Despite the meager beginnings of networks, vendors popped up everywhere selling their new technologies. Companies like Orchid, Fox, Novell, and others began selling network solutions, usually a combination of network cards and operating systems. The new software made printer-sharing a reality, and the networks became capable of locking files when they were in use by more than one person. Unfortunately, not much of the application software that existed at the time was smart enough to use the locks.

During this time, fearless PC coordinators pressed forward with plans for connecting all their personal computers to a network. After all, the users were storing a ton of information on their local computers that no one else could access. Files were often transferred via the "sneakernet," a low-cost network alternative involving a floppy, a pair of tennis shoes, and a five-minute walk to the recipient of the information. The coordinators wanted to eliminate the sneakernet and give users a place to store the growing number of spreadsheets and documents that people relied on to do their work.

As the industry matured, most of the network vendors left the hardware business and concentrated most of their efforts on the network operating systems. Products like Novell NetWare began to provide fairly stable and reliable server software that could support a large number of users. PC coordinators could make it through a full day without a major crisis.

Accounting software vendors were one of the first groups to take advantage of centralized servers to store company information. Besides the fact that it gave them a great opportunity to sell more copies of the software to a customer, these vendors could eliminate the elaborate importing and exporting schemes required to integrate information on separate PCs. They could also sell their software to larger customers who needed to store more information than one clerk could enter in a day.

Database vendors quickly adapted their software to the network environment as well. Popular products like dBase, Paradox, and Rbase gave users and developers a way to create custom applications that everyone could share. Developers could replace smaller minicomputer applications with PC-based software now that the PCs were networked to a common drive.

Almost from the start, most networks had the capability to send some kind of electronic mail. Initially, it was simply a sentence forced onto the bottom of your screen by another user. It quickly grew, however, from simple text messages sent between users to full-blown inboxes and folders for organizing mail messages, bulletin boards for sharing information, and files attached to messages to move the information to other users. As it became easy to send mail, more people wanted to jump on the bandwagon.

With all the sophistication of networks today, most people feel pretty good about what they get when they connect to the corporate network. Once you turn on your computer, the screen prompts you for a network login, and the system automatically maps several network drives to your PC. You can surf the network for the files you need with simple programs like the Windows File Manager or Windows 95 Explorer. The network software is often configured to automatically connect you to at least two laser printers somewhere near your workspace.

Most of the commonly used applications like Microsoft Word, Lotus 1-2-3, or WordPerfect now reside on the network where they are controlled by software metering products. Users often have a network directory called something like WORK where they can temporarily store files. They share a directory called TRANSFER where they can place files for other users to pick up. If one user can't access the other user-shared directory, he or she simply mails the file through the electronic mail system.

Due to its importance and the burden it places on the server, the accounting system usually resides on its own server somewhere in the bowels of the accounting department. Budget spreadsheets are e-mailed to managers each quarter and stored on the accounting server for consolidation. Database applications sit on a server close to the department that uses them the most. Guidelines, procedures, and handbooks generated by personnel departments are placed on a server, and users are mailed instructions on where and how to find those they need.

The Fruits of Change

For both the novice and the survivors of the network renaissance, the current systems are pretty good. There are plenty of ways to get a file from one user to another, application software is readily available, and there's always some room on the network for their files when their hard disk fills up. The electronic mail system brings them more than enough messages to keep them busy reading every day.

Much of the information that users need each day is available somewhere on the network, but often they still need to look in several places on the network to find it, and they often must launch two or more applications to load it. Unless the company has a sophisticated document management system, users have to decipher short DOS files names to find the document or spreadsheet that they need.

Also, in most cases, a traditional network environment does not effectively support ongoing electronic discussions. Typically, a person with an issue to discuss will send a question or concern to a list of interested individuals via e-mail. Several of these people respond, copying their response to the entire list and attaching the new message to the old one. As responses fly back and forth, everyone's inbox is clogged with incomplete threads of the conversation. The originator then spends an inordinate amount of time consolidating all the responses and feedback from all the messages into one cohesive document. Heaven help the person if a consolidated note is sent back out for comment or clarification.

For years, bulletin board operators have solved the discussion problem with user forums. People call into the bulletin boards on their modems, log in to them, and post messages in a public area. Other users can read the messages and post their responses in the same forum. Many electronic mail vendors also have bulletin board features built into their software that allow users to mail messages to a public mailbox. Powerful as they are, these bulletin boards still require users to search out the information they need, using an interface that isn't always the friendliest.

Along comes Notes with an innovative method for storing and retrieving information. You create a database for a given need and it becomes the repository for all the information that is associated with that need, including text, pictures, spreadsheets, and whatever files must be stored. You categorize and sort the information and build views to display the information in the order that you want to see it. If anyone wants to know about the database subject, you send them to the appropriate database.

Using Notes in a Proposal Process

A good example of how Notes can become a repository for information is a database for a proposal for providing services to a potential customer. Let's assume that we are creating a large proposal for our biggest client. The proposal requires everyone on the proposal team to review a document submitted by the client. The team needs to analyze what the client wants and come together to develop a theme for an answer. Each team member then prepares his or her response and circulates it to the other team members for responses and changes. Finally, the team brings all the components together and publishes the proposal.

We need a central place where everyone can store all the information about this proposal—a Notes database. We start by building the database and storing scanned images or an electronic version of the proposal-related documents. Team members can open the database, read the proposal, and analyze the contents, then attach comments, concerns, and follow-up questions.

As we develop a theme and an outline for a response, a member of the team enters it into Notes. Each issue that must be addressed will be represented by a document. The document will contain fields that hold a number for each section of the proposal, the issue to be addressed, and the names of the appropriate members of the team who will work on the section.

As we gather supporting facts, we update the documents with the information. We paste in electronic information or scan paper copies, and attach any electronic documents and spreadsheets that we can use. We attach separate documents to the issues documents, which hold a possible approach to the issue, an idea, or simply a white paper discussing the issue. Soon, we have a single repository for all the facts we need to respond to the proposal.

To help us organize this information, we categorize each document by proposal section, theme, author, and maybe even a ranking code for the best and worst ideas. We build views for each category so that it takes only seconds to find a document, and we create a full-text search index to help us locate key phrases in the text. As the team members read the supporting information, they also add their thoughts by attaching responses to the document.

Once the proposal is ready to write, we create another form in the same database for storing the drafts of each section, again categorizing the documents in ways that will help us organize and understand the information. The authors can use a sorted view to find all the ideas that back up what they are writing and create links to the supporting facts stored elsewhere in the database so that the editors can verify the points and arguments that they make.

Whenever someone edits a section, he or she pushes a button that marks the document as "Checked out" so others know that it is in use. With some development tricks, the document can even be locked, thus preventing users from making changes. After the changes are made, Notes can save a copy of the last version as a response document enabling editors to see the history of the document as it was built.

Often, some remote team members need to actively participate in the proposal process. They simply add their information to a database on their local PC, call the home office, and instruct Notes to synchronize their database with the master proposal database. If your company is partnering with another company and it has Notes, it can quickly become a part of the proposal with a few server changes.

As the proposal approaches completion, the team creates slide presentations and stores the files in a document in the database. The project leader changes the access on the database, enabling only a few people to make final edits to the product. The production department prints a copy of the proposal directly from the database, even as editors make last-minute changes to meet the deadline.

Because Notes isn't ideal as a word processor, if the editor wants a more professional-looking document, the production people can copy the documents into a word processor and generate such a final product. To impress the client, we make a copy of the database, strip out our internal notes and comments, and deliver both the Notes database and the paper document to the client just in time to meet the proposal deadline.

It's easy to understand why people get excited about Notes. It allows them to put all their data in a single place, control it, and disseminate it wherever it needs to go. Whenever someone asks about the status of the proposal, the answer is always "check the Notes database." If someone has something to add to the proposal effort, the instruction is "put it in the Notes database."

Using Notes for Process Improvement

The popularity of Notes also coincides with the increasing popularity of process improvement and process thinking. With process improvement, a company takes a detailed look at the way some or all of the tasks are performed in a process with the intent of saving time and money by doing things a better way. The people who perform the tasks in question usually come together as a team, document the flow of the old system, and try to come up with a better way of getting the task done.

As you would expect, many new processes require computerization. Before workgroup software existed, a company would typically build a system of screens that would capture information during the new process and add several reports to help users keep track of the process. The users would also write rules and guidelines around these systems to ensure that the proper approval and audit controls were in place. In many cases, rules meant paper forms, routing slips, and interplant mail. Users really didn't want another data entry screen and more reports; they wanted access to information and a very simple way to be more efficient. Users could see the benefits but they would sometimes question whether the "better" way was really going to save time and effort.

Workgroup software streamlines the systems that make process improvement work. Information resides in easily accessible databases, and Notes can keep people informed at any step in the process via electronic mail. Best of all, most people can just use the views and forms instead of reports to find the information they want.

The best way to see the connection between process improvement and Notes is to take a look at a typical process improvement activity and illustrate how a package like Notes can make a big difference. Let's assume that recently you have been put in charge of processing purchase requisitions. You lead a process improvement team and, during one of the meetings, you discover that there is a fairly predictable and somewhat automated process in place. Unfortunately, this process requires two or three weeks for your team to receive a requisition and another week to process it and place the order.

The requisition begins its journey after the originator enters the document into an automated system (see Figure 3.1). At the end of each day, the department clerk prints out the requisition and forwards it back to the originator, who signs it and puts it on the manager's desk for a signature (or, if it's important enough, on the seat of his or her chair). The manager signs the document and returns it to the clerk, who forwards it to your department, unless any line item is over $2,000, which means it must be signed by the vice president of the division.

Finally, the requisition arrives at your desk. Your team members recall the document from the automated system and they fill in the approval dates. If they are lucky, the requisition was filled out correctly and they can work on turning it into a purchase order. If not, the document heads back to the originator for changes and more trips through the approval process.

Next, your team wheels and deals with the vendors, updates the requisition, and prints a purchase order. For internal audit purposes, each purchase order must be approved by you if any line item is over $500. Finally, one copy of the order is faxed to the vendor, another is sent to the originator, and copies are sent to all of the approvers. Your file clerk diligently files other copies by vendor and by purchase order number (see Figure 3.2).

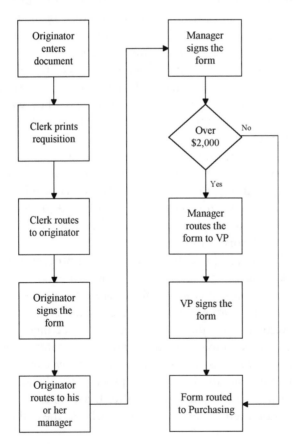

FIGURE 3.1 The requisition process, part 1.

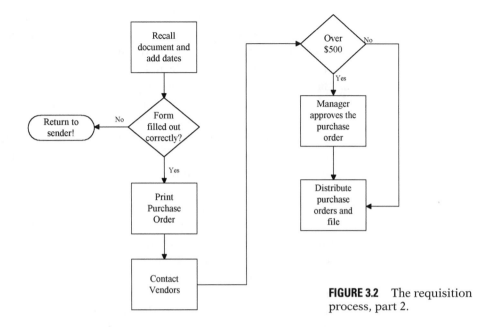

FIGURE 3.2 The requisition process, part 2.

Even with an automated system, no doubt the people who participate in this process will be frustrated by it. They always seem to be moving the document around, signing it, and filing copies of it to make sure the "system" doesn't lose it. The originator complains that your department is too slow; in reality, the approval process is the culprit. You are spending extra budget dollars on a filing clerk, on forms, and on a copier to make sure everyone is informed.

In contrast, let's apply the concepts of workgroup software to show how it can change the way your team works, while improving customer satisfaction. The problem with the process flow doesn't appear to be in the form that people use or any lack of ability to complete the form. Rather, it appears that the approval process and notification systems are cumbersome and labor-intensive. Let's see how Notes can be used to solve these problems. We need a system that eliminates the paper, reminds the approvers to sign the form, accepts electronic signatures, and prompts to add the extra approvals when required. When the order has been placed, the system needs to sort the information several different ways to meet the needs of all the people involved with the requisition.

We'll commission our trusty Notes developer to build a database for requisitions. We ask him or her to automate the requisition process based on the following scenario:

1. An originator enters a requisition into a Notes database. As he or she presses the Save button, Notes includes the originator's name in

the requisition and logs the date and time it was created. If the existing automated systems must be updated, the developer will use a tool like Notes ViP to update the systems periodically or interface Notes directly with the external system using the Notes API.

2. Based on the originator's employee ID or name, Notes determines who must approve the requisition and fires off a mail message to each of these people. If any line item is over $2,000, Notes adds the vice president's name to the list. The mail message includes a doclink that points to the requisition so the reader of the mail message can simply double-click on it to recall the requisition (see Figure 3.3).

3. The Notes mail system is customized to recognize the message as a request for approval. It prioritizes an approval message over the other mail messages, thus ensuring that it receives the appropriate attention. In fact, the mail system has a special view that shows only approval messages sorted by the originator's name and the date required.

4. In case the approvers become lax in giving their mail messages the appropriate attention, a background macro is scheduled to run every four hours to review the contents of the requisition database.

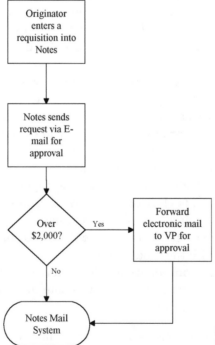

FIGURE 3.3 The new purchase requisition process, part 1.

If a requisition is missing the appropriate approvals or hasn't been put on hold in, say, two days, the program sends another message marked Urgent to the approver. If the approval is five days overdue, the program escalates it to the approver's manager.

5. The approvers display the requisition, review it for propriety, and click on an Approve button when they are finished. Notes adds the date and time of their electronic signature to the database and, when all the approvers have signed the document, it forwards a new message to the person in your group who is responsible for the department (see Figure 3.4).

6. Your reviewer reviews the requisition on the screen and notes any problems or questions in a special comments field on the form. If

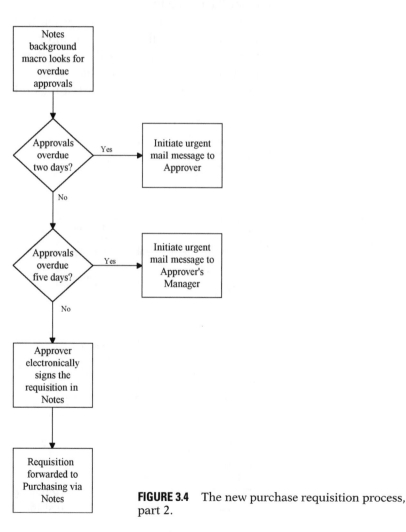

FIGURE 3.4 The new purchase requisition process, part 2.

further information is needed, the reviewer clicks a Needs more information button and Notes generates a mail message with the comments and a request for more information to the originator.

7. Once the reviewer is satisfied with the requisition, he or she places the selected vendor's name in the form and clicks the Place the order button. If the amount for any line item is over $500, it shoots a mail message to you to remind you to approve the form. In either case, Notes automatically faxes the document to the vendor, logs the time that the fax was sent, and notifies the originator (and the approvers if they still don't trust the system) via e-mail that the requisition was placed on a certain date with a certain vendor. If the vendor has Notes, your server could mail the order to them on a regular basis (see Figure 3.5).

8. If anyone needs to research the order, he or she simply calls up a Notes view that will provide the information. Orders can be displayed by originator, order date, purchase order number, or even vendor number. Instead of a file cabinet of paper, the Notes database contains a complete record of the entire requisition process.

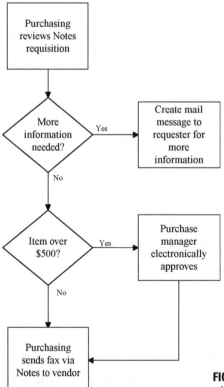

FIGURE 3.5 The new purchase requisition process, part 3.

As you can see, when our developer completes the database, we will be able to process, approve, and place an order in a very short period of time. The database has all the information detailing where the order is in the process, and your staff won't get calls every two days from people checking on its status. Users know that the approvers will immediately receive a message about the order, and all the approver has to do is read the screen and click a button to move the document on its way.

After the system is in place, you can assign your file clerk to much more important tasks or simply eliminate the position. The copier will stand idle a little more and mail room employees will be glad to see a lot fewer routing envelopes with copies of the requisitions in them. And you can review your team's work by browsing through a database instead of a pile of papers.

The key to the success of this and many other workflow applications is mail-enablement. As you can see in the example, the automated system that existed before Notes was limited by its inability to control the movement of the requisition throughout the system. The system cranked out a form and waited for it to arrive at the next destination where someone called it back up to add information. People had to pick up the form, move it somehow from approval to approval, and hope it arrived.

Notes and Mail Systems

With the Notes application, the requisition database is proactive, working with the mail system to make sure the requisition keeps moving forward throughout the process. Whenever someone performs a task, mail messages are issued to initiate the next step in the process. If someone forgets a step, the system reminds the person or escalates the urgency.

The mail system is also enhanced to improve the process. Notes Mail is simply another set of Notes databases that can be programmed and modified to support the processes in your company. By prioritizing approvals, the modified mail system raises the awareness of the approval process and helps the approvers separate the important messages from the flood of junk e-mail that comes across their desk.

Many non-Notes systems can be interfaced with most other mail systems, enabling them to generate messages based on certain events; but in such cases, the interface usually results in one-way messages that notify the recipient about an event that took place in the application. If the recipients want to see the record that generated the messages, they have to leave the mail system and load the other application first. In contrast, the connection between Notes Mail and other Notes databases is much more than an interface between two applications. Users can tap into the mail system at several levels, and application developers have a lot of flexibility in how they use the mail system to their advantage. Of course, you can always open your current mail database and send a message but, with Notes, there are many more opportunities to make mail do more.

The simplest access comes through the Mail menu in the Notes menu bar. No matter which databases or windows are open at any given time, you can select Mail Compose and create a mail message. How many times have you been working on one document and it sparked an idea or question that you need to discuss with someone else? When you select Mail Compose, Notes finds your mailbox and displays the mail form so you can create the message. If you want to reference something in the document that you were working on, you can insert a link to that document and place it inside your message. After you finish the message and send it off, Notes returns you to the place where you were before you started the message.

At other times, you may be reading a Notes document that you find important enough to send to another person. Perhaps the person is remote or doesn't have access to the document that you are reviewing. If you select another Notes menu choice, Mail Forward, Notes not only brings up a mail message form but also loads the entire document into the message area. Instead of cut and paste, you build a message quickly with all the information that you want to send.

And what if you need office supplies or want to notify the personnel department of your new address? The Notes mail system has the capacity to handle these tasks through the use of custom forms, which are usually lifted from an existing database and stored in a special database that the mail system accesses when you select Mail Compose Custom from the menu bar. Perhaps you're wondering why not just open the appropriate database and access the form directly. If you have a lot of forms, you are forced to fill your desktop with the icons that represent those databases that you may access only infrequently. Remote users would have to call the server and open the database just to get to the form. Custom forms gives you an electronic forms cabinet that centralizes the forms and saves you the hassle of figuring out where to go to get them.

Filling out a form doesn't do a lot of good if it ends up as a mail message for someone to key into another system. Notes solves the problem by allowing every database to become a mailbox that can receive mail from any other database. Most custom forms are set up to be automatically sent to the correct database after you complete the form. When it arrives at the database that contains the same form, Notes adds the message to the database as if it were keyed into it directly. The database owner doesn't really know how the message got there but he or she didn't have to key in the information.

Developers can tap into this same flexibility for any of the forms that they create in a Notes database. In the process improvement example, the requisition database automatically sent messages to the approvers. The users didn't have to select the Mail Compose menu or select a form from the Custom menu. Instead, the developer used information available in the database and created a mail message whenever the Approve or Save button was pushed. From within the application, the developer instructed Notes to send the information as a mail message.

Since any database can receive mail and all mail databases are programmable, the possibilities are infinite. When an application sends a message, it can send any or all of the fields that are on the form. It can be generated in a form called Memo and then modified to arrive at the destination database as a form called Action Item.

With this kind of flexibility, you can begin using Notes not only to improve processes but also to coordinate the movement of information to the culture of your workgroup, department, or even the entire company. Many organizations start by expanding the mail system to accommodate the personal management of their employees. After all, a lot of requests and task assignments come across on the e-mail system, usually as a followup to a meeting or an answer to a status report.

The mail system can easily become the hub for tracking mail and to-do's, personal goals, follow-up tasks, and status reports. If a message requires an action, you can push a button on the screen and Notes can convert it to a to-do form, where you add a due date and hourly estimates. When you send someone a message, you can use a follow-up field to flag it as a follow-up item, and then assign a date by which you need to check and see what happened. A developer can set up views that sort by to-do due dates or follow-up dates, ensuring that you review your tasks regularly and complete them.

Since Notes Mail is a programmable database, a developer can add a form to the mail database that displays the tasks and milestones arriving from databases, such as a project management or performance management database. As the messages come in, the recipient can associate them with one of the personal goals and save it for review time. A properly designed view can show users their progress toward personal goals and help them and their managers do a more effective performance evaluation.

Because Notes databases can be changed rapidly, users no longer need to wait patiently (or impatiently) for the changes required to implement the "idea of the month" coming out of management meetings. If this week marks the end of the old management system in favor of the hottest, latest version, for example, the Notes mail system can be modified in advance to quickly accommodate the newest theory. The Notes developers can create new forms and macros that move the old information into the new format and implement the changes within hours after the changes are needed.

The Evolution of the People

As Notes works its way through your organization, not only will you see a change in the way people do their jobs, you'll see a change in the people themselves. Once you've worked through a process improvement example with Notes, you will understand why some people get so excited when the lightbulb comes on about Notes. (A word of warning: the lightbulb comes on at different times for different people, which may cause some office battles if the implementation of Notes is not well controlled.)

We've already looked at how a company's process can change. Next let's take a look at the growth of Notes culture through the eyes of the diverse personalities that may emerge in its wake. Every organization is different and will react differently to a Notes implementation. Nevertheless, you will no doubt recognize some or all of the personality types discussed in the next sections.

The Zealots

We all know these people. They are the wild-eyed proponents of the latest word processor, fax software, and remote control mouse. They bug the IS staff for all of their computer magazines (they are seldom IS people because they are considered too dangerous), and they spend their evenings using America Online and watching *Star Trek*. They use (and sometimes abuse) their computer for everything, and they help those around them who haven't mastered the new technologies.

We've got to give them credit, nevertheless, for being visionaries about software products. They probably read about Notes in a magazine article or stopped at a trade show booth and listened intently as a salesperson extolled its virtues. They saw its value and immediately saw how it could revolutionize the office. They couldn't wait to tell everyone! Unfortunately, the Zealots have been pumped up so often about hot software that many of their colleagues may regard Notes as just another one of their crazy ideas. Notes is hard enough to explain to an attentive audience but to doubtful co-workers it's more difficult. In addition, Notes is tough to set up initially and some serious hardware is required to pilot a project in the department.

The Power Zealots

The Power Zealots (PZs) are usually managers with a keen eye for technologies that can contribute to the success of their departments and their careers. They usually come from one of the more creative departments like Marketing or Proposals, and they may have even been a Zealot until they realized that it took more than enthusiasm to get new ideas implemented. They probably introduced the first PC or Macintosh into the company and pushed hard for the overpriced color laser printer that everyone now depends on.

When they hear the Zealots expounding the virtues of Notes, they do a little checking on their own and, sure enough, they acknowledge that Notes has a lot of potential. In fact, they realize they could use it on an upcoming project and solve the current communications problem with the field salespeople. They check their budget, call in a couple of favors, and the hardware and software for the pilot project is on the way.

The IS guys catch wind of the project but, frankly, don't have time to do much more than approve the requisitions and write memos to the PZs about the guidelines prohibiting unauthorized network attachments. The PZs have already made sure that there was a little extra capacity on the network when they requisitioned the equipment to cover their "unexpected project contingencies." The memos don't worry them much.

While waiting for the system to arrive, the PZs check the budget again and see that they can bring in a college intern or two with a computer science background for the new project. The interns and the PZ's lead worker take a quick trip to the closest Notes training facility for classes on Notes administration and development. When they return, they begin in earnest to develop discussion forums, mail systems, and simple applications.

The Loyal Team Player

Working for the Power Zealot has required the Loyal Team Player (LTP) to learn how to adapt to rapid change, who finds the changes aren't too bad after the initial glitches are solved, and that, actually, the job stays fresh and exciting because of them. The Power Zealot gives the LTP a lot of recognition and some pretty good computer equipment, so the changes are taken in stride.

At first, Notes was hard to understand, but the interns were patient. They tweaked the systems quickly to match what the LTP wanted. The Power Zealot called meetings to discuss how effective the Notes applications were and asked the LTP to contribute. Soon, everyone felt comfortable with Notes, and the LTP even showed it off to friends in other departments.

The Operations Convert

The IS team wasn't blind to what was going on outside of the computer room. They've kept an eye on the rapid growth of Notes in the maverick department and they've noticed an awful lot of interest from other areas.

They've also noticed a steady increase in calls to the Help Desk to assist with the Notes server, to add users, and to possibly add a backup to the daily routine for all the Notes servers.

It's obvious to the Operations Convert (OC) that the Notes installation is outgrowing the capabilities of the college interns and, within a matter of months, the indispensable server will crash without some standards and periodic maintenance. More servers have already been requested by other departments, and clearly, someone must take control of the situation and clear up the chaos.

After lengthy discussions with the IS director, the Operations Convert builds a plan to consolidate the maintenance of the Notes servers under the control of the IS group. The OC proposes the plan to each of the department heads, who, in most cases, readily agree to turn over the most frustrating and least productive tasks for Notes servers—backup, adding and changing IDs, and capacity planning.

The Operations Convert works closely with the Help Desk to handle user requests, and, finally, moves the servers into the computer room. The OC rankles a few people by wrestling away control of the servers and limiting the number of people who can create a database on them. Now only the IS support team can put new Notes databases on the server but, overall, the server seems to crash less often and run a little faster.

Once the Operations Convert figures out Notes, it quickly becomes clear how the server can be configured to better support multiple departments and possibly even the loosely related sibling companies. After some interesting internal discussions with several IS compadres about replacing the company's electronic mail software with Notes, the OC interfaces Notes to the internal mail system and prepares for a transition of the users at a later date.

The Resistance

The announcement that IS is supporting Notes generates a lot of speculation, fear, and questions regarding the future of Notes in the organization. The success stories have filtered throughout the company, and managers are talking about how they might use Notes to solve their business problems. The IS team is even leading a group that is discussing how they can eliminate paperwork, handbooks, and forms by using Notes and Notes Mail.

The members of the Resistance are having a hard time with the rapid changes that they see in the company. They figure that if they ignore Notes, they won't have to use it. After all, they point out, they have done an excellent job for 23 years without Notes, so why try to learn it now. In fact, they question why the company should invest so much time and money in Notes without any quantifiable return. They add that it took them three years to master the electronic mail system, and they will keep using it because they know that the IS department can't just eliminate it until everyone has been trained and converted.

Despite their foot-dragging, the Resistance is often made up of some of the most valuable contributors in the company. Because of their lengthy tenures, they are often considered experts in their position. The latest upheaval not only disrupts their routine but also takes away the personal power that they have achieved through their longevity.

Of course, if you show the Resistance that Notes applications can be used to bring discipline and order to the chaotic systems that currently generate incomplete and inaccurate information, they will become some of your best supporters. Initially, they resist change partly because of the mess it makes and partly because it makes them uncomfortable. The members of the Resistance often just want people to follow the rules so that they can get their job done. If you propose a solution that fosters this activity, they'll soon get behind it.

The accounting department is often a haven for some members of the Resistance. By their very nature, accountants are conservative, and they really, *really* like their spreadsheets and accounting applications. In fact, they can be a stumbling block during the implementation of Notes because they control the purse strings for the company. They want justifications, one-year paybacks, and zero-cash flow options before they'll even consider Notes. But if you can show them that Notes can pay for itself, they can make it a lot easier to move your project forward.

The Notes Angel

At some point during the ramp up of Notes, the demand for small additions and changes to database forms and views begins to overwhelm the Zealots, their bosses, and anyone who has been pegged as the "Notes person." As the IS team begins developing Notes systems, it will have its hands full creating the new databases that are going to change the shape of the company. The backlog has already exceeded the meager resources that were allocated to Notes development so help usually doesn't come quickly from them.

The Operations Convert is usually the first to notice this phenomenon because the backlog for Notes calls is growing. The OC also gets the phone calls from department managers begging for more help with their Notes problems. The departments are already asking the personnel department for approval to hire a college intern to help out. After all, the Power Zealots were permitted to use interns, which worked for them.

Luckily, the Operations Convert has had an eye on the young and spunky support person who somehow manages to field 30 calls a day and visit 10 users before lunch. The OC realizes that the job is fun but even an enthusiast can install Windows and Netware drivers only so often before the routine gets a little dull. The support person already has installed Notes numerous times and even took it home to learn it. The OC knows that the backlog will become worse if one of the best support people is tied up, but knows that the support person really needs a change. When approached about the new job, the support person is a little nervous because of the lack of experience writing macros and creating very large databases. The OC expresses confidence in the support person, passes along all the small Notes development requests, and asks for only the best work that can be done.

After a couple of days with users, the support person realizes how quickly even one person can make a difference. Users seem to want only small changes, and the support person is able to make them in no time. In the users' eyes, the support person is an angel that came out of nowhere to solve their problems. The Notes Angel is ecstatic to be able to help, receive a lot of good feedback, and learn a new skill that will make him or her more valuable in the workplace.

The Notes Evangelist

The Power Zealots are happy to see Notes take off, but they just don't have time to take it beyond their department. Besides, to make Notes work well, someone needs to have a vision of what Notes can do for the company as a whole. That person must understand how Notes can link to or replace the mail system, know how to leverage replication and external communications to help the company, and discover where to find ways to tap the growing pool of external information services being offered to Notes users.

Enter the Notes Evangelists (NE). They can come from a variety of places but, usually, they are analysts in the IS group, the personnel department, or members of another department that could just as easily fit into IS or personnel. The NEs can temper a Zealot's hype with information, cajole a Resistor into looking at both sides of the issue, convince a Loyal Team Player to beta-test a new database, and show management how far they can leverage Notes to boost the bottom line.

Everyone wants to see Notes be more than just an amorphous information-gathering tool. They want someone to draw the "big picture" on paper, hear what others are using Notes for, and bounce ideas off someone who knows how it works. The Evangelists relish the task because they have seen all the opportunities for improvement in the company, and they have always wanted to find an automated way to take advantage of them.

The Notes Evangelists have an interesting mix of skills. They can build almost any kind of Notes database and show it to an audience with the gusto of a circus performer. They understand the inner workings of a Notes server, and can teach a beginner's class the ins and outs of using Notes. They scour the Notes Partner Forums for new ideas, then pepper the e-mail system with suggestions on how to use them. They fight the negative comments about Notes with enthusiasm and optimism.

The Refugees

In addition to the personality types already discussed, there will always be the stragglers who stayed out of the fray and now don't understand Notes. These people find their beloved e-mail system being discontinued as Notes Mail makes positive inroads. Slowly but surely, every piece of company information is now "out on Notes." In some cases, their boss finally tells them to just use it, period.

In many cases, there's not much you can do for the Refugees because they often deal with all change in this way. The smarter ones will get into Notes in their own time. The others may need special training, a little hand-holding, or simply an excuse to leave the company. It may also be that Notes hasn't yet made much of a difference in their job, and they need an application to help them join the crowd.

This evolution doesn't happen after someone rips open a carton of Notes. The time frame depends on the capacity of the culture for change. If a company is keeping pace in a rapidly changing industry, then the need for efficiency may necessitate full implementation in less than a year. That kind of time frame may cause serious conflicts between personality types because there isn't sufficient time for people to learn how to work together in the new environment. In such a situation, expect to invest in both Notes and conflict-resolution consultants.

On the other hand, it's not uncommon for two or three years to pass before Notes has sufficient acceptance in a company to be considered an integral part of its information systems. The employees can more slowly absorb the changes and assimilate the new systems that come online. If a company can afford to wait, the extra time can smooth the implementation.

Table 3.1 is a summary of the personalities discussed in this chapter. Can you identify them in your organization? Keep this list handy as Notes evolves. It may help you to understand your colleagues and how to deal with them.

TABLE 3.1 The Personalities in a Notes Culture

Personality Type	How It Fits in a Notes Implementation
Zealots	The wild-eyed enthusiasts who see what Notes can do and want everyone to share the excitement.
Power Zealots	The managers who have a vision for what Notes can do for their team and push hard to get it.
Loyal Team Players	The people who accept Notes early and begin the ground-swell of acceptance among the mainstream employees.
Operations Convert	The person who takes a big risk to organize the support requirements that Notes creates.
The Resistance	People who question the value of Notes and make sure that the Notes implementation is justified before it can move forward.
Notes Angel	A plucky support person who keeps an implementation going by helping users with all their requests.
Notes Evangelist	The visionary who helps everyone understand how Notes strategically fits into the organization.
Refugees	People who always wait to see if Notes is real, then hurriedly try to learn it and catch up.

The Evolution Behind Glass Doors

The integration of Notes into a company doesn't always depend on a few mavericks who decide to bring Notes in the back door. The Zealots and Evangelists in a company often belong to the management or IS team that has included Notes in their corporate strategy. Many IS groups, too, have spearheaded the push for Notes and taken a proactive, positive approach to bringing it into a company.

Whether the IS group leads or follows, it will experience its own metamorphosis as Notes invades its unique subculture. The IS staff will become users, developers, and caretakers—a great combination that will help them understand Notes and feel what their customers feel. In effect, they will have a professional as well as personal interest in its success.

The IS departments of the '90s are experiencing massive changes in tools and technologies. Notes may appear at first to be just another product that competes for their attention. A Notes project needs one or two people to get it off the ground, usually someone like the Operations Convert and the Notes Evangelist. They generate user excitement, get the pilot on the way, and take the heat on Notes, while the rest of the department worries about the other systems.

The operations team is often the first to accept Notes and move forward. These are the folks who have spent their lives adapting new technologies to an operational environment and making them run, and in many ways, Notes is just another challenge. They quickly learn how to bring up the Notes server, back it up, and load copies on users' machines. They'll discover that they can use Notes for their procedures manuals, backup schedules, and even Help Desk calls. They adapt as usual—nothing fancy... nothing splashy... Notes is operational.

The development team is a tougher nut to crack. Developers and analysts tend to want things to come to a standstill until they can get their projects done. They want known tools, minimal risks, and control of their computing environment. They are paid to make sure that solid systems are implemented on time and under budget. Notes offers them a potpourri of tools from Lotus and third parties, a sometimes quirky macro language, a Visual Basic equivalent, and a user environment that is less than bulletproof. Users figure out that forms and views are easy to create and they want developers to build a lot of them quickly. The users also create their own quick and dirty solutions to problems and then ask the developers to clean them up and implement them for a lot of other people.

It takes a Notes Development Guru to raise the Notes development effort to a serious and professional level. Whether the person is homegrown or specially hired, the Guru bridges the gap between traditional tools and methods and the Notes way of developing a system. This person answers the questions about connecting Notes to an SQL database or adding a special routine in the C language using the Notes API. The Guru connects with the Notes Evangelist to explain the technology and its implications and to describe the architecture of the systems to the database administrator, who is trying to make order out of the company's databases.

After one developer is immersed successfully into Notes, the rest of the team usually will follow suit. The Guru works with the team manager to bring in the best kit of support tools and helps the newer developers design the databases correctly and create good forms and views. The Guru contributes to the standards before there are too many databases to change.

As the team grows, its members will find that Notes encourages a closer working relationship between the users and the IS development team. Users will ask developers to venture out into the user community to build systems quickly and make changes on the fly with them. Although large-scale modifications will still require a controlled testing environment, many changes will be able to happen online in front of a user. Developers will become closer to the customers and enjoy the rewards of immediate feedback and improvements.

Throughout these changes in IS, the IS manager plays a pivotal role in making Notes a success. The IS job is a tough balancing act between heavy user demands, budget shortages, rampant technology changes, and managing a creative and often eccentric group of professionals who, seemingly, can make miracles happen. To implement Notes, the IS manager takes on a unique challenge that could be highly successful while possibly shifting the control of information and even development to the user community.

The purpose of an IS group is to provide to users information that improves the operating efficiency and decision making capacity of the organization. The IS group also ensures that all the support systems for hardware and software are efficient, cost-effective, and sufficient for the demands of the company. Notes will help the IS manager achieve all that more rapidly than many other tools, and the care and feeding of Notes is not much different from the support required for existing personal computer software, client-server databases, and applications.

Acknowledging the potential benefits of Notes, the IS manager will become a controlled Notes Evangelist. While the other Notes Evangelists will do the hard-core selling to the masses, the IS manager will create a vision for solid, dependable, well-managed information systems with the open and unstructured possibilities of Notes. Who better than the IS manager to alleviate top management fears that Notes is just a lot of expensive possibilities? The IS manager can demonstrate how the IS group will manage resources and bring development disciplines to the effort.

The IS manager is in a position to know, because the IS systems touch every aspect of an organization. With the help of the other Notes Evangelists, the IS manager can build a vision document that targets all the opportunities where Notes can make immediate and high-impact gains. The IS management staff comes together to deal with capital spending needs, capacity planning, support requirements, and development needs.

Once there is a vision, the IS manager drums up support in the ranks of the management team. The vision document gives the IS manager an opportunity to meet with other key managers to gather input and build a joint vision for Notes. They are pushed for a commitment to the plan and a willingness to contribute budget dollars, allocate manpower, and even reorganize current development plans if necessary.

As the vision solidifies and Notes moves forward, the IS manager maintains the vision and the commitment to making Notes work. Naturally, the new systems won't always be successful or meet all the user expectations, so the IS manager must be able to refocus the team on the objectives, modify the plans to adapt to business changes, and take the heat and exude confidence when department managers think the sky is falling.

Along the way, the IS team will experience its share of personality conflicts and developments, which will liven up the group and change it forever. The Notes developers will be in high demand, perhaps even altering the internal pecking order of the group and requiring some reorganization.

Nevertheless, as it has with other new languages, tools, and technologies, the IS team will assimilate Notes and make it one of their many tools to solve business needs.

Throwing Out the Paradigms

No matter how it is introduced, Notes changes the corporate culture, and people view information in a completely different way. They throw out all their old paradigms for storing and distributing information; instead of newsletters, faxes, memos, and bulletin board items, information is stored in databases that are accessible to everyone. Change becomes less threatening because users see Notes in action and know that the next new application will look and feel like those they already use.

The biggest shift occurs when people begin to understand the document orientation of Notes and how it differs from the record orientation they are familiar with. Those applications well suited to a transaction orientation have been automated over and over again for years. They often require a structured query to display a screen with fields filled with information. Each field can hold a certain number of characters, and, if the application is robust, a user can jump from one screen to another and follow the audit trail that backs up the original transaction.

In contrast, the information stored in Notes documents has seldom been automated and usually has been scattered in a variety of places on the network. People begin to realize that a Notes document contains fields of information, much like a transaction, and can hold attachments like word processing documents, spreadsheets, or embedded documents using OLE technology. Therefore, they begin to reduce their reliance on e-mail conversations and routing envelopes and focus on moving their documents to a system that can make the documents more available to everyone.

In fact, the lure of document orientation often makes people restless with their traditional applications. Instead of a single screen with a single record displayed on it, users can go into a Notes view and browse through a summary of the records until they find what they want. If the view is categorized, they can expand and collapse the view so that only the records under a single category show. Traditional systems often have more rigid search procedures, usually allowing users to search for a value or scroll through a lookup window with limited information.

However, Notes isn't robust enough to handle large-transaction volumes that require a lot of processing or complex calculations. This type of transaction still calls for the power and capacity of transaction-oriented systems. The ultimate solution, then, is a marriage of the two systems, where users have access to the transaction information in large databases and the flexibility of unstructured documents in Notes.

One solution is a database product to which Notes can connect, perform a query, and use the results on a Notes form. A good example of this kind of connection is a human resources application at a large corporation. The bulk of the processing for personnel information, government reporting, and feeds to the payroll system is done by a large, SQL-based application. When the human resources department receives a call for assistance, however, they log the call in a Notes database and use an SQL link to display employee information as they help the caller.

Another "happy marriage" is that between Notes and the concept of a data warehouse. A data warehouse is a repository of information, which is a snapshot of data at a point in time. This concept has become very popular in the '90s and, in addition to Notes, there are many other products that act as data warehouses.

The large, online systems prevalent in business meant that users often spent all day adding information and performing queries, while reporting was relegated to the night shift in order to reduce the processing loads on the system. If users wanted a report to sort differently, they waited for a developer to find some time to make the change or they used query tools that guzzled computing power and bogged down the central systems.

But users soon began to realize that most of their reports were created for a certain historical date or for a specific need. Further, they saw that if the data in the reports was processed in a timely manner and stored in a Notes database in a way that gave them some flexibility to sort and extract it, they wouldn't need all the paper reports. The database could even hold multiple snapshots and automatically clean out snapshots at regular intervals.

The repository for a data warehouse can be Notes, another database, or even a spreadsheet. Instead of creating reports based on a variety of permutations of the data, a user defines what data is needed, how it should be processed, and how often the snapshot should be taken. Once the information is placed in a Notes database, a developer can create a set of views for everyone to use. The users can then create their own custom views to help them do their specific tasks. Instead of paper reports, users scroll through information, drill down into the data, and extract what they need electronically.

Further, instead of running reports at night, developers can create data warehouse programs that process the data on the appropriate date and update Notes during the evening. The update can be as simple as an import of a text file or a more complicated routine written with the Notes API that merges and updates information. When users arrive in the morning, their snapshots are waiting for them.

Using Notes as a data warehouse is a timesaver for the IS group as well. Developers have to write only one program that creates all the necessary data elements. As users determine how they want to view information, developers can quickly create views to accommodate them. Users can easily create their own custom views rather than waiting for a developer; if the view becomes popular, the developers can simply add it to the design for everyone else to use.

To illustrate this concept, let's take a look at simple data warehouse for the management of XYZ Corp. Each day, a number of sales representatives take orders over the phone and enter them into the sales order entry system. Each night, the system prints invoices and updates its databases so that the representatives can research customer accounts and check inventory statuses the next day. Each week, the president of the company receives one report that lists total sales by product line, another that shows sales by territory, and a third that shows the YTD history for the top 50 customers of XYZ. During a special promotion, the sales manager requests daily reports to help evaluate the effectiveness of the campaign. The controller receives a product line analysis by profit margin once every two weeks.

To replace all of these reports, the IS manager asks the management team members if they would be willing to use a Notes data warehouse as their tool. Each night, a program would be executed that would update the database with the sales details, down to the line item on the invoice. The IS staff would develop detailed views by product line, territory, salesperson, and customer. Then, instead of printing the reports, the managers could simply open the database and look at a view designed for them.

Skeptical at first, the president and his or her managers agree to try Notes instead of reports. Every morning, the president selects a view categorized by product line and date and then another by territory and product line. Curious about the profit margins, he or she also uses the controller's view shown in Figure 3.6 to check them out.

The president then pops up the top 50 customer view and checks out the details of sagging sales to Smith Company, which once topped the list. When the president realizes Smith stopped buying products, he or she selects Mail Compose from the Notes menu to share the information with the sales manager.

The sales manager starts the morning by reviewing the details of yesterday's sales and sees a large spike in the revenue number. He or she creates a custom view to show only those sales exceeding $5,000 per invoice by customer and discovers a brisk business coming from a new customer. He or she makes a quick call to the owner of the company to offer a personal thanks for the orders. At month's end, the sales manager fends off questions about commissions by directing salespeople to the database to research details.

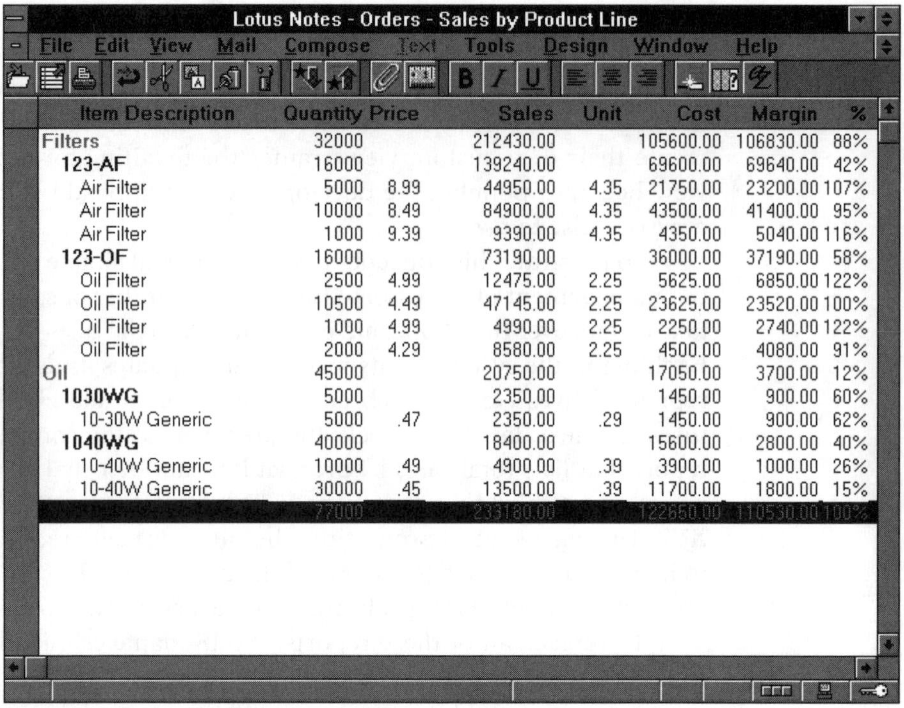
Lotus Notes - Orders - Sales by Product Line
File Edit View Mail Compose Text Tools Design Window Help
Item Description Quantity Price Sales Unit Cost Margin %
Filters 32000 212430.00 105600.00 106830.00 88%
123-AF 16000 139240.00 69600.00 69640.00 42%
Air Filter 5000 8.99 44950.00 4.35 21750.00 23200.00 107%
Air Filter 10000 8.49 84900.00 4.35 43500.00 41400.00 95%
Air Filter 1000 9.39 9390.00 4.35 4350.00 5040.00 116%
123-OF 16000 73190.00 36000.00 37190.00 58%
Oil Filter 2500 4.99 12475.00 2.25 5625.00 6850.00 122%
Oil Filter 10500 4.49 47145.00 2.25 23625.00 23520.00 100%
Oil Filter 1000 4.99 4990.00 2.25 2250.00 2740.00 122%
Oil Filter 2000 4.29 8580.00 2.25 4500.00 4080.00 91%
Oil 45000 20750.00 17050.00 3700.00 12%
1030WG 5000 2350.00 1450.00 900.00 60%
10-30W Generic 5000 .47 2350.00 .29 1450.00 900.00 62%
1040WG 40000 18400.00 15600.00 2800.00 40%
10-40W Generic 10000 .49 4900.00 .39 3900.00 1000.00 26%
10-40W Generic 30000 .45 13500.00 .39 11700.00 1800.00 15%
77000 233180.00 122650.00 110530.00 100%

FIGURE 3.6 The controller's profit margin view.

As you can see by this example, using Notes as a data warehouse gives the management team valuable information, when they want it, in a tool that's simple to use. Today's managers have had access to PCs for over 10 years, and, with a little instruction, they can manipulate Notes and reduce the requests for reports to the IS department. Soon, the management culture will change, and many reports will be eliminated in favor of a Notes database.

A New Culture

Company cultures don't change over night, regardless of whether we want them to change or they need to change. It may take several years for a company to assimilate all the changes that a product like Notes can produce. The company may experience an influx of applicants who want to work at the new, forward-thinking company. It may face turnover as members of the Resistance and Refugees decide not to accept the change. In any case, the company *will* change.

The exciting aspect of a Notes implementation is watching people use it after it has been in place a while. Users log in to Notes immediately to check mail, review the latest discussion databases, and check the latest information available in several data warehouses. Doclinks pop up in mail messages, and you'll hear "Go check Notes—I think it's in there" daily. When presented with an opportunity to improve a process, users will ask "Can we use Notes to make it better?"

C H A P T E R

4

Assimilating Notes

As people assimilate Notes into their company culture, they pass through phases of acceptance and understanding, as with any new technology. Notes changes their paradigm; in this case, the way they store and view information. Obviously, not everyone moves through these phases at the same pace. It will take patience and leadership from those spearheading the Notes effort to turn disagreement, frustration, and potential failure into positive discussions, compromise, and learning experiences. Notes also brings about some significant changes in the way users think about information. Many books are available that talk about accepting change and paradigm shifts and frankly, it's probably a good idea to pick one up for you and your colleagues. To date, users have learned to accept the traditional structured systems that are in place, relying on developers for changes to their systems.

With Notes, both users and developers are creating systems. Developers must connect unstructured Notes information to existing structured systems. The relationship between users and developers will change, and the company culture must adapt to be successful. As people pass through the acceptance cycles, one user may perceive an incredible benefit from the change, while another may view it as a dangerous threat to his or her orderly world. Again, remember everyone changes at his or her own pace and it is important to anticipate a variety of reactions. Only then can a Notes implementation be successful.

The five phase of acceptance are:

Exploration	What is Notes?
Discovery	This looks interesting. What can I do with it?
Euphoria	Wow! This is really cool! I'm going to do everything in Notes!
Reality Check	I can't do that?! That changes everything!
Control	I see. Yes, that would be a good approach. Let's do it!

There is no set time frame for how long people will spend in each of these areas. Some users will live and breathe Notes because everything they do depends on it. Others may only experience Notes once in a while and delay any opinions until they see what their co-workers do with it.

To help everyone through these cycles in a positive and constructive way, the group providing Notes should give everyone involved plenty of information about Notes, along with a healthy understanding of its capabilities. They should show users how Notes will benefit them and the company as a whole. When done sincerely, this flow of information will build a trust between users and providers.

Let's look at each cycle from the vantage point of both the user and the provider. In most cases, the provider is some kind of internal information systems department; but it may also be a consultant, a contract employee who is hired to assist in the implementation, or a zealot who pops up in the organization.

Exploration

The User Perspective

The previous chapter detailed the wide variety of user personalities in every organization. Except for the zealot, Notes will probably represent an unfamiliar technology to most users. Because it "kind of" looks like a word processor, a database, a Windows desktop, and an electronic mail system, they may not have ever imagined all of these applications rolled into one package, and they will need help understanding how it works.

For some, the journey through this cycle is often facilitated through question and answer sessions, brochures, and books—like this one. The internal Notes proponent should have Notes marketing literature from Lotus available and maybe even buy a few copies of this book so that people can study Notes, and learn what to expect when it arrives. One of the biggest dangers during this phase is that users may sense that the proponents are hiding information or making Notes seem too mysterious to understand. Just saying "Trust me" will not work. Actually, the more information given to the users early in the implementation cycle, the better!

Let's assume that the Notes proponent has put together a series of question and answer sessions using a well-respected Notes consultant. Let's also assume that the proponent has placed a good selection of Notes literature on tables in the room and that several books are now available to be checked out. The question and answer session may go like this:

Q: *What is Notes?*
A: Notes stores information, displays it, and moves information throughout your organization. It helps typical office users store information for others to share, and it helps them find and view information quickly. For the person who creates systems for the company, Notes provides a programming environment that supports rapid development of solutions to business problems. Remote users can view or download information with a few mouse clicks. The research analyst can arrive in the morning and find that Notes has polled several databases and retrieved the latest information during the night.

Q: *What kind of information can we put into Notes?*
A: Notes is a database that allows you to store text, numbers, and dates. It also has a special field called Rich Text where you can store huge documents. You can attach word processing documents, spreadsheets, pictures, and information generated from other packages, and launch those packages from Notes to view the information.

Q: *Can everybody put information into the same database?*
A: Yes. Notes allows many users to read and update information simultaneously.

Q: *What if I only want a few people to look at the information?*
A: Each Notes database has security at the form level where you enter information and at the view level where you browse through the information. You can limit who can open the database, who uses a form or a view, and who can read, add, or delete information in the database.

Q: *You talk about remote users. If I'm remote, won't it cost me a fortune to stay on the phone to look at all this information?*
A: When remote users dial in to a server, Notes regards them as a local network connection. It's true that a user could spend hours on the phone browsing around Notes databases. The more efficient way, however, is using the Notes replication function. As a remote user, you ask

Notes to make a replica, or copy, of a database on your local PC. When you dial in, you tell Notes to bring just the new information to your PC and to transfer your changes to the server. You hang up, and then you can use Notes locally without telephone charges.

Q: *If our remote people can dial in, can't hackers get in, too?*

A: Each user has to have an ID file that is certified by the Notes Administrator for the Notes installation. You can only connect to a Notes server with Notes, so if remote users aren't certified, they can't get in. If a user somehow has found a certified ID, he or she would still be limited to the security that we talked about before.

Q: *I only have a 386/33 on my desktop. Can my PC handle it?*

A: Notes will run on any Windows machine, but you should have a 486 or higher if you want acceptable performance in Notes.

Q: *I have a Macintosh. Can I run Notes on my Mac?*

A: Notes supports Macintosh clients. Again, the faster the Mac, the better the Notes performance.

Q: *Somebody told me that we'd have to use the Notes Mail system. I like our current e-mail system. Why do we have to change it?*

A: You don't have to change electronic mail systems. Notes Mail can integrate into your existing mail system through a software bridge that translates the message formats for you. However, one of Notes strengths is the integration of mail and databases. Notes Mail allows you to create forms that mail the information to a database. You can also send a message with a pointer to some information in a database that you'd like the recipient to read.

Q: *This whole Notes thing sounds like a big project. How much is this going to cost us?*

A: It is my experience that the hardware and software for Notes costs about $500 per user. Setup, training, development, and implementation costs vary, depending on how rapidly you want Notes put in place.

(Note: The following questions probably should be addressed by the internal proponent and his or her staff before this kind of meeting. Without thinking through the answers to these questions in advance, the provider and proponent risk being ill-prepared, and it subsequently may appear that there is some mystery to the Notes installation that he or she doesn't want to discuss.)

Q: *I don't have that kind of money in my budget for Notes! Who's going to pay for it?*

A: Because the Notes implementation affects everyone in the company, we are working with the controller to fund a company-wide project with a separate budget for Notes. In this way, you can concentrate on how to use Notes to make your department more efficient while we deal with the cost issues.

Q: *Who's going to load this stuff on our machines?*
A: My firm, Notes to You, has been hired to assist your internal staff in developing a plan for implementing Notes. They are also developing staffing plans to add the personnel needed to load and support Notes, and they would appreciate your help in reviewing those plans.

Q: *Who'll write the systems for us? Can we do it?*
A: Initially, we are considering the purchase of the XYZ Personnel System to replace the manual personnel system that you now use (a big cheer from the audience). This will reduce your workload and help us introduce Notes into the company. Your internal staff and I will be working with you to discuss development opportunities. The internal development staff will be trained in Notes to develop the applications. And yes, you *can* develop systems, and we encourage you to become active in using Notes. However, we'd like you to work with us and follow some basic guidelines, so that the systems can be maintained and supported successfully.

The questions could go on for quite a long time. And remember, you can't give the users too much information if you want them to buy into Notes! A big investment during this phase will almost guarantee a smoother transition through the other phases.

Users also need to feel that they can participate in the growth of Notes and that they can be involved in some development. They won't be patient for new applications when they discover that they can develop quick and dirty solutions in a short period of time.

The Provider Perspective

The best way to introduce Notes in an organization is through the proactive, positive support of the IS department. These departments have spent years adding vision and structure to information systems, servers, and networks, and a Notes implementation will impact each of these areas. From the outside, Notes seems fairly simple; on the inside, it's work to build a maintainable Notes environment.

If the IS department doesn't originate the use of Notes, those in the department who are charged with supporting Notes will be rushed through the exploration stage. And, because the IS department may already be more conservative than most, a rush job through exploration may cause resentment later. Instead of taking responsibility for the new challenges during the Notes implementation, IS staff may be tempted to *blame* the proponents instead of teaming with them to solve problems. Therefore, it's best for the provider to team up with the IS department as soon as possible to avoid these problems.

The IS people are always expected to be one step ahead of everyone else technologically, even if they are understaffed and overworked. In most cases, they are usually on the lookout for technologies like Notes. They travel in packs to trade shows, where, after a few demos of Notes, they will pelt vendors with technical questions and requests for demo copies of software. IS people will need to touch it, load it, and understand what it will do to their environment because, intuitively, they know it can make a big difference in their company.

The best way for a provider to get through this phase is to contact another provider at a similar company to find out how their implementation went. Everybody goes through these phases, and most companies are more than willing to brag a little about their great applications and how they survived the initial setbacks. The provider at the company with Notes already installed is probably an IS person too, so one or two phone calls should answer most questions.

Discovery

The User Perspective

I've seldom seen people leave a Q&A session without having their interest piqued by Notes. They may not be thrilled with the provider or proponent, the perceived budget problems, or the thought of such a huge project, but the concept of Notes and what it can do will stay with them. Once the seed is planted, the desire for Notes won't go away.

But whether users attend a Q&A or complete the exploration phase on their own, they will no doubt be reticent until they confirm their understanding by seeing Notes in action. Some may already have visions of the systems that they might be able to create in Notes, and they will want to know if those ideas are possible. Others will simply want to know if they are going to have to spend hours in Notes classes and how the mail works.

This is the time to identify for the "hot buttons" in each department— the labor intensive, time-consuming, irritating tasks that drive employees nuts every day. Talk with the managers of all departments; then consult the "spiritual leaders"—those people who seem to inspire others to action through their hard work and positive attitude. They will be key to the acceptance of Notes by the rest of the group.

Identify one of the simpler tasks in each department and build a prototype for it, preferably in front of the employees; or at least save the *piece de resistance* for the demonstration. In effect, you must sell the concept of Notes, and an "ah-ha" element or two will help convince them that they need Notes.

At the typical demonstration of Notes, you'll see the Zealots, the Loyal Team Player (LTP), and the Resistance. The Zealots will want to prove to the others that they were right, and to show everyone how much they know about Notes. The LTP will be truly interested in helping the department and the department manager. The Resistance will want to make sure that Notes isn't another lame-brained idea that will cause a ton of work. It's best to somehow diffuse the Zealots at some point because their questions and comments will draw the conversation away from how Notes can solve business problems, and the demonstration may veer into a technical discussion that bores the others, or into an esoteric discussion that should have been handled in the Q&A session. You might consider inviting the Zealots to a separate technical discussion or have a one-on-one meeting to give them a chance to discuss Notes.

In the Discovery phase, it's important that both the LTP and the Resistance leave the demonstration with confidence that Notes can do the job. The LTP will be willing to compromise if you can convince him or her that the long-term outlook of the Notes application is bright. The Resistance will be willing to go along with Notes as long as they're assured the application will work better than the existing system and save both time and money.

To better illustrate how the demonstration should proceed, let's assume that you've made a very simple prototype of the purchase requisition database that we used in a previous chapter. In this case, the LTP and Resistance are clerks in the purchasing department, and they want a better way to handle requisitions.

You've set up a form in which you can enter requisitions; you also have set up a view that sorts them by originator. You have added two buttons to the form: one to send a request for approval to the appropriate person shown on the screen and one that adds the user's name to the approval field.

The conversation might go like this:

> **Provider:** When we spoke earlier, you told me that the biggest problem you have right now is controlling purchase requisitions. I built this simple database to show you how it could work in Notes. Go ahead and enter a purchase requisition.

LTP: Okay. Let's see—it pops up my name as the originator along with my department. Where does it get my department?

Provider: I built a table with your names and your departments in it. We can ask the personnel department to help us update that every week so it's current.

R: What if someone changes departments? Personnel takes a month to make the change!

Provider: We can set it up so that the default is the department shown, but that it can be changed if necessary.

LTP: I'll fill in some more information, the default terms and due date. Great! On these line items, can Notes look at our inventory system and verify the part number? That would save us a lot of time and be a lot more accurate.

R: Without verification, the system is worthless. We already get enough bad part numbers as it is!

Provider: We'd have to talk to the development team about the best approach, but we should be able to do it. We could start using the system without verification, so we can get some early benefits and add verification later. We could even load the top 100 parts initially until the interface is ready.

LTP: The top 100 parts would certainly help. Okay, I've finished the requisition. Now what?

Provider: Add my name in the Approver field as the person who needs to approve the requisition, then click on the Send button. Next, open my mailbox and see what happens.

R: Can't the system automatically bring up the approver? We have a list of authorized approvers and the user should be able to choose one.

Provider: We can build a purchasing database to hold those names so that this application can automatically look up the originator's name then fill in the approver's name. You'd have to maintain it, but it could replace your paper log.

Provider: Now that LTP has sent the requisition to me, let's see what I received in my mailbox. Here's the message: "LTP requests approval of a requisition for a widget." If I click on this document icon called a doclink, it takes me to the requisition. Now I'll click on the Approved button. Notice that it puts my name and today's date and the time on the requisition. If you checked your mailbox, you'd receive an approval notice. Now let's look at the requisition database again.

LTP: There's the approval! Is there a way that I could be notified when a new requisition has arrived from someone in a department that I support?

Provider: We could update the approver list to add the name of the purchasing agent who supports the department. When a requisition is created, it could automatically add that person's name to the document. Each day, you would select a view that shows your requisitions, and the new ones could be marked to show that you haven't looked at them yet.

LTP: I'm sold! Could I play with this for a while and try it out? I might have some more questions.

R: Well, it doesn't look too bad. Are you sure we could get the automatic approvals built in?

You've accomplished your mission. Both the LTP and the Resistance have discovered what Notes can do, and they want to know more. If you can get them access to Notes at this stage, this may be a good opportunity to build a simple discussion database and give them more opportunities to explore Notes. They could post their questions in the database, read each other's comments, then you could respond to both of them without a lot of meetings.

Some departments may be slower to accept Notes because it still looks a little like "vaporware." They may have taken a risk on another project and gotten burned, or they are stretched for resources and therefore judicious about investing time in unknown projects. If credibility is still a problem, a pilot project in one department might help. A Notes pilot project appeals to most people in an organization for several reasons. They can minimize the cost of implementation by limiting the size of the pilot. They can try out the software and minimize their losses if it doesn't work. A pilot project will only impact one department or workgroup, while the rest of the company can continue with the business of making money.

The Provider Perspective

If the provider is not already a Notes consultant, it won't take long after the exploration stage for that person to understand what Notes can do. Consultants and IS departments spend a lot of time selecting software, reviewing features, and checking references, so they'll figure it out quickly. The main concerns will be how much it's going to cost to bring up Notes, how many people it will take to support it, and what kind of pressure it's going to put on servers and networks.

The Exploration stage answered some of those questions. As their understanding grows, they may need to call the references again for more information. At this stage, it pays to bring in a value added reseller (VAR) or a consultant to help them understand the scope of the Notes implementation that they are considering.

The Provider may have to spend some consulting time for a feasibility study, a requirements definition, and even an implementation plan to help move the upper management team and the finance department through the Discovery phase, to get company-wide approval for the project.

Euphoria

Whether you're selecting a new outfit or a new car, there's that moment when you cross the line and commit to a decision. You're happy and confident with your decision—at least for the moment. So it goes with Notes.

A few years ago, I saw a demonstration of a pocket organizer and thought it looked pretty slick. It had three phone books, expense tracking, a calendar/scheduler, memos, two clocks, a calculator, and external hookups for a printer and another computer. I agonized over the price and features, but finally bought it. I got it home, read the manual, and was convinced it was going to change my world. I transferred the contents of my DayTimer to the organizer and added every phone number and address that I could think of. I carried the organizer everywhere and even used it to enter notes at the meetings I attended. I knew it could do everything! I was in the Euphoria stage of using my organizer.

Like the organizer, Notes looks like it can do everything. Once people write their first database or create a simple view, their confidence grows, and Notes seems like the answer to all things. They have entered the Euphoric stage of their Notes implementation.

The User Perspective

After users complete the Discovery stage and experience a good application, they usually become supporters of Notes. Most of them welcome the move away from the drudgery of their manual processes and adapt quickly to Notes concepts. After a while, Notes becomes another application that helps them get the job done. These users will experience a little euphoria as they use Notes.

The idea that Notes can do everything is beneficial in that it can help dislodge people who are resisting change. Obviously Notes, however, can't do everything or even the majority of things. As we'll discuss later in this chapter, there are systems that should be developed in Notes and those that should not. If the euphoric users aren't moved through this stage quickly, they can slow down the development of important, *non-Notes* systems and even the progress of the users who have accepted Notes.

It's important to acknowledge the limitations of Notes in action. Recommend that the organization create a prototype of one of the systems that users propose. As they explore the @ functions and the limits of the Notes screens and views, the users will better understand what can and can't be done. Let them set up, maintain, and implement the database in a limited environment to experience the amount of work it takes to support a marginal application. If the application works, ask them to modify it to conform with the company's development standards, and encourage them to do more.

If users can't develop a system on their own, provide them with an estimate of how much it will cost for you to develop and what the limitations will be. Their idea may even warrant a prototype that you can create quickly. When users find that Notes can't produce the right kind of report, or that it's difficult to make changes to a complicated dataset, they will become more realistic about Notes.

The Provider Perspective

Providers often have one or two developers at the euphoria stage because Notes development can be much more rewarding at times than traditional development. Normally, providers get beat up over late schedules, budget overruns, and rigid systems, but when they assign developers to Notes development tasks, the developers usually find users who want simple systems that can be created in a couple of days. Users readily express their appreciation because they like Notes so much, and they don't ask for a lot of changes because they can create their own views if they need them.

One danger for developers at this stage is that it is very easy to walk away from years of standards and disciplines that they used to develop and maintain applications. Instead, a developer can slap together a quick solution for a user's problem and get immediate positive feedback. Down the road, however, another developer may struggle to understand how the application works because it doesn't follow the usual standards created by the provider. As the provider starts integrating Notes applications, his or her team may need to redo a lot because of inconsistent screens and buttons and programming methods.

Another danger during this stage is that a euphoric developer may view an inappropriate application as a challenge. After all, developers are trained to write code, and they revel in solving the tough problems. They try the elegant solution, but, if Notes won't cooperate, they try brute force to get the job done. The resulting system may disappoint the users and reduce their confidence in the provider's ability to solve their problems.

Like traditional development environments, providers need standards, such as libraries of common buttons and routines that the entire team will use. Databases and their field names need to be administered, and files on the servers need to be organized. Screens should have a consistent look so that users have a sense that all the Notes applications are part of a bigger plan. Potential systems must be analyzed, discussed, and selected to eliminate poor choices and to focus resources on the projects that return the most benefit. Because there are few developers with years of Notes experience, they need to be trained to avoid mistakes and develop efficient systems.

If the developers and the users have a balanced understanding of Notes capabilities and limits, they should be able to easily agree on how the application should be developed. The discussion that follows on the right and wrong ways to use Notes will help forge that understanding and possibly avoid situations described in the next section, the Reality Check.

Reality Check

There's nothing sadder than talking to a person whose bubble has burst. For me and my organizer, it happened when I discovered I couldn't type in my meeting notes fast enough and still pay attention to what was happening. Soon, I also found it was easier to just keep my expense receipts in an envelope. Then I found I couldn't read my appointments on the tiny screen. The organizer also became too bulky to carry around, and now I leave it in my briefcase and only use it as my phone book and calculator.

With Notes, the reality check usually happens in three ways: when users ask for an application and the provider says it can't be done with Notes; providers push the envelope too far for an application and it fails; or the provider simply messes up the project.

The User Perspective

By now, you can see how easy it is for users to become optimistic about Notes. Notes has become a company-wide project with its own budget. The provider has been schmoozing with the users to convince them that Notes is hot stuff and that the early applications look good. The users haven't had this kind of attention in a long time, and their hopes are high for their systems to get better.

When the novelty of the first successful applications wears off, the users begin asking for more sophisticated applications that take longer and may not even be possible. They won't want to believe the provider when they are told that it can't be done. In fact, they may threaten to find somebody else to do it for them.

If the provider truly feels that Notes can't do a certain job, he or she must prove it so that the users will maintain their confidence level. It may require a more technical explanation, a simple prototype that reveals the failure points, an alternative solution, or even an outside consultant's opinion. If the explanation is done properly, the users will better understand what to expect from Notes and how to ask for it.

If users don't back off from the request, they are asking for another reality check. As they press harder, either the provider will buckle under to pressure and try to do it, or an outside consultant will be brought in. Ultimately, the users will feel betrayed as soon as that first application goes bad.

Obviously, users can't be left in this state of unhappiness. A reality check is an event, not an ongoing process, and users need to have their problems solved. News spreads fast, so it's time for quick action. The first step to moving forward is to conduct a post mortem. It sounds a little gruesome, but the term is appropriate here. A project has died, the users are unhappy, and the Notes application isn't working. It's time to find out why and deal with it.

Once the key players are in a room and ready to talk, the leader of the meeting should list what good has come from the application and what the users would change. The meeting shouldn't be allowed to turn into a gripe session or none of the facts will come out. The leader simply listens for the good and bad points and gets them on the board.

Now the reality check can be turned into a positive event. The leader asks everyone to describe what went well and what contributed to the bad list. The users can voice their misunderstandings, and the developers can hear what needs to change to make it work. It may be that the users indeed expected more than Notes could do, the developers weren't capable of implementing the technology, or both sides simply didn't understand each other.

The tough part is to begin again. The developer needs to create an action plan and get everyone back on track. This time, expectations need to be set realistically, and the modified plan to be executed correctly so that the users will regain their confidence in Notes and the developer.

The Provider Perspective

The provider faces a dilemma with any Notes application. In general, Notes makes the users happy and gains the developers some brownie points. But, some applications are just beyond the capabilities of Notes, the staff, or both. There may not be a budget for outside consultants, the staff mix may be wrong or too small to get the job done right.

In some cases, a provider may just flat out screw up a project. The systems analyst didn't scope it right or the developer thought the API could do the impossible. The project manager may have quit halfway through the project and neglected to properly explain three key design elements. No matter what happened, the project is in trouble.

As we discussed in the user perspective, it's important to solve the problems as soon as possible and regain the users' faith in Notes and the provider's department. If the system is irreparable, then pull it from production, apologize for the failure, and put plans into place to find a better solution.

A failed system also brings the Resistance out in the open. He or she is often a C language guru, a low-level language purist, and someone who has been around for a while. He or she is fully aware that Notes and its macro language are weak in a number of areas. The morale of the Notes developers is already low when a failure occurs and criticism from the Resistance can quickly destroy the team. Remember, though, most Notes developers don't have years of experience, because the language didn't mature until version 3.0, and they will undoubtedly make mistakes. They should be allowed to fail. The provider should not tolerate the criticism and should change the focus immediately to how mistakes can be avoided in the future.

To further help the team, the Resistance may be a good candidate for projects requiring Notes API work and connectivity to non-Notes systems. These connections can be tricky and just the kind of challenge this person needs. As the Resistance and the Notes developers work together, they'll better understand each other's challenges and share the responsibility for the success of Notes. Whether the provider, the users, or Notes was responsible for the failure, the provider needs to clear it up and clear it up quickly. It's the only way to move on to the final phase of acceptance—control.

Control

After surviving all the bumps and bruises of the first four phases, the movement into the Control phase signals a maturity in both the users and the provider. The successes and failures have established the boundaries for what can and cannot be done. If there has truly been teamwork between users and providers, the question will be which project would be of the most value to the company instead of which tool to use to create the system.

Before Notes is introduced to the entire company, it's a good idea to have at least one group in the Control phase. These users can help direct colleagues through the other phases. The group will also be the best one for testing company-wide systems like Notes Mail and Personnel, because they will have reached a balanced outlook on what to expect and how a system should work. If your company opted for a pilot project, these pioneers will be the first control group. If your company opted for a pilot project, only one department will have reached the Control phase while the other departments, aware of the pilot, will anxiously await its results.

Don't assume that life in the Control phase is static. The provider will always be looking for new technologies to enhance new and existing Notes systems. And in proposing one of these technologies as a solution to a user problem, the provider risks moving those users back to the Discovery or Euphoria stage before the project starts. But the lessons learned the first time through a project should reduce the risk and improve the chances of success.

Both users and developers must also be prepared for changes in Notes itself. Lotus upgrades Notes every 18 to 24 months. Usually, the upgrades are significant in scope, and users will require training and more information. The Notes developers and support people will be swamped with upgrading user machines, adapting applications to the new environment, and retesting customized links between Notes and external systems.

Summary

It's only a matter of time before all five phases of acceptance are in progress simultaneously in an organization. It's best that users are in different phases, because no provider could handle the chaos of everyone either in euphoria or dismay. Still, the sooner all the users reach the Control phase, the sooner the organization will be using Notes and improving the way they do business.

5

The Best and Worst Ways to Use Notes

We've talked a lot about the dynamics of bringing Notes into an organization and making it a success. Part of that success comes from using Notes correctly in an application so that it enhances your ability to store and view information instead of inhibiting it. For many people, discovering the right and wrong way to use Notes comes through a process of trial and error, and although that may be acceptable on a small project, it can be a very expensive lesson if a large project has to be abandoned.

There are no hard and fast rules about the best and worst way to use Notes, but there are areas more prone to failure. Naturally, there are always exceptions to the rules, so regard the examples in this chapter as guidelines. Let's look at these areas and weigh the risks of using Notes for them.

The Best Ways to Use Notes

Everyone has an opinion on the best way to use Notes. True knowledge, however, comes from experience with Notes and from good advice provided by seasoned consultants and developers. There is no argument, however, that Notes has strong capabilities in a number of areas that when exploited properly will result in powerful applications that will improve the way your company and you do business.

Connectivity with Remote Sites and Employees

Consultants and technicians have been setting up networks, implementing electronic mail, and installing shared applications for years. Ask them to set up a network in a single building and they will quickly say "No problem!" But ask them to include two remote sites, three field salespeople, and three of your largest vendors, and they'll say "Oh, I'll need a couple of days to work on that one!" Remote communication has always been a pain. It has been around for a long time, and there are plenty of horror stories about connecting to the home office and trying to transmit information. Thankfully, Notes was architected with strong remote communication features to make information easily accessible and to get people off the phone as quickly as possible.

The replication features discussed in Chapter 1 can be leveraged to get information out to the field quickly and in an organized fashion. Instead of a stream of electronic mail and faxes, information can be centralized into a couple of databases at the home office. When the field people can get to a phone, they simple highlight the database icons and request Notes to connect to the server and download information. All new information is flagged as not yet read, and they can browse through the new documents when they have the time.

We also spoke earlier about selective replication, where a database designer can specify which documents will move between replicas of the same database. Let's look at another example that shows why replication is one of the best ways to use Notes. Let's say, for example, that you have a database of helpful information about the products your company manufactures. You want customers to have access to price lists, press releases, product descriptions, and training schedules for classes offered at your site. And when customers call for help, you want employees to have access to the procedures for taking orders and handling support calls.

With selective replication, you can create a filter that determines what information customers will copy when they connect to the Notes server. The developer of the database can add a check box to each form with two options: Internal only and Internal/External. Every document is thereby marked for the appropriate audience, and the replication formula is set to only send documents marked for Internal/External. The customers will get their price lists, but not the internal procedures.

Large databases, and ones that only a manager needs to review once a week probably should not be downloaded to the remote person's local personal computer. Instead, Notes allows the remote person to call up and connect to the server as if he or she were attached to the company network, look for the tidbit that he or she needs, and disconnect when he or she is done. Because most of the processing in Notes happens at the server, the low data speed won't slow things too much, and a user can still get quick access to the database.

If you have key suppliers or customers that you work with on a regular basis, Notes to Notes replication can build even closer ties to them. With automatic replication, your server can call their server and transfer information several times a day without operator intervention. You can establish effortless electronic mail, share databases for key discussions, and keep them updated regularly. If they don't have Notes, offer them a copy, give them access to your server, and encourage them to use it so you can keep the lines of communications open and active!

Workflow and Moving Information

We've already talked a lot about how Notes moves information throughout a company, and how to exploit that strength. Recall that the mail system is available to every application, databases can receive documents through the mail system, and documents can be referenced and made readily accessible to other documents using doclinks.

Almost every form in a database contains some information that should be mailed to someone. A purchase requisition has to be approved. An electronic order confirmation should be mailed to the originator. A project schedule should notify employees about tasks to which they've been assigned and let the manager know when a milestone is complete. Even a discussion database could generate an FYI mail message to someone who might benefit from something you just read. By using custom forms in the mail system, anyone can mail requests and submit information to databases without requiring access to the database. You can periodically add new surveys as custom forms to encourage employee and customer feedback. It certainly saves remote employees from having to replicate a bunch of databases that have forms they use only once or twice a year.

Doclinks are a powerful way to tie documents together and eliminate redundant information. If document 1 has information related to something in document 2, then a doclink should be placed in 2 with a short description such as "click here for more information." Instead of traversing a bunch of databases for information, a click on a doclink brings the related document to the screen. Doclinks are an important element in using Notes effectively, so let's take a look at another example of how they work. Let's say that you were looking at a view of the company information database that shows descriptions of this week's hot topics. As you click on an item, it displays a one-paragraph document giving you a synopsis of the topic followed by a doclink icon. The icon points to the full text of the topic, and, if you are interested, you click the icon and display the document, which may also contain doclinks that take you to further related topics.

Quick Applications

Notes is a great tool for quick applications. You can throw together a discussion database in a matter of minutes or you can borrow someone else's database design and create a more customized database that matches your needs in an hour or two. In other words, you don't have to invest a lot of time to develop something that could solve many business problems.

Notes is also good for prototyping and rapid application development (RAD) techniques. Developers can create a database shell based on what the users requested; then everyone can come together and make changes immediately. Beta copies of databases can easily be placed on the network, and selected people can be asked to try it out. The database can simply grow from suggested changes, and it may never be really finished as users continue to recommend improvements.

Be aware, however, that Notes flexibility doesn't mean that all Notes systems can be written in a day or should be in a state of flux forever. Large projects that affect many groups or the entire company still require the rigors of a development methodology and a disciplined implementation. Even in these cases, however, the development group can divide up the project into "bite-size" pieces and put parts of the Notes application into production as soon as possible.

There are many, many processes for which people need a simple solution. Why not use Notes to fill those gaps quickly and help users get on with their work.

Data Warehousing

In Chapter 3, we discussed data warehouses and how Notes makes an excellent, static repository for snapshots of information. Most data warehouses require only nightly or weekly updates, so the processing of documents and rebuilding of views can take place at night or at off-peak times. Notes can even clean out old documents automatically after a predetermined period of time.

You don't have to limit Notes to simply holding documents or records from a transaction database. Notes accepts just about any kind of file in a rich text field, enabling you to create databases that store files from other applications. The database becomes a basic document management system. For example, let's assume the management team wants to standardize its electronic presentation formats and store all presentations in a library of some kind. For letters and forms, they want everyone to have access to the company logo. In addition, the team just spent two weeks analyzing a new business venture, and they want to store the spreadsheets for further reference. All these files could be stored in documents that categorize them by project, description, or date.

The only danger with data warehouses is that they grow, and grow, and grow, and grow. Just ask a Notes administrator how fast the hard drives fill up on the server, then watch their eyes roll as they try to come up with an answer. Put a few presentations in a database, add daily sales summaries, and sprinkle in 50 or so mail messages with 200KB attachments and you're looking at 50MB to 100MB of information *each day!* Forewarned is forearmed: data warehouses have to be managed and kept clean, or they can get out of hand very quickly.

The suggestions just given of the best ways to use Notes is only a sampler. Notes is good for just about any application where you need to store structured and unstructured data. Chapter 9 gives you 50 ways to use Notes, and once you start playing with it, you'll probably find at least 50 more.

The Worst Ways to Use Notes

As with the best ways to use Notes, there aren't any hard and fast rules about the worst ways to use Notes, but certain tasks are more risky and may not even work.

Ad Hoc Queries

As stated, Notes is a great tool for displaying information. You can build very impressive views that highlight the information that you want people to see. By using colors, the multicategory views can make information stand out so that users can find exactly what they need. The categories in a view collapse and expand with a double-click of the mouse, and a single category can be found easily by typing the first letter of that category. But, if you want to limit what a view displays or see just one or two documents, it takes a lot more work. The only way to limit a view is with its selection formula. This formula is made up of Lotus macro language commands and functions, and you can only have one selection formula for each view. If you want to limit the view to a different set of documents, you must create a personal view that uses a *new* selection formula, or you need developer access to get into the view and change the formula. Unfortunately, the view would then be changed for everyone.

Views aren't that difficult to create, but many people aren't comfortable with the task. While they know what information they need, they will struggle and often call for help, especially if they need to create a new view each time they want to select a group of records or find three or four items in a database. But as users gain experience with the database, they can better help developers understand what information they want and need most often. The developers can then create an extensive set of views to accommodate those requirements.

Building macros that prompt for values to search for in the database are also useful. The macro then writes the values to the Notes INI file as environment variables. The developer can modify the selection formula in a view to read the variables and select only those items that match those variables. Each time users want a different set of documents, they run the macro and enter the values that they are searching for.

Lotus also manufactures Approach, an excellent database product that you can buy as a separate package or as a part of Lotus SmartSuite. Approach enables users to read Notes databases and tap its much more friendly query-by-example capability to find the documents they want. The only drawback is that they must purchase and learn another database to perform queries.

Transaction-Based Applications

Transaction-based applications are systems in which a large volume of similar, succinct pieces of information must be batched together, entered, balanced, totaled, and posted. A good example of such an application is an accounts payable system, where invoices are bundled together for the day, entered into the system, balanced to a tape total of the dollar value of the invoices, and posted to the vendor's open account, month-to-date and year-to-date balance.

Although Notes is capable as a transaction system, its features do not strongly support it as the best solution, because data entry is almost always slower in Notes than in a transaction system, especially during file lookups and save operations. To print a single batch of information, you have to create a custom view that selects only the items in that batch, and for every batch, you have to modify the selection formula.

Optionally, you can display a view of all transactions, select the items that belong in a batch, and just print all of them, but, the entire process becomes a completely manual one that could easily cause the user to skip one or more of the items that were supposed to be in the batch. The users would regard such a process as a step backward, not forward.

Although Notes can create totals in its views, Lotus did not implement the most attractive method for displaying totals on the screen. They appear on the same line as the sort category that you used, instead of at the bottom after all the items in the category have been listed. As a result, totals in Notes are confusing if you are not used to them and Notes 4.0 does nothing to change that.

For periodic totals, you can create a view that summarizes the transactions by month and year. However, it is difficult to have the view show a beginning balance based on a summary of the year-to-date transactions, followed by a detailed list of transactions in the current month. Notes can summarize and show detail, but it can't really handle running balances.

There is currently no good solution, so you must just live with the limits of Notes views. Notes is good for documents, not transactions, and, the best advice is to use "canned" applications for transactions systems. Use the Notes API or some other means to calculate summaries, and move the summaries and totals to a Notes data warehouse every evening so that users can take advantage of Notes' strong view features.

Bulletproof Applications

A bulletproof application is a system that:

1. will never let bad information into the system no matter how inept the user may be,
2. will facilitate the entry of information quickly, and
3. will never damage or lose information.

It sounds like a lot to ask, but we all have come to expect these requirements in most of the applications that run our businesses.

IS departments have been trying to build these kinds of applications for years, and many canned packages are successful because they meet a company's need for a bulletproof application. Companies purchase an accounting application, for example, because it won't allow unbalanced transactions, randomly skip a few customer statements, or write a few extra payable checks because of a bug.

Unfortunately, there is no guarantee that Notes will not allow bad information into the system. Notes can restrict information, validate it, and even perform lookups on tables and other databases. Nevertheless, a user can still go to a view, highlight a document, and use cut and paste to duplicate it. No matter what programming has been done in the form to restrict the database to only unique records, the user can just work around it.

Users can also set up a view for importing information and completely bypass the entry forms. If the view isn't set up correctly or the data to be imported is not formatted properly, Notes will still accept the data. The data entry forms may have fits when you call up a document, but the document is still in the database, but the information may be bad or have missing fields until you clean it up and save the information again.

When several forms are related to each other, developers often copy key information such as an order number into each form as new documents are added. But Notes is not a relational database, and changes to a key field in one document do not automatically update that field in other documents. A user can change the order number in one document, but the developer will have a difficult time updating all the other documents with that number. Some of these problems can be mitigated with the right kind of security controls on the database, forms, and views. But, again, if users can create documents, they can cut and paste and delete them. The only thing a developer can do is redesign the database or create macros to help the users change the order number correctly.

In general, it's easy to add information to Notes but some of its quirks can make data entry difficult and confusing. It's almost impossible, for example, for a clerk to master the many applications when the tab and arrow keys don't react consistently. When you are in a nontext field, tab moves you to the next field; when you are in a text field, however, the tab becomes a part of the text. Further, the arrow keys don't always take you in the direction that you're expecting, and a carriage return in text fields adds a line and changes the look of the form.

Even after users become acclimated to some of these inconveniences, they will encounter slowdowns in fields that do lookups. If a database is large and is updated by several people, Notes will be constantly reindexing the information. When users hit a view that hasn't been updated, they will have to wait until the indexing is complete before the value is returned.

Notes doesn't damage information, but it does create duplicate records if there is a conflict between users. Say, for example, that two people are working on the same document. Notes doesn't allow a developer to lock a record so when the two users save their documents, Notes can't determine which document is the one that should be saved. Instead, it saves one and creates another labeled as a replication conflict, leaving two records that must be cleaned up to put the database back in order. Most users don't have time or even know how to resolve replication conflicts.

If a database does become corrupt for some reason, the corruption will spread to all the other servers as soon as they replicate. Many times a Notes administrator isn't aware that a database was corrupted until a user calls in for support. If the corruption is a day or two old, the database has probably replicated the errors to all the other copies of the database. The nightly backup will also record the corruption, and the administrator may have to go back two or three days to find a good copy.

In short, it's next to impossible to build a bulletproof application in Notes. There are just too many opportunities in Notes to corrupt the database. It's also problematical to plunk an untrained or inexperienced user in front of a Notes application and expect that person to circumvent some of Notes' quirks. Notes is a valuable tool, but, if you need to dodge bullets, it may not be the best candidate.

Applications with Large Files and Complex Views That Require a Quick Response

The ability to build views in a database with up to 1 gigabyte of information is one of the most powerful features of Notes. A view can be a simple, unsorted list of information in the database, or it can be a complex list of documents with several sorts, complicated formulas that define each column, and selection formulas that filter out unwanted documents.

Whenever documents are added to the database, Notes refreshes the views and executes each of the formulas and filters for each document to determine what should be displayed in the view. Needless to say, the refresh time can take a minute or two for a very large or complex view, especially if the server is busy. Most Notes applications don't require immediate response, though, because users are simply looking up a discussion document or reviewing historical documents. If the database is fairly static, users can tolerate a periodic rebuild of the view. If you are 1 of 30 people on a support line, however, and you have an irate customer on the phone, you need information quickly to solve the problem. A support database is usually in a constant state of flux, and the views require frequent rebuilding to display new calls and eliminate closed calls.

If you aren't tracking a lot of history records, the database will remain small and the rebuilds won't be too inconvenient. But, assume that 30 people take 25 calls a day and they maintain one year of history (260 workdays); the database would grow 750 documents a day to over 195,000 documents by year's end. In this case, Notes would definitely need some time to rebuild all the views whenever another record is added to the almost 200,000 that already exist.

The workaround is for developers to replace complicated views with one or two basic views that get the job done in a reasonable amount of time. They can then create a replica of the database and add the more complicated views to it. The database could be replicated several times a day while specifying that the views do not replicate back to the original database. Support team members and supervisors can then access the replica when they need the special views.

Systems with Complex Data Relationships

Notes works well for databases in which one form can hold all the information for a document. For example, in the mail system, each document is unique and contains a sender, a subject, and the message. It's easy to create views sorted by subject or sender, and a change to one document doesn't really affect any other document.

Without using Notes ViP or some other similar add-in product, Notes can be only be programmed to handle data relationships in which a form can perform a lookup on a view in the same database or another database. In most Notes applications, developers use the Inherit Fields feature that was discussed in Chapter 2 to bring a copy of a field into a form. Maintenance of those relationships can be difficult, though, because the information in one form is not linked to the other form, nor do changes in one automatically force a change in the other.

This point is best illustrated through an example using a database in which sales leads are entered and maintained. It has three forms, one for tracking information about the company that was contacted, another for entering the contact people at that company, and a third form to log all the sales activities that occur as followup on the sales leads (see Figure 5.1). We would like the views to show the company document first, all the contacts underneath it, and all the sales activities under each contact. We would also like to have a view sorted by contact that shows the company name. At times, we'd like to sort the sales activities by the name of the person who was sent information and by that person's company name.

All of the documents must contain the company name so that the views we specified can be created. Both the contact document and the sales activities log need the contact name for the other views. We only want to enter the company name and contact name once, then have Notes copy them on each document as appropriate.

To make sure that every form contains the company name, only the form for creating company documents is added to the Compose menu. The developer places a button on the company form that opens the form for entering contact people, bringing the company name with it. Next the developer

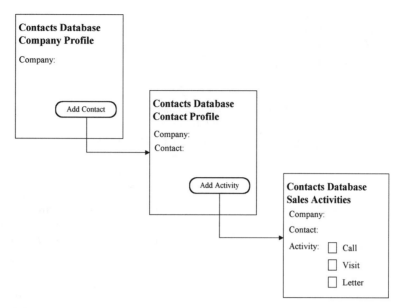

FIGURE 5.1 Three forms in a contact database.

places a button on the contact document that opens the sales activity form, bringing with it the company name and the contact name (see Figure 5.2).

The database works well until someone notices that the name of a new company is misspelled. The company document can be recalled and fixed, but that action won't repair the contacts and sales activities documents. The fields in those documents could be set up to automatically do a lookup into the company view to update all fields in common, but this would add a significant amount of processing time to bring up a form and execute several lookups every time a document is viewed. The only thorough way to repair the database is to edit all the related records manually or to create a macro that changes all selected documents to the new company name. Unfortunately, macros are still a manual process that users must initiate themselves, and one document may be overlooked and not receive the changes.

To avoid complicated data relationships, you must compromise and accept fewer views. A developer can use response documents, which always stay attached to the original document, and, with a properly designed view, they will always appear below that document. This relinquishes some flexibility in the type of views you create to display the log information.

If the application is simple, you may just decide to buck the rules of data normalization and put all the information on a single form. The company document in our previous example could have had name and address

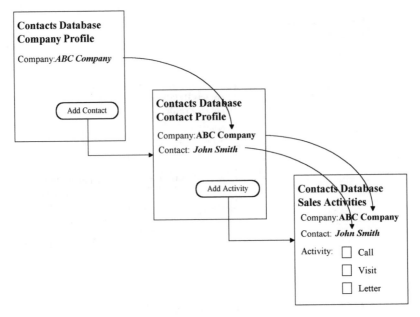

FIGURE 5.2 Moving fields between forms.

fields for three or four contacts on one form. Again, the views are more limited, but the data is easier to maintain.

The Only Way to Use Notes

Notes can be used in more ways than most of us can imagine; concomitantly, there are tremendous opportunities for Notes to be successful, but also plenty of potential for it to fail. When it comes right down to it, the only way to use Notes is to be bold, ask a lot of questions, and try to stretch it whenever possible. Prototype an idea, load up the database with test information, and see if it will fly. It may lead to a fantastic system, or it may prevent a mistake.

Summary of the Best and Worst Ways to Use Notes

The Best Way to Use Notes
♦ Connectivity with remote sites and employees
♦ Workflow and moving information
♦ Quick applications
♦ Data warehousing

The Worst Way to Use Notes

- ◆ Ad hoc queries
- ◆ Transaction-based applications
- ◆ Bulletproof applications
- ◆ Applications with large files and complex views that require a quick response
- ◆ Systems with complex data relationships

6

Presenting the Vision for Notes

The implementation of Notes will have far-reaching effects on the way an entire company conducts business. It takes a serious commitment of time, money, and personnel to bring Notes into an organization properly and to care for it. Like any big project, it should be well planned, adequately funded, and executed with confidence. A successful Notes implementation also requires a champion on the management team. He or she doesn't have to be a technical person, the IS Manager, or even a power user. The champion must, however, believe in change and process improvement and what it can do for the company. The champion needs to be able to fight politically for Notes, and be willing to push hard for the time and money required to make it happen.

Setting the Stage for Notes

A company-wide or department-wide implementation of Notes not only brings a new tool in to the company, it also implements new systems and a new electronic mail package. The project is equivalent to such stress-producing tasks as changing word processing or spreadsheet programs.

A well-executed Notes project, whether company-wide in scope or simply a pilot, should start with a clear vision of how the project will unfold from planning through implementation. The vision must be presented in down-to-earth terms that can spark the interest of people who care about the company and want to improve the way it does business, but it must also contain enough high-level, detailed information so that the management team understands what is being proposed and can properly analyze it and make a decision.

The best way to propose the Notes project is to write a proposal document. The document should include a number of topics, including:

- ◆ An executive summary of the project
- ◆ A full description of the project and its scope
- ◆ The expected benefits from implementing Notes
- ◆ Justification of the costs
- ◆ A project time line

That may seem like a lot to put in one document, but the research and planning performed up front will reap benefits throughout the project. This is the time for the management team to ask the tough questions, and it's your opportunity to sell them on the Notes project using facts and figures. If the project is well planned, adequately funded, and good for the company, you will get management to buy in early, and their backing will carry you through the entire project.

To best illustrate each element of the proposal document, we'll build portions of a proposal for the purchase requisition project described in Chapter 3. In some areas, we'll expand the discussion to cover a more extensive implementation of Notes as well.

The Executive Summary

The executive summary is just that. It's for those top few who make million-dollar decisions every day but can only give you 10 minutes of their time. Therefore, the summary has to make an impact fast, and without a lot of background. In one or two pages you have to explain the project adequately and pique their interest enough to want more.

The executive summary is usually created after the full proposal document is completed, because you'll have all the facts already on paper and you can quickly distill them to just the key points. The executive summary should of course reference the more detailed document so that readers can do further research if they want.

Let's develop a draft of an executive summary for our purchase requisition project.

PURCHASE REQUISITION IMPROVEMENT PROJECT

Our process improvement initiative has shown that we have a tremendous opportunity to improve the purchase requisition process, reduce costs, and maintain existing staff levels through the implementation of improved information systems. ABC Company has become the leading manufacturer of widgets in the United States, and it has experienced rapid growth in all areas. This growth has created enormous challenges for the Purchasing department as they struggle to service a larger employee base that is now spread out in several buildings.

The project will involve the use of Lotus Notes to move requisitions electronically throughout all company departments. The system will replace the large number of paper documents that currently move slowly, thus causing delays in Manufacturing. The system will also be integrated into our existing purchasing application to feed information into the MRP system.

With the new system in place, we anticipate a 10 percent reduction in errors, a 50 percent reduction in filing requirements, and a savings of 10 hours per month for every department manager who currently approves requisitions. In addition, we anticipate faster turnaround of orders to vendors and lower inventory levels due to shorter lead times. We expect the project to pay for itself in less than one year.

The plan calls for developing a pilot system using the Industrial Widget Department (IWD) in Manufacturing as our test site. We anticipate needing four months to set up Notes and develop the system, and two months to test and implement with IWD. Once the system has been fully tested, we anticipate a six-month roll out to all remaining departments. A detailed time line is provided on page 27 of the planning document. A full cost justification is also provided on pages 28–30.

In a matter of minutes, we have provided the decision makers with everything they need to know to start forming opinions, asking questions, and determining who should look into the project. Let's examine each paragraph and see how the major themes were presented:

Paragraph 1: Introduce the Project

The project description (Purchase Requisition Improvement Project)

Why the project is being proposed (process improvement activity)

How will the company benefit (reduce costs and maintain staffing levels)

Paragraph 2: How and What

Notes to move information and feed it to other systems

Replace paper systems to reduce delays in Manufacturing

Paragraph 3: The Benefits

Reduce errors and filing

Provide quicker turnaround of documents and reduce inventory levels

Improve productivity

Payback in less than one year

Paragraph 4: Who Does What, and When

The Industrial Widget Department will be the test

Four-month development and test cycle

Six-month company-wide roll out

This executive summary is very brief and assumes that the decision maker is somewhat aware of the background of the project. For someone less knowledgeable, text should be added to further explain the process improvement activity and introduce Lotus Notes. There may also be a few more important reasons to do the project that should be included. And, if you learn that the implementation may positively affect an area dear to the reader's heart, by all means, include that information.

Just remember that the executive summary is a *summary*. It must be able to be evaluated quickly or it may get put aside. Pull the reader into the proposal, and quickly, or the proposal may end up on the corner of someone's desk.

Description of the Project and Its Scope

The project description is the product of a long period of feasibility studies, planning, and analyses. The executive summary may get the project noticed, but the people who analyze the project need a lot more information. They must feel that they are making the best decision for the company before allocating people and money to the project.

One way to build an effective project description is to break it up into smaller sections that guide the reader through the same thought process that you used to research, analyze, and recommend the project. Break it down this way:

- ♦ Describe the current situation and the problem to be addressed
- ♦ Explain the approach to studying the problem
- ♦ Divulge our findings
- ♦ Make recommendations for change

Describe the Current Situation

This section tells the audience the purpose of the project, how the process you propose replacing currently works, and how it is failing. It should cover enough history to adequately describe how and why the current situation developed. To begin selling the importance of the project, this section should also lay out the consequences of *not* changing the current process.

Let's describe the current situation for the Purchase Requisition Improvement Project. The opening sounds familiar because, remember, the executive summary is a shortened version of this document.

PURCHASE REQUISITION IMPROVEMENT PROJECT

ABC Company produces widgets for industrial, commercial, and home markets; it is the leading manufacturer of widgets in the United States. The company manufacturers its products in New Widget, Massachusetts and has sales offices in 14 cities across the United States. In just two years, ABC Company has increased its market share from 10 percent to 37 percent and is expected to reach 52 percent by 1997.

The rapid expansion of ABC Company has resulted in a significant growth of facilities and employees. During the last two years, 300 employees and 100,000 square feet of manufacturing and administrative space have been added. Production has increased 200 percent, and home widget sales in 1995 increased by 150 percent. We anticipate that the employee base will continue to widen in all areas of the company, and that manufacturing will continue to grow to meet the demand for widgets.

The Purchasing department supports all other departments at ABC. It is responsible for ordering all goods and services required by ABC Company to maintain its current level of business activity. All purchase requisitions are handled by the Purchasing department, which places the orders with the appropriate vendors.

The existing purchase order process was developed five years ago when the purchasing process was centralized under one department. A requisition form was created in 1990 for use by employees to describe what they want to order and when they need it. Guidelines were also created to assign responsibilities for approving purchase requisitions and placing purchase orders.

An automated purchase order system was implemented in 1993 to facilitate the ordering process. Approved requisitions are routed to the Purchasing department, where they are entered into the automated system and tracked from order placement to receipt of goods or services. Information affecting the manufacturing process is sent to the automated MRP system each evening.

The rapid growth of ABC Company has created an enormous challenge for the Purchasing department. The number of requisitions has increased 300 percent over the last two years as production increased and the facility was expanded due to high demand for our products. Further, we have added over 100 new vendors to meet the need for the more complex raw materials required for widgets for the home market.

The current purchasing process was adequate when ABC Company was fairly small, but after studying the process, we found that both the manual and automated processes are now failing to adequately support all departments. Specifically, we found that:

♦ The Manufacturing department relies heavily on the services of the Purchasing department to procure the raw materials needed to keep the shop floor at 100 percent production levels. They are experiencing four- to six-week delays from the time a requisition is submitted to the time the materials are received.

♦ Stock levels have been rising by 5 percent a quarter to avoid shortages on the shop floor.

♦ There has been an increase in incorrectly ordered items, from one a month to one a day.

♦ At the last company-wide manager/supervisor meetings, the approval process for requisitions was chosen as the most time-consuming and least efficient process.

If the requisition process does not improve, we expect these situations to worsen and impede the growth of the company. The Purchasing department has already requested an additional purchasing agent to handle the current load, and we expect the need for more employees in the near future to reduce the requisition backlog.

Studying the Problem

Once we have discovered the problem, it is necessary to explain how the conclusions we made were reached. This is the point at which we establish our credibility and the value of our findings. Let's continue the description of the project.

In September of last year, members of the Purchasing and Manufacturing departments met to initiate a process improvement project for purchase requisitions. A team of six people were chosen to review the purchase requisition process, apply process improvement techniques to it, and recommend a new process. The team used the company's internal process improvement methodology, and the meetings were facilitated by a representative from the Human Resources department.

The project spanned three months and involved over 100 ABC employees. The team interviewed the people involved with purchase requisitions, and they created flowcharts of the entire process. They measured turnaround times for the requisitions, isolated bottlenecks in the flow of the documents, and prepared a detailed analysis of their findings to the managers of the Purchasing and Manufacturing teams.

The team proceeded to develop a new purchase requisition process. They worked closely with the Purchasing and Manufacturing employees to eliminate problem areas and improve efficiencies. The results of their work were then presented to the managers of the Purchasing and Manufacturing teams for approval to proceed on an automation project.

Findings

The stage is set for the punch line. Now we want to let readers know what we found and what kind of benefits they can realize. A little later, we will expand on those benefits, add values to them, and calculate the cost savings that will be realized from this project. At this point, though, let's continue with this section of the project description.

The process improvement project showed that we have a tremendous opportunity to improve the purchase requisition process, reduce its costs, and maintain existing staffing levels in the Purchasing department through the implementation of better processes and improved information systems. The company has grown such that impersonal communication, interplant mail routing, and paper forms no longer support the purchasing needs of its employees.

The team identified several areas in which we could vastly improve the purchase requisition process:

◆ Inventory levels are rising because stock clerks are ordering more to cover the long lead times. By reducing the lead times, we can reduce inventory levels by ordering less but more often.

◆ Each member of the Purchasing department spends over 25 percent of their time handling requisitions, checking for signatures, and entering information into the purchase order system. Two full-time clerks are required for filing documents. By automating the requisition form, we can reduce these requirements and eliminate the work of one full-time employee.

♦ The increase in errors on the requisitions is due to inadequate part lists at the originator's desk. By providing up-to-date part lists and descriptions, the errors could be significantly reduced or eliminated.

♦ Managers and others who originate a requisition spend at least 20 hours a month handling requisition approvals and tracking down missing forms. Automation of the requisition process could reduce that by at least 10 hours.

The process improvement team has created a report that describes its analysis and presents flowcharts and findings. A flowchart for the new processes will be attached as Exhibit 1. Examples of the use of flowcharts can be found in Chapter 3.

Recommendations for Change

Finally, we get to Notes. Notes is the means by which we are going to make all these recommendations happen. We have shown that the process is faulty, but that we have an answer to the problem. Now we need to explain Notes and what it can do.

To implement the recommendations of the process improvement team, we are advising that an automated purchase requisition system be built using Lotus Notes. Notes is a product that can deliver information to every desktop in ABC Company in a way that will eliminate many of the purchase requisition bottlenecks. It can automate the purchase requisition workflow, thereby eliminating the paper form, encouraging quick approval of requisitions, and providing all managers with up-to-date information on the status of their requisitions.

The proposed Notes requisition system will allow users to electronically enter requisitions, approve them, and move them onto Purchasing in a matter of hours. Users will be able to view the latest parts list as they create requisitions, and Purchasing clerks will have fewer documents to file.

We also recommend that the Notes system be interfaced to the existing purchase order processing system. Doing so will eliminate the duplicate entry of requisition information, and allow complete closure of the purchasing cycle once an item has been received.

The project description is complete. Naturally, there are numerous places where you could embellish the description, and you should do whenever the information would help sell the project.

Expected Benefits from Implementing Notes

Now that the project has been laid out, it's time to show how it will pay for itself. As this chapter explains later, you could end up spending over $2,000 per person for Notes. For a group of even 100 people, that adds up to a serious chunk of change. Therefore, it's necessary to demonstrate the payback on a Notes project to assuage the concerns of the "bean counters."

Any project can be justified by showing how it can generate revenue, eliminate costs, avoid costs, and/or improve productivity. The total savings that will be realized from the project can be calculated and compared to the total cost of the project over a one- or two-year period. Some analysts prefer return on investment (ROI) as a good measure of a project's value, while many downsizing, budget-constrained companies prefer to predict how soon the project will pay for itself.

Obviously, defendable numbers for revenue generation and cost elimination are hard to dispute, so we want to identify as many of these items as we can. Cost avoidance and productivity improvements are softer items that are helpful but harder to prove and sell. Some analysts even discount the soft numbers by 50 or 75 percent to show the riskiness and uncertainty of any measurable return from them.

Because every organization is different, it is difficult to come up with a canned description of how to justify Notes. Instead, we'll look at examples of activities that can help justify the costs of implementing Notes, which should give you ideas for your organization.

Revenue-Generating Ideas

The best way to justify a Notes project is to demonstrate how to generate revenue from it. Almost any company can generate revenue by selling the expertise that has helped it grow, and everyone has customers and suppliers that would be willing to pay for better service, more information, and faster turnaround. There are revenue opportunities in every company just waiting for a creative person to locate. Some examples are:

- *Subscriptions:* Currently, the company sells subscriptions to newsletters, policy and procedures manuals, and knowledge databases that are sent to subscribers on disk or on paper. The company implements its product in Notes and, for a higher subscription fee, it connects to the customer's server and transmits the information automatically.

- *Support:* The company offers support services for their products for a per-call fee. Using Notes, it builds a knowledgebase of support questions, hints, and product technical tips for the support staff. With Notes, the staff is able to answer and invoice 10 percent more calls. They sell access to the database to resellers and end users for an additional $200 a year.

- *Competition:* The company's five largest customers buy products from your company, but purchase similar products from another vendor, which are critical to their business. Their purchasing agents spend a lot of time calling for ship dates and prices. The company creates a data warehouse containing an order form and the information that the purchasing agents need to keep them up-to-date. A server-to-server connection is implemented that updates a copy of the database hourly. Studies show increased customer satisfaction, a preference for your company's products, and an increase in sales of 5 percent. The database is so successful that the company sells it to other customers for $1,000 a year with $1,000 in rebates toward products purchased through the system.

Ideas for Eliminating Costs

There are always costs that can be eliminated. Unfortunately, most projects promise to do that but rarely follow through. Any justification must show believable cost reduction, and the costs *must* disappear. To really sell the savings, project managers should be willing to submit a budget reduction form with the project justification to prove that they are serious about making the cuts. There are many cost-cutting ideas lurking in every budget. Some of the following examples make spark some ideas for your organization.

♦ *Electronic mail:* The company currently pays about $30 per person each year for software support and upgrades for the electronic mail system. Notes Mail can replace the electronic mail package in phases over six to twelve months and eliminate the upgrades. Since Notes includes electronic mail, new users will not require an additional mail package.

♦ *Paperwork:* Two full-time clerks are now required to file all the paperwork generated by the Purchasing department. The new automated purchasing system uses Notes and eliminates the forms and most of the paperwork. One or both of the clerks are no longer required, and can be moved to another department or let go.

♦ *Orders:* Customers currently place phone and fax orders based from a catalog of the company's products. The company implements the catalog in Notes and offers customers a 5 percent discount if they order via Notes. The change results in 1,000 fewer catalogs sent out each month and a 10 percent increase in sales volume. The company can take more orders with the same number of people, or can eliminate one position.

♦ *Personnel:* Two people are currently necessary to process resumes, track applicants, schedule interviews, and route documents throughout the organization. The company creates a document tracking system in Notes that stores a scanned image of resumes, tracks all the activities that surround recruiting and hiring, and maintains performance reviews and other personnel-related tasks. The Personnel department no longer has to store hundreds of documents, and they may be able to increase services or reduce their staff by one or more people.

♦ *Forms:* The company currently has 30 locations all across the United States. All administrative, personnel, and purchasing functions are handled at the home office. The company replaces all forms with electronic versions in Notes, eliminating all paper forms. Postage, fax charges, and express delivery costs are reduced by 25 percent.

◆ *Information Delivery:* The company publishes a number of documents for its employees including class schedules, newsletters, phone lists, product information, and policy manuals. They eliminate the publishing of all paper documents by distributing them via Notes, reducing the number of copies generated by 30,000 per month.

◆ *Outdated Systems:* The technical library at the company is out of space to store research papers and internal technical manuals. It is faced with spending a significant sum of money to expand the facility. Instead, the company decides to use Notes and document imaging to store the older manuals. All electronically generated papers and manuals are stored in Notes documents. The total cost of the project is 25 percent less expensive than the expansion, and more information is available.

Avoiding Costs

Avoiding costs requires us to trek into the murkier side of cost justifications. Most cost avoidance involves those that are forced onto a company by law or outside authorities. If a cost is eliminated by replacing it with a Notes system, it's often regarded as cost savings, not cost avoidance. The following example is a typical situation.

◆ *Government Mandate:* A new bulletin from the U.S. Government requires that all employees have access to information on toxic materials in the workplace. You purchase the information in a Notes format and obtain approval to use Notes as the method of access instead of printing and storing paper copies. This innovative use of Notes saves the cost of producing and updating 100 manuals every month.

Eliminating Costs by Improving Productivity

Any time the buzz phrase "improve productivity" shows up in a justification, you might as well put a red pen through the apparent savings. Productivity gains is a favorite haven for people who can't come up with enough hard savings. These savings are generally viewed with skepticism and distrust. That doesn't mean you can't use them to justify a Notes project; it just means that the productivity improvements better be measurable and visible. The project managers should be willing to trim their budget over the project period to show their support for their proposed productivity gains.

The following examples have a good chance for acceptance. Note that each of them is measurable:

- *Orders/Support:* The company stores all of its policies, procedures, and support information in a Notes database. Personnel on the phone are able to field 10 percent more calls every day because they are able to find accurate information that they need more quickly.
- *Salespeople:* All product-related information, technical specifications, and ship dates are stored in a Notes database. Customer data is also summarized and stored in a data warehouse every night. Remote salespeople download the information every morning and are better able to prepare for customer visits. The sales staff shows a 5 percent increase in sales and a reduction of five days in the sales cycle. Final approval on large sales is also handled via a Notes database, reducing the sales cycle time by three days and closing 5 percent more sales.
- *Personnel:* All performance evaluations are replaced with electronic versions. The Personnel department spends 100 fewer hours a month routing documents and tracing lost evaluations. Managers spend 20 fewer hours during every performance review cycle requesting forms and routing evaluations for approval. The mailroom experiences a reduction in workload of 2 percent.
- *Purchasing:* All purchase requisitions and approvals are replaced with electronic forms. The Purchasing department sees a 10 percent reduction in errors and its clerk spends 50 percent less time filing and sorting forms. Department managers report that their staffs save 10 hours a month processing and following up on requisitions.

As you can see, there are numerous ways to justify the use of Notes in your company. The more believable justifications are those that contain measurements that can be put in place before the project begins. Without measurements, you can't prove the anticipated benefits such as "a 10 percent increase in productivity" or a cost saving such as "10 percent fewer hours the phone." A review committee may be reticent to move forward on a project unless it knows you can be accountable for measuring the success of the project.

Even with all your ducks in a row, it may be difficult to justify Notes unless you have some great revenue figures or cost elimination numbers, in which case, it may be better to propose a pilot project as discussed in Chapter 3. Once the pilot project proves to be a success with measurable results, the larger project will be easier to sell.

Let's continue to use the findings from the process improvement project to build a benefits statement. The acceptance of the project hinges on how well we propose these cost savings to the decisions makers, and how clearly we explain them. If they don't buy the cost savings, the project is dead before it can be discussed.

The Statement of Benefits

PURCHASE REQUISITION IMPROVEMENT PROJECT

Expected Benefits from Project Implementation

The improvements that were recommended for the new purchase requisition process offer us several opportunities to significantly reduce costs in the Purchasing department. Our analysis of the purchasing process shows that the reductions are realistic and attainable in the first year. Through the use of process improvement and new technologies such as Lotus Notes, we can realize the following cost savings:

Reduce inventory levels in the Industrial Widgets area by 10 percent.

Cancel the open position for a Purchasing agent.

Eliminate the cost of product returns by reducing errors.

Eliminate purchase requisition forms.

Increase the productivity of the requisition originator by 10 hours per month.

Reduce Inventory Levels

The Industrial Widgets Department (IWD) has suffered the most from the weaknesses in the purchasing process. We interviewed several IWD stock clerks and found a high level of frustration with their inability to meet the demands of their team members on the manufacturing floor. They reluctantly admitted that they will order 10 to 20 percent more product than they need and stockpile it so that they are not responsible for delays in the schedule.

Our study also showed that IWD currently manages an inventory valued at approximately $1 million. The clerks agreed that, assuming that the purchase requisition process time could be streamlined, they could stop ordering more than they need. Our analysis shows that inventory levels could drop approximately $100,000 to $200,000 in the first year as stockpiles are used up and replenished on a more regular basis.

Cancel an Open Position

The Purchasing department has an open position for a Purchasing agent. The position is required to handle the increased number of purchase requisitions entering the Purchasing department. Based on the results of our process improvement activities, we could reduce filing and paperwork enough to eliminate the need for one of the two existing Purchasing clerk positions. We would promote and train one of the clerks to fill the open agent position and eliminate a $15,000/year clerk position.

Eliminate Product Return Costs

Requisition originators do not have access to the automated Purchasing system. Many of the parts and part numbers in our Inventory system are similar, and we have experienced a growing number of errors on the requisitions. These errors result in incorrect product orders, which must be returned at our expense. The average cost of a return was calculated at $50.

Based on our process improvement activities, we found that users are working off outdated printouts to make their parts selections. Part numbers have been superseded by newer numbers, and new vendors have been selected. In six months, there were an average of 20 product returns based on incorrectly completed purchase requisitions. Using a preliminary systems design, we found that the Lotus Notes system can query our existing inventory system from within a purchase requisition form. In addition, we can store additional information about the parts and possibly images of the parts. With this information, users have assured us that they would be able to create error-free requisitions.

Eliminate Purchase Requisition Forms

The purchase requisition form is required so that the appropriate approvals can be obtained from departmental managers. Using the purchase requisition system created in Lotus Notes, managers can electronically approve requisitions. The system will maintain all the information about a purchase requisition and interface with the existing purchase order system. We can eliminate the forms for an annual savings of $1,000.

Increase Productivity by 10 Hours per Month

The IWD stock clerks said that they spend at least 10 percent of their days tracking down purchase requisition approvers to obtain signatures. These approvers, in turn, must often expedite the process and search out the vice president of Manufacturing for approvals. The approvers also felt that they spent about 10 percent of their time searching their in-baskets for requisitions, signing them, and routing them to the appropriate destination. We conservatively estimate a savings of 10 hours per month by implementing the improved purchase requisition and eliminating these activities.

The detailed analysis that supports these cost savings is provided in Appendix A of this document. Our estimates tell a conservative, yet compelling, story of how we can reduce costs through process improvement and technologies such as Lotus Notes. We anticipate that the cost savings shown for IWD are a precursor to the larger benefits that we can realize across the entire company.

The statement of benefits provides a concise explanation of each of the five cost savings efforts, clearly defines the issue, and shows how the new system will help the company realize the savings. Instead of bogging down the reader in details, the statement points to an appendix with all the information that backs up the claims. If the reader wants more detail, it's available.

The scope of the pilot project can be small, but the implementation of Notes should be handled as if Notes were going to be distributed across the company. It doesn't pay to take shortcuts and scrimp on the first project. Issues not addressed up front will require rework and additional funds to deal with them later. For example, if the server isn't set up initially with hierarchical naming conventions, a lot of work will be required to change it later. If the server is underpowered to save money on the initial project, it will have to be replaced out of future funds.

Presenting the Cost Justification

Everything we've discussed so far sets the stage for the project. By now, the reader should understand the value of the project and its importance to the company. The cost section of the proposal can quickly cool everyone's jets unless a convincing case for the project has been established.

At first, the decision makers will be more concerned with the validity of the revenues or costs saving statements. Remember, they may not understand workflow and Lotus Notes applications, but they definitely understand budget dollars. If the numbers look fishy, and the decision makers don't quite understand the project, they'll probably send everyone back to the drawing board before wasting more time on the project. Chances are, though, that the decision makers will not dwell on the details of the costs if the Information Systems department has a track record of planning, monitoring costs, and delivering good products. In fact, they may approve the project based on the proposed savings and your commitment to turn over the budget dollars. More likely, the decision makers want to trim costs; they will question higher-ticket items such as for consultants and training. But if you explain them clearly in the project description, they should be defendable.

To illustrate how the cost justification should look, let's continue to use the purchase requisition project. We'll summarize the costs savings that were realized in our discussion of benefits, and then contrast them against the costs of implementing the project.

In this example, we'll assume that we engaged a Notes consultant to help us estimate the costs. (Chapter 7 goes into greater detail on all the issues regarding the costs for a more complex Notes implementation.) We'll also assume that we have done studies on the amount of time that everyone spends on the purchasing process, and the costs of forms and employees. Ten people will participate in the project.

PURCHASE REQUISITION PROJECT
Cost Justification

The following cost savings were created based on estimates generated by the Purchase Requisition Process Improvement Team during the last six months. Although we anticipate seeing 100 percent of the proposed productivity gains, we realize that it will take longer than we expected, therefore we factored the gains by 50 percent. A copy of the study is attached in Appendix A of this document.

Costs Savings

Reduce inventory levels in the Industrial Widgets area by 10 percent (currently at $1,000,000).	$100,000
Cancel open position for a Purchasing agent and train existing Purchasing clerk due to 50 percent reduction in filing requirements and 10 percent improvement in productivity.	$15,000
Eliminate cost of product returns by reducing errors by 20 per month at $50 in shipping and handling costs.	$12,000
Eliminate purchase requisition forms.	$1,000
Increase originator's productivity by 10 hours per month— 8 originators in test @ $35/hr. Factor savings by 50 percent.	$16,800
Total savings	$144,800

A feasibility study was performed by Notes Consultants, Inc. to assist ABC Company to estimate the project costs. A preliminary plan was drawn to generate the development costs. Notes Consultants, Inc. also worked with the Information Systems department to estimate the hardware, software, and training costs. The feasibility study is attached to this document as Appendix B, and the preliminary development plan is shown in Appendix C.

PROJECT EXPENDITURES

Hardware costs

Notes server with backup capabilities	$15,000
Memory upgrades for six PCs	$ 2,000

Software costs

Notes server license	$ 275
Notes client licenses (10 @ $275)	$ 2750

Training

Basic Notes class @ $150/person	$ 1,500
Developer training @ $1,000/person	$ 1,000

IS Resources

Development time—coding and testing—100 hours @ $35/hr	$ 3,500
Operations—setup—50 hours @ $35/hr	$ 1,750
Analyst time—implementation—40 hours @ $35/hr	$ 1,400
Support—on-going—2 hours/week @ $35/hr	$ 3,640

Consultants

Planning and assistance—100 hrs @ $100/hr	$10,000

Total expenditures	$ 42,815
Net savings in the first year	$101,985

PROJECT SUMMARY

Savings realized from the project	$144,800
Costs expended to complete project	$ 42,815
Net saving in the first year	$101,985

Payback in months	5
ROI	238 percent

Not bad! We can show that the project pays for itself in five months, with a pretty impressive return on investment. Of course, Purchasing still needs to handle the purchase requisition backlog for a while without hiring a new employee. Next, the project needs to be added to the IS department schedule and completed, then the project manager must be ready to measure the results after the project is started to help justify further Notes projects.

A larger Notes project would naturally require a lot more research and preparation before the costs for hardware and software could be estimated, because these needs are heavily dependent on the scope of the project, the number of users, the location of the users, and the amount of information they want to store. It may be necessary to develop a preliminary design of the system and consider the implementation issues in Chapter 7 first to accurately estimate the total costs.

A Project Time Line

By now, the reader should be anxious to find out when this project is going to happen, which means you're going to need a time line. The time line will give the reader a good idea of when the project will start, how it will proceed, and when the funds will be needed. Like the cost estimates, the management team will expect you to honor the time line. They may not remember the details of the project, but they always remember how much it costs and when it was supposed to be completed.

When drawing the time line, you must of course factor in the availability of people, hardware, software, and funding. Project managers may try to preallocate resources before a project is approved, but often those resources disappear as other projects compete for them. Therefore, the time line for the proposal can be only tentative at best and should be presented as such.

At a minimum, the proposal time line should include the major milestones for the project. (In Chapter 7, we will prepare a more detailed task plan that is divided into several phases, such as Gather Detailed Requirements and Develop Notes Architecture.) For the proposal, these phases should suffice and should be presented with dates or placed on a Gannt chart.

Let's complete our on-going proposal with a time line. Figure 6.1 also illustrates a simple time line.

PURCHASE REQUISITION IMPROVEMENT PROJECT

Project Time Line

We would like to begin the project on January 1, 1998. Based on preliminary estimates, we expect the project to require four months for development and Notes setup, and another two months for implementation. We have divided the project into several milestones and expect to complete them as follows:

	Task	Completion Date
Phase I:	Gather detailed requirements.	01/31/98
Phase II:	Develop Notes architecture.	01/15/98
Phase III:	Develop training plan.	02/15/98
Phase IV:	Procure hardware and software and schedule implementation.	01/31/98
Phase V:	Create Notes infrastructure.	02/28/98
Phase VI:	Develop purchase requisition system.	04/15/98
Phase VII:	Implement hardware and software for users; train users.	04/30/98
Phase VIII:	Test new purchase requisition system.	04/30/98
Phase IX:	Implement purchase requisition system.	06/30/98

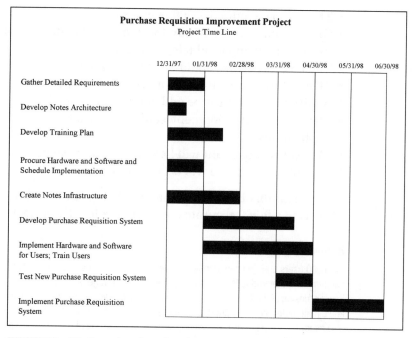

FIGURE 6.1   Project time line for the purchase requisition system.

Go for the Whole Enchilada!

All that's left now is the proposal presentation, and the go-ahead for the pilot project. Although the project is small, Notes probably will be there to stay once the first server and software are purchased. Probably, every department will soon want its own pilot, and before long, the pilots will become a full-blown Notes installation. For this reason, let's take a look at the costs of a larger project, one that encompasses an entire company. We'll assume that Notes is new to the company, but that it has a Notes champion who has convinced management to go for the whole enchilada. A pilot project has started and is moving forward successfully.

The company has decided to fully implement Notes, purchase and modify applications for the Human Resources and Product Support departments, and replace their poorly performing electronic mail system. They calculate that the productivity improvements resulting from the new applications and electronic mail system will pay for the costs of the system in one year. Further, a team has been formed to identify future opportunities for improvement using Notes applications. A Notes consultant helped the project team with its analysis, and they gathered the following information to help calculate hardware, software, and training costs:

- The company employs 500 people.
- Of those employees, 25 are located out of state and another 25 call in from home using local telephone lines.
- Each Notes server should be able to handle about 75 users.
- All employees are already connected to the network.
- Additional staff must be added for Notes support.
- The internal development staff will do all the modifications to the applications.
- The Notes consultant will help plan and implement Notes.
- The implementation will occur over one year.

Based on this information and the help from the Notes consultant, we can generate a fairly accurate cost estimate for the project.

Hardware Costs

With 500 users and 75 users per server, we will need seven servers. Our standard server will be a Pentium computer with 64MB of memory, 2GB of disk storage, and a 5GB tape drive. Based on a preliminary design of the Notes architecture, we will also need one server to act both as a domain server and a mail router. We need another server as a communications server to the outside world. We will also maintain a spare server in case of a system failure in one of the others. To handle the telephone traffic, we will install three phone lines and assume that each remote person will spend 1 half-hour a day replicating with the server.

Approximately 10 percent of the users must replace their PCs to enable them to run Notes. Another 20 percent will need 8MB of memory to improve the performance of their machines; 5 percent of the users need additional hard drive space.

Software Costs

Each user requires a Notes client license, and each server requires a Notes server license. The company uses Novell Netware as its server operating system, and each server requires a Netware 4.1 five-user license. Each server uses automated tape software to back up the systems each night.

The Notes developers require one copy of the Notes API for C and one copy of Notes ViP. Remember to allow some funds for licenses. We will allocate additional funds for software that connects Notes to our SQL databases in anticipation of future applications requirements.

Training

Every employee will be required to attend two 16-hour classes, Introduction to Notes and Using Notes Mail and Company Standard Applications. These will be offered by an outside trainer in company facilities, and there will be 10 students per class. Another 30 percent of the employees have requested a 16-hour class on Creating and Changing Notes Forms and Views. It will given by the same trainer.

The development staff will attend external classes on LotusScript and Notes macros. One developer will attend a class on the Notes API for the C language. The entire support staff will attend the Notes Administration class, and one member will attend an advanced Notes Administration class. Two members of the team will attend LotusSphere, the Lotus-sponsored trade show that spotlights Notes and related applications.

Personnel

Additional IS staff is required to support the installation. Over the implementation year, the company will add two Notes support specialists, two Help Desk specialists, one network administrator who focuses on Notes, and three Notes developers. The existing management team will supervise the new additions.

Consultants

A Notes consultant will be used throughout the installation; that person will invoice for 80 hours of time in the first two months, 40 hours for the next six months, and 20 hours for the remaining four months.

Cost Summary

Now let's calculate the costs of the company-wide implementation. At the end, we'll come up with a cost per user and compare it to the $4,000-plus per user that we found in the pilot.

Hardware

Servers (9) @ $20,000				$180,000
Phone connections (3)	Installation, 800 #	$ 600		
	Monthly 800 fee @ $100/month	$ 3,600		
	25 users, 30 minutes,			
	250 days/year @ $.11	$20,625		
			$ 24,825	
New PCs (50) @ $3,000			$150,000	
Memory upgrades (100) @ $200			$ 20,000	
Hard drives (25) @ $250			$ 6,250	
				$381,075

Software

Notes client licenses (100) @ $275	$ 27,500
Notes run-time licenses (400) @ $155	$ 62,000
Notes server licenses (9) @ $275	$ 2,475
Netware 4.x five-user licenses (9) @ $600	$ 5,400
Notes development tools (API for C, Notes ViP)	$ 3,000
Allowance for additional connectivity software	$ 20,000
	$120,375

Training

Introduction to Notes classes (50) $1,000/class	$ 50,000
Using Notes Mail and applications classes (50) @ $1,000/class	$ 50,000
Creating and changing forms classes (15) @ $1,000/class	$ 15,000
LotusScript and macros classes (3) @ $2,000/student	$ 6,000
Notes Administration classes (6) @ $2,000/student	$ 12,000
LotusSphere conference/lodging/airfare (2) @ $2,500/attendee	$ 5,000
	$138,000

Support Staff

Notes support specialist (hired Jan. 1) @ $40,000	$ 40,000
Notes support specialist (hired July 1) @ $20,000	$ 20,000
Help Desk specialist (hired Jan. 1) @ $30,000	$ 30,000
Help Desk specialist (hired July 1) @ $15,000	$ 15,000
Notes Network administrator (hired Jan. 1) @ $60,000	$ 60,000
Three Notes developers (hired Jan. 1) @ $45,000	$135,000
	$ 300,000

Consultants

Consulting fees, 480 hours @ $150/hour	$ 72,000
Total cost of the company implementation for 500 users	$1,011,450
Cost per Notes user	$ 2,023

Bottom Line for a Company-Wide Implementation

As you can see, the cost of bringing Notes into a company can add quickly. Based on our estimates, it will cost over $2,000 per user to install Notes. We've made a lot of assumptions that increase the amount, such as the size of the support staff and the number of users that a server can hold. There are also places to shave costs, including using internal trainers for the Notes classes and cutting back on hardware purchases. But the bottom line is, Notes is going to cost about $2,000 per user, plus or minus a couple of hundred bucks.

C H A P T E R

7

Implementing Notes

It feels great when you finally get approval for the Notes project. You proved through hard work that Notes can make a difference and management is behind you. Expectations are high, though, and management is looking forward to all the revenue and cost savings that were promised. It's time now to take action and bring up Notes. The planning process for the proposal effort helped everyone understand the scope of what has to get done. Next, the cost estimates and the basic time line have to be fleshed out in preparation for the more detailed plan that will keep you on time and budget.

At this point, the company is going to spend some serious money and commit a lot of people to the implementation effort. Recall that we included a Notes consultant in the proposal in Chapter 6. It's time to bring that person on board. Most of the critical decisions in the implementation will have to be made early in the project, and you want someone with experience to help you make those decisions.

First, we are concerned with the operational issues of rolling out Notes. The operational side of our plan should include the following phases:

- Developing the Notes architecture
- Designing the Notes infrastructure
- Upgrading user hardware
- Finding the people to get Notes started
- Adding the people for the long haul
- Training users, developers, and the support team
- Building a workplan for implementation
- Expanding to the outside world

The discussions that follow will help you define the tasks that should be included in your plan. Where applicable, we will also discuss the costs that will be incurred during each phase. In most cases, the information included in the proposal in the previous chapter was derived from this chapter.

Developing the Notes Architecture

The Notes architecture serves as the blueprint for the deployment of servers, operating system software, networks and telecommunications equipment, and databases used for Notes throughout the company. This is the most critical phase in the plan because decisions made early affect the implementation in its entirety. Notes consultants often pay for themselves during this phase, so again, hire a good one.

Let's examine the four elements of the architecture and dig into the issues that must be addressed during the implementation plan. The technologies for each of these elements change monthly, so the discussions will center more on what to consider instead of selecting actual configurations. Each section will cover estimated costs and the time required to implement the hardware or software.

Hardware

Notes affects almost every piece of hardware in the organization. Servers must be purchased to make Notes accessible to the users and to hold their databases. The network must be beefed up to support the new network traffic and telephone lines must be deployed to support remote communications. Frequently, you'll find that the equipment on the user's desk may be underpowered and need a boost.

Let's look at hardware from the Notes administrator's perspective to determine what we need to buy to support Notes.

Server Hardware

There are any number of machines out there that can act as a Notes server. In this area, however, it pays to stick with whatever internal standard the company has, so that spares are available and repair contingencies are in place. (We'll talk about hardware limitations caused by the network operating system in the next section.)

Because most Notes tasks running on the server are processor-intensive, invest in a powerful server up front. Consider a multiprocessor system that will allow you to simply add another processor to boost performance instead of buying a new server. A Notes server can handle a lot more users simply by adding memory and processing power. If you buy a scaleable hardware product, you can grow Notes incrementally for a while without major disruptions. Some operating systems, like Novell Netware, have not tapped the power of multiple processors yet, but they will if they intend to stay competitive.

The number of users who can be connected to one Notes server depends on the power of the server and the user level. One server can handle over 100 remote users if they only call in once a day for 10 or 15 minutes. On the other hand, a single user can keep the server busy by constantly changing documents, rebuilding views in a large database, and setting the database with high-priority replications to another server every five minutes.

Plan conservatively, say 20 to 60 users per server. Consider the power needed to support the databases and run the applications planned for those users. You can easily add users to a server that is underutilized, but it's a lot of work to move users and their databases from one server to another to balance the load. After working with a server or two, you'll know the limits of the hardware and be able to gauge the effects of usage on them.

When the servers are in production, monitor the peak number of concurrent users on the server, and start planning for another server as the first approaches the planned maximum. Keep in touch with users to get feedback on the server's speed. They will notice first that their databases open more slowly, their views take more time to refresh, and their documents take longer to save. If possible, add a server *before* you hear the complaints.

Notes users are notorious information pack rats. Frankly, the Notes project team has sold them on the idea of using Notes to store all their information, and they happily go forth and multiply that information. Initially, the disk drives will fill slowly as people learn Notes and discover what they can do with it. But as more applications come on line, users will eat up the hard disk space rapidly.

Don't expect users to help you manage the server storage requirements. They are seldom aware of the size of a database until they replicate it locally and fill up their local hard drives. Besides, most database owners usually want to keep the information forever; if you're lucky, they may be willing to let Notes automatically erase something after a year or so. They also know that hard drives are cheap so, unless you want to have database police on staff, you are probably better off with an architecture that supports a lot of storage.

It pays, too, to invest in hardware that supports an array of disk drives on one server. Most major manufacturers have disk subsystems that can hold at least six or seven drives, making it very easy to bump up the storage simply by sliding another one in. One server may appear to be in good shape until the users on it need to replicate several monster databases from another server to implement a new application. You want to be able to meet their demands without a major hardware upgrade.

Notes servers must be backed up nightly, therefore, the server should have its own tape drive or be included in the backup cycle of a remote backup system. The ability of Lotus Notes to replicate databases, however, offers some latitude in how the backup is done. One server could be used as a single "mega"-server that replicates all the databases from all the servers. Then, instead of backing up every server, only the mega-server is backed up nightly (see Figure 7.1). In a more decentralized topology, only certain databases on server 1 may need to be backed up because there is a replica of those databases on server 2 that is updated hourly and already backed up each night (see Figure 7.2).

Replication should be regarded only as an excellent alternative to daily tape backups; it shouldn't replace it. Notes databases can become corrupted for a variety of reasons, and the corruption can go undetected for hours or even a couple of days until someone hits a document or view that causes the corruption to show up as an error. With replication turned on, the damaged database will replicate the corruption to all other replicas of that database on all the servers. If the replication cycle is set to run every hour, the cor-

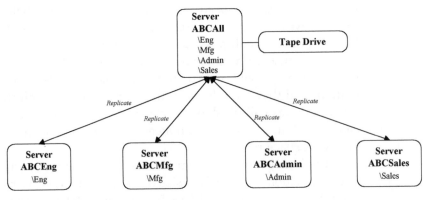

FIGURE 7.1 Backing up a mega server.

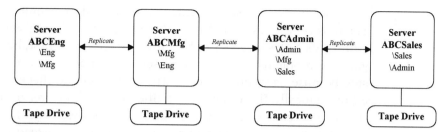

FIGURE 7.2 Backing up a decentralized server.

ruption will take its toll in an hour. Then, when the nightly backup to tape occurs, users could find themselves reentering a lot of information, unless daily and weekly tapes are maintained.

Notes needs to execute mail routing on at least one of the servers. This server monitors the outgoing Notes Mail mailbox on each Notes server, and distributes the mail to its intended destination. If the mail is addressed to external servers, the mail router calls the external server and sends the mail to it.

The task of routing mail adds a load on the mail server, as shown in Figure 7.3. The larger the installation, the more horsepower that server will need to process the volumes of mail, in addition to all of its other user activities. Since mail is an important process that supports almost all workgroup applications, the reliability and speed of this server is very important. A server should be dedicated to the task, if possible, and included in the Notes architecture. Plan to implement it well before the server that currently routes mail starts to slow down under the strain of all its tasks. People quickly become accustomed to the immediate mail delivery that Notes provides. Their jobs often depend on the mail system, so it had better work and work well.

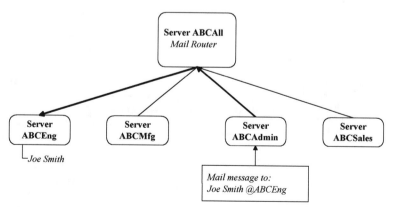

FIGURE 7.3 Mail routing with Notes.

Companies will soon decide that they want to communicate with their business colleagues using Notes. Providing external users with access to the company's Notes servers can be a little unnerving at first, but you can mitigate the problems with a firewall server. Remote access to Notes is fairly safe because users encounter all the same security checks as if they were attached locally. If they are not certified to use the server or they don't have the right access to a database, chances are, they won't get in.

Another level of control can be achieved if, instead of letting users connect via modem to a production server, a separate server is set up with replicas of only the databases that they are allowed to access. Then, if a production database on a local server is left unprotected, remote users won't even see it. Using the techniques that we discussed in Chapter 2 for firewall databases, those replicas can be further limited to hold information that is fit only for external publication. In fact, all communication activities to the outside world can be easily turned off if all modems and remote connections are funneled through firewall servers (see Figure 7.4).

Server Hardware Costs

A good administrator buys enough processor power, hard disk space, and redundancy to allow for growth into the server without bankrupting the company. By the time this book is published, the cost of hardware will have dropped again, or the same dollar will buy 10 to 20 percent more. Traditionally, manufacturers add more features, hotter technologies, and all sorts of other goodies to keep the prices at about the same level, so we'll come up with a dollar amount and assume you'll keep getting more for it.

Let's take a shot at building a practical and powerful Notes server. After considering the number of users, the sizes of the Notes databases, and the internal company server standards, the Notes administrator speci-

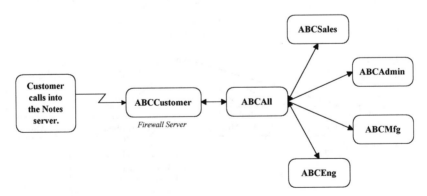

FIGURE 7.4 Firewall servers.

fies a server with an Intel processor that is expandable to four CPUs. It comes with 128MB of memory, plenty of expansion slots, and a drive array that can hold six hot-swappable drives. The system includes two 2GB drives that will be mirrored, a 10GB tape drive for backup, two 32-bit network adapters to balance the network traffic, and a couple of high-speed modems for connecting remote users. After a few phone calls to two or three local computer stores, the price comes in somewhere between $15,000 and $20,000.

The system sounds like a pretty nice server, and it is. If pushed, you could reduce the cost by forgoing some of the memory, the extra tape drive capacity, and one of the network cards. Further, a vendor could be found who sells comparable, but not standard, equipment that costs less and has received good reviews. If you want to take those risks, the price can definitely be less. Still, it is wise to plan for the higher price then hope it comes in lower. It's always more difficult to go back to the well for funds than it is to say you didn't spend the initial investment.

Perhaps the first project is a small pilot that only extends to 10 people in a single workgroup. The review team has agreed to fund the more expensive hardware only if the project proves successful. In that case, a decent desktop unit can handle the task and be recycled later as a user workstation when the bigger server is approved. Let's assume that the smaller server is an Intel-based processor with 64MB of memory, one 2GB hard drive, a network card, a modem, and a good-quality tape drive. After a call to the same computer stores, the price comes in at around $5,000, including a free mousepad.

During the planning process, make sure to include the costs of the larger server when estimating all the servers that will come online after the pilot is complete. The plan should also indicate that the first server will be swapped out as soon as the larger server is available. The management team will probably balk at the difference in price and ask detailed questions about the need for the bigger server, but by explaining the need for redundancy, expansion, reliability, more users, and ease of maintenance, you should be able to easily justify the larger server.

Our Plan

To summarize, our plan should include the following tasks for implementing Notes servers:

- ◆ Identify the number of users and their location
- ◆ Determine their disk storage requirements
- ◆ Forecast growth in users and storage requirements

- Identify the need for servers to support external communications
- Calculate the number of servers required, including a mail router and firewalls
- Use the forecast to calculate future server requirements
- Specify equipment configurations
- Purchase servers

Network Operating Systems

Lotus has done a great job of expanding the types of servers that now support Notes. Two years ago, the only option for a Notes server network operating system (NOS) was OS/2. Now, with a Notes version for Netware, Windows NT, Sun, and more to come, an administrator can pretty much pick whichever server will do the best job for your installation.

Because OS/2 was the first and only NOS for Notes for quite a while, administrators had no choice but to resign themselves to its quirks. Notes was notoriously unstable on OS/2 and the "Server not responding" message sent shivers down administrators' spines on a regular basis. New hardware was a gamble because it was often difficult to find the device drivers that OS/2 needed to recognize it. But Iris Associates used the best tool available at the time to get Notes to market.

Administrators waited longingly for the Notes NLM for Netware, which offered them a stable server environment, disk mirroring, and access to almost any device driver known to man, via CompuServe. The Notes NLM itself had to be administered from a client station with a less-than-adequate program, but the inconvenience was considered a small price to pay by Netware administrators who were down to one NOS.

Then the Windows NT platform became popular, and support of it poses an interesting paradox for both Microsoft and Lotus. Microsoft desperately wants to yank the workgroup computing market away from Lotus. They discourage corporate accounts from moving forward on Notes until they've seen Exchange. Microsoft also wants these same customers to jettison their Netware servers, OS/2 servers, and any other NOS in favor of Windows NT 3.5.

Although Lotus doesn't encourage its customers to use Notes on an NT server, if that's what they want, Lotus has to support the platform. As a result, Notes runs on NT. The Notes server software installation is almost identical to the client version, and, similar to OS/2, Notes uses the multitasking capability of NT to run its processes as background tasks and allow administration on the server.

Sun hardware put Notes in its first Unix environment and tapped a fairly tightknit circle of engineering and design groups. These users preferred native applications on their Sun servers and, although they could connect their Sun machines to Notes on an Intel server. The Sun platform gave Lotus a chance to feel out the Unix market while reaching a highly technical and sophisticated group of workstation users.

With all these operating system choices, it's best to just stick with the company's internal standards. Each operating system has its quirks, and Notes is a handful to take care of by itself without adding a new network operating system to the to-do list of the network administrator. Just bring up the Notes server on the NOS you know, add it to existing backup routines, and get on with loading Notes.

Notes can also communicate with users via several network protocols. The administrator should use the company's default protocol with Notes to simplify network support and troubleshooting. Using a different protocol requires the support team to add software to the user's workstation, which eats up memory and adds one more thing to support.

Network Operating System Costs

The cost of a network operating system depends on the latest marketing plan that exists. Users don't log in to the server as individual users, therefore a license pack for only a minimum number of users is required. Assume $1,000 for the operating system for estimating purposes.

Our Plan

To summarize, our plan should include the following tasks for implementing the Notes network operating system:

◆ Review internal standards for network operating systems
◆ Identify protocols used on the user workstations
◆ Select a network operating system
◆ Purchase a network operating system

Network Hardware

Notes is a client-server application, which, by definition, is designed to minimize network traffic and rely on the power of the server to process information. Notes offloads much of the processing for views, replication, and maintenance to the server, and requires a powerful processor to maintain good performance. This doesn't mean that Notes can't put a load on the network, but it does mean that casual users will have very little effect on network performance.

Most networks are designed to localize traffic into smaller networks, called subnets, using routers or etherswitches so that users will only compete with a smaller group of users for network bandwidth. Servers are placed within the subnet whenever possible to improve performance. Other users can enter the subnet, but the routers introduce some slowdowns while processing their requests.

There are many Notes databases that will appeal to a large audience of users spread throughout the network. But, if the database resides only on one server, all the users will be entering the subnet of that server and hurting network performance. To mitigate the problem, the Notes administrator can identify those databases and place replicas on the other Notes servers on the network. Instead of steady access from the larger audience, the traffic will be reduced to automatic replication once every several hours.

There are a few things you can do to improve network performance for Notes users. Most network servers can hold multiple network interface cards, which means that if one network card is saturated, a second card can be added and the network can be broken up into two segments. (OS/2 had a noticeable weakness in this area in that the administrator could not bind the protocols that used the NDIS standard to the same card as those protocols that used the ODI standard. If a server needed to communicate using Appletalk (NDIS) and NetBEUI (ODI), then two cards were required for just the protocols; further segmentation required additional network cards.)

Replication is one of the few threats to network performance in Notes, because users may attempt to move gigabytes without really knowing what they are doing. For example, say new user Joe is very excited about the prospect of having the company's knowledgebase on line and he taps into it immediately on a daily basis. He decides that he wants the 100MB database on his local machine so that he can work at home and still use the database. All he has to do is select Tools Replicate, select the database, choose his local PC for the destination, and send 100MB of information over the network.

Unfortunately, there is no way to stop users from transferring large files. Luckily, most users don't have the luxury of 100MB of spare hard drive just waiting for a Notes database to arrive. For those who do, a company policy may be required to enlighten them about the effects of large transfers on the system, and directing them to do it in off-peak hours.

Electronic mail and document attachments pose the same threat to network performance. It's a snap to attach a 2MB Freelance presentation or

Excel spreadsheet to a document and mail it off to 20 people located on five servers. The mail router will find the message, send it to every server that has a mailbox for the message recipients, and eat up $5 \times 20 \times 2$ or 200MB of disk storage. It's tough to plan around these kinds of events and another policy may be required. Notes Mail cannot stop a user from sending a file based on a size limit. However, be aware that there are times when the 2MB file really must be sent to one person. If someone needs to send a file to a lot of people, he or she should create a document in a database shared by everyone, attach the file to it, create a doclink to the document, paste the doclink into a mail message, and send the message to everyone. The recipients can select the doclink and download the attachment if they really want it, eliminating a lot of network traffic and saving disk space.

As the number of servers grows, so will the amount of data that has to move between the servers. At a minimum, each server will have to send mail messages to the other servers. Traffic will increase significantly during the period when automatic replication of databases is initiated and the servers begin moving information among each other.

The best way to control replication is to plan for and control the automatic replication information stored in the connection records of each server's name and address book. Each server can be scheduled to replicate anywhere from every minute of every day to just once a week. A separate schedule can even be created for each of the replication priorities (high, medium, low). Subsequently, with the correct tuning, the task can be spread evenly throughout the day or done during the night when the network isn't busy.

If you still find Notes causing a network problem, you can isolate Notes users and their servers on their own network segment using a router or an etherswitch. Unfortunately, there isn't a good way to build a separate network segment just for replication. Although the Notes server can have multiple network cards, Notes cannot be instructed to replicate over a specific card. If Notes thinks that Server A can reach Server B through two different paths, it may take either one.

Outside the company's walls, obviously, the power of remote access and replication with Notes requires modems and phone lines. Of course, how many depends on the number of remote users and the amount of information sent each day. That number will grow rapidly, too, as remote users require access to more databases and local users replicate databases to their home computers.

Modems are fairly inexpensive, so plan for two initially. Use the Notes communications log to keep track of how often the modems are used and how many times both are in use at the same time. As usage on the second modem grows, you can assume that the percentage of people that aren't getting through to the server is also growing, in which case it's time to plan for another modem before the remote users start complaining.

Remote communications is a fairly simple task in Notes, but, without some guidance, remote users can abuse the feature. When Notes connects remote users, those users often regard the Notes server as a local connection. They can open databases, select views, add records, and tie up the modem for hours. They can also replicate huge databases and rack up some pretty high phone charges. A little training and a copy of the first phone bill in hand will usually clear up any confusion about how to communicate remotely. It's easy for the novice to misunderstand the Tools Call process and forget to have Notes hang up the phone. The Notes administrator can use the remote access log to accumulate information on users' activity and politely notify them of the problem when he or she notices some bad habits forming.

All databases targeted for remote users should be kept lean and mean to keep transmission times to a minimum. Notes compresses the attachments added to a document, but it does not compress information as it is transmitted remotely. If possible, use a selective replication formula so that the caller receives only what's absolutely necessary. For example, a regional sales manager may only need information on his or her region, not the entire database.

In version 3.x of Notes, remote users can only access databases on the server that has the modem. If they need access to two databases on two different servers, they are required to make two phone calls—and they will definitely complain about it. A workaround is to identify the databases that the remote users will need and place replicas of them on the server used for remote users.

Version 4.0 allows a Notes server to become a gateway to all other servers. When users dial in, they will be able to see all of the Notes servers attached to the network. The feature defeats the benefits of a firewall server, however, so it should be turned off on any Notes server used for that purpose.

Network Hardware Costs

Network topologies are so unique that we can't begin to guess the costs of upgrading the hardware. Most users are already hooked up to the network, so there will be no additional costs for network interface cards. If the network has a fairly low traffic load on it, you shouldn't need any new equipment. On the other hand, if a workgroup currently uses the network only for printer sharing and they implement a major Notes application, then an investment in something such as an etherswitch may be required to improve throughput.

The server will require at lease two modems and two phone lines. The cost of a high-quality modem is about $400. (In our previous server discussion, we included the modems in the cost of the server hardware.) An 800 number can be set up to make it easy for remote users to call the Notes server. It minimizes tracking phone bills, and allows employees to call from anywhere whenever they need to. If you assume that two users will call twice a day for 15 minutes at $.11 a minute, a typical phone bill for the Notes server would look like this for the first year:

Installation of an 800 number	$ 200
Monthly 800 fee @ $100/month	$1,200
Two users × 15 minutes × 250 days × $.11	$1,650
	$3,050

You can assume that the phone bill will rise about $825 a year per user as the number of remote users increases. The number will surely rise as the number of databases increases, so bump the number to 30 minutes or higher in future years.

Our Plan

To summarize, our plan should include the following tasks for implementing changes to the network hardware:

♦ Identify databases with potentially broad appeal, determine the best location for replicas based on the network topology, and update the server plan for more disk space on those servers.
♦ Analyze network topology based on proposed server locations and Notes applications, and identify areas where performance may be a concern.
♦ Identify the hardware required to handle performance issues that were found.
♦ Develop a policy concerning replication and transfer of large files.
♦ Define a high-level server-to-server replication schedule that avoids peak network traffic periods.
♦ Identify the databases that remote users must access, and place replicas on the servers that will service those users.
♦ Schedule the installation of remote phone lines and an 800 number.
♦ Develop procedures for monitoring remote communication logs for capacity issues and misuse.
♦ Select network hardware and telecommunications equipment.
♦ Purchase network hardware and telecommunications equipment.

Databases

The size and usage of each database has a big impact on the number of servers, the placement of the servers, and the storage required on each server. A Notes database can reside on any Notes server, and it can have replicas on all the other Notes servers on the network. A replica can be placed on a server in a way that reduces network traffic and improves performance by allowing a user to reach the database via the shortest and least-traveled network path. On the flip size, each replica adds twice the disk storage requirements as the original, and the replica must be updated regularly over the network.

The only way to identify databases and estimate their impact is to review the development plan for Notes applications. Even though the development plan may only include major milestones at this time a project manager should be able to use it to figure out where the large applications will be used and who will need access to them. The project manager can create very conservative estimates of the file sizes, calculate disk storage requirements, and modify the server hardware plans if it appears that another server may be needed.

The implementation plan should also include a periodic review of usage statistics to determine if and when replicas are necessary. A database may start out small and stay that way until another department discovers its value. After 40 or 50 new users start generating network traffic and bogging down the server by accessing the now-popular database, the Notes administrator should be aware of the changes in user habits and create a replica on a server close to the new users.

Costs

There are no costs associated with database architecture except for the staff required to manage it. Depending on the size of your company, it may be prudent to have someone on board who manages the capacity available on the server, monitors usage, and recommends ways to improve the deployment of databases and replicas on the servers.

Our Plan

To summarize, our plan should include the following tasks for implementing databases:

♦ Estimate database size requirements based on existing development plans

♦ Identify servers that will hold replicas of the database and update sizing estimates

♦ Develop procedures for reviewing database usage patterns and recommending replicas

Designing the Notes Infrastructure

Once the Notes architecture has been defined, it is important to define how Notes servers work with each other, how users are added to the system, and how databases are organized on the servers. This step is crucial to the Notes support team because proper planning of server domains, certificates, user names, group names, and database placement can greatly simplify the task of managing the Notes implementation.

Domain Names

Before you even name a Notes server, you should consider how you would like to group the servers for administrative purpose. Notes allows you to group servers into domains, an entity that shares a common Notes Name and Address Book. A domain usually includes all the servers for an organization, but it can also refer to a division or even a large department.

The decision to create multiple domains should be made based on how you want to manage the Notes Name and Address Book. You need only one domain if you want users to see every name throughout the organization when the Name and Address Book is displayed; but if you have a server for external users and you want them to see only the names of other external users, you can create a separate domain for them (see Figure 7.5). Users can still send mail between domains, because the Notes administrator can replicate copies of the Name and Address Book from one domain onto the servers of another and make it available to users. Even if the Name and Address Book from a domain does not exist on the server, a user can simply enter the person's name followed by an **@ sign** and the domain (for example, **Joe Blow @ Domain1**) if they know both components.

There's really no need to establish numerous domains unless the company is very large or you want to protect the Name and Address Book. Multiple address books just mean multiple databases to administer, so, if possible, it's best to keep things simple and use one domain and one Name and Address Book.

The domain name itself should be simple and easy to associate with the servers and company it represents. Whenever someone outside your domain addresses a message to you, that person will be adding it to your

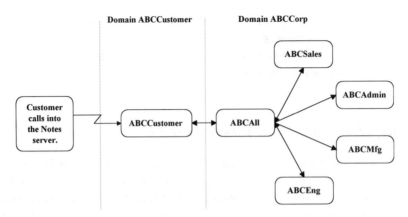

FIGURE 7.5 An example of domains.

name, so you want a domain name that is easy to remember. The best domain name is the company name (ABC, SmithCo, whatever), although a company name like The Great American Manufacturing Company should be shortened to GAMCo or something like it.

Server Names

Every Notes server must be assigned a name. The server name is used actively by Notes in dialog boxes, on desktop icons, and during replication to identify the servers to the user; it is the first access point to all the databases on the Notes servers. The name must be easy enough to remember because users must include it when they are identifying where a database can be found. Without the name, users will struggle in their search for databases. And, once a server name is chosen, there is almost never an opportunity to change it; therefore, it's important to take some time and assign an appropriate one.

Many administrators, especially those who spent time with the Unix crowd, are tempted to name servers after birds, cartoon characters, trees, and anything else you can imagine. It's fun at the time, but it may ultimately detract from the business purpose of Notes, and users will have a hard time remembering which bird is which after about the fourth server. External users may also question the company's professionalism, unless the eccentricity of the company is legendary.

At a minimum, the name should contain something that identifies it with the company. If the domain name is made up of the initials or a shortened version of the company name, then use the domain name for the first part of the server name. The rest of the name should be made up of mnemonics that help users relate to the location or contents of the server.

Corporate America is constantly on the move, posing a challenge to any administrator who wants to name a server after a department or location. If a department is able to bring its server with it when it moves, it's probably safe to add the department name in the server name. If servers stay put when people move, then building numbers or location IDs can be included as part of the the server name. A name such as ABCNotes3 doesn't help a user find a server as easily as ABCMarketing or ABCBldg2001East.

Some servers handle a diverse group of users who share no common name or location. In this case, the name could include a number that can be incremented as new servers are added. For example, the servers at ABC Company could be called ABC1 and ABC2. However, if the Notes administrator expects the number of servers to grow significantly, then more descriptive names should be developed up front.

No matter which method you select, the names should be informative and succinct so that users don't have to try to decipher them each time they use Notes. And remember that external users will probably need the server name when the company allows them to connect, and the name should also be clear enough to be understood by other than local employees.

Let's generate a few server names for ABC Company and see how they might work:

ABCMarketing
ABCBldg2001West
ABCWesternRegion
ABCBostonSales

These names seem to describe their purpose fairly well. Again, simple is the best.

Certificates

We touched on the topic of certificates in Chapter 2 as a means of determining which servers can be accessed by users and other servers. Notes allows both hierarchical certificates, where you can create up to four organizational units and certify at each level, and nonhierarchical certificates, where all the servers are certified under one certificate. Hierarchical certificates are a little more work, but they allow you to fine-tune a user's access to servers. If there is a group of servers in the executive suite that users should not access, for example, then a hierarchy could be created as shown in Figure 7.6. All users are certified at the Admin and Public levels for access to most of the servers, and only a few users are certified at the ABCCorp level for access to all servers.

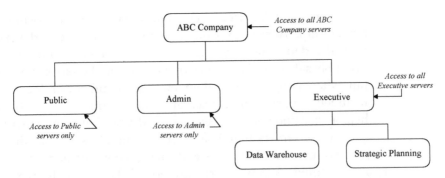

FIGURE 7.6 Limiting access using a hierarchical certificate.

Only one certificate is necessary if everyone will have access to every server; in such a case, it's tempting to just use a nonhierarchical certificate because the administrator can manually cross-certify other certificates and emulate the hierarchy fairly well. If the servers in the previous example were nonhierarchical, however, the executives would need to be certified for all three certificates (Management, Admin, Public) instead of requiring only one. If there are only a few people on the server or few organizational levels, a non-hierarchical certificate is fine.

Notes uses the structure of certificates to more fully describe user in the Name and Address Book. A user's name will also contain the names of the organizational units to which it belongs if hierarchical certificates are used. This information is often included in mail messages to give users more information about the person who sent the message.

Set up the Notes server as if you were going to be a multisite, multi-departmental organization. To start, you need only one level; the Notes architecture can be adapted later to any structure needed to support changes in the company structure. Notes applications can mask any super-fluous information.

User Names

Most of us have experienced the evolution of user names as we have tried to access different kinds of networks and host computers. We were assigned an ID such as 250,17 to access the minicomputer, then graduated to eight characters such as JSMITH so we could use MHS gateways. Now most mail systems let us use the name we were born with to say who we are.

User names in Notes are very important. Workgroup applications display them in a window during approval processes, on a view sorted by author, and to control database access. Users can electronically sign documents when they mail them, and their name is displayed when the recipient reads the message. A Notes name is more than just a first and last name. When an ID is created, Notes includes users' first and last names, then adds the name or names of the organizations or departments included in their certificate. The name also includes the country and the domain of the users' mail servers.

This fuller version of the user name is referred to as Notes Distinguished Naming. Notes doesn't just build a lengthy text string with all of the information in it and call it a user name. Notes stores the name internally with the following format:

```
CN=John Smith/O=ABC/C=US @ ABCCorp
```

where:

CN= John Smith	represents the full name of the user
O = ABC Corporation	represents the user organization
C = US	indicates that the organization is in the United States
@ ABCCorp	represents the domain name of the server that John Smith uses for his mailbox

Most Notes users follow this convention and it's recommended that you follow it as well. The Notes macro language understands how to parse such a name into each of these pieces, enabling developers to use them in applications. As you reach out to other Notes servers, the recipients of your mail messages will be assured that their applications will find all of the components of the name in the correct place.

The most common abuse to the standard is caused by playing games with the first and last name. For external users who access only your Notes servers, it's tempting to put their full name in the first name field and their company name in the last name field so that everyone can distinguish employees from external users. The problem, of course, is that any applications that sort by last name will actually be a mix of employee names and company names. External users with their own Notes servers will follow the naming standard and they will look like employees, unless someone notices the different domain name. A better solution is to set up external users on their own server with a separate domain that identifies them as external users. Their company name should be in the department field of the Name and Address Book, so that any application that needs the name can do a lookup and find it.

Although a user's fully distinguished name can be displayed in any Notes application, most users don't like to do so because the name takes up a lot of space on screen and they have to decipher it to figure out who the person is. Therefore, before implementing applications, developers should use the Notes functions that strip out the extra information and just show the user name. The Notes administrator can also store a short name for each user. When this name is used to address mail, Notes searches the address book, finds the short name, and converts it to the full name. If the company is converting from another mail system to Notes, the short name provides a nice way to transition users to the new naming convention.

The security of every database is also controlled by placing a user name in the access control list. It's not difficult to add a user to the list, but it becomes more tedious when a request comes in to add all 50 users in a department to the list. Be aware: Notes is picky about the exactness of user names, and if someone enters a name into an access control list incorrectly, Notes won't complain, but it won't let the user in either until you correct the error.

You can reduce administrative hassles of updating access control lists by creating group names in the Name and Address Book. A group name is a document in the Name and Address Book that holds a list of user names or other group names. Instead of adding 50 users to an access control list, for example, you just create a group name with the 50 people in it, call it DepartmentX, and add the group name to the list. The group name can be reused in any database, and, any time you make changes to the department group, the access control will automatically be changed (see Figure 7.7).

Before the Name and Address Book is deployed, the support team should agree on how group names are going to be used. Group names for the support team should be created immediately and be added to every database access control list as it is placed on the server. Company mailing lists should be defined and people assigned to administer them.

Database Placement

It doesn't take long for a new Notes server to become a disorganized mess as users randomly add their databases to it. Like any network server, standards should be established that define where Notes databases will reside on the server. The standards can be simple, organizing the files on the server by department or workgroup. If standards already exist for other servers, take advantage of them and reuse them for Notes. For example, if Marketing has a MARKETING directory on its Netware server, employees would be more likely to remember where to find their Notes databases if you used the same name on their Notes server.

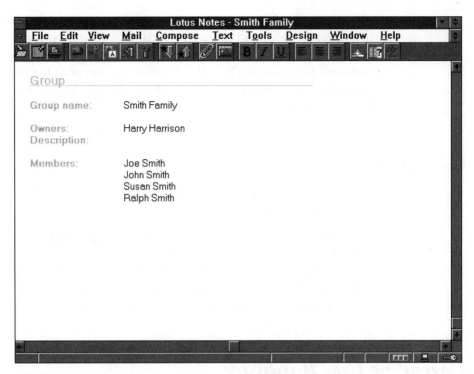

FIGURE 7.7 Group names in an access control list.

Unlike other servers, Notes allows many replicas of the same databases to exist on different Notes servers. Two Netware servers may have completely different directory structures because they support the applications for two different departments. You could use the same directory structures for Notes and put replicas in different directories or, preferably, create the same directories on both servers so that replicas of a database are always found in the same directory anywhere in the company.

One sensitive issue with users is the Notes administrator's ability to limit users from placing databases on the Notes servers. Anyone can create a database locally if he or she has the development version of Notes. Unfortunately, not all users are organized enough to place the databases in the correct directories on the server, and many don't know the pitfalls of using the wrong access control on the database. Nevertheless, many of them will create valuable databases that belong on the servers. The best way to control the movement of databases onto the server is by permitting only the Notes support group to replicate databases onto the server. This ability should be given to more than one person so that the support team can react in a timely manner to a request to put a database on the server. Users will probably accept that they can't put new files on the server if the support team responds quickly.

Users should be required to explain why a given database belongs on the server. They should prepare a document or mail message that describes the purpose of the database, why it is important to the company, and who will need to access it. Once the database is approved for placement on the server, the database should also be checked that adequate access control has been moved onto the server.

Our Plan

To summarize, our plan should include the following tasks for designing the Notes infrastructure:

♦ Organize the proposed servers into domain and create domain names
♦ Develop a server naming convention
♦ Create the organizational hierarchy and set up certificates
♦ Define user naming conventions and standards for using group names
♦ Develop a directory structure for the servers

Upgrading User Hardware

Users need adequate horsepower to use Notes or they will quickly become frustrated, and their first experiences will set the tone. Although most Macintosh computers and Windows-based PCs can run Notes, some of them are painfully slow, and an investment in the right computer configuration for each user will eliminate one barrier to a smooth implementation. A user may need only an upgrade to run Notes. In addition to the storage needed for Notes, users often store replicas of their favorite databases locally so they can work on them off the network. Some users replicate their Notes Mail database locally, a file that can grow well beyond 10MB if attachments and old messages are seldom cleaned out. Remote users replicate a lot of database so they can disconnect from the server and keep the phone bill down.

If Notes is to have a good shot at success, you must agree on a minimum acceptable configuration for all Notes users, and plan to upgrade everyone to it. Notes will be implemented in phases, so the cost of the upgrades can be spread over the entire project. While the upgrades will put a load on the technical support staff, spreading out the upgrades will enable them to schedule the upgrades and complete their current workload without adding staff or hiring temporaries.

Cost of Upgrading User Hardware

Any configuration recommended here would be obsolete by the time this book is published. However, while computers seem to get faster, the price continues to hover around the $2,500 mark. Memory and hard drive costs are volatile, too, but let's assume that 8MB of memory will cost approximately $450 and a 850MB hard drive will cost $250. And we have to factor in labor time for installation, especially if the upgrades are going to contracted out.

Our Plan

To summarize, our plan should include the following tasks for upgrading user hardware:

- Develop a minimum Notes hardware configuration for all users
- Identify the users who must be upgraded and their upgrade requirements
- Develop a schedule for upgrading user equipment
- Create a purchase requisition for new equipment
- Purchase the new equipment
- Install upgrades as purchases arrive

Finding the People to Get Notes Started

As discussed, a small pilot project is a great way to initiate users, developers, and support people to the Notes environment. The project should be controllable, and, with one server and a small number of users, the support people should be able to handle the Notes installation and their existing jobs as well.

When the company is ready to implement Notes comprehensively, it will have to hire various professionals to ensure its success. They won't have to be hired all at once, but their functions need to be filled or Notes may flounder. One person may assume several of the roles until the demand warrants adding more people. As mentioned earlier, consider hiring a Notes consultant. There are many Notes consultants available, and most of them are reputable. They can handle development, installation, and ongoing support. Of course, they'll charge you dearly, but it will be worth it in the long run as the Notes support staff picks up tricks from the consultant. You will also have a little more time to identify, hire, and train the right full-time employees.

The following job descriptions define the kind of help you'll probably need. Again, qualified Notes experts can be expensive, so don't forget that pool of talent in your company. Many of them are itching for an opportunity to expand their horizons and learn a new technology.

The Operations Guru

The Operations Guru knows servers, likes operating systems, and gets a kick out of running networks. This person dabbles in programming, writes clear and descriptive manuals, plays with technologies into the wee hours of the morning, and will teach an Introduction to Notes class at 8 A.M. the next day without any prior notice. This first hire must be a Jack or Jill of all trades, because Notes touches on almost all aspects of the information systems business. Initially, this person must select the correct server hardware, develop a long range strategic plan for Notes, and install Notes to fit into those plans. The Guru must integrate Notes into the network topology and connect outside users to it.

The Operations Guru is also the first Notes evangelist, developing quick and dirty applications that inspire others to join and use Notes. This person installs Notes on user PCs and trains those first users. The Guru is always on the lookout for new Notes products and services that can streamline the operation of the company.

An Operations Guru, like Novell Certified Network Engineers (CNE), command a hefty and well-deserved salary. The field is fairly new, and the demand is high for the small group of people who actually have a couple of years' experience with Notes. If you decide to look internally, find the most energetic network support person available and get him or her into training classes. Be sure this person thrives on challenges. After Notes administrator training, hook up the person with a Notes consultant and have them bring up the first installation together. Immerse the new Notes person in some of the development efforts.

For a small project, you should need only the Operations Guru to keep things afloat. If there are some very technical development needs, you may need a developer or consultant as well.

The Developer

Once Notes is installed and there are databases in use, people will start to demand changes. Initially, the changes come in small requests to the Operations Guru, who gladly whips them out in a minute or two. Soon, they take an hour or two, then an extra hour or two after work, and then, they don't get done for a week. The once happy user community starts complaining as its desire for development exceeds the capacity of the Operations Guru.

This is when the Developer steps in to balance the Notes support equation. This person does nothing but database development and spends a little time with users to get specifications and try out the changes. The Operations Guru should immediately pass on longer assignments to the Developer, knowing that the project can be completed more quickly by someone with an uninterrupted schedule.

Much of the initial development efforts outside of the main project often require light development skills because users don't need the world reinvented yet. They want a couple of views for their discussion database or some fields added to a form. The lure of Notes for many beginners is the speed at which a simple application can be developed. Therefore, the first developer does not have to be a seasoned programmer. Often, the programmers who have been around a while prefer traditional development solutions to a package like Notes that offers nontraditional capabilities. A novice programmer often has the ability to adapt to a new way of thinking with a refreshing zeal that results in innovative solutions. If a seasoned developer shows interest and is open to a different kind of development environment, then give him or her a shot at it.

The first developer could even come from the intern program at the local college. These young adults have been playing with compilers and languages without a taste of the real world. Under the tutelage of the Operations Guru or a Notes consultant, the intern can rapidly gain a sophistication in a matter of months at an incredibly good price.

No matter who ends up in the job, the person should attend Notes development classes and the Notes administrator class to gain a full understanding of the way Notes looks and operates. The classes are taught by trainers certified by Lotus, and they are a wealth of ideas and tricks. In most cases, they work for local consulting firms, and the classes will give you an opportunity to check out the consultant in action.

Our Plan

To summarize, our plan should include the following tasks for building a new Notes staff to support the Notes implementation:

♦ In the project time line, budget for support positions
♦ Search both inside the company and externally for an Operations Guru and a Developer
♦ Select a candidate for the Operations Guru position and obtain training as needed

♦ Select a candidate for the Developer position and obtain training as needed
♦ Assign the new employees to tasks as needed on the Notes implementation project

Adding People for the Long Haul

It's never too soon to plan for the day when the first small project is complete. When people see what Notes can do, projects will quickly come out of the woodwork. Because it takes a long time to build and train a Notes staff, don't wait for the pilot to complete before making staffing plans. If you are planning for a large Notes implementation, it's time to start looking for people to fill the positions that we will be describing in the next sections. As we cautioned before, experienced people are very hard to find, and inexperienced people will need a lot of training.

Help Desk Operator

Once things are hopping, the Operations Guru will have worn out his or her sneakers, and the Developer will be knee-deep in code. Users will grow more sophisticated and begin asking more questions about how to create views and forms. They will want more databases placed on the server and more access control lists changed. Name and address books will have to be updated and users will need more group names set up.

Now is a good time to move Notes to the Help Desk. In most organizations, the Help Desk has people who know how to answer tough questions over the phone. They usually are Operations Gurus in training, and should be able to pick up Notes quickly. If possible, their call tracking systems should be converted to Notes so that they can work with Notes every day.

The Help Desk Operator can leverage the now-swamped Operations Guru by answering the questions and the administrative tasks mentioned. By having someone only a phone call away, users can get their questions answered quickly.

The Help Desk is also a great place for support people to learn Notes firsthand, to experience what the users are experiencing, and learn more about the company. It's tougher to explain a Notes problem over the phone than it is to solve it at the user's desk, so the Help Desk Operator will learn how to help the users solve problem themselves. They will see the good and bad database designs as they help users, and, over time, they will be exposed to almost all of the databases for the entire company.

The biggest challenge with Help Desk Operators is keeping them happy for more than one or two years. Phone support is stressful, and eventually even these sharp, energetic people will grow tired of the hassles, the same questions, and the mundane tasks. If possible, set Help Desk Operators free once a week to serve as junior Operations Gurus so that they can meet the people they serve. They can build a rapport with users, who may be a little kinder once they can visualize the face that goes with the person on the phone.

The Integrator

As Notes hits its stride, people will want to hook in to existing systems and access information from their applications. A link into an accounting package, for instance, can return the financial status of the company, mail-enabled approvals, even sales forecasts and actual information. Personnel systems can grab names from the payroll system, and updated histories can be fed into the production planning process.

It's wonderful, but it ain't easy. Version 3.x tools required an experienced programmer, and, although Version 4.0 adds a wealth of new tools to Notes, you'll still need a seasoned developer who can figure them out. You want developers who prefer the C language to the English language, who build Visual Basic applications at night for fun, and who can't wait to get hold of the integration kits that vendors are shipping for Notes.

If you are lucky, you will find Integrators who can apply their technical expertise to Notes integration without sacrificing the "feel" of Notes. However, while most Integrators enjoy connecting the technologies, they prefer that someone such as the Developer add the polish. Consultants charge a lot of money for this kind of integration, so let the Integrator have fun while the developer/intern adds the human side to Notes.

Database Manager

Notes databases don't appear to require a lot of maintenance, but as databases increase in size and replicas start popping up all over, someone has to monitor the growth and make sure it doesn't get out of hand. This task should be given to a Database Manager. This person should be almost invisible to the user community as they tend to their databases. His or her job is to implement the guidelines for directory structures and replication and take the responsibility for capacity planning and usage monitoring. He or she is also responsible for the integrity of all the databases on the servers and their efficient use.

As noted earlier, users love to fill Notes databases with information, which in turn, eats up a lot of disk space. The Database Manager should monitor the capacity on each server and plan well in advance for the purchase of additional disk storage. Instead of blindly adding drives, however, the Database Manager should analyze where the growth is occurring and determine if it is warranted or if steps can be taken to clear out old information.

The Database Manager should also handle any task that involves replication. A replication schedule needs to be developed for all the servers and reviewed regularly so that adjustments can be made as the characteristics of the network change. The Database Manager should monitor database usage and create new replicas on other servers to help balance usage and network load.

The support team should work closely with the Database Manager to decide which directories should be added and where new databases should be placed. The Database Manager will create the new directories, propagate them to the appropriate servers, check new databases for proper access control, and place new databases and their replicas of new databases wherever they are needed.

As time passes, users will need the Database Manager to create firewall databases, archive old information, and split up databases that may have gotten unwieldy. As time permits, the Database Manager should also review the database catalog to find databases that aren't properly documented and to identify databases that appear to be duplicating information or function.

Although the Database Manager may be responsible for all of these tasks, many of them can be shared by the Operations Guru and the Help Desk Operator. After all, everyone needs a vacation, and the entire team should be crossed-trained in all support areas. However, one person must be responsible for the management of all the databases or the task may be set aside as the Notes support people struggle to handle all the requests for help.

Visionary

By the time you need a Visionary, Notes is in full swing in the company. Applications are popping up all over, users are getting their questions answered, and people are wondering how they worked without it. They still have some concerns about the disruption caused by current installation, but Notes is making a visible difference in the success of the company, so complaints are low level.

For Notes to become a truly strategic tool for the company, however, there has to be a focused Visionary who wants Notes to succeed, and knows how to make that happen. This person understands how the business runs, who is in charge of what, and how it all could be better. The Visionary has some technical background and recognizes the potential of new add-in products and software tools. Most of all, the Visionary has the confidence of management, and its blessing for creating and executing plans across the company.

Ideally, the Visionary was instrumental in bringing Notes into the company in the first place, and he or she had an active say in its deployment. If not, one of the other Notes support people already defined can carry the banner until one is assigned. In most cases, IS directors or development managers are a good choice for the Visionary role, because every department has discussed its information needs with them. Their staffs have the technical background to brief them on the development, implementation, and maintenance issues of Notes. They understand the company's financial position because they spend a lot of time working with budget managers to fund equipment and systems. In short, they know more about the company than most other employees.

In companies that don't have a centralized IS environment, the individual IS managers should come together and become a group Visionary. The company needs standards for screen designs, integrating applications, and moving information around, and as long as the team members work well together, they may actually be stronger in the Visionary role than a single individual because they will contribute more ideas and new perspectives based on their diverse backgrounds.

But no matter who fills the role of the Visionary, the role will change as the user community grows more sophisticated about Notes. Initially, someone is needed to explain the big picture, to build a support team, bring in hardware, and propose pilot projects. As systems come on line, however, the Visionary becomes more of a facilitator. By having Notes on their desks, users will finally understand what it can do. They will explode with new ideas, and the Visionary will help them prioritize those ideas, turn them into projects, and keep their eyes on the long range needs of the company. The Visionary can also help users through the sales cycle and get their projects on the time line.

Consultants

Yep, consultants again. Just staying abreast of the latest Notes technologies can be a full-time job, and most companies can't afford a technologist to do it. Consultants earn their keep by being the technologist and the operations guru and the developers—in short, by playing all those positions.

A consultant can be of most value to the Visionary. Frankly, any Visionary who really knows Notes is probably a consultant, too. A consultant can review the ideas and plans developed by the Visionary and explain what it will take to follow through on them. The consultant can also brief the Visionary and IS staff on new ideas, and solve tough problems that have the internal staff stumped.

Our Plan

To summarize, our plan should include the following tasks for increasing the Notes support staff to handle the long range needs of a Notes implementation:

- ♦ In the project time line, budget for additional support positions and consultants
- ♦ Identify the need for the position and initiate internal and external searches
- ♦ Select and train candidates as they become available
- ♦ Reassign tasks for the support team as new members come on board

Training the Users, Developers, and Support Team

Whenever you implement Notes and Notes applications, you'll see significant and positive changes in the way people work. But change also disturbs a once-stable work environment, and it sends employees scrambling for ways to cope. One of the best ways to alleviate fears and prepare employees for Notes is through training. The more proactive the training, the better prepared the employees will be to accept new systems.

Notes should be regarded as more than just another application—it's a new way of thinking. Notes culture has its own jargon, which everyone should learn so that they can communicate their needs to developers and support people. For example, data entry screens are called forms; the information entered and saved on that screen is called a document; and the report-like screen of information that lists documents is called a view.

The distinction between user and developer also blurs because users can customize databases locally and build their own views. If you properly train users to customize their own views and some forms, you can significantly reduce the load on the support people. But you'd be wasting their time and yours if you try to train them to write C code and use the Notes API.

Training can also be used as a vehicle to implement company-wide standards, replacing a lot of heavy-handed announcements. In a classroom setting, the instructor can explain the concepts behind Notes, explain how those concepts are being standardized at the company, and explain why they are being applied in that way.

Training Users

There should be two kinds of training offered: classes for general knowledge of Notes and specific classes on new applications. Every employee in the company should attend one Notes introduction class to gain a basic understanding of how the company is using Notes, the Notes jargon, and any Notes standards that have been put in place. New application classes should be offered at the same time each application is being created so that users are ready to roll when the application is implemented.

Like good Notes support people, good Notes instructors and classes are fairly expensive. It costs a lot of money to set up a certified Notes training center, and if you intend to do so, include it in the price of training. It shouldn't be a difficult cost to justify, because these instructors have valuable experience with Notes installations which they can pass on to students, often saving the company a lot of future headaches—and expenses—when problems arise.

If possible, assign at least one or two key support people to attend a broad range of external classes so that they can help build an internal curriculum. These same people can work with internal training resources or part-time instructors from local colleges to customize a series of classes for your company. Lotus and other companies sell training materials that can jump-start the effort and serve as the basic classroom text.

Once Notes is in place, some users will pick it up quickly and should be given the opportunity to teach others how to use it. It gives them a chance to broaden their skills and gain the respect of their peers. Offer these people some kind of "train the trainer" classes to help them prepare for the task.

It will probably be more difficult to justify the development of training materials for new applications because the audience is usually small and the application is company-specific. One option is to find a local training company or even a teacher in the area who is willing to develop the course for a fee and possibly do the training. As the instructors become familiar with the style of the company, it will take less time to develop the new courses, users will grow comfortable with the instructor, and the training will become more effective.

At a minimum, you should plan on at least four classes so that users can attain a basic level of competence in Notes. This competence level is, of course, variable, depending on users' role in the company and their usage of Notes. These classes are:

An Introduction to Notes
Using Notes Mail and Company Standard Applications
Creating and Changing Forms and Views
Remote Communications and Replication

An Introduction to Notes

This class is very important to the success of a Notes installation because it is during this time that users will form their first impressions of Notes. If Notes was brought into the company in a planned and organized fashion, the class will introduce the program and demonstrate its power and ease of use. If Notes initially "had a life of its own" and was only recently brought under control, the class can clear up misconceptions and pass on tidbits to help even the most sophisticated or the most overwhelmed users.

Above all, the instructor must help users understand Notes. As you saw in Chapter 2, Notes can be difficult to explain because of its many unique capabilities. The user needs to learn the concepts of storing and viewing documents, workflow, replication, and remote communication to be able to work with the applications. They also must be told the number of servers and their names so they will know how and where to find databases.

The Notes desktop also deserves attention because it is the key to reaching all Notes information. Users may be confused by the desktop because, although it has some similarities to Windows, it represents only Notes databases. Version 4.0 raised the level of complexity, and users will need guidance in order to harness its power.

The database view is possibly the most important feature for a user to understand because it is the vehicle for locating and retrieving information. There is no formula for a "typical" view, and users should be shown a great variety of view examples so that they know how to deal with any view they may encounter. They should also become familiar with useful methods for finding information, such as full-text searches and unread marks.

Include discussions on forms and doclinks to the class and the introduction should be complete. Although forms are simply used for data entry, the Notes interface has some quirks that can cause frustration unless users are aware of them. Doclinks make it exceptionally easy to follow related information from document to document, and users should leave the class knowing what a doclink is and how to use it.

Using Notes Mail and Company Standard Applications

Notes Mail is often the most visible application in a core set of administrative applications that span the entire company. Other standard applications include personnel changes, purchase requisitions, and expense reports. A lot of thought goes into the design and development of these systems, and users need training to take the best advantage of them.

The mail system seldom handles just mail. Usually, it becomes a repository for to-do's, company goals, task assignments, meeting notices, and many other pieces of personal information. Therefore, the instructor must break the paradigm that electronic mail is just for messages, and explain how a Notes database can receive mail and turn it into something other than a mail message.

Like the training for Notes Mail, training for standard applications should explain not only how to use the application, but also how information flows throughout the system. The class gives the instructor the opportunity to explain the process behind the system and the reasoning behind the application design. Users should be given a chance to play with the application without fear of destroying anything important; then, when they are assured that their paperwork will not disappear into a black hole, they are often more willing to take more time and fill out forms correctly.

Creating and Changing Forms and Views

Many users are going to discover that they can create databases and custom views in the databases that exist. In most cases, though, because they are not trained developers and won't have access to developer's guides, they will run into a snag and call the support people or the Help Desk. The people taking this class should be the more adventurous users who have some knowledge of how to develop Notes. A little training up front can eliminate a lot of their questions, and empower them to take full advantage of Notes. The class is also a good opportunity to give them some of the internal Notes development standards and insist, in a positive way, that they use them as they develop their forms and views.

Obviously, this class should not go into the same depth that a developer needs to create systems. If the view or form is too complicated, users will defer it to the development staff after they have spent 10 or more frustrated hours on it anyway. Instead, the class should focus on the basics of simple forms and views.

Remote Communications and Replication

Remote communications and replication can be taught fairly quickly and, at times, explained fairly well over the phone. Invariably, remote users face obstacles like bad phone lines, busy signals, and server crashes that they don't how to deal with. Eliminating misunderstandings about how to dial up the server and disconnect when Notes is finished can save the company a pretty penny in phone charges alone. This training class can also eliminate a lot of problems for the Notes support team. It's easy for someone to call in and think he or she has replicated a database when that's not the case. Remote users may also attach a huge file or database to a mail message not understanding how they affect other users when the replication ties up the modem for an hour. A good training class will explain the ground rules for remote communication and give the users plenty of hands-on examples to bring the point home.

Often, the best time for the class is during a group meeting at the home office. Many times, remote employees come to the home office for an annual sales meeting or quarterly updates. To save expenses, the employees could stay in town for an extra day or two and take the Introduction to Notes class along with this one. If they are scheduled to receive Notes when they visit the home office, the Notes support team can schedule a time to load their laptops with Notes, Notes Mail, and replicas of all the standard company applications.

Training the Development Staff

Notes developers have a menagerie of tools available to them. In addition to the ever-growing and quirky Notes macro language, Lotus added LotusScript to version 4.0 and improved the API for Notes. The third-party market for Notes applications, integration software, and connectivity tools continues to grow, adding still more for the developer to learn. Because of the amount of information, if possible, immerse one of the best developers on staff in a training regimen that covers development of views and forms, Notes administration, and both the Notes macro language and LotusScript languages. This person's mission should be to query all the instructors about the tools that are available and to get the names of companies that have successfully implemented them. This person should return from class ready to help the rest of the team launch a development methodology and select tools.

In addition, all the developers should be formally trained in the Notes macro language and LotusScript once the team has agreed on a development approach. The Notes macro language doesn't always follow the logic of more traditional languages, and a good class will save the developer from a lot of debugging time. Although Lotus doesn't publish hard and fast standards for development, many consultants have developed their own standards for applications, and there are many standards generally accepted in the Notes community.

At least one developer should be trained on the Notes API for the C language. Notes version 4.0 enables a developer to access almost any feature of Notes through the API and someone should be able to tap those features at any time. Often, it takes some low-level code to tie an external application to Notes, and the training will pay for itself after the benefits of the connections are realized. Without training, the company will have to rely on a consultant to integrate applications with Notes, and the development staff will not have gained the knowledge to do it themselves the next time.

Training the Support Team

The Notes support team should be the guinea pigs for the Notes curriculum. They should take the Introduction to Notes and the Changing Forms and Views classes at a Notes training center. These classes will demonstrate how other people teach the classes, and they will make valuable contacts with other companies that are bringing up Notes. The instructors will probably also be consultants, and the support people can get a preview of their work in case they ever need to hire one of them.

Although only one or two support people will administer Notes, every person on the Notes support team should sit in on a Notes administration class. This class details all the tasks required to keep the Notes servers running. When users want to replicate their databases or reorganize a workgroup, the support people will be in a better position to make recommendations and explain how the changes will affect the servers and other users.

The support team should also receive training in the Notes macro language and LotusScript. Many user problems can be solved with a simple macro or a new button on a form, and the support team will be better prepared to troubleshoot a database problem and make suggestions to help the developers solve it. In a pinch, a support person can also help complete an application when a crucial deadline is approaching.

Our Plan

To summarize, our plan should include the following tasks for training users, developers, and the Notes support team:

- ♦ Identify authorized Notes training centers
- ♦ Schedule training for the Notes support team and development staff

- ◆ Work with the training department to develop a curriculum for new users, which will be added as the Notes implementation moves forward
- ◆ Schedule classes for new users to coincide with the implementation of Notes on their desktops

Building a Workplan for Implementation

It would be convenient if everyone could just come up on Notes right away and start loading information. Unfortunately, it's not possible unless you build a huge support staff immediately and hire an army of consultants and temporaries to support them. The Notes implementation will take time— time for user training, time for the users to acclimate themselves to the new environment, and time to roll out all the hardware and software.

Implementing Notes can be a complex task that requires a strong project manager and a good time line. Realistically, the time line is dependent on the number of users, the availability of training classes, the complexity of upgrading user hardware, the availability of support staff, and many other milestones that we've covered in this chapter. Some plans are open ended, while others have a fixed end date. Nevertheless, let's review all the tasks we have developed in this chapter and build a basic workplan for a Notes implementation. We will add a few tasks to the workplan, including Procure Notes Client and Server Licenses, that were not discussed previously but are obviously necessary. The plan will not include hourly estimates or start and end dates because every company has unique requirements and resources.

We'll assume that a parallel effort is being made by the development team to scope out the Notes applications that justified the project in the first place. In the meantime, we'll assume that users will receive only Notes Mail and some basic databases with their installation in anticipation of the new applications.

Notes Implementation Workplan

Phase I: Gather Detailed Requirements

1.1   Identify the number of users and their locations.
1.2   Develop a minimum Notes hardware configuration for all users.
1.3   Identify the users who must be upgraded and their upgrade requirements.
1.4   Review internal standards for network operating systems.
1.5   Identify protocols used on the user workstations.
1.6   Determine user need for full-client licenses or run-time version of Notes.

1.7 Estimate database size requirements based on existing development plans.

1.8 Determine disk storage requirements for user databases and applications databases.

1.9 Identify databases with potentially broad appeal that will require replicas.

1.10 Identify the need for servers to support external communications.

1.11 Identify the databases that remote users must access.

Phase II: Develop Notes Architecture

2.1 Forecast growth in users and in storage requirements.

2.2 Determine the best location for replicas with broad usage based on the network topology, and update server plan.

2.3 Determine the best location for databases required by remote users, and update server plan.

2.4 Calculate the number of servers required, including a mail router and firewalls.

2.5 Forecast future server requirements.

2.6 Identify servers that will hold replicas of the database, and update sizing estimates.

2.7 Specify equipment configurations.

2.8 Select a network operating system.

2.9 Analyze network topology based on proposed server locations and Notes applications, and identify areas where performance may be a concern.

2.10 Identify hardware required to handle performance issues that were raised.

2.11 Select network hardware and telecommunications equipment.

Phase III: Add Notes Support Staff and Develop Training Plan

3.1 Search internally and externally for an Operations Guru and a Developer.

3.2 Select a candidate for the Operations Guru position and obtain training as needed.

3.3 Select a candidate for the Developer position and obtain training as needed.

3.4 Assign the new employees to tasks as needed on the Notes implementation project.

3.5 Identify authorized Notes training centers.

3.6 Schedule training for the Notes support team and development staff.

3.7 Work with the Training department to develop a curriculum for new users, which will be added as the Notes implementation moves forward.

Phase IV: Procure Hardware, Software and Schedule Implementation

4.1 Purchase new equipment and upgrades for users.

4.2 Purchase servers.

4.3 Purchase a network operating system.

4.4 Purchase network hardware and telecommunications equipment.

4.5 Purchase Notes client and server licenses.

4.6 Purchase the upgrades for user equipment.

4.7 Schedule the installation of remote phone lines and an 800 number.

4.8 Develop a schedule for upgrading user equipment.

4.9 Define a high-level server-to-server replication schedule that avoids peak network traffic periods.

4.10 Develop an operational plan for ongoing Notes maintenance.

Phase V: Create Notes Infrastructure

5.1 Organize the proposed servers into domains and create domain names.

5.2 Develop a server naming convention.

5.3 Create the organizational hierarchy and set up certificates.

5.4 Define user naming conventions and standards for using group names.

5.5 Develop a directory structure for the servers.

5.6 Develop procedures for reviewing database usage patterns and recommending replicas.

5.7 Develop procedures for monitoring remote communications logs for capacity issues and misuse.

5.8 Develop a policy concerning replication and transfer of large files.

Phase VI: Implement Hardware and Software for Users

6.1 Install servers and network hardware.

6.2 Install user equipment upgrades.

6.3 Select users for Notes software installation.

6.4 Schedule classes for new users to coincide with the implementation of Notes on their desktops.

6.5 Install Notes client software.

6.6 Train Notes users.

Phase VII: Add Additional Support Staff

7.1 Initiate an internal and external search to fill additional Notes positions.

7.2 Select and train candidates as they become available.

7.3 Reassign tasks for the support team and new members as they come on board.

The first three phases are vital to the success of the project. As we discussed throughout this chapter, many of the decisions made up front will determine how successful the ongoing maintenance and support of the installation will be. Once users are on-board, it's more difficult to stop everything and make significant changes to the software or hardware architectures.

The first few months of Notes installation usually run smoothly because there are only a few users and plenty of capacity on the servers. But as new systems come online and more users are added, it becomes more difficult to add new users and still support the existing ones. New users often depend heavily on the support staff for a few weeks. As a reminder, make sure that users receive basic Notes training and hands-on experiences with Notes before they begin using internal applications.

Expanding to the Outside World

As soon as the implementation is successful, however, the management team will see the opportunities to generate revenues and reduce costs by connecting their internal systems to customers and vendors. A number of customers and vendors already have Notes and will be more than happy to hook up to your systems.

You can easily expand the scope of your Notes installation to include suppliers and customers by just thinking of them as remote users. The customer or supplier will have an easy way to communicate with the company and share information databases that help them better understand the company's products and procedures. In many cases, your company will gain a competitive edge because your vendors have access to more information.

The cost of expanding outside the company, however, can be daunting. Assuming you have 3,000 customers and a Notes server can handle 200 remote users, you would need 15 servers, a lot of phone lines, and two or more support people to take care of it all. The infrastructure needed to support external users could be larger than what you have for your internal systems! Instead of sinking a ton of money in your own installation, however, you can take advantage of new Notes services offered by companies like AT&T and CompuServe. They have invested a sizable chunk of change in placing Notes servers all over the United States so that users anywhere can have local access to a Notes server. You contract with them to store databases on their servers, set up a replication schedule to keep them updated, and your company is online everywhere the services are available.

To a user, the AT&T and CompuServe Notes servers are just an extension of your own servers. Remote users connect as often as they want to the closest Notes server and replicate the databases that you have published. Although users don't pay any long-distance charges, they must still pay for the time they spend communicating with the service provider.

From an operational standpoint, these services are a gift from heaven. You don't have to administer extra servers, maintain a huge telecommunications network, or handle support calls from users. No big hardware investments are required, nor does anyone need to do capacity planning and upgrades. Further, these services offer users more than just a place to access your databases. CompuServe offers access via Notes to newsletters, information services, mail gateways, and user forums. AT&T offers Help Desk services for users who are struggling with Notes. Other service providers are sure to jump on the bandwagon as Notes becomes more popular.

Implementing Notes for external users is not a complex task and can easily be included on the workplan as part of the Notes Architecture phase. It's a good idea for the internal staff and employees to be comfortable with their Notes implementation first, however, so that they can deal professionally with the outside users when they are brought online. If the Training department designs a good curriculum for your employees, there may even be an opportunity to generate a little revenue from training your suppliers and customers.

8

Developing Applications in Notes

Nothing happens in Notes until someone writes an application. True, Notes ships with a bunch of applications and templates to get you started, but in most cases, users want the templates customized to their unique requirements on a fairly regular basis. Clearly, there will always be a demand for Notes development.

The purpose of this chapter is to discuss an approach to development and introduce the processes and procedures that should be in place to do it right. It is beyond the scope of this book to explain the details behind the Lotus macro language, LotusScript, Notes ViP, and the Notes APIs, therefore we will cover technical details only where it adds to your understanding of the development process.

What Is Notes Development?

Notes development is the process of designing, creating, and implementing Notes databases, a definition that isn't much different from that of any other database package. Many of the same development disciplines used for building applications in traditional or fourth-generation languages can be applied to Notes development.

But Notes poses a challenge to the developer because it lacks many of the amenities or tools found in other development environments. All forms, views, and macros are stored with the data in one database which means the entire database must be backed up to save the latest version of the code. The database synopsis is a barely usable method of reviewing forms and view settings, field names, and field types.

Despite its shortcomings, Notes enables us to create an environment that facilitates the efficient development and deployment of Notes applications. The ideal time, however, for building the development environment is well before the first applications are created. Once a pilot program is in place or third-party applications start rolling in, it is extremely difficult to go back and standardize Notes systems and try to keep up with new development requests.

Let's break down the development process into phases and discuss how we can make it productive and efficient. These processes are:

♦ Setting up an infrastructure
♦ Setting up a library
♦ Creating a data dictionary
♦ Planning and scoping an application
♦ Creating the application
♦ Implementing
♦ Updating the application

Setting Up a Development Infrastructure

As with Notes' hardware and system software architectures, the decisions that you make initially regarding the development infrastructure will enhance or plague your applications for a very long time. A global change to a form name, view name, or field name requires a lot of effort in Notes, so correct names should be selected up front based on organizational standards. The Training department will take screen shots of existing applications and use them in training manuals, and any big changes could cause them a lot of rework. Set standards at the start and stick to them.

Database Standards

Every new database means more work for the Notes administrator. Access control must be set up and maintained, the database must be replicated to the appropriate servers, and someone must monitor the existing database for redundancy and obsolescence. Provide standards that effectively control database access and minimize the administrator's workload.

With the goal of improving the life of the Notes Administrator, consider the following standards when designing and developing a database:

Access Control	Implement all access control using group rather than individual names. This allows all changes to access rights to be made through the Name and Address Book, instead of in the individual databases. The group name can also be used as a mailing list for the people using the database.
Database Names	Database names should stand on their own on the desktop, even if they are set up in subdirectories. A calendar database should say Manufacturing Calendar of Events, not the general Calendar of Events, in case there is more than one calendar database on the server. Avoid names like Jon's Calendar of Events, and use Calendar of Events (Jon) so that all databases sort in logical order in the File Open Database scrolling window.
Help Documents	Include in every database a complete description of its purpose in the About Database document, along with detailed instructions for using the database in the Using Database document. The version number of the database should appear in both documents.
Icons	When practical, icons that serve the same purpose should look the same. For example, all address books should have the same icon, with different text; or, all mail-enabled databases should have an envelope somewhere on the icon. Department icons should have the same background color, for example.
Updates	Perform all development in a copy of the database that is isolated from the production version. Developers

should either refrain from replicating the modified database until it is fully tested, or use the Refresh or Replace design options to update the production copy of the database.

Forms Standards

Users will be entering information into many forms that reside in many databases. The standards you create will help them to move between forms and databases without a lot of retraining. The screens should have a consistent look, and buttons should always result in the same action. And only the forms that the users need should appear on the Compose menu. The standards to consider in meeting these requirements are:

Buttons

Agree on a minimum set of buttons that will reside on all screens, and place them in the same position if possible. For example, each screen should have an Edit button and a Save button in the upper right-hand corner of the screen. Standardize the titles of all buttons; for example, Change Status, Save and Exit, Calculate, Submit Request, and so on.

Copyright

Include the company name and a copyright notice in any form that contains a document available to external users.

Field Colors

Choose one color for the fields that capture information and another for the text descriptions. And define a separate color for fields that should be highlighted or emphasized in the application.

Fonts

Select one font for all forms, preferably one that every computer in your workgroup possesses. Agree on the size and position of the screen title. Define the font size and attributes (bold, italics, and so on) for the fields that capture the information and for the text that describes the fields. Define special fonts for fields that must be emphasized.

Form Names

Keep form names to one or two words, and do not include verbs. To control the Compose menu, precede the name with numbers or letters; for example, 1. and 2. or A. and B. Include an alias with every form.

Hidden Fields

Define one or two areas where hidden fields will be placed on the form so that every developer knows where to look for them. Change their color to red so they can be spotted easily.

Last Edit Field	Include on every form a field that displays the name of the last user to edit the document and the date of last edit.
Logos	Select a company logo to include on all forms, and define its location. For forms that are embedded in documents or transmitted remotely, develop a text substitute to conserve space.
Read/Compose	For forms, use the same access control rules as for databases. Implement all access control through group names and the Name and Address Book.
Screen Colors	Choose one or two colors as the default background color for forms. You may want to use one color for documents and another for responses to help users recognize the document type.
Subforms	New to version 4.0, use subforms whenever possible to reduce reprogramming the same fields in several forms.
Tabs	Use tabs to position text and fields on the screen. Avoid placing fields on the same line when filling one field with a lot of information will force another field to move to the right. Use hanging indents to align the left margin of fields that will display multiple lines of text.
Window Titles	Assign a window title to every form. The title will change to indicate the current state of the document. For example, the document may be New, Waiting for Approval, Received, Sent, and so on.

Field Standards

A Notes field is a memory location in which Notes stores information gathered from a user or an existing document. A developer places a field on a form so that Notes knows where to prompt the user for information or where to place the information that already exists in the document. The field can also be computed based on the information found in other fields.

The field name gives developers a way to identify the fields. It allows them to create formulas and macros that manipulate the fields, and to create views that display them. Fields can be unique to each form or shared by more than one. Many users won't even see field names because a developer created the entire application for them. However, many users are capable of adding their own views, and they will be affected by the standards you choose.

Field standards should help the developer become more efficient and allow other developers to modify and update the database without a lot of training. Let's consider the following field standards for Notes databases:

Formats	Assign all numbers and dates a format.
Keyword Display	If possible, display all keyword fields as radio buttons or check boxes. For those keyword fields displayed with the standard format, place a special graphic or text symbol next to the field to indicate that it is a keyword field.
Keyword Lists	Do not hard code keyword lists unless they will never change, such as Yes/No. Store the elements of the list as documents in the same database or an external database, and access them using a lookup into a view.
Shared Fields	Use shared fields whenever a field appears in more than one form in the database.
Temporary Fields	Set aside field names for the temporary fields that are allowed by Notes in formulas. For example, use Temp0 through Temp9 as temporary variables, and specify that they never be used as permanent variable names in a database.

As noted, field names are important to both the developer and user. The standard should be clear without being oppressive. Most Notes programmers use a single word for a field name or they concatenate several words into one and capitalize the first letter of each word. For example, a field that holds customer names could be given the name CustomerName.

Full names should be used for clarity whenever practical. CustomerName is much easier to understand than CstNm or even CustName. However, a field name like PartDescriptionAfterPartLookupIntoInventoryControlDatabase may be overdoing it a bit, when PartDescription is sufficient.

As more databases come online, it becomes more difficult to remember which field names belong to which database. The Notes Data Dictionary Database can help with views sorted by database name. Another option is to assign every database an alias in the data dictionary, then add it to the field name. Using the preceding example, the customer name field in a database with the alias Cust could be identified as Cust_CustomerName.

Let's add another standard to our field standards:

Names	Enter the field names as one word. If the name must include multiple words, concatenate them and capitalize the first letter of each word. Use full names whenever practical. The Database Administrator for the Notes databases will decide whether a database alias should precede all variable names.

Environment variables are used in formulas to temporarily store information while the form processes the formulas. These variables are written to the NOTES.INI file, where they remain indefinitely. The standards should define a set of temporary and permanent environment variable names to reduce the growth of the NOTES.INI file and to keep the number of variable names small.

We'll add still another standard to our field standards:

Environment Variables	Environment variables will be assigned by the Database Administrator as if they were field names. The names ENV0 through ENV9 will be set aside as temporary variables that can be reused by any formula.

View Standards

Views show us which documents are in a Notes database, and allow us to access them by selecting and opening the documents. Views are used for creating reports, searching for information, and as a filter for the database. In short, views are the user's window into a Notes database.

View standards are tougher to enforce because users have no incentive to follow them. They will be creating only a few of their own views, and they may not want or remember to take the extra time to add standards. Nevertheless, here are some view standards to consider:

Attachments	Display an icon in all views that indicate file attachments.
Fonts	Define the font size and attributes (bold, italics, and so on) for most columns. Select special font attributes for fields that will be emphasized (bold in red, for example).
Formats	Assign a format to all number and date columns.
Private Views	Define a naming standard for private views so that new application development doesn't delete the view when the database design is refreshed. In conjunction with the upcoming View Names standard, consider including, a separate letter or number to precede the view name; or perhaps determine that private views are those *not* preceded by a letter or number.
Read Access	Views should use the same access control rules that were discussed previously for databases. Do all access control through group names and the Name and Address Book.
Unread Marks	All views should display unread marks.
View Names	Assign view names of one or two words, and do not include verbs. To control the view menu, precede the name with numbers or letters. Include an alias with every view.

View Colors   Choose one or two colors as the default background color for views. Select separate colors for unread documents and totals. Define a hierarchy of colors for categories (14 point, blue, bold for the first category; 12 point, red, bold for the next category, and so on).

Interfacing with Third-Party Applications

All of the preceding standards sound reasonable, and they should help us maintain control of our applications. But it is also necessary to insist that third-party developers follow our standards when we hire them to create applications for us. It may cost a little more, but our staff will be able to maintain the databases long after the third-party company has gone.

Unfortunately, we can't force our standards on third-party developers when we buy canned applications, unless we intend to spend a ton of money retro-fitting their product. If the developer is any good, they will have their own set of standards and their applications will appear professional. If you are just beginning to build Notes applications, the developers may be willing to share their standards in hopes of locking you in as a long-term client.

The best thing to do is to adapt their software to our standards wherever practical and train users to handle the differences. We can still maintain operational standards such as access control, and update our data dictionary with their variables. And it may not be too difficult to change the form and view colors and fonts in order to bring the application closer to our standard. Anything that will bring the third-party applications in line with internal standards will help both the user and the developer.

Future Standards

More standards issues will arise as you begin developing Notes applications. It's important to remember to address issues as early as possible in the development process to eliminate the rework required to adapt existing database to a new standard. If a new standard is needed, it's best to implement it right away instead of waiting as more databases are put in production that will need to be updated later.

Setting Up Development Libraries

With a traditional language, developers store finalized applications in a development library. The library is controlled by a fearless Librarian who won't allow anyone to add, change, or remove any complete applications from the library without his or her permission. If developers want to make a change to an application, they must request the library copy. The Librarian checks the application out to the developer and checks it back in only after the new application has been tested and accepted for implementation.

Notes development should be handled in the same way. A developer should check out the latest Notes database from the library and make the appropriate changes in a development directory or on the local personal computer. When the application is successfully tested, the Librarian can replace the design of the library copy with the more recent version and update one of the replicas in production so that all the other replicas will get the change.

The Librarian doesn't have to be a full-time person and, in fact, most people can't afford to dedicate someone to the task. However, one of the developers or operations people should be assigned the Librarian task to ensure that the process is being followed. Without a library, it doesn't take long for many versions of the same database to end up floating around all over the company.

As we'll see later, Notes also encourages development "on the fly" at the user's desk. The library concept shouldn't interfere with a developer's ability to respond quickly or to be a more efficient developer. Developers should continue to solve problems and work as required with users, but make sure that the Librarian is notified when a project is completed.

Developers also should maintain a library of commonly used programming routines that they will share as they create applications. By using the library, developers can avoid reinventing a routine that already exists, and standards can be enforced from a single location. The fearless Librarian would allow any developer to use a routine only that originates out of the library to ensure the integrity of applications.

Notes developers can also benefit from a similar library for macros and formulas. The library would be a single Notes database that held standard forms and macros. With the advent of subforms in version 4.0, the library should also contain any subform that may be used in many applications. One of the forms in the library, for example, could contain the company logo, an Edit button, and a Save Button. Another form could contain Notes 4.0 subforms for approving a document or displaying a customer name. To use the form, the developer would open the database, use the Design Forms menu, copy the library form to the clipboard, and paste it into the new database. The library would also contain a single form for buttons and for fields with standard formulas. To add a button to a new form, the developer would open the library form, copy the button to the clipboard, and paste it into the new form. For formulas, the developer would again use cut and paste, then modify the field name as needed.

Creating a Data Dictionary

Most development tools employ the concept of a data dictionary. The data dictionary is a repository for all the field names that exist in all the applications that are created by the development tool. Developers define fields as they develop applications, then the fields are added to the data dictionary permanently when the application is implemented.

The data dictionary is very helpful because it enforces standards and reduces redundancy. A developer who needs to create a field that inherits values from another field called AccountNumber can set up the new field with the same format. Developers will avoid creating duplicate field names that represent a different piece of information. Notes does not have a tool that remotely resembles a data dictionary, therefore, we would need to create one as a Notes database. It would require a single form to capture the field name, the field type, the name of the form that holds it, and the name of the database. It needs a view by field name, by database, and by form to provide the information in the most useful way.

A data dictionary is not required for effective Notes development, but it can certainly help developers avoid duplicate field names and keep track of the fields in their applications. A small development group may not want to invest the time in creating a data dictionary, however, because probably everyone knows everyone else's formulas and databases. But if they expect the number of databases and their staff to grow, they may want to start one now before they are too busy to create one later.

Planning and Developing an Application

The users of the '90s have high expectations from the developers of the '90s. Gone are the days when a systems analyst could build a specification over several months and throw it over the wall to a developer who works in a dark room, drinks a lot of caffeine, and wolfs down Twinkies until 2 A.M. Today, users want developers to quickly understand their project, prototype a system, tweak the specification, and get on with it. The developer, of course, views this approach as dangerous and rushed. The user skimps on a specification and the developer is locked into a never-ending cycle of changes because he or she never pinned down the user. The developer ends up running 200 percent over budget and the user is never happy.

In reality, many users don't understand Notes sufficiently to know what they really want. The concept of mail enabling is new to them, as are the concepts of replication and doclinks. Without proper education on the capabilities of Notes, they may agree to a specification based on their knowledge of traditional screens and reports. Instead of reaping the benefits of Notes, users may suffer to due to our insistence on a specification without a prototype or a demonstration.

Therefore, our planning must include some of the rigors of traditional application design integrated with the speed of rapid prototyping and fluid specifications. In high-profile applications, the changes to a Notes database are indeed never-ending. We must do our best up front to understand and design the application as quickly as possible to get something in front of the user, while acknowledging that it is phase 1 of many improvement efforts.

These are the steps we should follow to plan and develop an application. The next sections provide more details:

- ◆ Develop a process flow
- ◆ Identify data elements and data types
- ◆ Define the databases
- ◆ Define the forms and their relationships
- ◆ Define views
- ◆ Develop a prototype
- ◆ Finalize requirements
- ◆ Implement a prototype and enhance the product

Develop a Process Flow

A process flow diagram shows the reader how information flows through a process that we intend to automate, and it defines what happens to the information at each step along the way. Creating the diagram clarifies the process for users and helps them to understand its strengths and weakness. Most users discover that there are plenty of opportunities to improve the process as they help create the process flow diagram.

Users should be encouraged to start a process improvement team to clean up the process before they try to automate it. The developers, with their knowledge of Notes, can help users visualize a better way to approach the task using Notes. Without this interaction, the developer may create an application that will perform the wrong tasks faster or more efficiently and not really give the user the maximum benefit of automation.

As the flow is documented, the developer should also encourage the users to minimize the use of paper forms in favor of Notes. It's usually easy to eliminate one copy of a five-part form, but the real benefits are seen when the need is reduced to one copy that can be output on a laser printer instead of on a multipart, high-cost form.

The final product should be a flowchart that represents the most efficient way to approach the process, using Notes as the automation tool. The process improvement team can move forward and make the necessary changes to manual processes while the developer moves onto the next steps in planning the application. There are several good flowcharting tools available that can cut down on the time required to actually draw the diagram, enabling you to concentrate more on the content instead of the form.

Identify Data Elements and Data Types

The process flow diagram sets the stage for identifying data elements, in that every process box with an action will generate data elements. Recall from our previous example of the purchase requisition process that there was a step called Originator Enters Requisition into Notes. To discover the data elements, we ask the person who processes requisitions to list the items that he or she would want to enter into a system.

Even an action such as Mail Requisition to Approver generates data elements. The name of the approver may already be present, but we should also store the date and time sent and the name of the person who sent the message. Notes requires certain fields to be present before it can mail a document, so those must be added to our list as well.

There are not a lot of data types in Notes, so it's pretty easy to figure out which data type to assign to each element. There is only one number field type, one date and time field type, a text field type that holds thousands of character with no formatting, and a rich text field that holds any kind of file attachments and accepts formatting. None of the Notes data types requires or even accepts a field length, so you have one less detail to worry about.

Every Notes field type except Rich Text and Sections can have a default value, translation formula, and a validation formula. Ask users if a data element requires a default or if the incoming text should be translated a certain way (all text in uppercase, for example). Some data elements must fit in a range or be restricted, giving you a clue as to whether the data element requires a keyword data type.

Keywords are used when the data element represents a list of values and the user must pick one or several of them. As you interview the person who performs the process, ask not only for the data element, but also try to discover if the data is limited to one or more choices or requires verification using another set of data elements. Based on the interview, you should be able to determine if the keyword can be shown as a radio button, check box, or in the standard format.

Some Notes data types help you control access to information, which means you'll need to discover if any data elements are restricted for use by only certain people. For example, if everyone in the Purchasing department can read a requisition, but only the supervisors can change a field called Approved By, then you may need to use the Section field type to control access, or create multiple forms and use the Reader Names field type.

Use Table 8.1 to help you document all the data elements that you find. It will also remind you to ask for the additional information you will need to develop the Notes application.

Define the Databases

Once you have the data elements, you can begin to define the databases that you need to support the application. Notes is not a relational database, however, so you can't just pull out the old database theory book, normalize the data, and be done with it. Sometimes, you will have to store a copy of the same data element in more than one document to speed up Notes or to build a certain kind of view.

A single Notes database can also hold any number of unrelated groups of documents that could be considered a database on their own. For example, a Notes database could hold purchase requisitions, inventory items, department names, and vendor names. This feature gives you the flexibility to have one file that holds all the documents for an application. It also requires every view to have a filter that eliminates any documents that don't belong in that view.

TABLE 8.1 Data Elements Worksheet

Data Element	Full Description	Data Type	Restrictions (Range or List of Values)	Access Limits
Purchase Requisition	Purchase requisition number	Text	6 letters	None
Requisition Date	Date on which the requisition was issued	Time	None	None
Requisition Status	The status of the requisition	Keyword	A List: New Submitted to Mgr Approved by Dept Submitted to VP Approved by VP Submitted to Purch Approved by Purch Order Placed Order Received	Users can only change this using buttons— no editing allowed

The more documents that you have in a database, the longer it takes to sort views and maintain the database. Therefore, it's best to include only the documents that you need in a database to display the views properly. In our requisition database, we should move the inventory items and vendor names to a separate file and use lookups to retrieve information. We may need a field in the document that is a copy of the item description or vendor name, but having the field will eliminate slow lookups into the other database.

On the other hand, the Notes Administrator would go nuts if you created a database for every little list and then asked to store it on the server. Be aware that every Notes database takes up at least 125KB of disk space even if it has only a few items in it. If you have a keyword that can have, say, 25 values, and the list is changing regularly, go ahead and add the 25 documents to the same database.

In most cases, you'll find that each application usually fits in a single database unless it must verify information in a large database of master records such as customers or vendors. Having one database for the entire application makes it easier for developers to maintain. It's also easier for remote users to replicate one database instead of trying to remember to replicate two of them.

Define the Forms and Their Relationships

Even though an application may require only one database, it will have related data elements that should all be entered at the same time. These logical groups of data elements are the basis for defining the number of forms that the applications will need. For example, the data elements for a purchase requisition are one group and the data elements for department names and personnel are another.

Logical groups don't necessarily equate to a single form, however. All the data elements may be related to a process, but a subgroup of the elements may be required only once for each document (purchase requisition number, requisition date), while another subgroup of elements may be required several times (items to order, quantities to order). The relationships between the subgroups defines how many forms are needed and the order in which the forms are used.

The terms used for defining the data relationships between data element groups are *one-to-one* or *one-to-many* relationships. For instance, one purchase requisition requires one department number and manager, making it a one-to-one relationship between the requisition data elements and the department data elements. One purchase requisition number and its associated data elements requires many items, quantities and prices, making it a one-to-many relationship between the purchase requisition setup data elements and the purchase requisition ordering data elements.

Figure 8.1 illustrates the relationships between groups of data elements. With a one-to-one relationship, all the data elements can exist on a single form. If we design the form and find that it contains multiple occurrences of the same data element, then we really have a one-to-many relationship.

With a one-to-many relationship, some of the data elements must be moved to a form that is executed once. The rest of the data elements will be used on another form that must be executed after the first as many times as necessary to capture all of the information. The second form must contain one or more of the data elements from the first form so that the two can be related to each other in a view.

Once the one-to-one and one-to-many relationships are established, we need only to plug in the data elements to decide what goes on each form. Let's plug some of the data elements into Figure 8.1 to illustrate the next step, as shown in Figure 8.2.

It is possible in a one-to-many relationship between data elements that only one data element is required many times. In such a case, instead of creating an entire form to capture the information, it's better to use a Notes keyword field formatted as a standard field or a check box. Notes views recognize the significance of a keyword field that holds multiple values, and, if the keyword is used as a category in a view, Notes will display the document once for each keyword field without making duplicate copies of the document in the database.

Multiple forms are essential in one-to-many relationships, but Notes has a limitation that makes them a little bit frustrating for a user. Notes can-

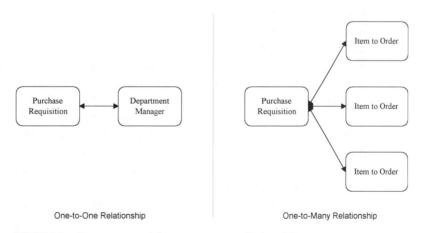

One-to-One Relationship   One-to-Many Relationship

FIGURE 8.1   One-to-one and one-to-many relationships.

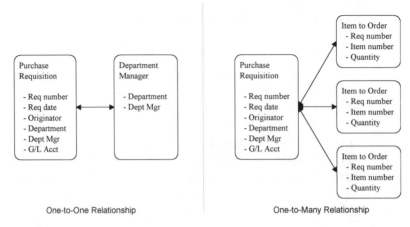

FIGURE 8.2 Data elements in one-to-one and one-to-many relationships.

not display two forms in the same window. Unless the data elements on the first form are inherited by and duplicated on the second form, the user cannot see the two screens at the same time. The user could manually use Windows to minimize the two screens and resize them to fit on the screen but it wouldn't be practical, considering the time required to do it.

This limitation may make it tempting to ignore one-to-many relationships and just repeat fields on the same form. But that strategy works only when you have just two or three occurrences of the repeated data elements, the repeated information is used for display purposes only, and you can be *sure* that the number of occurrences will never increase. The user is happy and can see everything on one screen and the developer is happy because none of the fields has to be moved to another form and synchronized.

The drawbacks to this approach are twofold. It is impossible to create a sorted view on the repeated data elements because a view cannot sort on two different fields as equals nor can it display the results. Someone will always come up with an exception to the rule and want one or two more sets of repeated data elements on the screen. If you cut corners and only use one form, chances are, you'll end up reworking the applications.

Once all the data elements have been defined, there's not much left to do for fields in a one-to-one relationship but to create the fields on the Notes form and place them in the proper locations. The developer should review the standards and add the logo, buttons, text, fonts, and colors as needed. If any access control is required, the developer should arrange the fields so that a section can be created around them.

Forms in a one-to-many relationship need some additional attention to ensure that the information from the first form is transferred properly to the second form. The first form in the relationship, the one form, must be filled out before the second form, the many form, can be completed. In addition, the developer doesn't want the second form executed before the first form because some data elements in the second form are copied from the first form. Those fields would be blank if the first form didn't precede it. The developer can control the order of execution by using the Design Form Attributes menu to turn off the Include in Compose Menu option and to turn on the Inherit Default Field Values option for the second form. The developer then adds a button in the first form that becomes the only way that a user can execute the second form. The second form automatically copies key information from the first form, and all the necessary data elements become available in the document.

Figure 8.3 illustrates the use of buttons to control the order of execution. The user enters information into the Requisition Master and pushes the button to add a detail item. The second form inherits the purchase requisition number from the first form, and the user adds the detail information. The user pushes the Add Another Detail Item to Order button, Notes saves the document, and it displays an empty form for the next item.

If the developers have—or want to form—a good relationship with the users, this is a good time to bring the forms that have been developed to the users for feedback. They will probably be amazed at how quickly the forms were developed, and it will give them a sense of how the application might work. The developers could even sit down with the users and note the changes as the users give them feedback. This kind of interaction bolsters the confidence of the users and gives them the feeling that they are really participating in the project.

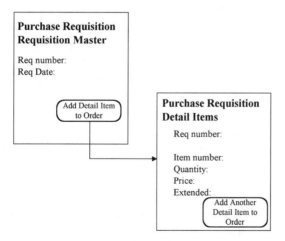

FIGURE 8.3 Forms controlled in a one-to-many relationship.

Of course, there is a danger that the users may think the project is almost complete and it will only be a matter of days before implementation. This kind of situation can be avoided by including the visits as a part of the original plan. If the users hear up front that there will be prototypes coming to them often for feedback as the project progresses, they will understand the process and have the correct expectations.

Define Views

Notes views provide users with access to the information entered into Notes forms. The design of these views determines how much effort users will expend to find a document, how quickly they will be able to bring it up, and how clearly they can print information from the database. A form can be poorly designed and still capture information, but a poorly defined view will severely limit users' ability to find the information that they need.

Most views are not difficult to create, and developers often can do so without a formal design document. But before they perform their magic, developers have to spend time understanding the application from the user's perspective by reviewing the process flow document and listening to how the users expect the system to work. By the time they are ready to design, they know why users want the view, what they want on it, and what kinds of sorts and totals they require.

Complicating the process, however, is that some users may not know how to express what they want, while other users will have only experienced traditional development environments and may express their needs in terms of the report writer that they've always used. The developer may need to educate users in the power and limitations of Notes views to help them break out of their paradigm and come up with the view they really want. The purpose is not to change their requirements to fit Notes but to rework their expectations based on the kinds of views that can be created.

Sample databases are a valuable tool for helping users define their view requirements. If users can't visualize what they need, developers can focus in on why until they find a similarity between the requirement and an existing database. The developer can bring up a sample database and demonstrate how it performs a similar task. Assuming that the database is just a sample, the developer can even tweak the views in front of users to help them refine what they want. There are basically four why scenarios for creating a view:

- ♦ to visually locate documents
- ♦ to act as a front end for the full-text search engine
- ♦ to summarize information
- ♦ to import and export information from and to external files

A developer can either use an existing database or build one that covers all four scenarios and have it available for demonstrations. Each of the four views has unique design characteristics that users will be able to identify with their needs. Users may see more than one view that fits what they want, in which case the developer can merge the features. Let's take a look at the four why scenarios and the characteristics of the views that represent them.

To Visually Locate Documents

One of the primary purposes of a Notes view is to help users locate documents. After all, a view is the only way that a user can recall a document, so there must be at least one view of this kind in the database. In fact, most of the views in a database are used for this purpose.

These views will make heavy use of sorting and categories. One or two fields in the document represent information that will help a user drill down to the specific document. For example, the categories may be Region, Territory, and Salesperson, or perhaps Product Line and Product. These fields will be used as the first columns in the view, and Notes will show the category value on a single line preceding the information it represents.

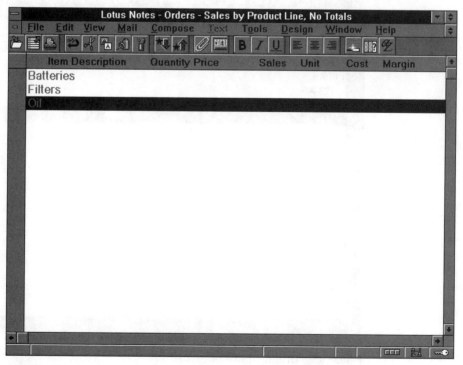

FIGURE 8.4   A view with collapsed categories.

Figures 8.4, 8.5, and 8.6 illustrate how categories help users locate information. The Orders database is categorized by Product Line and Part Number. In Figure 8.4, the view shows only the Product Line categories without the detailed records beneath them. This is accomplished by displaying the view with all categories collapsed, giving users a high-level view from which to start locating the document that they want.

Once the user selects a product line, Notes lists all the products for the selected product line only. A database with thousands of records may have only 25 items in the top category, enabling the user to skip most of the database and quickly move down to the next category level. A double-click on the category brings out the next level of information, as shown in Figure 8.5.

As with the first category, this category shows a subset of the entire database, again helping users move quickly to the information that they need. One more double-click on the appropriate product, and users can view all the documents that they need. Categories enable the drilldown into information to occur, and formatting enhances the look of the view to make it even easier for users to operate. In the view shown in Figure 8.6, each cat-

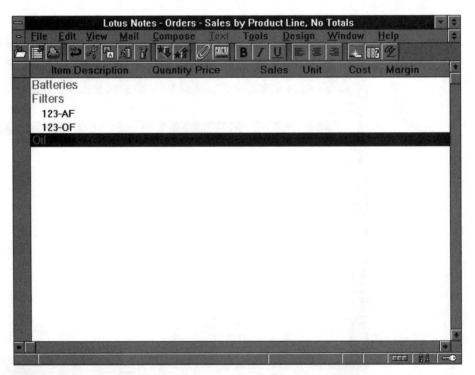

FIGURE 8.5 Drilling down one level.

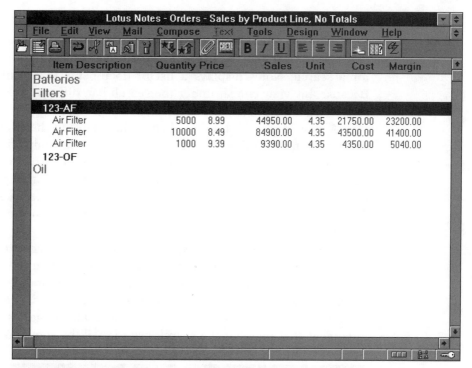

FIGURE 8.6 A full view with documents.

egory is indented to give it an outline look. Indenting is a natural consequence of how categories are created in a view, and you can control the width of the indent as you design the view.

Fonts and colors add the final touch to this kind of view. Users need some way to easily differentiate the categories or they will spend all of their time trying to figure out the screen. The indents help, but a view with five categories can still be difficult to follow. In our example, the main category uses a 12 point bold font so that it stands out from the rest of the 10 point text. Although the black and white image doesn't show it, the category could be changed to a red color to make it stand further. The second category is only 10 point, but it is bold and in a blue color to help differentiate it from the other category. The detail document lines are simply 10 point black text to indicate that we are at the bottom of the drilldown.

In these views, fields that help find information are more important than the details. If our example had five categories instead of two, we would have eliminated many of the number columns so that the full description would be visible. Here, a user and a developer would be able to sit down with the view and add whatever fields would fit in the space that remains.

To Act as a Front End for the Full-Text Search Engine

The full-text search feature in Lotus Notes uses a view to display the results of a search. The search bar sits above the view and, after a user enters text for a search, Notes displays a list of documents that contain that text. Because any view can sit under the search bar, different views can be created to enable the kind of searches each user performs.

A view for a search differs from other views in that Notes ignores all categories in displaying the results. The search bar only affects the way a Notes view displays the information; the view maintains the sorting order defined by the categories. The view can contain categories, and it will display them when used without a search filter, but when a search is performed, Notes will ignore the categories and display the columns as if no categories exist.

Figure 8.7 shows a fully expanded view of the Orders database with the search bar over it. We will search for all parts with Filter in the description. Note that although the view shows the categories before the search, Figure 8.8 shows the results of the search *without* the categories. The view that supports text searches should be developed without categories because every document that matches the search criteria will be shown on a single line

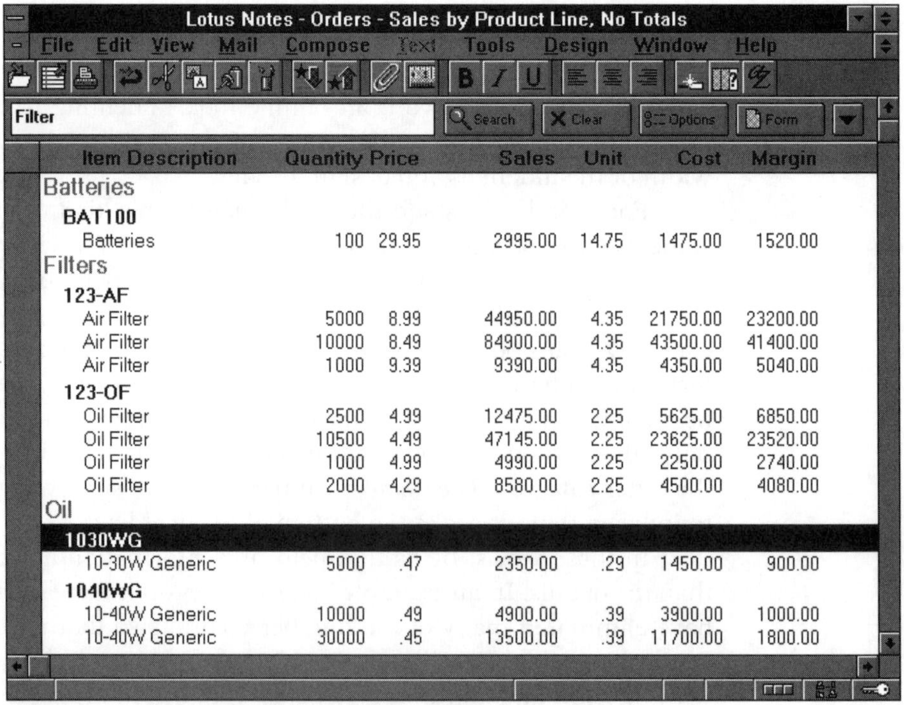

FIGURE 8.7   Using a search bar with a view.

anyway. The fields selected for the view columns should provide users with significant clues about the contents of the document so they don't have to waste time on stray hits.

For our search example, let's use a modified version of the view that repeats the categories on every detail line, as shown in Figure 8.8. It will look redundant before the search but the results will give the user more clues as to the content of the document. The views in this category are very similar to the views used to visually locate documents because users want the same information with subtotals and totals. The only difference between these views and the others is that totals in a Notes view are a visual nightmare and can turn an attractive view into a monster. If a user wants this kind of view, the developer may need to make some subtle changes to an existing view to show totals and subtotals in a more pleasing manner.

Notes displays all totals on the line that displays a category. Since the category is shown before the detail lines, all of the totals are displayed above the detail lines instead of below them, where one would expect to find them. It's often hard for users to get used to this, and they may request some changes.

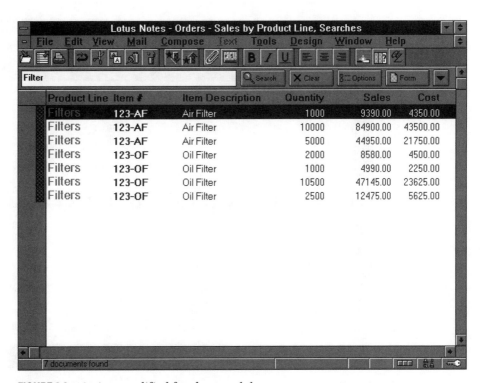

FIGURE 8.8   A view modified for the search bar.

Figure 8.9 shows a view of the Orders database by Product Line with totals. The view doesn't look too bad, but the screen is very busy and it's difficult to separate the totals from the detail. (On a color screen, the totals show up as blue so they are easier to identify.) This view can be useful if the user has only a high-level summary total of one category. When the categories are collapsed, the view provides a clear summary of the totals (see Figure 8.10).

For our detail totals, however, we need some way to separate the totals from the details. Figure 8.11 shows a view where each numeric column was duplicated. One column was not totaled; the other column was totaled and set to Hide Detail Lines. The view isn't perfect, but it does separate the detail from the actual totals. The only drawback is that it requires a lot more space on the view, eliminating a lot of the detail columns that made up the amounts.

Users need to understand the limits of views and totaling up front, otherwise they are sure to be disappointed by the outcome. Two or three examples of different totaling schemes would go a long way in helping them decide what they want. If they really need fancier reports, then a package like Lotus Approach may be necessary to complete the application.

Item Description	Quantity	Price	Sales	Unit	Cost	Margin	%
Batteries	100		2995.00		1475.00	1520.00	11%
BAT100	100		2995.00		1475.00	1520.00	100%
Batteries	100	29.95	2995.00	14.75	1475.00	1520.00	103%
Filters	32000		212430.00		105600.00	106830.00	78%
123-AF	16000		139240.00		69600.00	69640.00	42%
Air Filter	5000	8.99	44950.00	4.35	21750.00	23200.00	107%
Air Filter	10000	8.49	84900.00	4.35	43500.00	41400.00	95%
Air Filter	1000	9.39	9390.00	4.35	4350.00	5040.00	116%
123-OF	16000		73190.00		36000.00	37190.00	58%
Oil Filter	2500	4.99	12475.00	2.25	5625.00	6850.00	122%
Oil Filter	10500	4.49	47145.00	2.25	23625.00	23520.00	100%
Oil Filter	1000	4.99	4990.00	2.25	2250.00	2740.00	122%
Oil Filter	2000	4.29	8580.00	2.25	4500.00	4080.00	91%
Oil	45000		20750.00		17050.00	3700.00	11%
1030WG	5000		2350.00		1450.00	900.00	60%
10-30W Generic	5000	.47	2350.00	.29	1450.00	900.00	62%
1040WG	40000		18400.00		15600.00	2800.00	40%
10-40W Generic	10000	.49	4900.00	.39	3900.00	1000.00	26%
10-40W Generic	30000	.45	13500.00	.39	11700.00	1800.00	15%
	77100		236175.00		124125.00	112050.00	100%

FIGURE 8.9   A Product Line view with totals.

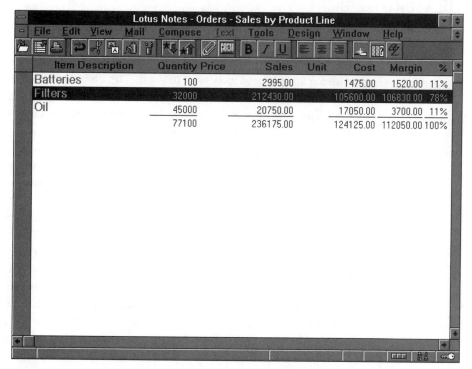

FIGURE 8.10 A Product Line view with category totals only.

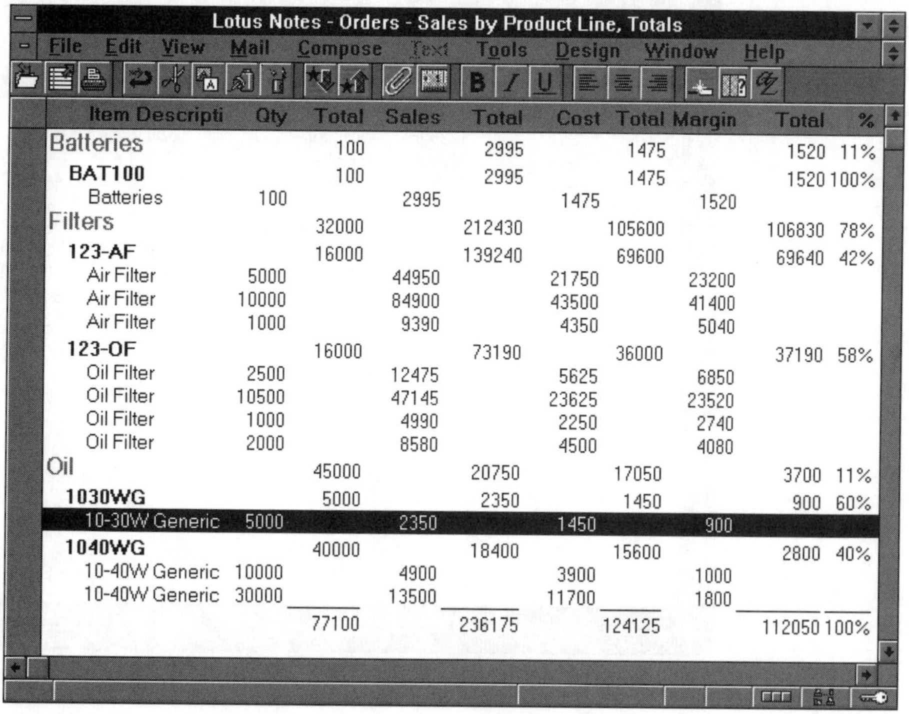

FIGURE 8.11 A modified detail Product Line view.

To Import and Export Information from and to External Files

Users may want to import or export information using Notes, and a view provides a simple and easy way to do it. The view becomes a map that takes the information from a text file or spreadsheet and assigns the first column in the import or export file to the first column in the view, the second column to the second column, and so on.

If a user wants to import information, the developer must find out which fields on a form need to be filled in and how the columns in the spreadsheet or text file are ordered. For exporting information, the developer must know in what order the user expects the data to be exported.

These views will be plain and unattractive, but they get the job done. Figure 8.12 shows a typical view for an import or export. Note that there are two fields, Sales and Cost, that are calculated whenever the information is imported or exported. A column can represent a constant value as well.

Once developers know why a user wants a view and the kind of view, they need to know which data elements to include in the view. All that information should already reside in the document, because lookups into other Notes databases would severely degrade the performance of the view. The

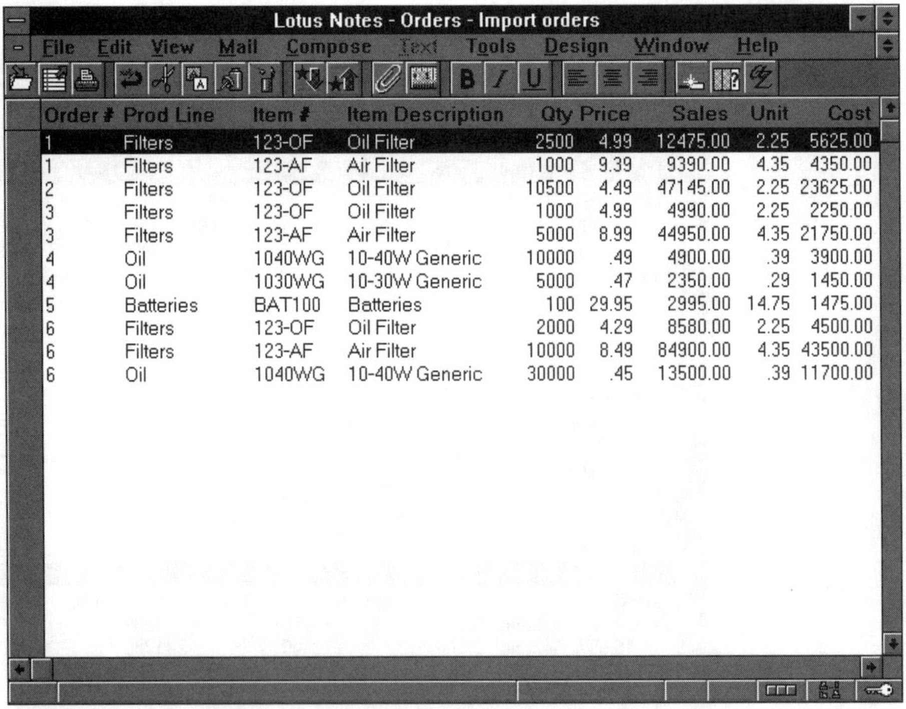
Lotus Notes - Orders - Import orders
File Edit View Mail Compose Text Tools Design Window Help
Order # Prod Line Item # Item Description Qty Price Sales Unit Cost
1 Filters 123-OF Oil Filter 2500 4.99 12475.00 2.25 5625.00
1 Filters 123-AF Air Filter 1000 9.39 9390.00 4.35 4350.00
2 Filters 123-OF Oil Filter 10500 4.49 47145.00 2.25 23625.00
3 Filters 123-OF Oil Filter 1000 4.99 4990.00 2.25 2250.00
3 Filters 123-AF Air Filter 5000 8.99 44950.00 4.35 21750.00
4 Oil 1040WG 10-40W Generic 10000 .49 4900.00 .39 3900.00
4 Oil 1030WG 10-30W Generic 5000 .47 2350.00 .29 1450.00
5 Batteries BAT100 Batteries 100 29.95 2995.00 14.75 1475.00
6 Filters 123-OF Oil Filter 2000 4.29 8580.00 2.25 4500.00
6 Filters 123-AF Air Filter 10000 8.49 84900.00 4.35 43500.00
6 Oil 1040WG 10-40W Generic 30000 .45 13500.00 .39 11700.00

FIGURE 8.12 An import view.

process of defining a view may result in changes to the forms if the necessary information doesn't exist in the correct document.

All that remains in the design of the view is to identify the fields that need to be sorted, categorized, and totaled. Each of these features is merely a check box or two in the column definition of the view, and they can be changed quickly. Often, one view can be cloned over and over again, with only the category field being moved to support a different sort.

Throughout the view design process, we have used examples to help the users decide on the kind of view that they want. If the users are anxious to get started and willing to help, the developer may want to use prototyping to design and implement views at the same time. As the users decide what they want in the view, the developer can be creating the view on the spot. For more complicated views, the developer could create 90 percent of the view, then come back to the users to add the last 10 percent of the changes.

There is one other kind of view that a user will not need, but that a developer must set up if a field in a form requires a lookup table for verification. To perform a lookup into a Notes database, that database must contain a view that is sorted in the order necessary for the lookup. Developers should review their form designs to identify any views that are required for lookups.

Develop a Prototype

The users of the '90s also expect developers to spend a lot of time with them while an application is being built. The development tools in Notes support this expectation, by enabling developers to tweak screens and forms in no time right in front of the user. And users prefer receiving their systems in pieces, rather than waiting months for the entire application to ship. They will live with shortcomings and fewer features as long as they can immediately improve part of the process for which the system is intended. If you give them a time estimate of 12 months, you'll see them looking for someone who can do better.

In other words, the best approach to Notes development in most cases is to abandon the traditional methodologies and use prototyping. A prototype is a version of the application that is functional, but not ready for final implementation. It gives the users a chance to play with the application without any consequences, and it gives them the opportunity to catch design flaws well in advance of the release to production date. The prototype doesn't have to be pretty, it just has to give the user an idea of how things work and how far the project has come.

We talked about prototyping when we created views and forms. The importance of this step depends on how actively the developers have been meeting with users with interim versions of the application. If the developers and users have been meeting daily, and the users know the application intimately, then you have already delivered the prototype. If ongoing prototyping hasn't occurred, then you will have to create one. There isn't a Notes application in existence that was implemented without change. If someone tells you that there is such a database, then the database probably isn't being used or the original developer quit and the users don't know how to make changes.

Reviews of the prototype should happen regularly and as early as possible during the development stage. And no matter how often they occur, the results of the prototyping sessions should be documented and passed on to the project manager for review. As the project progresses, these status reports will help track the reasons for changes that were made and document the causes of any delays that have occurred.

Be aware that this kind of development activity *can* cause problems if users never firm up their requirements and make drastic changes during the prototyping sessions. But if the requirements were gathered correctly up front, there shouldn't be any big surprises during prototyping, and the users should just be catching misunderstandings.

Don't make the mistake of thinking that using prototyping methods negates the need for application libraries and control of the distribution of databases onto servers. The developer can still check out a database from the library, prototype the change with the user, and coordinate a quick implementation of changes with the database Librarian. The users receive their changes quickly and the application libraries stay current.

Finalize Requirements

At some point during the prototyping, the requirements for the application must be finalized. Users will be excited by the prototypes and they will try to increase the scope of the application to include more and more features, but remember, the application will never be finished if the requirements aren't nailed down and a cutoff date for feature additions is not set. Be prepared, though, even after a date is set, users will continue to want to add features. When this occurs, the developers must be firm and remind the users that they agreed to a deadline. They should then assure users that the changes will be included in the next update. They create a Phase 2 Feature List for this purpose.

Implement Prototype and Enhance the Product

Essentially, prototyping is continuous, as users strive for the perfect application. But never lose sight of the goal, which is to put a solid product into production. Constantly tweaking will provide smaller and smaller returns in the end product. When the prototype works well and has been tested thoroughly by the users, it should be put into production as soon as practical.

Once the users understand the ease with which Notes can be enhanced, they should be willing to accept a product that is 95 percent completed. Having it in production allows them to get valuable work done while minor changes are made.

Updating the Application

Every application ever written will change. It will either be updated with new features, modified to meet new business requirements, or be replaced by another system. Maintenance is a fact of life in development. In a traditional environment, the developer and librarian updated the production library with new application code, and everyone was able to use it. But when the application was distributed over many systems, servers, or personal computers, the update required a highly coordinated effort involving many people and several hours of work.

In contrast, replication is Nirvana for a developer who must distribute an update to a Notes database. No matter how many replicas of the database exist, the developer need only update one replica to implement the change. The updated replica sends the latest forms, views, and macros to the other replicas the next time that they swap new information and changes.

But replication can also backfire if the developers don't do their job correctly. Any bugs that infest one of the replicas will travel throughout the company during the next replication cycle. In other words, never forget to test the application *before* it is placed into production because a bug will spread worldwide in a matter of minutes.

Other Developers

Our discussions so far have focused on developers and applications that are planned and take time to develop. A typical Notes installation has two other groups of developers actively involved in creating applications: The Notes support staff and the users themselves.

Working with the Notes Support Staff

The people on the Notes Support team fill the void caused when an application is a little too difficult for the user, but not important enough to send to the development team. A simple application may not initially appear to be meaningful to the entire company but making one Notes user more productive affects everyone, ultimately. Clearly, there is a need for someone who can bypass the bureaucracy and just get these databases done.

Notes Support, however, is always in the middle, between the user, who wants the application quickly, and the development team injunction to follow the standards. Many times the users don't want anything fancy, just a simple discussion database or a database with one form and a couple of views, and will accept whatever they can get to help them out, in which case, Notes Support can probably whip something out and get the application done in a couple of hours.

This should not become a regular practice, as developers are not anxious to maintain an application that doesn't follow their standards. All too often, the quick and dirty database turns into a full-blown application that the user can't do without, thereby shaking up development schedules and causing friction between the Notes support person and the developers.

The only way to effectively handle these situations is to insist that Notes Support follows the standards. Recommend that they borrow an existing template that already has the standards in place. Notes Support shouldn't be taking on tasks that take more than a day or two anyway, and using the standards will add only a little time to a small project.

The user should also be involved and help out more with these applications. Notes Support should agree to the task with the stipulation that the user create the help documents. The user should be willing to accept a longer development schedule and allow Notes Support to complete other support tasks. In other words, there should be a give and take.

If the number of small projects continues to grow, Notes Support should be replaced with a developer dedicated to small tasks. Good developers can keep a lot of users happy by quickly completing the small projects. The extra developer will free up Notes Support to deal with operational issues.

Because small Notes projects are often time-consuming but not complicated, these are great opportunities to use interns from the local college. You'll probably find a few that you'll want to keep.

Working with Users Who Develop Applications

Many Notes users are potential developers, and they will try just about anything in Notes. To stop them, you would have to take away their full copy of Notes and give them the run-time version, thus preventing them from developing applications. But taking away the ability for some users to develop database in Notes is akin to eliminating macros from their spreadsheets.

They know how to use them, and they feel it's their right to do so. The best way to work with users who want to develop applications is to give them access to the Notes standards and send them through the internal Notes training courses. Many users have not experienced a disciplined approach to development—they are closet developers at heart. They will probably enjoy the training and follow the standards if someone invests the time to explain them.

There is not much you can do about the user mavericks who refuse to buy into the standards. You can block them from implementing their systems by not allowing them to replicate on a server, or by removing their access control. However, the negative control is almost like declaring war on the users, and it certainly won't help build positive relationships. Unless these users create an application that is a massive violation of corporate standards, allow them to implement their systems. If the application is innovative and well done, then the development team can learn from it and adapt it to the standards whenever they have time. If the application stinks, the other users will complain about it, stop using it, and it will die a slow, quiet death.

Summary

There are many opportunities for solving business problems in any organization through the use of Lotus Notes. It takes a dedicated team of developers, willing to take on the challenge of Notes, to turn those opportunities into realities. The release of version 4.0 with its upgraded development tools has provided developers with even move options to perform miracles with Notes.

9

50 Ways to Use Notes

In this chapter, we will describe the 50 different databases that the employees of ABC Company use to make their everyday tasks a little easier. These databases are located on the CD-ROM that is included with this book, and they can be installed onto your local hard disk drive if you would like to use them as you read this chapter. Follow the instructions in Appendix B to install the databases.

As you will see, you don't have to build huge and complicated applications to gain efficiencies in the workplace. All you need is a tool that can automate the entire process and move information easily between users.

Common Features

As with any application package, Notes developers built a library of tools that can be used over and over again to reduce the development time for new applications. For example, the sample databases include a template called the Empty Database that contains a simple form that holds a company logo, mail-enabling fields, and some commonly used buttons. Most of the databases were created using that template. In some cases, two databases will look very similar because one was built from a copy of the other. As you review the 50 sample databases, you'll find a number of features or techniques that are common to almost all of the databases. These common features and techniques are:

◆ *Hiding buttons on forms depending on the document mode:* A Notes document can be viewed in read-only mode or in edit mode. Some Notes buttons are unnecessary depending on the document mode. For example, there is no reason to save a document if it is in read-only mode and can't be changed; therefore, the Save button shouldn't appear. Or, using the Text Paragraph menu choice while designing a form, a developer can hide a line on the form depending on the document mode. Each form has two lines at the top, one with the form title and an Edit button, and another line with the form title and a Save button. The first line is hidden when the document is in edit mode; the second line is hidden when the document is in read-only mode. This technique takes up less screen space and places the buttons on the screen only when they are needed.

◆ *Mail-enabling all forms:* Every form has the basic fields necessary to mail-enable an application. In most cases, a database will end up needing mail capabilities, even if not apparent initially.

◆ *Automatic insertion of names, dates, and other fields:* Notes already "knows" the user name of the person entering information and on what day and time it was entered. In some applications, it's also handy to automatically store the user name so that there is proof of who created the document. Many applications store the user name, and some also search the Employees/Departments database for supervisor names and department information. Of course, these databases must be kept accurate or the techniques will fail.

◆ *Adding a Save button at the bottom of the screen:* Some forms require more than one screen to display all of the information in a document. The Save buttons are a good way to help users save a document, but it's inconvenient when the button disappears as the user moves down a long screen. If you find yourself using the scroll bars to get to any button, it probably means you should place a copy of the button somewhere more convenient on the form. Many of the applications have two Save buttons to make life easier for the user.

◆ *Using auto-refresh to calculate form values:* A Notes database can be set up to automatically calculate all the fields in a form each time the user moves from one field to the next. Although this feature keeps all of the fields updated, it can also slow down the application if there are a lot of fields. The 50 databases are set to automatically refresh all fields.

♦ *Only allowing access to certain forms from within another form:* Notes allows you to remove a form from the Compose menu so that users cannot access it. This feature can be used when a developer wants to control the flow of information entered into a database and pass information automatically from one form to the next. In the purchase requisition database, for example, detail items can only be created from the requisition form so that the requisition number can be automatically passed to it. In several of the forms, there is a button that opens the hidden form and copies information into it from the original form.

♦ *Automatically adding doclinks to forms called from another form:* When information is split between two forms, users may want to view information on one of the forms while they are looking at the other. When a user opens a second form using a button, as described in the previous technique, a doclink will be automatically stored in a field to provide immediate access to the first form.

♦ *Using views to select a link to a second database:* Notes allows a developer to use a column of information from one database as the contents of a data entry dialog box in a form in another database. The user can then select one of the items on the list to store it in a field in the form. However, a user may need to view an entire document before they can select the right one; one column of information isn't detailed enough to help the user select the proper information. Several of the sample databases have a button in a form that opens a second database and displays a view. The user is instructed to select an item on the view and press a button in the form that comes up after the item is selected. That button saves key information, exits the second database, and loads the information in the first form. This technique works well as long as the user follows the proper steps: **1.** select the button, **2.** select an item on the resulting view, and **3.** push the proper button on the second form that moves information to the first form.

Digging into the 50 Databases

Now it's time to get into the 50 databases and learn how they work. Each Notes database has been documented using the two customizable help documents, Help About and Help Using, that are accessible via the Help menu. The Help About document describes the contents of the database, its purpose, and any information that will help you use the database more efficiently. Help Using describes the steps that you should take to use the database properly.

The following descriptions were pulled directly from the help documents in the databases, and each help document was created and formatted in Notes and pasted with very little change into the document that became this book. As you can see, wise use of the Notes help documents can allow developers to virtually eliminate the need for user manuals.

Mail (1)

PURPOSE

The Notes Mail database is the hub of activity for every Notes user. Not only do users receive typical mail messages, they also receive messages from applications that spur them to action in another database. The Mail database can also be modified to support productivity activities such as goal tracking, to-do lists, and calendars. Version 4.0 of Notes drastically changed the mail database, and it now has much of the functionality of cc:Mail but still can be modified.

FORMS USED

Actions	Captures an action item that the user is expected to perform, and includes the name of the person requesting the action (see Figure 9.1a).
Meetings	Captures meeting information, including the names of the attendees and the date and time of the meeting.
Message	Creates a mail message and allows a user to add follow-up dates, priorities, and delivery methods (see Figures 9.1b and 9.1c).
Other, Goals	Captures a goal that can be attached to an action item to assist the user in demonstrating how actions performed matched the goals assigned to the user.

VIEWS

Actions, All, Category	Categorizes all the projects by the person requesting the project and by project name. Displays the project document, all the tasks, and all time entries for the project.
Actions, Completed	Categorizes the projects that are in progress by the person requesting the project and by project name. Displays the project document, all the tasks, and all time entries for the project.
Actions, by Goals	Categorizes all project tasks and time entries by project name, and displays estimated and actual hours worked.
Actions, Meeting Only	Categorizes all the projects by the week in which time was logged, by the name of the person performing the task, and by project name. Displays the project document, all the tasks, and all time entries for the project.
Actions, Meet Timeline	Categorizes the projects by status and by the system name stored in the project document. Displays the project document, all the tasks, and all time entries for the project.

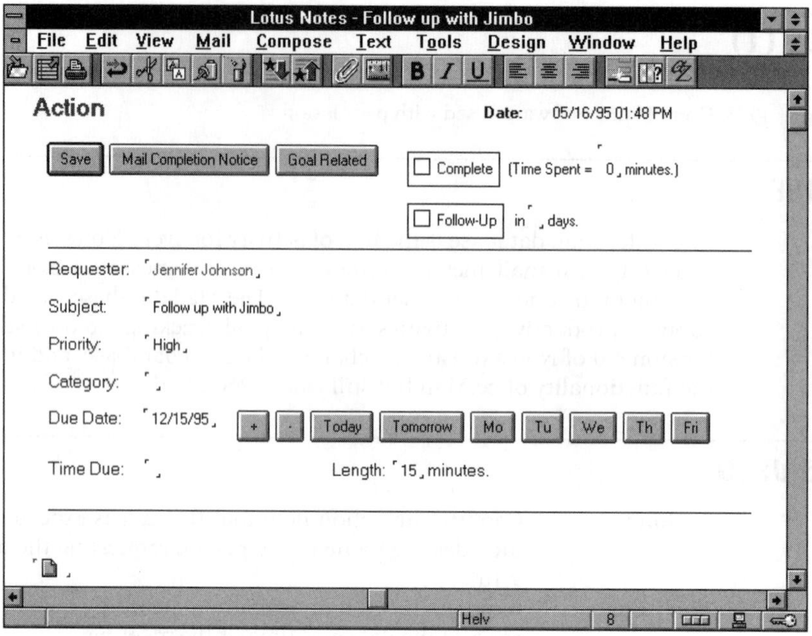

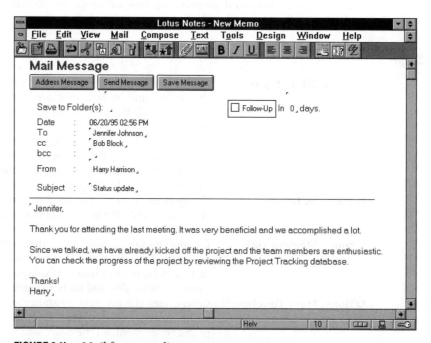

FIGURE 9.1a   Action item form.

FIGURE 9.1b   Mail form, sending a message.

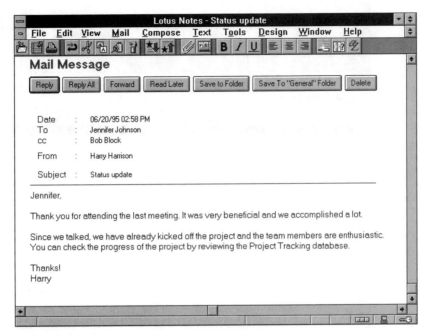

FIGURE 9.1c   Mail form, receiving a message.

Actions, Pending	Categorizes all the projects by the person leading the project and by project name. Displays the project document, all the tasks, and all time entries for the project.
Actions, by Requester	Categorizes all time entries by the person who entered the time and by the date of the entry for all projects that are in progress.
Mail, by Date	Categorizes all the projects by project name, and displays the project document, all the tasks, and all time entries for the project.
Mail, by Folder	Categorizes the projects by project name, and displays only those projects that are completed. Displays the project document, all the tasks, and all time entries for the project.
Mail, by Mail Box	Categorizes the projects by project name and displays only those projects that are not complete. Displays the project document, all the tasks, and all time entries for the project (see Figure 9.1d).
Mail, by Sender	Categorizes all the projects by direct report (person reporting to the president of the company) and by project name. Displays the project document, all the tasks, and all time entries for the project.
Mail, by Subject	Categorizes all the projects by manager and by project name. Displays the project document, all the tasks, and all time entries for the project.

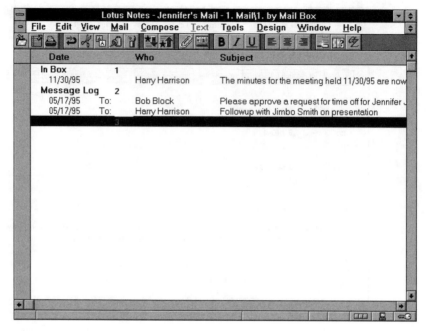

FIGURE 9.1d   Mailbox view.

Mail, with Attachments	Categorizes all the projects by the project manager and by project name. Displays the project document, all the tasks, and all time entries for the project.
Other, Followup	Categorizes the projects by status and by project name. Displays the project document, all the tasks, and all time entries for the project.
Other, Goals	Categorizes all project tasks and time entries by project name, and displays actual hours and costs.
Phone	Categorizes all project tasks and time entries by project name and displays variable costs only.

BUTTONS

+, −, and Date Buttons	Adjusts the due date in the Action Assignment form by one day (+, −) and by the values listed on each button.
Address Message	Displays the Name and Address Book so that a user can select the recipients of the message.
Delete	Marks a document as deleted.
Edit	Places the document in edit mode so that the user can change the document. It is only visible when the document is being read.
Forward	Copies the mail message and addresses that are displayed on the screen into the body of a new mail message that has been composed.

Goal Related	Allows a user to relate a goal to the action item that is displayed.
Mail Complete Notice	Prompts the user for the amount of time spent on an action item, changes the action item's status to Complete, and sends a completion message to the person who requested the action.
Mark Action Complete	Prompts the user for the amount of time spent on an action item, and changes the action item's status to Complete.
Mark Meeting Complete	Prompts the user for the amount of time spent in a meeting, and changes the action item's status to Complete.
Notify Attendees	Sends a mail message to everyone who will be attending a meeting.
Read Later	Changes the mailbox category from In Box to Read Later, allowing message to be saved in the Mail Box view without showing in the In Box category.
Reply	Copies the body of the mail message that is displayed on the screen into the body of a new mail message, and changes the Send to field to the person who sent the message.
Reply to All	Copies the body of the mail message that is displayed on the screen into the body of a new mail message. Changes the Send to field to the person who sent the message; also sends the message to all the people listed in the cc field.
Save	Saves the document and exits to the last open view. This button is visible only when the document is being edited.
Save Message	Saves the message displayed and exits to the last open view. The message is saved in a Draft folder and can be recalled to be sent later.
Save to Folder	Prompts users for the name of a folder to assign to the mail document, saves the document, and exits to the last open view.
Save to General Folder	Saves the mail message in a folder called General and exits to the last open view.
Send Message	Mails the mail message displayed.
Today, Tomorrow, etc.	Changes the meeting date to today, tomorrow, or the day of the week listed on the button.

MACROS

Clear Flag	Sets the followup flag to blank so that all the items selected do not appear in the followup views.
Mail Paste Macro	Automatically applies to any document mailed to this database.
Mark Completed	Marks an action or meeting as completed, and asks for the amount of time expended to complete it.

Move Date	Prompts the user for the number of days that should be added to the followup date for all action or meeting documents selected in a view.
Move to Next Weekday	Adjusts the followup date for an action or meeting document by one day or the number of days needed to make the date a weekday (Monday through Friday).
Move to Today	Changes the followup date for an action or meeting document to today's date.
Relate to Goal	Displays the goals in a dialog box, allows the user to select a goal that is related to the action item, and saves the goal in the document.
Set Priority	Allows the user to select a priority from a list and assign it to the document.
Set User Preference	Displays a user preference form where users can add defaults for the Notes Mail database.

ACCESS CONTROL

The default access control should be set to Editor for the owner of the database. No other user should have access to the database.

ENHANCE IT!

You can make this database even more powerful by:

1. Integrating other databases with the Mail database so that they create action items that are sent to the Mail database.

USING MAIL

The database is intended for all **Users.** To create a mail message:

1. The **User** adds a document using the Message form.

To reply to a mail message:

1. The **User** displays the Mail by Mail Box view and selects a mail document.
2. The **User** pushes the Reply button to compose a mail document. The name of the sender is placed in the Send To field and the text from the old document remains in the message area.

To forward a mail message:

1. The **User** displays the Mail by Mail Box view and selects a mail document.
2. The **User** pushes the Forward button to compose a mail document. The name of the sender is left blank, and the text from the old document remains in the message area.

To store mail messages:

1. The **User** displays the Mail by Mail Box view and selects a mail document.

2. The **User** pushes one of the Save to Folder or Save to General buttons. Notes will either prompt the **User** for a folder name or automatically save the document with a folder name of General.

To create an action item:

1. The **User** adds a document using the Action form.

To convert a mail message into an action item:

1. The **User** displays the Mail by Mail Box view and selects a mail document.
2. The **User** selects the Action form from the View menu.
3. The **User** pushes the Save button to save the document.

To create a meeting:

1. The **User** adds a document using the Meeting form.

To create a goal:

1. The **User** adds a document using the Other, Goal form.

Moves (2)

PURPOSE

Employee moves are commonplace as companies co-locate their personnel by project, department, or function. The Moves database provides Operations personnel with a central database where all the connection information can be stored, accessed, and updated.

FORMS USED

Moves   Captures the information needed to schedule the move of employees from one building to another (see Figure 9.2a).

VIEWS

Move Date   Categorizes the move by the date on which the move is scheduled to occur.

Move from Building   Categorizes the move by the building from which the employees are moving.

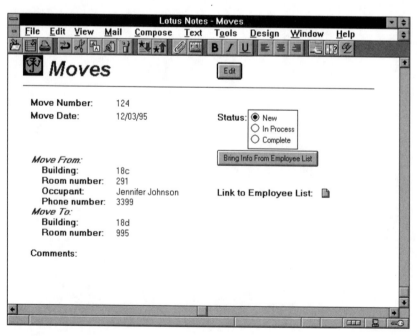

FIGURE 9.2a   Moves form.

Move Number	Categorizes the move by an internal move number assigned by the person entering the move information (see Figure 9.2b).
Move to Building	Categorizes the move by the buildings to which the employees are moving.
Status	Categorizes the move by the status of the move. A hidden column was added to sort the documents by New first, In Process next, and Completed last.

BUTTONS

Edit	Places the document in edit mode so that the user can change the document. It is visible only when the document is being read.
Save	Saves the document and exits to the last open view. The button is visible only when the document is being edited.
Save and Compose	Saves the document but also opens a new form so that a user can enter another document. The button is visible only when the document is being edited.
Info from Emp List	Assists users in bringing employee information from the Employees and Departments database. The button opens a view in the Employees and Departments database. The user selects a document and presses a button in the form

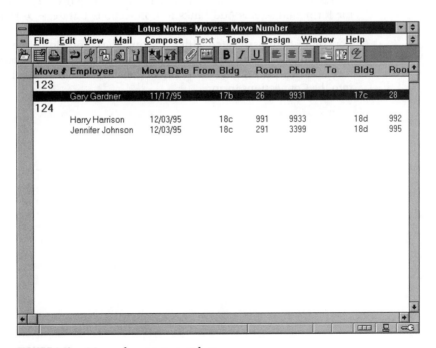

FIGURE 9.2b   Moves by move number.

to return to the Connections form and paste in the employee's building, room number, name, and a doclink to the Employees and Departments database.

ACCESS CONTROL

The default access control should be set to Editor for all Operations users. All other users should be given Read access to this database so that they can check on the status of their move.

ENHANCE IT!

You can make this database even more powerful by:

1. Adding a button to automatically generate a Help Desk call for the move.
2. Adding fields for technicians assigned to the move.
3. Adding an import view to bring the move information into the database from a spreadsheet that holds the information for a major move.

USING MOVES

The database is intended for all **Operations Users.** To create a move entry:

1. The **Operations User** adds a document using the Connections form.
2. For connections associated with a user, the **Operations User** selects the Bring Name from Employee List button, chooses an employee from the view, displays the form, and selects Add Links to Connections Database to bring information back into the Connections form.
3. For connections associated with a meeting, the **Operations User** selects the Link to Meeting Room button, chooses a meeting room from the view, displays the form, and selects Add Links to Connections Database to bring information back into the Connections form.

TCP/IP Addresses (3)

PURPOSE

TCP/IP has become one of the de facto network protocol standards for most corporations. To operate properly, it requires that users have a unique TCP/IP number, called an address, that identifies their workstation. Users can also be grouped into subnets using the third octet of the address, allowing network routing devices to perform a variety of tasks that make the network more efficient.

The TCP/IP Addresses database provides a central location for the issuance of TCP/IP addresses. It allows the Information Systems group to control the numbers so that there are no duplicates, and it gives the Help Desk the flexibility to assign numbers to users as needed.

FORMS USED

TCP/IP Addresses Assigns the TCP/IP address, and captures information about the user and the name of the computer assigned the TCP/IP address (see Figure 9.3a).

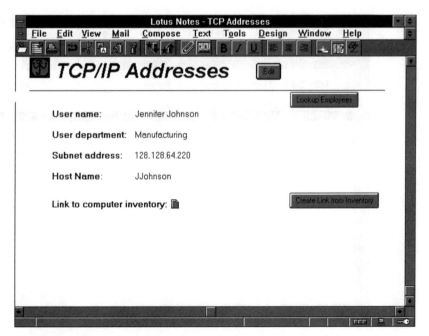

FIGURE 9.3a TCP/IP address form.

VIEWS

Department	Categorizes the addresses by the department to which the owner of the address belongs.
Employee	Displays the addresses by the names of the employees who received the addresses.
Subnet	Categorizes the addresses by subnet number to help the users find the next available address to be assigned in that subnet (see Figure 9.3b).
TCP/IP Address	Displays the TCP/IP addresses by address number so that users can check for duplicates.

BUTTONS

Create Link from Inventory	Assists users in linking a TCP/IP address to the Computer Physical Inventory database. The button opens a view in the Inventory database. The user selects a document and presses a button in the Inventory form to return to the TCP/IP form and paste in a doclink.
Edit	Places the document in edit mode so that the user can change the document. It is visible only when the document is being read.

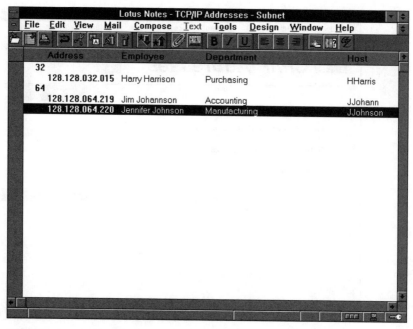

FIGURE 9.3b   TCP/IP addresses by subnet view.

Lookup Employees	Builds a dialog box that displays all of the employee names in the Departments and Employees database. Once an employee is selected, the button automatically fills in the employee name and department fields.
Save	Saves the document and exits to the last open view. The button is visible only when the document is being edited.
Save and Compose	Saves the document but also opens a new form so that a user can enter another document. The button is visible only when the document is being edited.

ACCESS CONTROL

The default access control should be set to Editor for all of the Information Systems or Help Desk users. They will all be adding or changing the TCP/IP addresses, and any one of them may need to update a document.

All other users should be given Reader access so that they can read all documents and find an address when they need it.

ENHANCE IT!

You can make this database even more powerful by:

1. Adding a button that automatically mails a message to a new user with his or her new TCP/IP address.

USING TCP/IP ADDRESSES

The database is intended for use by all **Information Systems Users** and **Help Desk Users.** To create a TCP/IP address:

1. The **Information Systems User** or **Help Desk User** determines which subnet the assignee will belong to.
2. The **Information Systems User** or **Help Desk User** adds a document to the database to assign the new TCP/IP address to the user.

Telecomm Connections (4)

PURPOSE

Companies are always moving people and equipment, and it doesn't take long for wiring information to become obsolete. Without up-to-date information about the telephone and network connections, technicians spend extra time tracing wires before they can complete their work. The Telecommunications Connections database provides Operations personnel with a central database where all the connection information can be stored, accessed, and updated.

FORMS USED

Connections Captures the information needed to track telecommunications connections (see Figure 9.4a).

VIEWS

Building Categorizes the connection by the building and room number at which the connection is located (see Figure 9.4b).

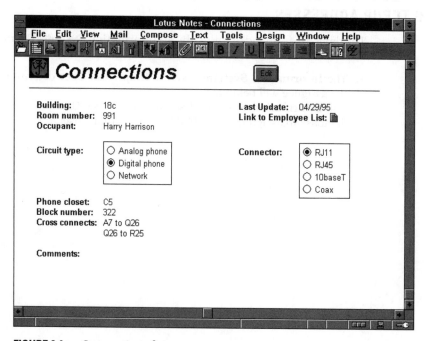

FIGURE 9.4a Connections form.

Circuit Type	Categorizes the connection by the type of circuit that the connection supports.
Employee	Displays all connections by employee.
Phone Closet	Categorizes all connections by the phone closet in which they reside.

BUTTONS

Edit	Places the document in edit mode so that the user can change the document. It is visible only when the document is being read.
Link to Meeting Room	Assists users in bringing meeting room information from the Meetings database. The button opens a view in the Meetings database. The user selects a document and presses a button in the form to return to the Connections form and paste in the meeting room building, room number, name, and a doclink to the Meetings database.
Name from Emp List	Assists users in bringing employee information from the Employees and Departments database. The button opens a view in the Employees and Departments database. The user selects a document and presses a button in the form to return to the Connections form and paste in the employee's building, room number, name, and a doclink to the Employees and Departments database.

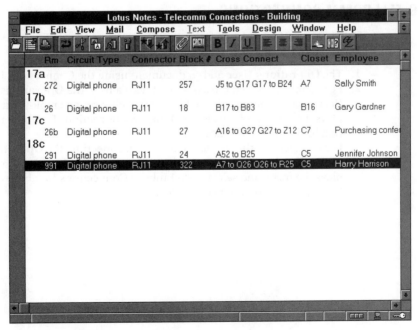

FIGURE 9.4b Telecomm Connections by Building view.

Save   Saves the document and exits to the last open view. The button is visible only when the document is being edited.

Save and Compose   Saves the document but also opens a new form so that a user can enter another document. The button is visible only when the document is being edited.

ACCESS CONTROL

The default access control should be set to Editor for all Operations users. No other user should need access to this database.

ENHANCE IT!

You can make this database even more powerful by:

1. Adding a button that allows you to link the connection to the Computer Inventory database.
2. Changing the form attributes so that any changes are stored as response documents.
3. Adding an import view to bring the inventory information into the database automatically.
4. Creating a field that indicates that a connection is unused, and building a view that displays only empty circuits so they can be easily identified and used when a new connection is required.

USING TELECOMM CONNECTIONS

The database is intended for use by all **Operations Users.** To create a telecomm connection entry:

1. The **Operations User** adds a document using the Connections form.
2. For connections that are associated with a user, the **Operations User** selects the Bring Name from Employee List button, chooses an employee from the view, displays the form, and selects Add Links to Connections Database to bring information back into the Connections form.
3. For connections that are associated with a meeting, the **Operations User** selects the Link to Meeting Room button, chooses a meeting room from the view, displays the form, and selects Add Links to Connections Database to bring information back into the Connections form.

Help Desk Call Tracking (5)

© Copyright, 1995, Great Plains Software. Used with permission.

PURPOSE

The Help Desk is the hub of activity where sharp and energetic support people field a barrage of tough phone questions daily. Many of these calls must be dispatched to other support people who roam the corridors of the facility solving problems that must be handled at the desktop. The Help Desk Call Tracking database files all of the calls that come into the Help Desk, which allows the Help Desk personnel to track time, dispatch calls, and monitor open calls to ensure that all of the work is being completed on time.

FORMS USED

Call Report Captures information about the help call, the person taking the call, the person assigned to the call, and the date and time the call is completed (see Figure 9.5a).

Category Creates a list of categories to help group the calls into related areas of concern.

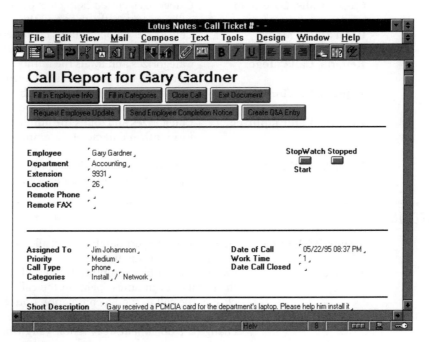

FIGURE 9.5a Call report form.

Open Status   Creates a list of open help calls for a support person, and allows the composer to send that person the list as a mail message.

VIEWS

All Calls, Category   Categorizes help calls by category and subcategory, ordering them by number of days since the calls originated.

All Calls, Department   Categorizes help calls by department and employee, ordering them by number of days since the calls originated.

All Calls, Employee Name   Categorizes help calls by employee, ordering them by number of days since the calls originated, and displays the department next to the name (see Figure 9.5b).

All Calls, Last Update   Categorizes help calls by the status of the call, the date that the call was last updated, and the employee. The calls are ordered by the number of days since they originated.

All Calls, Technician   Categorizes help calls by the technicians assigned to the calls and by the status of the call. The calls are ordered by the number of days since they originated.

Categories   Displays a list of the categories entered into the Categories form.

Closed Calls, Date Sent   Categorizes closed help calls by the date the closed call was sent to the user and the technician's name.

Open Status Memo   Categorizes all open status documents by the person to whom the memo was sent, usually the technician.

Reports, Call/Category   Categorizes and totals the number of help desk calls by month, category, and subcategory.

Reports, Call/Department   Categorizes and totals the number of help desk calls by month, user department, and technician.

Reports, Call/Employee   Categorizes and totals the number of help desk calls by month and name of the employee who placed the call.

Reports, Call/Technician   Categorizes and totals the number of help desk calls by month, employee, category, and subcategory.

BUTTONS

Create Q&A Entry   Opens the PC Expert database and allows a user to add a tip or solution to the database.

Close Call   Closes the call by prompting the user for a resolution and the number of minutes spent on the call. Allows the person closing the call to send a completion notice.

Edit Document   Places the document in edit mode so that the user can change the document. It is visible only when the document is being read.

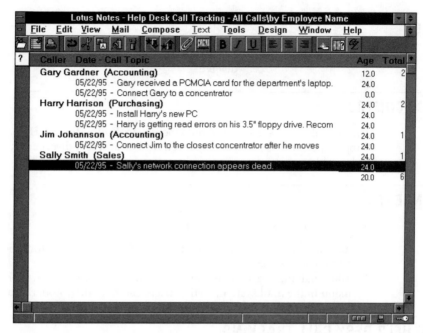

FIGURE 9.5b All Calls by Employee Name view.

Exit Document	Closes the form without saving. Notes will prompt you to save the document if changes have been made.
Fill in Categories	Displays the categories and subcategories, and fills in those fields with the results.
Fill in Employee Info	Prompts the user for an employee name, and fills in the department, room number, and phone number fields.
Query Open Projects	Searches the database for all open calls for a technician, and places the list in a text field so that the list and comments can be mailed to the technician.
Request Employee Update	Asks a user via electronic mail if the status of their help call has changed.
Send	Mails the open status memo to the technician referenced in the memo.
Send Employee Notice	Sends a notice via electronic mail to the user who generated the help call that the call has been closed.
Stopwatch 1	Activates a timer that tracks the length of time that a call has been in progress.
Stopwatch 2	Turns off a timer that tracks the length of time that a call has been in progress.

MACROS

Delete Closed Calls   Selects all calls that have been closed so that they can be deleted.

ACCESS CONTROL

The default access control should be set to Editor for all Help Desk users and Support personnel. Users can be given Author access if direct entry of help requests is desirable.

ENHANCE IT!

You can make this database even more powerful by:

1. Adding buttons to link the calls to the Computer Inventory, Communications, and Move databases.
2. Mail-enabling the database and including a Help Desk form in the Custom forms menu in the mail system, so that users can mail their noncritical help requests.

USING HELP DESK CALL TRACKING

The database is intended for use by all **Help Desk Users** and **Support Users.** To create a Help Desk Call document:

1. The **Help Desk User** adds a document using the Call Report form.

To process help desk calls:

1. The **Support User** displays the All Calls by Technician view and identifies calls that must be completed.
2. The **Support User** completes a call, recalls the appropriate call document, and pushes the Close Call button to mark the call as closed and mail a completion notice to the person who logged the call.

To monitor the technician's progress on the calls:

1. The **Support User Supervisor** displays the All Calls by Technician view, composes an Open Status Memo, and sends it to the technician.
2. The **Support User** reads the electronic mail messages, adds status information, and sends a reply to the **Support User Supervisor.**

PC Expert System (6)

PURPOSE

Many common problems arise as employees use their personal computers. Instead of having a Help Desk or support person solve the same problem over and over again, the PC Expert System can be used to store the answers to frequently asked questions.

FORMS USED

Add A Document Stores the solutions to problems and allows the author to categorize the text in several ways to facilitate the search process (see Figure 9.6a).

VIEWS

Decisions Categorizes all documents that contain the category code Decisions by system.

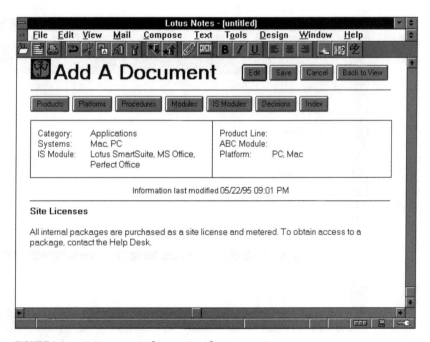

FIGURE 9.6a PC expert information form.

Help Desk	Categorizes all documents that contain the category code Help Desk by system.
Index, Alphabetic	Categorizes all documents by a keyword that contains the values stored in the fields Category, Systems, ISModule, GPModule, ProdLine, Platform, and Title (see Figure 9.6b).
IS Modules	Categorizes all documents by IS Modules.
Modules	Categorizes all documents that have a value in the Modules field by module.
Platform	Categorizes all documents that have a value in the Platform field by platform.
Procedures	Categorizes all documents that contain the category code "Procedures" by system.
Product Line	Categorizes all documents that have a value in the Product Line field by product line.
Systems	Categorizes all documents by system.

BUTTONS

Back to View	Exits a document and returns to the view from which the document was selected.
Cancel	Exits a document and returns to the view from which the document was selected.
Decisions	Displays the Decisions view.

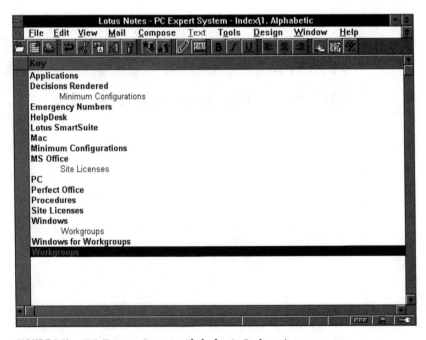

FIGURE 9.6b PC Expert System Alphabetic Index view.

Edit	Places the document in edit mode so that the user can change the document. It is visible only when the document is being read.
Index	Displays the Alphabetic Index view.
IS Modules	Displays the IS Modules view.
Modules	Displays the Modules view.
Platforms	Displays the Platforms view.
Products	Displays the Products view.
Procedures	Displays the Procedures view.
Save	Saves the document and exits to the last open view. The button is visible only when the document is being edited.

ACCESS CONTROL

The default access control should be set to Read for all users. The department responsible for creating the database should be given Editor access.

ENHANCE IT!

You can make this database even more powerful by:

1. Creating a macro that deletes documents that have expired.

USING PC EXPERT SYSTEM

The database is intended for all **Users.** To create a PC Expert System document:

1. The **User** adds a document using the Add Document form.

Computer Inventory (7)

PURPOSE

Personal computers have become as common as calculators and telephones on users' desks. There are many models with a myriad of configurations, and users are constantly requesting upgrades and changes. When repairs are required, computer vendors need a copy of the invoice as proof of purchase. The Computer Inventory database holds all the information required to track a computer purchase, its configuration, and any repairs that were made. The document can be linked to the Purchase Requisition database, allowing the technician to retrieve a scanned image of the invoice, and to the Vendor database. The form also creates a link to the TCP/IP database.

FORMS USED

Computer Inventory   Captures all the details about a computer and its configuration. It also holds the warranty expiration date so that the technician can easily determine if a repair is covered by a warranty (see Figure 9.7a).

Computer Inventory Log   Captures information about repairs, changes, and upgrades to the computer equipment (see Figure 9.7b).

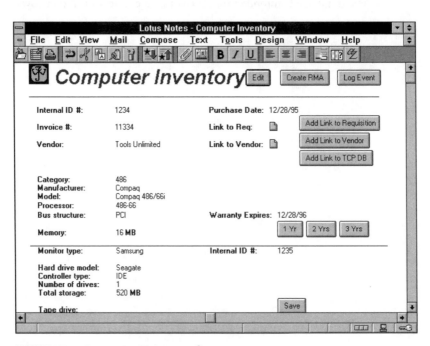

FIGURE 9.7a   Computer Inventory form.

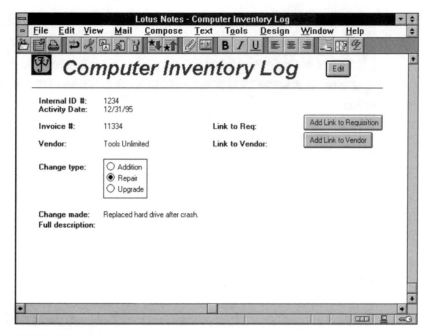

FIGURE 9.7b   Computer Inventory Log form.

VIEWS

Category, with Log	Categorizes the inventory by the type of computer, and includes any activity logs in the view.
Category, without Log	Categorizes the inventory by the type of computer, but does not include activity logs in the view.
ID Number	Categorizes the inventory by the internal asset number assigned to the machine (see Figure 9.7c).
Invoice Number	Categorizes the inventory by the vendor's invoice number.
Purchase Date	Categorizes the inventory by the date on which the computer was purchased.
Warranty Expire Date	Categorizes the inventory in reverse chronological order by the date on which the warranty will expire.

BUTTONS

Add Link to Requisition	Assists users in creating a doclink to the Purchase Requisition database. The button opens a view in the Purchase Requisition database where the user selects a document. After the document is displayed, the user presses a button in the form to return to the Computer Inventory form and paste a doclink to the purchase requisition.

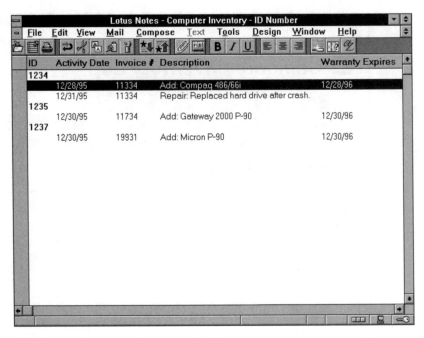

FIGURE 9.7c Computer Inventory by ID view.

Add Link to TCP DB	Completes a process in the TCP/IP Addresses database. A user presses a button that opens a view in this database. When a document is displayed, the user presses this button to create a doclink and paste it into the TCP/IP Addresses database.
Add Link to Vendor	Assists users in creating a doclink to the Vendor database. The button opens a view in the Vendor database and the user selects a document. After the document is displayed, the user presses a button in the form to return to the Computer Inventory form and paste a doclink to the vendor database.
Create RMA	Creates a document in the RMA database so that a technician can track RMAs for computer inventory items. The button also inserts information about the inventory items into the form.
Edit	Places the document in edit mode so that the user can change the document. It is visible only when the document is being read.
Log Event	Creates an Inventory Log document for the inventory item.
1 Year, 2 Years, 3 Years	Adds one, two, or three years to the purchase date and saves the results as the warranty date.
Save	Saves the document and exits to the last open view. The button is visible only when the document is being edited.

Save and Compose	Saves the document but also opens a new form so that a user can enter another document. The button is visible only when the document is being edited.
Send Comments	Sends the contents of the Subject and Comments fields to the originator of the job via electronic mail.
Send Complete Notice	Sends a message that the print shop job is complete to the originator. The button also updates the completion date with the current date if the field has not been filled in.

ACCESS CONTROL

The default access control should be set to Editor for Operations personnel. All other users should have Read access.

ENHANCE IT!

You can make this database even more powerful by:

1. Adding fields and buttons to link the inventory items to the Telecomm Database.

USING COMPUTER INVENTORY

The database is intended for all **Users** and **Operations Personnel.** To create a Computer Inventory document:

1. **Operations Personnel** adds a document using the Computer Inventory form.
2. **Operations Personnel** creates doclinks to the Purchase Requisition and Vendor databases.

To create a Computer Inventory Log document:

1. **Operations Personnel** selects the Create Log button on the Computer Inventory form.
2. **Operations Personnel** updates the form and saves the document.

To create an RMA document:

1. **Operations Personnel** selects the Create RMA button on the Computer Inventory form.
2. **Operations Personnel** updates the form and saves the document.

RMAs (8)

PURPOSE

Many pieces of equipment must be returned to a vendor to be repaired under warranty. The vendor typically issues an RMA (Return Material Authorization) number to the transaction, and that number is used to trace the item until it is returned to the company. The RMA database helps the technical team track the many RMAs that are issued.

FORMS USED

RMAs   Captures information about the RMA number and the dates that the equipment is due to return from repair. It also brings in the computer inventory information when the form is created from the Computer Inventory database (see Figure 9.8a).

VIEWS

Expected Date   Categorizes RMAs by the date on which the equipment is expected to return.

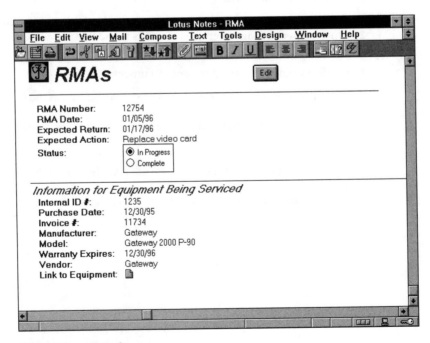

FIGURE 9.8a   RMA form.

RMA Number	Displays RMAs in RMA number order (see Figure 9.8b).
Status	Categorizes RMAs by their status (In process, Completed). Displays RMAs by the date on which the equipment is expected to return.
Vendor and Status	Categorizes RMAs by the vendor who is processing the RMA and by status (In process, Completed). Displays the RMAs by the date on which the equipment is expected to return.

BUTTONS

Edit	Places the document in edit mode so that the user can change the document. It is visible only when the document is being read.
Save	Saves the document and exits to the last open view. The button is visible only when the document is being edited.
Save and Compose	Saves the document but also opens a new form so that a user can enter another document. The button is visible only when the document is being edited.

ACCESS CONTROL

The default access control should be set to Author for all Operations users. No other users require access to the database.

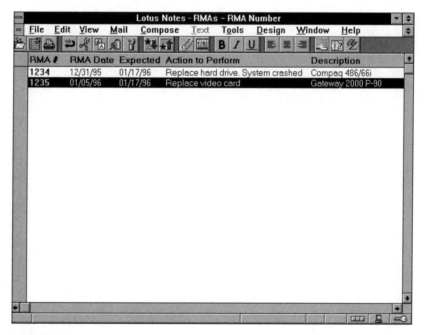

FIGURE 9.8b   RMAs by RMA Number view.

ENHANCE IT!

You can make this database even more powerful by:

1. Adding buttons to create links to the vendor if the item is not in the Computer Inventory database.
2. Adding a response form that tracks all the telephone activity created during followup of the RMA.

USING RMAS

The database is intended for use by all **Operations Users.** To create an RMA:

1. The **Operations User** adds a document using the RMA form.
2. The **Operations User** can also add a document by using the Create RMA button in the Computer Inventory form.

Purchase Requisitions (9)

PURPOSE

Purchase requisitions require a lot of paperwork and routing before all the approvals have been completed and an item can be ordered. The Purchase Requisitions database controls the entire process from entry of the requisition to the placement of the resulting purchase order with the vendor.

FORMS USED

Purchase Requisition Fax

Builds a single-page requisition out of the requisition document and all the detail documents so that the requisition can be faxed to a vendor. The form can be called only from the Requisition form, and it assumes that the user sends faxes through the Windows printer driver (see Figure 9.9a).

Requisition

Captures requisition information about the originator, the suggested vendor, and the purchasing agent who will process the requisition. Often called the requisition header document (see Figures 9.9b and 9.9c).

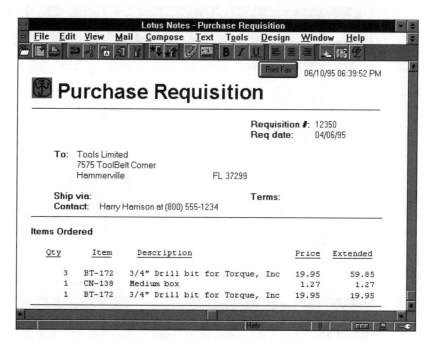

FIGURE 9.9a Purchase Requisition fax.

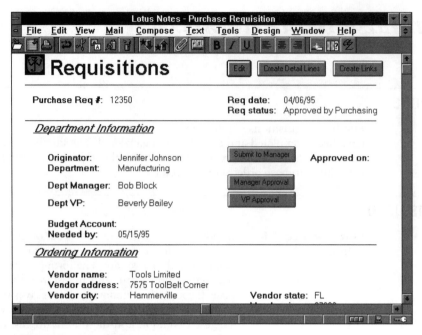

FIGURE 9.9b   Purchase Requisition form.

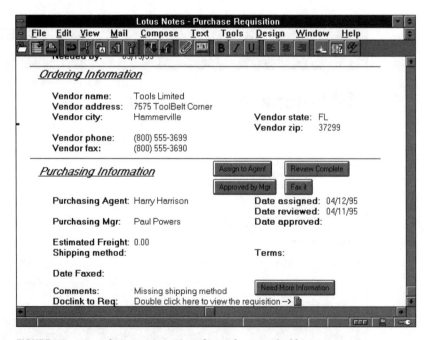

FIGURE 9.9c   Purchase Requisition form, bottom half.

Requisition Detail	Captures the detail information on one item ordered on the requisition. The form can be accessed only from the Requisition form (see Figure 9.9d).

VIEWS

Purchase Requisition	Categorizes a requisition by requisition number, displaying the requisition header first, followed by the detail lines (see Figure 9.9e).
Requisition by Department Manager, Manager	Categorizes a requisition by department manager and requisition number, displaying the requisition header first followed by the detail lines.
Requisition by Department Manager/Status	Categorizes the requisition by department manager, requisition status, and requisition number. Displays the requisition header first followed by the detail lines.
Requisition by Originator	Categorizes the requisition by originator and requisition number, displaying the requisition header first followed by the detail lines.
Requisition by Purchasing Agent	Categorizes the requisition by purchasing agent and requisition number, displaying the requisition header first followed by the detail lines.

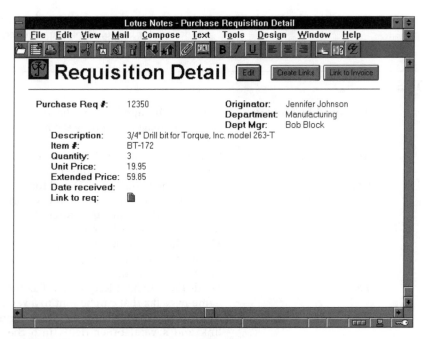

FIGURE 9.9d Purchase Requisition Detail form.

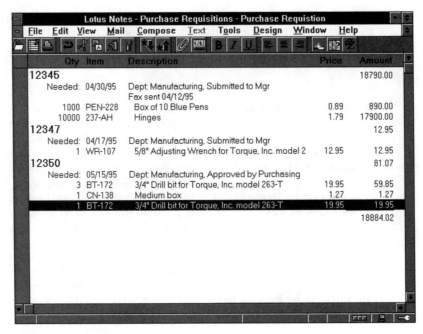

FIGURE 9.9e Purchase Requisitions by requisition number.

| | Requisition by Vendor Name | Categorizes the requisition by purchasing agent and vendor name, displaying the requisition header first followed by the detail lines. |

BUTTONS

Approved by Manager	Indicates the approval of the requisition by the Purchasing manager by adding the manager's name and the date of the approval.
Assign to Agent	Changes the name of the agent assigned to process the requisition to the current user's name.
Create Detail Lines	Displays the Requisitions Detail form.
Create Links	Returns the Computer Inventory form and pastes a doclink to the requisition after the Add Link to Requisition button has been pressed.
Edit	Places the document in edit mode so that the user can change the document. It is visible only when the document is being read.
Fax It	Loads the Purchase Requisition Fax form, which builds a one-page fax that can be sent to a vendor.
Link to Invoice	Returns the Invoice Approval form and pastes a doclink and several other fields into the approval form after the Create Links to Requisition button has been pressed.

Manager Approval	Indicates the approval of the requisition by the department manager by adding the date of the approval to the form. Changes the status to Sent to Purchasing or Sent to VP, depending on the dollar amount of the requisition, and notifies the originator via electronic mail.
Need More Information	Sends the contents of the comments field to the originator.
Print Fax	Executes a Print command to send the one-page requisition to the vendor. It assumes that the fax driver is the current printer driver.
Review Complete	Changes the status of the requisition to Review Complete, and notifies the Purchasing Manager that an approval is necessary if any item is over $500. Otherwise, the button changes the status to Approved by Purchasing.
Save	Saves the document and exits to the last open view. The button is visible only when the document is being edited.
Save and Compose	Saves the document but also opens a new form so that a user can enter another document. The button is visible only when the document is being edited.
Submit to Manager	Changes the status of the requisition to Submitted to Manager, and uses electronic mail to request approval of the requisition.
VP Approval	Indicates the approval of the requisition by the department vice president, adding the date of the approval to the requisition.

MACROS

Test for Approval	Tests the approval status for Submitted to Manager and, if found and the approval is overdue by more than two days, sends a mail message to the manager requesting approval.
Update Detail Docs	Updates the detail requisition line items with the requisition status, purchasing agents, and vendor name.

ACCESS CONTROL

The default access control for all users should be Author. The Purchasing department and all managers and supervisors should be given Editor access.

ENHANCE IT!

You can make this database even more powerful by:

1. Adding a button to send the requisition information to a third-party accounting package for use as a purchase order.
2. Adding a test in each button to ensure that the user pushing the button is the person who can approve parts of the purchase requisition.

USING PURCHASE REQUISITIONS

The database is intended for all **Users, Supervisors, Vice Presidents,** and **Purchasing Users.** To create a purchase requisition:

1. The **User** adds a document using the Purchase Requisition form.
2. The **User** presses the Create Detail Lines button to add a document using the Requisition Detail form.
3. The **User** continues to add detail documents until the requisition is complete.
4. The **User** presses the Submit to Manager button to notify the supervisor that the requisition is ready for approval.

To approve the requisition:

1. The **Supervisor** displays the requisition using the doclink in the mail message. The **Supervisor** must go into the Purchase Requisition database if detail is needed.
2. The **Supervisor** pushes the Manager Approval button to approve the requisition.
3. If **Vice President** approval is needed, the Requisition form sends a mail message requesting approval and follows the same steps as the **Supervisor** using the VP Approval button.

To process the requisition:

1. The **Purchasing User** reviews the Requisitions by Status view for items that are Submitted to Purchasing.
2. The **Purchasing User** pushes the Assign Agent button to be assigned to the requisition.
3. The **Purchasing User** processes the requisition and pushes the Review Complete button to mark the requisition as Approved by Purchasing. If any item costs more than $500, the button sends a message to the Purchasing Manager for approval.
4. The **Purchasing Manager** reviews the requisition and pushes the Approved by Manager button to mark the requisition as Approved by Purchasing.
5. The **Purchasing User** pushes the Print Fax button to create a one-page fax, then pushes the Fax It button to send the fax to the appropriate vendor.

Print Shop Requests (10)

PURPOSE

The Print Shop is a busy place in most companies. Everyone always wants a lot of copies in a hurry. More and more often, brochures, reports, and presentation materials are created electronically with word processors, spreadsheets, and graphics packages, and users want to be able to simply mail a file to the Print Shop for final output. Print Shop employees need a tool to track the projects submitted by their customers and a simple way to notify customers that the project is completed. The Print Shop Requests database gives users an easy way to submit their jobs to the Print Shop. Users can attach a file to the job and track its progress. Print Shop employees can ask questions via electronic mail and send a job completion notice with the push of a button.

FORMS USED

Print Shop Request   Captures a request for print shop services and allows users to add the detail requirements for services. Allows the print shop employees to assign tasks, update the status of the job, and send completion notices to employees (see Figures 9.10a and 9.10b).

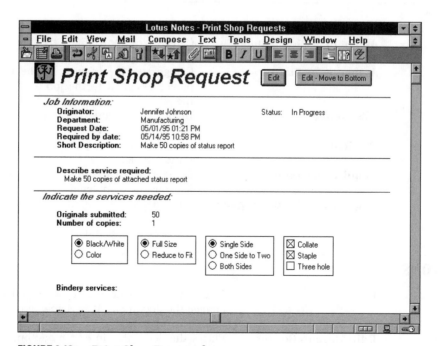

FIGURE 9.10a   Print Shop Request form.

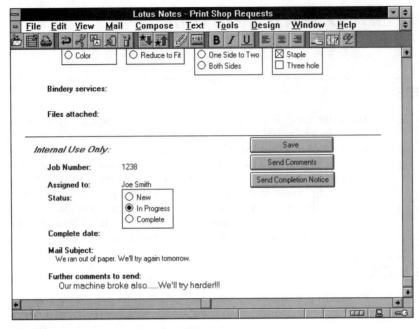

FIGURE 9.10b   Print Shop Request form, bottom half.

VIEWS

Assign to, by Job Number	Categorizes the request by the Print Shop employee assigned to the job.
Assign to, by Status	Categorizes the request by the Print Shop employee assigned to the job and by the status of the job.
Job Number	Displays the request by the internally assigned job number (see Figure 9.10c).
Originator	Categorizes the request by the person who submitted the job.
Required by, Date	Categorizes the request by the date on which the job must be completed.
Required by, Date, Assigned	Categorizes the request by the date on which the job must be completed and by the employee who has been assigned the job.

BUTTONS

Edit	Places the document in edit mode so that the user can change the document. It is visible only when the document is being read.
Edit–Move to Bottom	Places the document in edit mode but also moves the cursor to the bottom of the document. This saves the

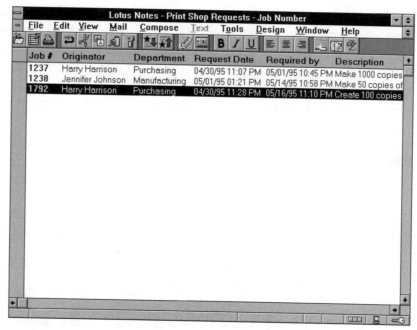

FIGURE 9.10c   Print Shop Requests by Job Number view.

	user from relying on the scroll bars or Page Down to see the part of the form that isn't visible when it is first opened. The button is visible only when the document is being read.
Save	Saves the document and exits to the last open view. The button is visible only when the document is being edited.
Save and Compose	Saves the document but also opens a new form so that a user can enter another document. The button is visible only when the document is being edited.
Send Comments	Sends the contents of the subject and comments fields to the originator of the job via electronic mail.
Send Complete Notice	Sends a message to the originator that the print job is complete. The button also updates the completion date with the current date if the field has not been filled in.

ACCESS CONTROL

The default access control should be set to Author for all users. The Print Shop staff should have Editor access so that they can update the request as needed.

ENHANCE IT!

You can make this database even more powerful by:

1. Adding a section field to limit access to the Internal Use Only section of the form.
2. Creating the request as a custom form in the mail system and changing the database into a mail-in database. The form would contain only the top part of the form, and the database that receives the mailed-in form would allow Read access to all users. The mailed-in message would be modified by the mail paste macro to use the form in this database.
3. Adding fields to store estimated completion dates and mail them to the originators.

USING PRINT SHOP REQUESTS

The database is intended for all **Users** and **Print Shop Personnel.** To create a Print Shop Request:

1. The **User** adds a document using the Print Shop Request form.
2. The **Print Shop Supervisor** reviews the database, adds a job number to each new task, and assigns an employee to a task.
3. The **Print Shop Personnel** reviews the database several times a day to see which tasks have been assigned to that department.
4. The **Print Shop Personnel** sends questions to employees when the request is not clear.
5. The **Print Shop Personnel** completes tasks and sends an electronic completion notice.

Suggestions (11)

PURPOSE

Employees of every company have a wealth of good ideas that can improve the way a company does business. A suggestion plan often encourages employees to submit those ideas to the benefit of both the company and employee. The Suggestions database allows Notes users to easily submit a suggestion. They enter a detailed description of their suggestion along with their cost justification, then simply save the document. They can also attach a word processing document or spreadsheet in the field for detailed suggestions.

The database also gives Suggestion Plan Administrators a central location for storing and processing employee suggestions. It eliminates paper routing and gives them an easy way to send comments and suggestion status back to the submitter. The person submitting the suggestion can also watch its progress as work is done on it.

FORMS USED

Suggestions Captures the basic suggestion information from the user. The lower section, marked Internal Use, allows the Suggestion Plan Administrator to communicate with the person submitting the suggestion. It also stores research information and allows the administrator to change the status of the request, keeping the submitter informed of its progress (see Figures 9.11a and b).

VIEWS

Originator Categorizes the documents by the person who entered the suggestion, which makes it easy for users to find the suggestions they have submitted.

Status Helps the Plan Administrator keep track of the age of each suggestion. The documents are sorted in descending order by activity date so that the newest suggestions are always at the top of the category. A hidden column is used to show the New documents first followed by In Progress, Approved, and Not Approved.

Suggestion Number Shows all the suggestions sorted by the internal suggestion number assigned by the Suggestion Plan Administrator. It is helpful when the user has several suggestions and the administrator wants a unique number to refer to when he or she answers questions about the suggestion (see Figure 9.11c).

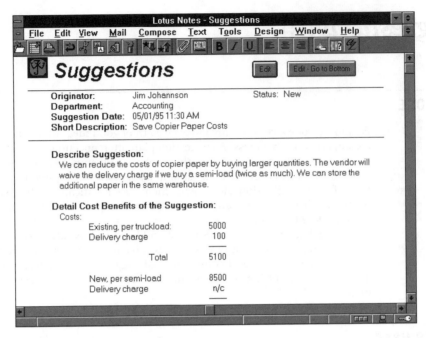

FIGURE 9.11a   Suggestions form.

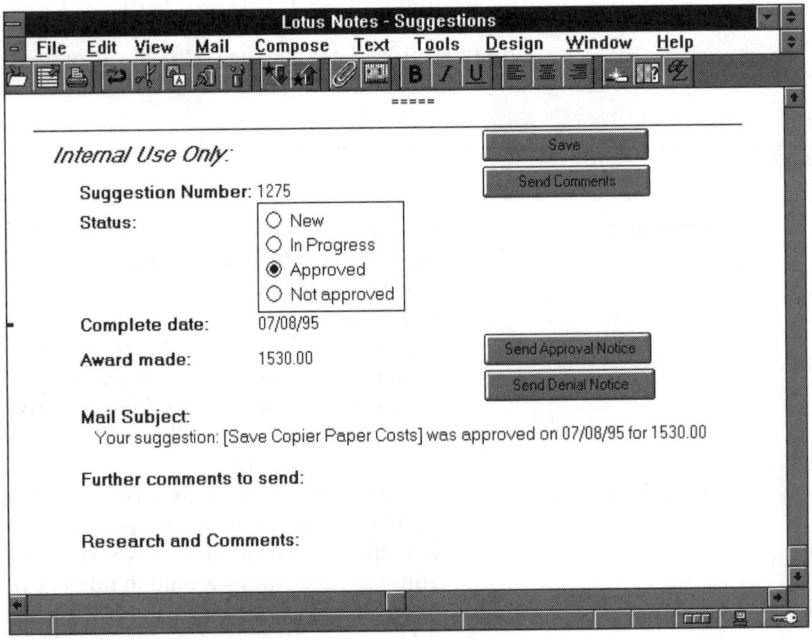

FIGURE 9.11b   Suggestions form, bottom half.

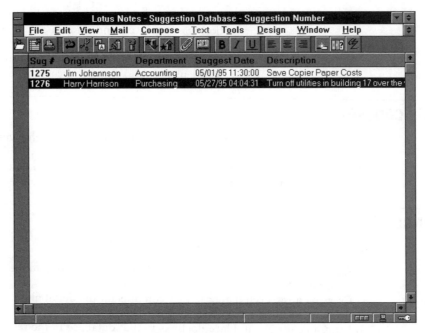

FIGURE 9.11c   Suggestions by Suggestion Number view.

BUTTONS

Edit

Places the document in edit mode so that the user can change the document. It is visible only when the document is being read.

Edit—Go to Bottom

Places the document in edit mode but also moves the cursor to the bottom of the document. This saves the user from relying on the scroll bars or Page Down to see the part of the form that isn't visible when it is first opened. The button is visible only when the document is being read.

Save

Saves the document and exits to the last open view. The button is visible only when the document is being edited. A second Save button is located in the lower section of the form so that the user doesn't have to move to the top of the form to use the first Save button.

Save and Compose

Saves the document but also opens a new form so that a user can enter another suggestion. The button is visible only when the document is being edited.

Send Comments

Sends a message to the person who submitted the suggestion. This is useful when the Administrator needs to ask a question or update the submitter on the progress of the suggestion.

Send Approval Notice	Sends a message to a submitter that his or her suggestion was approved and that an award will be given. It also changes the status to Approved.
Send Denial Notice	Sends a message to a submitter that his or her suggestion was denied. It also changes the status to Not Approved.

ACCESS CONTROL

The default access control should be set to Author for users who will be submitting suggestions. The Suggestion Plan Administrators should have Editor access. By adding section controls, the lower section of the database can be restricted so that users cannot edit or view the information.

ENHANCE IT!

You can make this database even more powerful by:

1. Adding sections to limit access to the Internal Use section to the Suggestion Plan Administrators.
2. Creating a research database that contains all the detail about the work that is done to verify the database. Set the access control so that only the Administrators can view it. Place doclinks to that database in the research field of the Suggestion database. All users can then view the status but not the research/candid comments.

USING SUGGESTIONS

The database is intended for all **Users** and the **Suggestion Plan Administrator.** To handle a typical suggestion:

1. The **User** composes a suggestion and completes the upper section of the form.
2. The **Suggestion Plan Administrator** reviews the database daily for new suggestions. The **Administrator** adds a suggestion number and changes the status to In Progress when work begins on the suggestion.
3. The **Suggestion Plan Administrator** mails comments and questions to the **User.**
4. The **User** reviews the database periodically to check on the progress of the suggestion.
5. The **Suggestion Plan Administrator** approves or denies the suggestion, fills in the award amount (if applicable), and sends the appropriate message to the **User.**

Inventory Data Warehouse (12)

PURPOSE

The Inventory Data Warehouse provides users with an audit trail of inventory purchases and receipts, as well as periodic inventory balances. Although much of the inventory is available through an accounting module of some kind, Notes provides users with more options for viewing the information, and the data warehouse does not have to have a user license in the accounting software.

FORMS USED

Inventory Data Warehouse	Captures detailed inventory transaction information, including inventory item, transaction date, and transaction amount (see Figure 9.12a).

VIEWS

Import View	Contains all of the fields in the Inventory Data Warehouse, and accepts a text file or spreadsheet information from which to load the database.

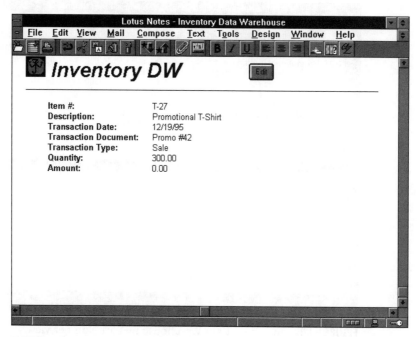

FIGURE 9.12a   Inventory DW form.

Part Number	Categorizes and totals sales by inventory item number, and sorts the transactions by date in reverse chronological order (see Figure 9.12b).
Sales Type	Categorizes and totals sales by the transaction type (balance, sale, purchase) and inventory item number. Sorts the transactions by date in reverse chronological order.
Transaction Date	Categorizes and totals sales by transactions by date in reverse chronological order. Sorts the transactions by inventory item number.

BUTTONS

Edit	Places the document in edit mode so that the user can change the document. It is visible only when the document is being read.
Save	Saves the document and exits to the last open view. The button is visible only when the document is being edited.
Save and Compose	Saves the document but also opens a new form so that a user can enter another document. The button is visible only when the document is being edited.

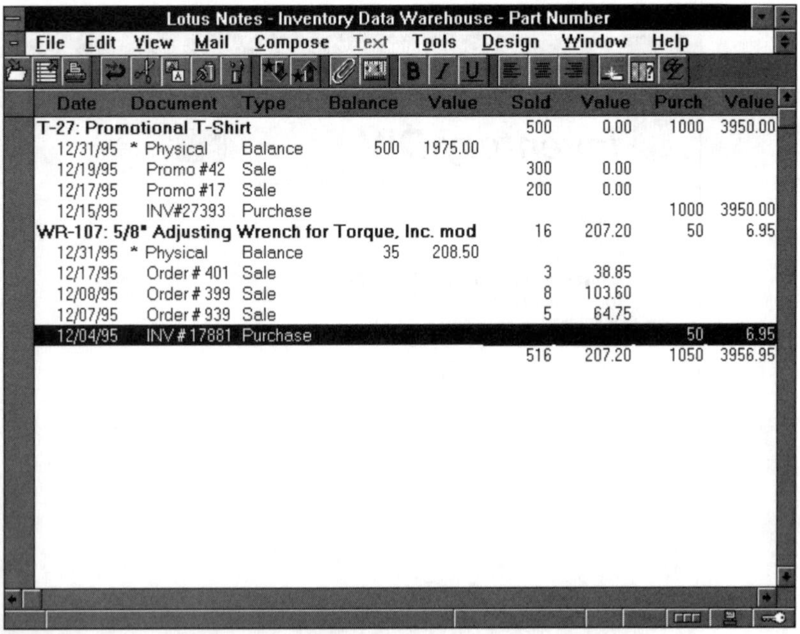

FIGURE 9.12b   Inventory Data Warehouse by Part Number view.

ACCESS CONTROL

The default access control should be set to Read for all users. Those responsible for updating this database should be given Editor access so that they can perform the imports and clean up any problems with the database.

ENHANCE IT!

You can make this database even more powerful by:

1. Using development tools to automate the import of information into this database.

USING INVENTORY DATA WAREHOUSE

The database is intended for all **Users** and the **Inventory Database Administrator**. To create sales documents in the Sales Data Warehouse:

1. The **Inventory Database Administrator** extracts the new inventory transactions from the accounting system and imports them into a text file or spreadsheet.
2. The **Inventory Database Administrator** imports the transactions into the Inventory Data Warehouse using the Imports view.

Budgets (13)

PURPOSE

At least once a year, ABC Company prepares detailed budgets using the standard company spreadsheet. The departmental spreadsheets are on the network and automatically roll up via formulas linking them to a summary spreadsheet. However, it is difficult to analyze all of the information because it is contained on several spreadsheets.

The Budgets database is a mail-enabled database for receiving spreadsheets from managers. It can be used as a tool for the review of preliminary budget numbers, after which all documents are erased; or it can represent the final budget figures. See Using Budgets for the assumptions about the format of the spreadsheet that is sent in.

FORMS USED

Mailed-in Spreadsheets	Holds the spreadsheet and spreadsheet name that is received as a mail message. The Mail Paste macro should be set up to change the form name to this form when the item arrives.
Spreadsheet Imports	Displays the documents that are created when the mailed-in spreadsheets are imported (see Figure 9.13a).

VIEWS

Full Budget	Categorizes and totals the budget items by organizational unit and by supervisor (see Figure 9.13b).
G/L Account	Categorizes and totals the budget items by major G/L Accounts (revenue and expense) and by G/L account numbers.
Mailed-in Budgets	Displays a list of budgets that have been received from department managers.
Product Line	Categorizes and totals budget items by major G/L Accounts (revenue and expense), by product line, and by G/L account numbers.
Spreadsheet Import	Used to define the fields for importing budget spreadsheet information.

BUTTONS

Edit	Places the document in edit mode so that the user can change the document. It is visible only when the document is being read.
Import	Detaches the spreadsheet that was mailed into the database and imports it into the Spreadsheet Import view. The button assumes that the file resides in the \Notesbk\Budgets directory.

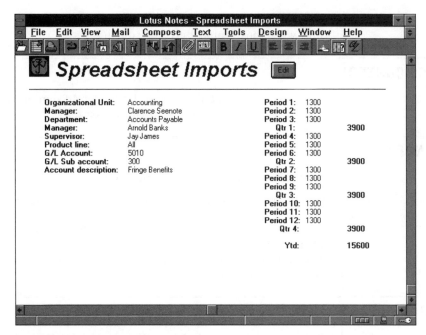

FIGURE 9.13a Budgets Import form.

Description	Period 1	Period 2	Period 3	Period 4	Period
Accounting (Clarence Seenote/Arnold	26235	26235	26235	26235	262
Accounting (Arnold Banks)	2910	2910	2910	2910	29
Salaries	1050	1050	1050	1050	10
Hourly Employees	960	960	960	960	9
Overtime wages	90	90	90	90	
Fringe Benefits	270	270	270	270	2
Travel	120	120	120	120	1
Training	120	120	120	120	1
Telecommunications	210	210	210	210	2
Office Supplies	30	30	30	30	
Postage	30	30	30	30	
Miscellaneous	30	30	30	30	
Accounts Payable (Jay James)	13625	13625	13625	13625	136
Salaries	5000	5000	5000	5000	50
Hourly Employees	4500	4500	4500	4500	45
Overtime wages	450	450	450	450	4
Fringe Benefits	1300	1300	1300	1300	13
Travel	500	500	500	500	5
Training	500	500	500	500	5
Telecommunications	1000	1000	1000	1000	10
Office Supplies	75	75	75	75	
Postage	100	100	100	100	1
Miscellaneous	200	200	200	200	2

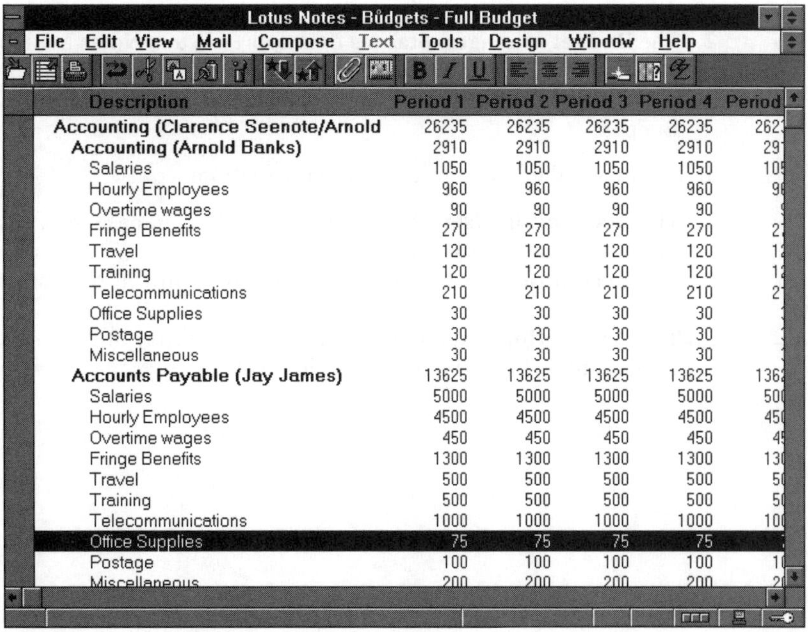

FIGURE 9.13b Full Budget view.

Save   Saves the document and exits to the last open view. The button is visible only when the document is being edited.

ACCESS CONTROL

The default access control should be set to Editor for Accounting users. All Budget Managers should be given Read access to this database.

ENHANCE IT!

You can make this database even more powerful by:

1. Adding fields and forms to allow mid-year changes and budget to actual comparisons to the G/L data warehouse.
2. Using third-party tools to read the spreadsheet directly and write information directly into Notes.
3. Adding a field that marks the version of the budget or the budget year so that multiple years can be stored.

USING BUDGETS

The database is intended for all **Accounting Users** and **Budget Managers.** The design of the database includes the following assumptions:

1. The spreadsheet used to calculate the budgets creates an export file in the WK1 format shown in the spreadsheets stored with the sample documents in this database.
2. The **Budget Manager** attaches the export file to a Notes Mail message and mails it to an address set up in the Name and Address Book that sends the message to this database. For example, the mail message could be sent to a name called Budget.

To update the database with budget information:

1. The **Accounting User** checks the Mailed-in Database view to locate any documents that have not yet been imported.
2. The **Accounting User** selects a document with the New status and opens the form.
3. The **Accounting User** pushes the Import button and selects the Spreadsheet Imports form from the Import dialog box.

Bad Debt (14)

PURPOSE

The Accounting department spends many hours following up on debt problems. The process soon becomes paper-intensive as folders are created for each problem, phone messages are stored, and copies of letters and faxes are saved. The Bad Debt database assists the Accounting department in tracking all activities associated with collecting bad debts.

FORMS USED

Customer Information   Captures the name, address, and the overdue balances on the customer's account (see Figure 9.14a).

Daily Call Information   Captures the details of each contact made with the customer in an attempt to collect on the overdue amounts (see Figure 9.14b).

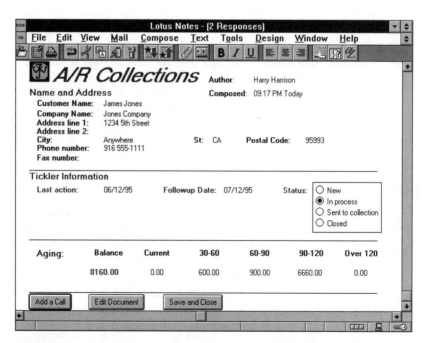

FIGURE 9.14a   A/R Collections form.

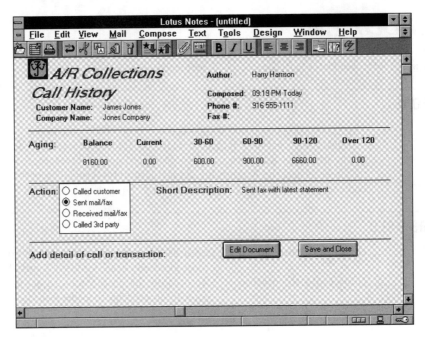

FIGURE 9.14b A/R Collections Call History form.

VIEWS

By Followup Date Categorizes the customer documents and call information by the date entered for the next followup effort and by customer. The customer document is displayed as the first line in the first, preceded by an arrow (see Figure 9.14c).

Customer View Categorizes customer documents and call information by customer name. The customer document is displayed as the first line in the view, preceded by an arrow.

BUTTONS

Add a Call Displays the Daily Call Information form.

Edit Document Places the document in edit mode so that the user can change the document. It is only visible when the document is being read.

Save and Close Saves the document and exits to the last open view. The button is visible only when the document is being edited.

ACCESS CONTROL

The default access control should be set to Editor for all Accounting users. No other users should have access to the database.

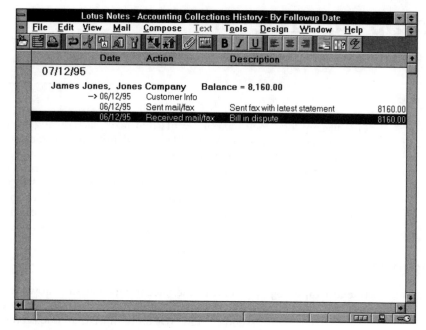

FIGURE 9.14c   A/R Collections by Followup Date view.

ENHANCE IT!

You can make this database even more powerful by:

1. Using the API or a third-party package to automatically create the customer set-up document and to update it on a weekly basis.
2. Adding buttons and fields to forward information to the Accounting Supervisor when all actions have failed.

USING BAD DEBT

The database is intended for all **Accounting Users.** To create a customer document:

1. The **Accounting User** uses the Customer Information form to set up a customer for followup.

To create a call document:

1. The **Accounting User** accesses the Followup view to display the name of the customer that needs to be processed.
2. The **Accounting User** selects the Customer Information document and displays it.
3. The **Accounting User** pushes the Add Call button and adds a Daily Call document.

Backup Tape Log (15)

PURPOSE

Tape backup logs document all events that take place during a backup session. It allows system operators to locate files and identify any problems with the backup session. Tapes are often kept off-site, and the logs allow operators to locate a tape that they need instead of having to mount each one and perform a search.

The Backup Tape Log database allows backup operators to store the backup log and attach extra information to the document, such as backup type (full, incremental) and server name. It also provides Help Desk personnel with easy access to the log so that they can help users without requiring the assistance of other IS staff.

FORMS USED

Backup Tape Log   Captures the backup tape log and allows users to add information about the servers backed up, the date of the backup, and the tape IDs used. More than one server can be listed in a single document (see Figure 9.15a).

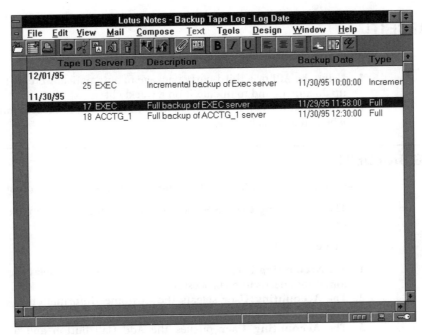

FIGURE 9.15a   Backup Tape Log form.

VIEWS

Backup Date	Displays the logs by the dates of the backups in reverse chronological order.
Backup Date/Server	Categorizes the logs' backup dates in reverse chronological order, then by the server IDs of the devices backed up.
Log Date	Displays the document by the date of the log entry (see Figure 9.15b).
Server ID/Backup Date	Categorizes the logs by the server IDs, then by the dates of the backup logs in reverse chronological order.

BUTTONS

Edit	Places the document in edit mode so that the user can change the document. It is visible only when the document is being read.
Save	Saves the document and exits to the last open view. The button is visible only when the document is being edited.
Save and Compose	Saves the document but also opens a new form so that a user can enter another document. The button is visible only when the document is being edited.

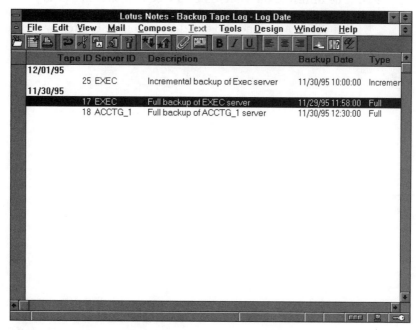

FIGURE 9.15b   Backup Tape Log by Log Date view.

ACCESS CONTROL

The default access control should be set to Editor for all Information Systems users, as they will all be adding the tape logs to the database, and since, usually, no one person is responsible for all backups, any one of them may need to update a document.

Help Desk users should be given at least Reader access so that they can read all documents and find a file that a user has requested.

ENHANCE IT!

You can make this database even more powerful by:

1. Adding a button that automatically inserts a tape log into the database.
2. Writing an application to automatically mail a log into the database after the tape software is finished.
3. Changing the rich text field in the form to a text field, and pasting the text of the log into the field, instead of attaching a file. Create a full-text search index so that a user can search the database for file names and dates.

USING BACKUP TAPE LOG

The database is intended for all **Information Systems Users.** To store a backup tape log:

1. The **Information Systems User** creates a backup tape log document.
2. The **Information Systems User** moves to the bottom of the form and uses File Insert File Attachment to add the tape log file created by the backup software to the database.

Widget Catalog (16)

PURPOSE

ABC Company wants its customers and salespeople to have information about the entire Widget line at their fingertips. With the Widget Catalog, these users can view information about any widget, view pictures of each item, and bring up a view of the items that are on sale.

FORMS USED

Add Widget Items	Captures detail information about Widget Inventory items. The form contains Save and Save and Compose buttons to help users create the documents more efficiently. Once a document is completed, its form is changed to the Widget Catalog form.
Widget Catalog	Displays the Widget Catalog items in a more visually appealing format than the Add Widget Items forms. The form has a top section that matches the Add Widget Items form that is hidden when the user is just reading the form. The bottom section contains calculated fields, which show the item details, and displays sales prices and special comments in a bold, red text (see Figure 9.16a).

VIEWS

Description	Lists the Widget catalog items by part description (see Figure 9.16b).
Model Number	Categorizes all the Widget parts by model number so that all parts and accessories are displayed together.
On Sale!	Lists all Widget items that are on sale.
Part Number	Lists all Widget items by part number.
	Note: The database is indexed for a full-text search so that a user can search for any text information in any view.

BUTTONS

Edit	Places the document in edit mode so that the user can change the document. It is visible only when the document is being read.
Save	Saves the document and exits to the last open view. The button is visible only when the document is being edited.
Save and Compose	Saves the document but also opens a new form so that a user can enter another document. The button is visible only when the document is being edited.

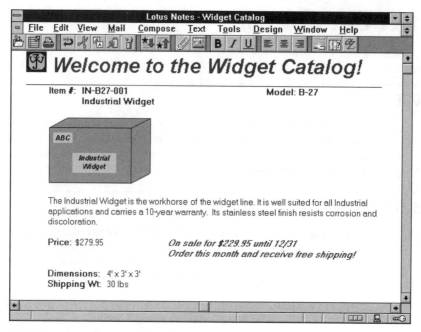

FIGURE 9.16a   Widget Catalog form.

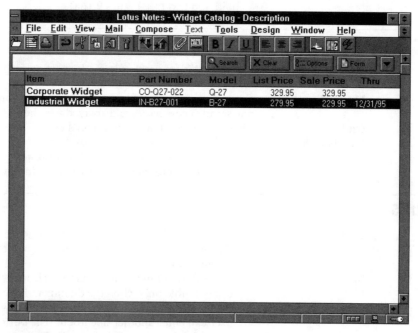

FIGURE 9.16b   Widget Catalog by Description view.

ACCESS CONTROL

The default access control should be set to Read for all users. The Catalog Manager should have Editor access to all of the documents.

ENHANCE IT!

You can make this database even more powerful by:

1. Adding a button that allows a reader to create an order.
2. Including doclinks to the Widget Technical Notes database.
3. Adding an import view to bring the inventory information into the database automatically.

USING WIDGET CATALOG

The database is intended for all **Users** and **Catalog Managers. Users** see only the catalog information, and they should not be permitted to enter information. To create a catalog entry:

1. The **Catalog Manager** adds a document using the Add Widget Items form. The form is automatically changed to the Widget Catalog form that the **Users** see.

Order Form (17)

PURPOSE

The fax machine has become a popular method of submitting orders. However, handwritten forms are time-consuming for resellers, and the information must be entered manually into an order processing system. With Notes, the reseller can enter an order into the system, send it to ABC Company, and maintain the document in the local database for future reference. Order personnel can also include additional information using the Related Support Information form, and they can give access for the database to the Support group to help them provide better service.

FORMS USED

ABC Order Form   Captures the details of the order, including addresses for the reseller, bill to and ship to addresses for the customer, the item details, and special order information. The status field allows sales managers to approve the order.

Related Support Info   Stores text information that will help the Support department deal with issues after the sale (see Figures 9.17a through 9.17c).

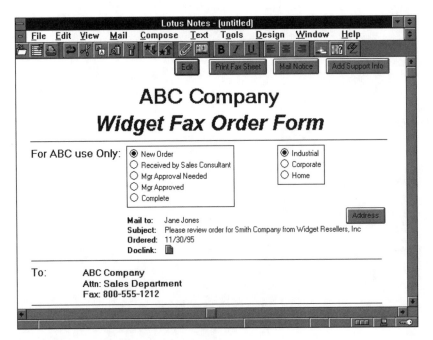

FIGURE 9.17a   Widget Fax Order form, part 1.

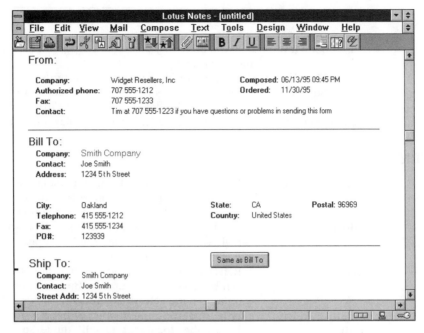

FIGURE 9.17b   Widget Fax Order form, part 2.

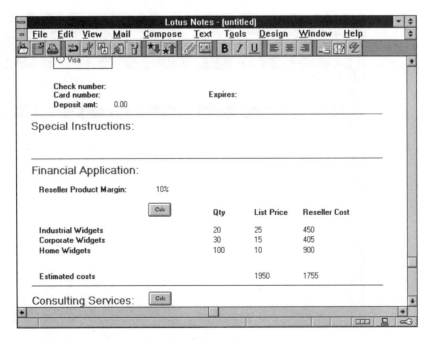

FIGURE 9.17c   Widget Fax Order form, part 3.

VIEWS

Customer View	Displays orders by customer name, and lists the reseller name and order date.
Order Month	Categorizes orders by month and status.
Order Status	Categorizes orders by status; also lists customer name, reseller name, and order date (see Figure 9.17d).
Reseller View	Categorizes the orders by the reseller responsible for them.

BUTTONS

Add Support Info	Creates a response document using the Related Support Information form, which gives the Support department more information about the details of the order.
Address	Displays the Name and Address Book so that the person reviewing the order can send a supervisor or reviewer a doclink to it for approval.
Calc	Refreshes all of the fields so that the total cost of the order can be calculated accurately. Be aware, though, that turning on automatic refresh significantly slows down the database because of the large number of fields in it.
Edit	Places the document in edit mode so that the user can change the document. It is visible only when the document is being read.

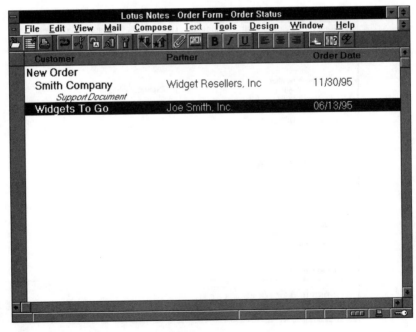

FIGURE 9.17d   Order by Order Status view.

Go to Top	Moves the cursor to the top of the document. This eliminates having to use the scroll bars or Page Up to return to the top.
Mail Notice	Sends a doclink directing the person listed in the Send To field to the order form.
Print Fax Sheet	Outputs the order form to the default printer, assuming that the Windows printer driver is a fax device.
Same as Bill To	Fills in all of the Ship To fields with the Bill To fields so that the user doesn't have to enter the same information twice.
Save	Saves the document and exits to the last open view. The button is visible only when the document is being edited.

ACCESS CONTROL

The default access control should be set to Author for all resellers and the Support team. The Order Processing users should have Editor access. The reseller's version of the database should be set up so that it replicates only the reseller's order forms. No other users should have access to the database.

ENHANCE IT!

You can make this database even more powerful by:

1. Using the API or a third-party package to automatically add the order to the order processing system.
2. Integrating the form with the Inventory Data Warehouse or an inventory file in an accounting package to allow users to select from a parts list.
3. Adding buttons and fields to better document the approval process and make it easier to approve.
4. Adding fields for actual ship dates and integrating the order processing system with the order form database so that resellers know when their product has shipped.

USING ORDER FORM

The database is intended for use by all **Order Processing Users, Order Reviewers,** and **Resellers.** To create an order document:

1. The **Reseller** uses the ABC Order form to create an order.

To process an order.

1. The **Order Processing User** reviews the database regularly for orders with a New Order status.
2. The **Order Processing User** changes the status to Received by Sales Consultant and processes the order.
3. The **Order Processing User** either changes the order to Complete or notifies an **Order Reviewer** to review the order.
4. The **Order Reviewer** updates the status to Manager Approved.
5. The **Order Processing User** finishes processing the order.

ABC Knowledge Database (18)

PURPOSE

Employees and resellers want and need to be informed about all aspects of ABC Company. They will gather information from a variety of sources, including newsletters, memos, electronic mail, the grapevine, and bulletin boards. Unfortunately, these disparate sources of information almost guarantee inconsistent messages and gaps in the facts for many users. The Company Knowledge database replaces most of the information sources with one central repository that can be relied on as the official source. Users and resellers can review the database regularly and keep up with the products, events, and all other happenings at ABC Company.

FORMS USED

Add to Knowledge database   Captures company information along with categories that help sort and distribute the information in the appropriate view for easy search and recall (see Figure 9.18a).

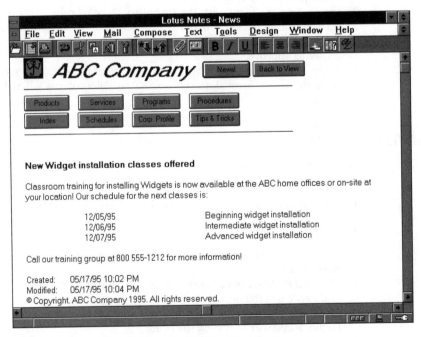

FIGURE 9.18a   Company Knowledge Database form.

VIEWS

Corp. Profile	Categorizes all documents that contain any value in the Company field by category.
Dates Created	Categorizes documents by the date they were created.
Date Created by Owner	Categorizes documents by the person who created them and by the date on which the document was created.
Dates Modified	Categorizes documents by the date on which the document was modified.
Index, Alphabetic	Categorizes documents in alphabetic order based on a keyword field created by combining the values in the company, category, topic, and subject fields (see Figure 9.18b).
Index, Class	Categorizes documents in alphabetic order based on the values in the Class field.
Index, Category	Categorizes documents in alphabetic order based on the values in the Category field.
Index, All Topics	Categorizes documents in alphabetic order based on the values in the Topic field.
News!	Displays all documents that contain the class code News!
Procedures	Categorizes all documents that contain the class code Procedures by category.
Products by Name	Categorizes all documents with the class code Products according to the category stored in the document.
Product by Platform	Categorizes all documents with the class code Products according to the platform stored in the document.
Programs	Categorizes all documents that contain the class code Programs by category.
Schedules	Categorizes all documents that contain the class code Schedules by category.
Services	Categorizes all documents that contain the class code Services by category.
Tips & Tricks	Categorizes all documents that contain the class code Tips & Tricks by category.

BUTTONS

Back to View	Exits a document and returns to the view from which the document was selected.
Corp. Profile	Displays the Corporate Profile view.
Index	Displays the Alphabetic Index view.
News!	Displays the News! view.
Products	Displays the Products view.
Procedures	Displays the Procedures view.
Programs	Displays the Programs view.
Schedules	Displays the Schedules view.

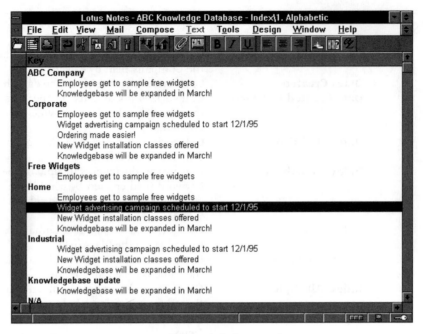

FIGURE 9.18b   Company Knowledge Alphabetic Index view.

Services	Displays the Services view.
Tips & Tricks	Displays the Tips & Tricks view.

ACCESS CONTROL

The default access control should be set to Read for all users. The department responsible for creating the database should be given Editor access. For resellers, a separate database should be set up that filters out any documents during replication that are marked for internal use only.

ENHANCE IT!

You can make this database even more powerful by:

1. Creating a macro that deletes documents that have expired.
2. Creating a replica of the database that doesn't include deletions so that there is an archive of *all* documents added to the database.

USING ABC KNOWLEDGE

The database is intended for all **Users.** To create a Knowledge database document:

1. The **User** adds a document using the Add to Knowledge database form.

Widget Technical Notes (19)

PURPOSE

Customer service is often an excellent way to elevate a company above its competitors. Phone support is usually the preferred service method, but it is also very expensive and labor-intensive. With a Widget Technical Notes database, the Customer Service department can eliminate a lot of phone calls by providing its customers with a wealth of technical information that will solve many of their problems 24 hours a day.

FORMS USED

Adding Technical Notes   Captures the technical information for a part number and allows the author to categorize the technical information by type of service. Documents created with this form are assigned to the Technical Notes form when they are saved.

Technical Notes   Displays the same information as the Adding Technical Notes form, without the Save and Save and Compose buttons (see Figure 9.19a).

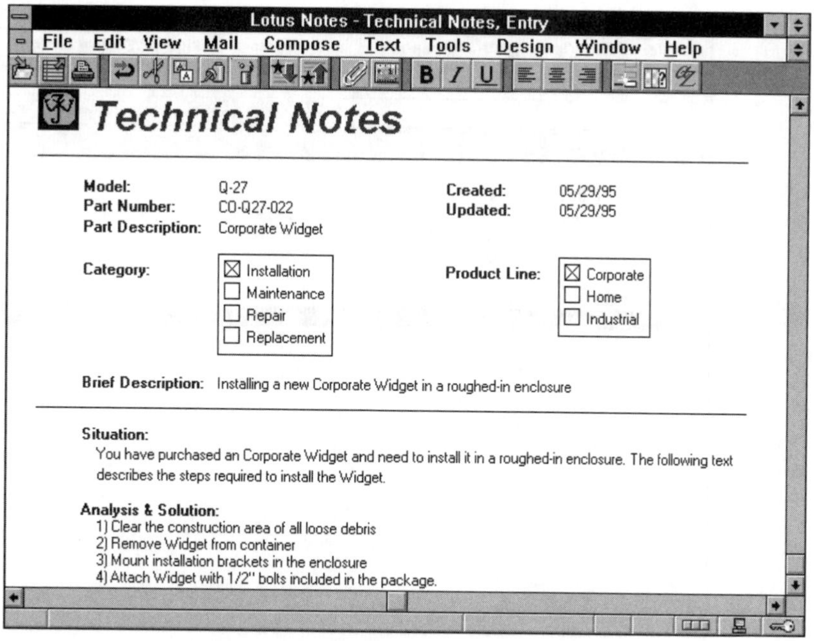

FIGURE 9.19a   Technical Notes form.

VIEWS

Category	Categorizes the technical notes into one of four categories: Installation, Maintenance, Repair, and Replacement.
Date Updated	Categorizes the technical notes by updates in reverse chronological order to help users find the technical notes with the most recent changes.
Model Number	Categorizes the technical notes by Widget model and part number (see Figure 9.19b).
Part Number	Categorizes the technical notes by part number and description. *Note:* The database is indexed for a full-text search so that a user can search for any text information in any view.

BUTTONS

Edit	Places the document in edit mode so that the user can change the document. It is visible only when the document is being read.
Save	Saves the document and exits to the last open view. The button is visible only when the document is being edited.
Save and Compose	Saves the document but also opens a new form so that a user can enter another document. The button is visible only when the document is being edited.

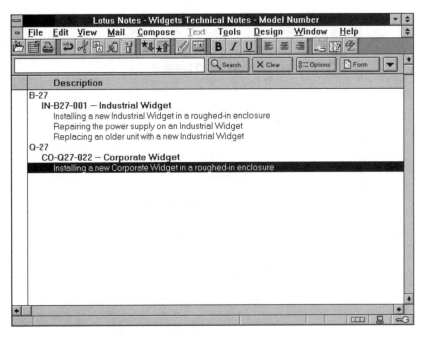

FIGURE 9.19b Technical Notes by Model Number view.

ACCESS CONTROL

The default access control should be set to Read for all users. The Customer Support staff should be given Author access so that they can add tips. Customer Support supervisors should have Editor access so that they can modify or remove tips.

ENHANCE IT!

You can make this database even more powerful by:

1. Changing the form so that new technical notes are shown in their own view. Only supervisors with Editor access can approve the form and put it into production.
2. Adding an expiration date and a macro to clean out old technical tips.

USING WIDGET TECHNICAL NOTES

The database is intended for all **Users** and **Customer Support Personnel.** To create a Widget Technical Note:

1. **Customer Support Personnel** adds a document using the Adding Technical Notes form.

Presentations (20)

PURPOSE

Seldom does an important meeting take place without some kind of presentation. Presentations are expected to look very professional, and often they are done using a package like Freelance or PowerPoint on a personal computer hooked up to an overhead projection device. The presenter is often asked for copies of certain slides or even of the entire presentation.

The Presentations database gives presenters a place to store their presentations, thus making them available to everyone in the company. Instead of asking for a copy of the rather large files to be sent through the electronic mail system, employees can search the database for the proper presentation, download or launch the file, and copy the slides they want.

FORMS USED

Presentations   Captures information about a presentation and allows the author to categorize the presentation. The rich text field at the bottom of the form allows the user to store the presentation file (see Figure 9.20a).

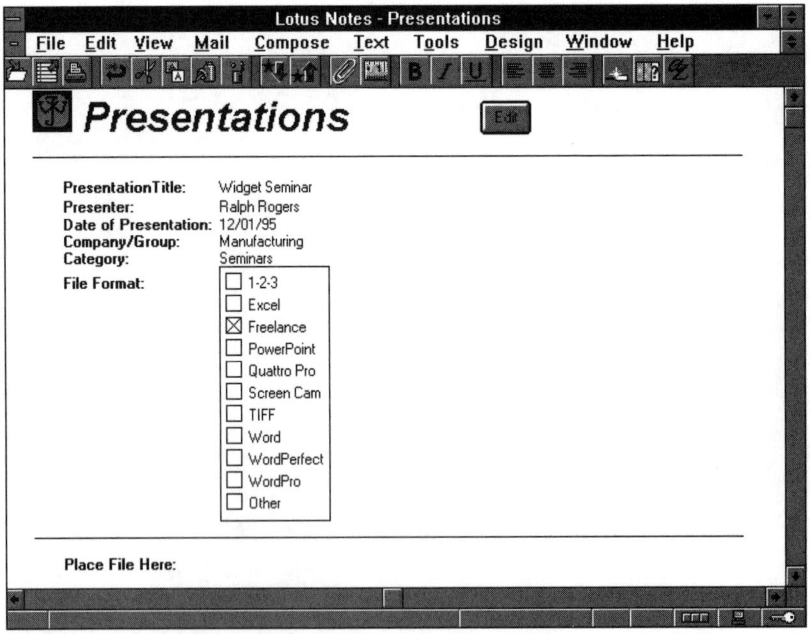

FIGURE 9.20a   Presentations form.

VIEWS

Category	Displays the presentations by a user-defined category field.
Group	Shows the presentations by the name of the group that gave the presentation.
Presentation Date	Displays the presentations in reverse chronological order (see Figure 9.20b).
Presenter	Shows the presentations by the name of the person making the presentation.

BUTTONS

Edit	Places the document in edit mode so that the user can change the document. It is visible only when the document is being read.
Save	Saves the document and exits to the last open view. The button is visible only when the document is being edited.
Save and Compose	Saves the document but also opens a new form so that a user can enter another document. The button is visible only when the document is being edited.

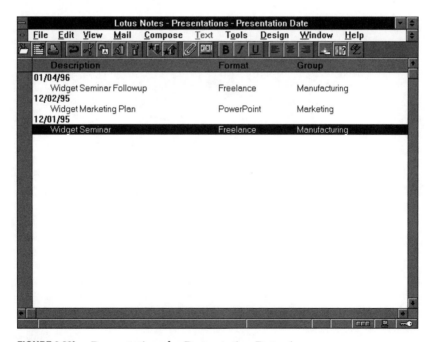

FIGURE 9.20b   Presentations by Presentation Date view.

ACCESS CONTROL

The default access control should be set to Author for users who will be adding the presentations.

USING PRESENTATIONS

The database is intended for all **Users.** To handle a typical presentation document:

1. The **User** creates a presentation document.
2. The **User** moves to the bottom of the form and uses File Insert File Attachment to add the presentation file to the database.

Contact Tracking (21)

PURPOSE

Good salespeople have a unique ability to juggle hundreds of prospects and current customers while keeping appointments and remembering all the details about the key players in the sales process. Most of these people also rely on a system that helps them manage their network of contacts and prospects. The Contact Tracking database holds information about a company, the contacts at the company, and all the activities that occurred during and after the sales processes. In addition, the user of the database can create to-do's and action items in the Notes Mail system, as well as send faxes and letters to prospects.

FORMS

Action Assignment	Captures an action item for another user and mails the item to that user's Notes mailbox. The item will show up in the user's action item list.
Activity Log	Captures a response document that lists some activity associated with a contact. The form can be accessed only from the Contact Document form (see Figure 9.21a).
Company Doc	Captures all the information needed to set up a company document. All other documents are called from this form or from the forms called by this form (see Figure 9.21b).
Contact Doc	Captures the information about a sales contact. The form is called from the Company Document form or Reseller Document form (see Figure 9.21c).
FaxR2R	Builds a response document from a contact document, which can then be faxed to a contact. The user must add comments to the form before faxing it.
Leads	Gathers lead information for a contact. The form is called from a Contact document (see Figure 9.21d).
LetterR2R	Builds a response document from a contact document, which can then be used as a letter to a contact. The user must complete the letter before printing it.
Reseller Doc	Captures all the information needed to set up a reseller document. All other documents are called from this form or from the forms called by this form.
To-do	Captures a to-do item for the user and mails the item to that user's Notes mailbox. The item will show up in the user's Notes Mail to-do list.

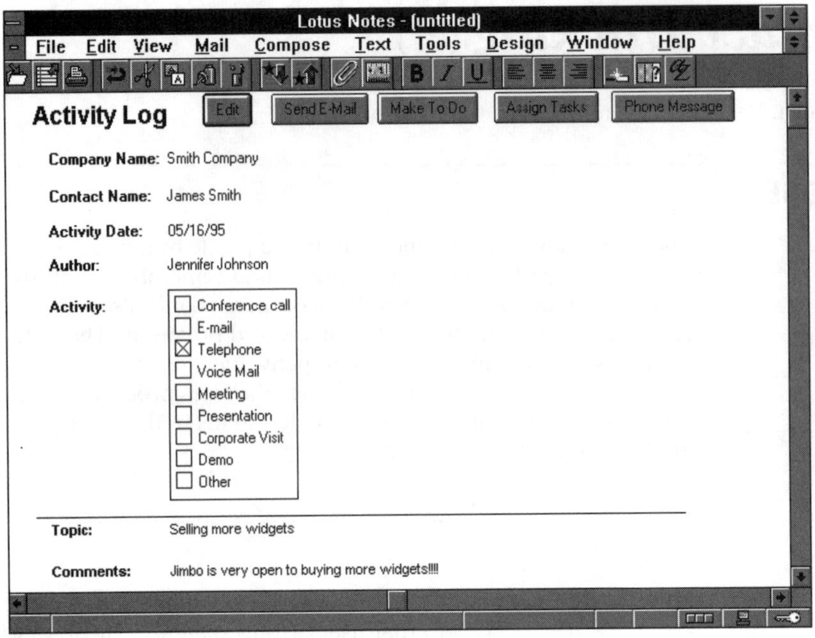

FIGURE 9.21a Activity Log form.

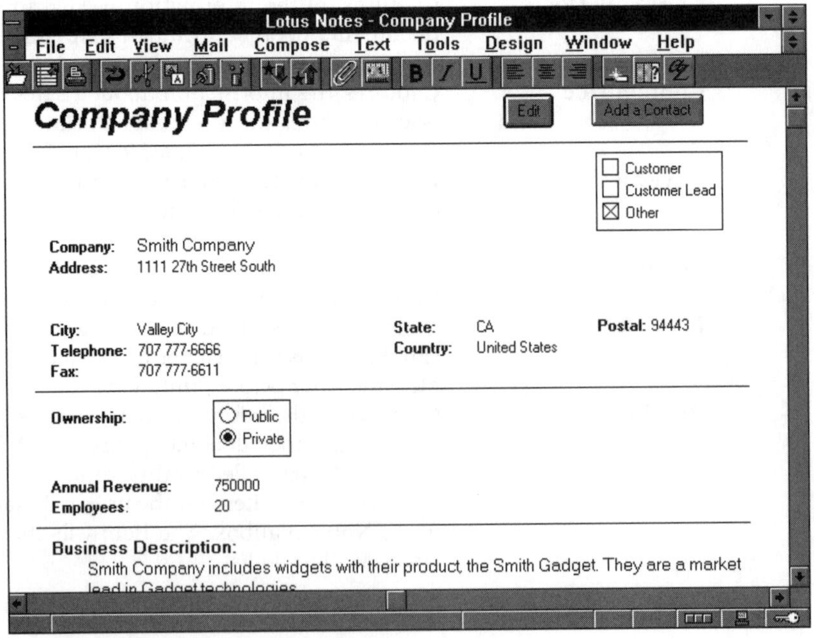

FIGURE 9.21b Company Profile form.

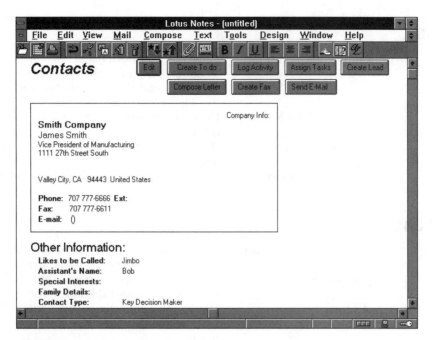

FIGURE 9.21c Contacts form.

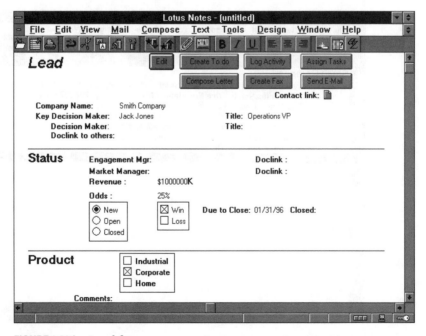

FIGURE 9.21d Lead form.

VIEWS

Companies by Name	Categorizes the documents by company, and displays all documents related to that company with contact documents first and all activity for that contact beneath them (see Figure 9.21e).
Contacts, Last Name	Displays all contact documents alphabetically by last name.
Contacts, First Name	Displays all contact documents alphabetically by first name.
Contacts, Company	Displays all contact documents alphabetically by company name.

BUTTONS

+, −, and Date Buttons	Adjusts the due date in the Action Assignment form by one day (+, −) and by the values listed on each button.
Add a Contact	Creates a contact document and adds the company name to the Contact Document form.
Address	Displays the Notes Name and Address Book so that the user can add the name of the person who will be assigned to a task.
Assign Tasks	Creates an action item and sends it to another user's Notes Mail database.

FIGURE 9.21e   Companies by Company Name view.

Compose Letter	Creates a letter and fills it in with the contact name and address.
Create To-Do	Creates a to-do item in the user's Notes Mail database.
Create Fax	Creates a fax cover letter, with fields for adding comments, to be sent to the contact.
Create Lead	Creates a lead document and fills in company information from the contact document.
Edit	Places the document in edit mode so that the user can change the document. It is visible only when the document is being read.
Log Activity	Creates an Activity Log document to store the results of activities with a contact.
Mail Assignment	Sends an action item to another user's Notes Mail database.
Make To-Do	Creates a to-do document in the user's Notes Mail database.
Phone Message	Composes a phone message document in the user's Notes Mail database.
Print Fax Sheet	Prints the fax cover letter created by the Create Fax button and assumes that the default printer output is sent to a fax card.
Print Letter	Outputs the letter created by the Compose Letter button to the default printer.
Save	Saves the document and exits to the last open view. The button is visible only when the document is being edited.
Send E-mail	Composes an electronic mail message with the user's Notes Mail database.

MACROS

Store Company Name	Stores in an environment variable the name of the company in the document that has been selected in a view.
Change Company Name	Replaces the company name in all documents selected in a view with the contents of the environment variable created by the Store Company Name macro.
Store Contact Name	Stores in an environment variable the name of the contact in the document that has been selected in a view.
Change Contact Name	Replaces the contact name in all items selected in a view with the contents of the environment variable created by the Store Contact Name macro.

ACCESS CONTROL

The default access control should be set to Author for all users. Sales Supervisors and Database Administrators should be given Editor access.

ENHANCE IT!

You can make this database even more powerful by:

1. Integrating the database with the order form database so that the name and address information can be automatically added to the order form.

2. Integrating fax software so that faxes that are received can be stored in an activity log record.

USING CONTACT TRACKING

The database is intended for use by all **Sales Users**. To add a company or reseller:

1. The **User** adds a document with the Company Document form or the Reseller Document form.

To add a contact:

1. The **User** displays the Companies by Company Name view and selects a company or reseller document.
2. The **User** pushes the Create Contact button to compose a contact document.

To create leads, send e-mail, create faxes and letters, create action assignments and to-do's:

1. The **User** displays the Companies by Company Name view and selects a contact document.
2. The **User** pushes the appropriate button to display a form.

To update all documents when a company name or contact name changes:

1. The **User** selects a company, reseller, or contact document and edits the contents of the form.
2. The **User** executes the Store Company Name or Store Contact Name macro to store the changes.
3. The **User** selects all documents that must be changed to the new company or contact name.
4. The **User** executes the Change Company Name or Change Contact Name macro to make the changes.

Advance Requests (22)

PURPOSE

Employees are often asked to attend classes, seminars, and trade shows as a part of their job duties. They naturally incur expenses, but rather than being reimbursed after the fact, ABC Company doesn't want them to use personal funds. The Advance Requests database allows users to submit a request for a cash advance to cover these expenses, and allows supervisors to approve the advance electronically.

FORMS USED

Advance Requests   Captures the details of the advance, mails a request for approval to the employee's supervisor, and allows the supervisor to approve the advance (see Figures 9.22a and b).

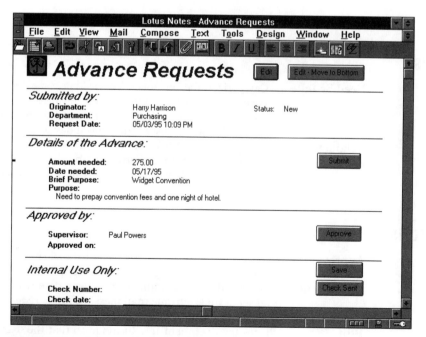

FIGURE 9.22a   Advance Requests form.

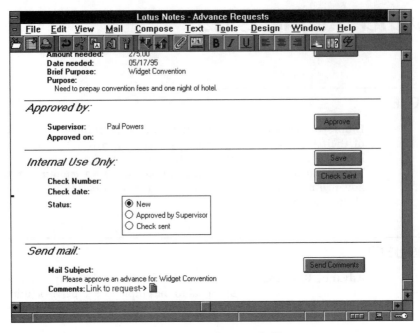

FIGURE 9.22b   Advance Requests form, bottom half.

VIEWS

Need by Date	Categorizes the advances by the date on which the advance is needed and by the status of the advance, which helps the Accounting staff monitor the requests and determine the number of checks that are necessary on a given day or week.
Originator	Categorizes the advances by the employees who requested them.
Status	Categorizes the unpaid advances by the status of the advance—New, Approved by Supervisor, Check Requested—(see Figure 9.22c).

BUTTONS

Approve	Changes the approval fields to add the current user's name as the approver and the current date as the approval date.
Check Sent	Requests the check number and check date from the current user, and sends an electronic mail message to the requester that says that a check was sent to him or her on the check date.
Edit	Places the document in edit mode so that the user can change the document. It is visible only when the document is being read.

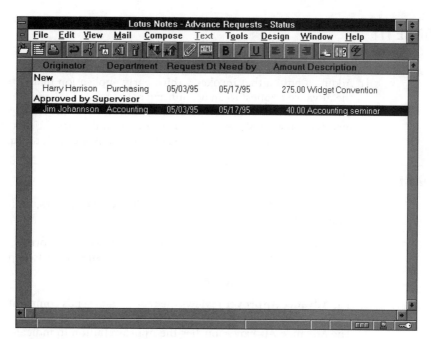

FIGURE 9.22c   Advance Requests by Status view.

Edit—Move to Bottom	Places the document in Edit mode, but also moves the cursor to the bottom of the document. This eliminates having to use the scroll bars or Page Down to see the part of the form that isn't visible when it is first opened. The button is visible only when the document is being read.
Save	Saves the document and exits to the last open view. The button is visible only when the document is being edited. Another Save button is placed lower in the form so that the user can save the document without moving to the top of the screen.
Save and Compose	Saves the document, but also opens a new form so that a user can enter another document. The button is visible only when the document is being edited.
Send Comments	Allows the person reviewing the request to send comments and questions via electronic mail to the requester.
Submit	Sends a message to the requester's supervisor asking that the supervisor approve the request.

ACCESS CONTROL

The default access control should be set to Author for all users. All advance approvers should be given Editor access to this database so that they can approve the advances.

ENHANCE IT!

You can make this database even more powerful by:

1. Adding a button that invokes a third-party application that automatically sends the Advance Request to an accounting package.
2. Changing the Advances form into a custom form for the Notes Mail system, and modifying the database so that it is a mail-in database. Users should not have access to the database; that is, be able to see anyone else's advance.

USING REQUESTS

The database is intended for all **Users, Advance Approvers,** and **Accounting.** To create an advance request:

1. The **User** adds a document using the Advance Requests form.
2. The **User** pushes the Submit button, asking the supervisor to approve the request.

To review or approve the request:

1. The **Advance Approver** reviews the request and sends comments or questions to the requester.
2. The **Advance Approver** pushes the Approve button to indicate that the request has been approved.

To generate the advance and notify the requester:

1. **Accounting** reviews the database daily for items marked with an Approved by Supervisor status.
2. **Accounting** generates a check to pay the advance, and either mails the advance or uses direct deposit.
3. **Accounting** presses the Check Sent button to log the check date and check number. An electronic mail message notifies the requester that the check is in the mail.

Expense Reports (23)

PURPOSE

Many activities that support ABC Company require employees to incur expenses when they participate in those activities. The Accounting department needs detailed receipts and information about each expense, and employees wants quick turnaround of expense reports so that they can pay off charge cards and be reimbursed.

The Expense Reports database controls the entire expense reports process as employees enter expenses, managers approve them, and accounting pays them.

FORMS USED

Expense Detail Captures the expenses using one document per vendor per reporting week. Scanned documents can also be included. The form can be accessed only from the Expense Reports form (see Figure 9.23a).

Expense Reports Captures the employee information and a summary of expenses. The form also controls the approval process (see Figure 9.23b).

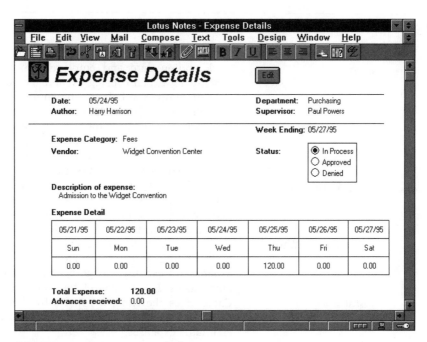

FIGURE 9.23a Expense Details form.

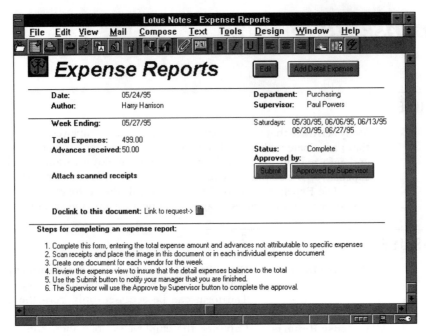

FIGURE 9.23b Expense Reports form.

VIEWS

Balance Expenses Categorizes and totals the expense report and detail by week ending date and employee name. Displays each expense by expense category and includes a column to help the employee balance the summary information to the detail (see Figure 9.23c).

Expense Detail Categorizes and totals the expense report and detail by week ending date and employee name. Displays each expense by expense category and shows the amounts by day of the week for each expense.

Exp Detail W/Descr Categorizes the expense report and detail by week ending date and employee name. Displays each expense by expense category and shows the full expense description and the amounts by day of the week for each expense.

Exp Detail W/Totals Categorizes and totals the expense report and detail by week ending date and employee name. Displays each expense by expense category and shows and totals the amounts by day of the week for each expense.

Status Categorizes the expense reports by their status and the week ending date. Displays the employee name and the estimated expenses.

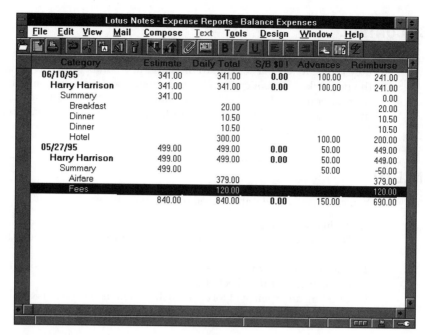

FIGURE 9.23c   Expense Report, Balance view.

BUTTONS

Add Detail Expense	Creates a detail document for entering the expenses for an entire week for one vendor.
Approved by Supervisor	Changes the status of the expense report to Approved by Supervisor and notifies the user via a mail message that it has been approved.
Edit	Places the document in edit mode so that the user can change the document. It is visible only when the document is being read.
Save	Saves the document and exits to the last open view. The button is visible only when the document is being edited.
Submit	Changes the status of the expense report to Complete and sends the supervisor a request via a mail message to approve the expense report.

MACROS

Approve All Items	Changes the status in all selected Expense Detail documents to Approved.
Deny All Items	Changes the status in all selected Expense Detail documents to Denied.

ACCESS CONTROL

The database should be set up so that users have access to it only via a database that they replicate to their local hard drive or via a database that is assigned to them on the network. The replication formula should be set so that only the user's expense information is replicated to a consolidated database, which the Accounting department uses to process expense reports. The Accounting department should have Editor access to the database.

ENHANCE IT!

You can make this database even more powerful by:

1. Adding a button to integrate third-party scanning software into the Expense Detail form so that receipts can be scanned and inserted automatically into Notes.
2. Adding a button that marks the expense report Paid and prompts the Accounting department for the check number and date paid.
3. Building an expense report spreadsheet and using Notes FX technology to create detail expense records from it.

USING EXPENSE REPORTS

The database is intended for all **Users, Supervisors,** and **Accounting Users.** To create an expense report:

1. The **User** adds a document using the Expense Reports form.
2. The **User** presses the **Add Detail Expense** button to add a document using the Expense Details form.
3. The **User** continues to add detail documents until the expense report is complete.
4. The **User** presses the Submit button to notify the supervisor that the report is ready for approval.

To approve the expense report:

1. The **Supervisor** displays the expense reports using the doclink in the mail message. The **Supervisor** must go into the Expense Reports database if detail is needed.
2. The **Supervisor** pushes the Approved by Supervisor button to approve the report.

To pay the expense report:

1. The **Accounting User** reviews the Status view for items that are Approved by Supervisor.
2. The **Accounting User** processes the expense report and issues a check to the appropriate employee.
3. The **Accounting User** marks the expense report as Paid in the Expense Reports form.

Sales Leads (24)

PURPOSE

Sales leads are obtained from a variety of sources within ABC Company. The Sales Leads database allows users to enter those leads and transmit them to sales personnel for further action. Leads that require more followup can be transferred to the Contacts database for more detailed tracking.

FORMS USED

Sales Leads   Captures the name and address of the lead and allows comments to be added (see Figure 9.24a).

VIEWS

Leads-Salesperson   Categorizes the leads by the salesperson who must act on the lead (see Figure 9.24b).

FIGURE 9.24a   Sales Leads form.

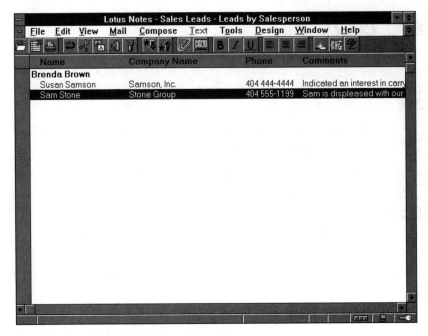

FIGURE 9.24b Sales Leads by Salesperson view.

BUTTONS

Add to Contacts DB   Opens the Contacts database included with this book and automatically creates both a Company document and a Contacts document.

Edit   Places the document in edit mode so that the user can change the document. It is visible only when the document is being read.

Save   Saves the document and exits to the last open view. The button is visible only when the document is being edited.

ACCESS CONTROL

The default access control should be set to Editor for all remote sales users. Sales telemarketers or administrative personnel should be given Author access to this database so that they can create sales leads.

ENHANCE IT!

You can make this database even more powerful by:

1. Adding a status field to mark items as Moved to Contacts Database.
2. Enhancing Notes Mail to recognize sales leads as another mail message type and creating a view for sales leads.

3. Changing the replication filter so that the remote salespeople receive only the leads with their name on them.

USING SALES LEADS

The database is intended for use by all **Sales Users**. To create a sales lead:

1. The **Sales User** adds a document using the Sales Leads form.

To add a sales lead to the Contacts database:

1. The **Sales User** selects a sales lead from the database.
2. The **Sales User** pushes the Add to Contacts database button to automatically create company and lead documents.

Invoice Approval (25)

PURPOSE

One of the toughest tasks for the Accounts Payable department is to match requisitions to invoices and receive approval from budget managers. Managers must handle paperwork, sign it, and send it back to Accounting. Documents often become lost or misplaced during mail routing, resulting in unpaid invoices and more work for Accounting.

With the Invoice Approval database, Accounting personnel can scan an invoice, store it in a document, link the document to the original requisition, and electronically receive approvals. Managers can simply check their electronic mail boxes to discover that approvals are necessary. They can also follow doclinks to review transactions and approve them.

FORMS USED

Invoice Approval   Captures information about an invoice, connects the invoice to the appropriate requisition, and coordinates the approval process for the invoice (see Figure 9.25a).

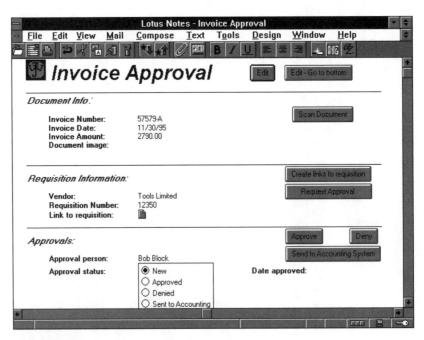

FIGURE 9.25a   Invoice Approval form.

VIEWS

Invoices	Displays the invoices by invoice number.
Invoices by Approver	Categorizes the invoices by the person who must approve them.
Invoices by Date	Categorizes the invoices by invoice date for all those that have not been sent to Accounting. This helps the Accounting department track old invoices and remind approvers to review them.
Invoices by Status	Categorizes the invoices by the status of the invoice (New, Approved, Denied, Sent to Accounting). This helps Accounting follow up on invoices that haven't been approved or denied.

BUTTONS

Approve	Changes the invoice status to Approved and changes the Date Approved to the current date.
Create Links to Requisition	Assists users in bringing the approver's name and a doclink to the Purchase Requisition database for the requisition that preceded the invoice. The button opens a view in the Purchase Requisitions database. The user selects a document and presses the Link to Invoice button in the form to return to the Invoice Approval form, then pastes in the approver name and a doclink to the Purchase Requisitions database.
Deny	Changes the invoice status to Denied and changes the Date Approved to the current date.
Edit	Places the document in edit mode so that the user can change the document. It is visible only when the document is being read.
Edit—Move to Bottom	Places the document in edit mode, but also moves the cursor to the bottom of the document. This eliminates having to use the scroll bars or Page Down to see the part of the form that isn't visible when it is first opened. The button is visible only when the document is being read.
Request Approval	Sends a mail message to the invoice approver to approve the invoice. If the document has not been doclinked to a requisition, an error appears asking the user to create the link.
Save	Saves the document and exits to the last open view. The button is visible only when the document is being edited.
Save and Compose	Saves the document but also opens a new form so that a user can enter another document. The button is visible only when the document is being edited.
Scan Document	This button is inactive. It is placed on the form to show how scanning software could be used to attach a scanned image of the invoice as a part of the workflow process.

Send to Accounting	This button is inactive. It is placed on the form to show how the approved invoice could be automatically sent to the Accounting system as a part of the workflow.

ACCESS CONTROL

The default access control should be set to Editor for all Budget Managers and Accounting users.

ENHANCE IT!

You can make this database even more powerful by:

1. Adding the capability to mail comments to Accounting without approving or denying an invoice.
2. Adding the scanning software to activate the scan button.
3. Adding the interface required to activate the button that sends the invoice to the Accounting module.
4. Adding a section field to limit access by Budget Managers to just the approval area.

USING INVOICE APPROVAL

The database is intended for use by all **Budget Managers** and **Accounting Users.** To create an invoice approval document:

1. The **Accounting User** adds a document using the Invoice Approval form.
2. The **Accounting User** scans the invoice document and adds the image to the document.
3. The **Accounting User** creates a doclink to the appropriate requisition, bringing over the name of the invoice approver (**Budget Manager**).
4. The **Accounting User** sends a request for approval via electronic mail to the **Budget Manager.**
5. The **Budget Manager** approves or denies the invoice.
6. The **Accounting User** sends the approved invoice to ABC's accounting package.

Candidate Tracking (26)

PURPOSE

Hiring employees involves a lot of time, people, and paperwork. A number of people have to review a candidate's resume, and the Personnel department is required to keep detailed documentation of hiring practices. The Candidate Tracking database allows the Personnel department to track the entire hiring process and store a copy of each candidate's resume.

FORMS USED

Candidates   Captures detailed information about an employment candidate, the position for which they are applying, and the manager who is doing the hiring (see Figure 9.26a).

Activity Log   Stores information about any activity that relates to the employment process. This form can be accessed only through the Candidates form.

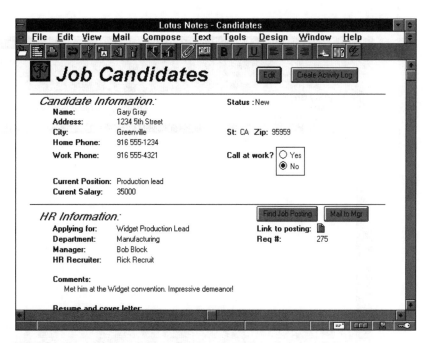

FIGURE 9.26a   Job Candidates form.

VIEWS

Candidate	Categorizes the candidate information and activities by the candidate who is applying for a position.
Department	Categorizes the candidate information and activities by the department filling a position and by the candidates who are applying for a position.
Recruiter	Categorizes the candidate information by the recruiter coordinating the hiring.
Requisition Number	Categorizes the candidate information by an internally generated position requisition number (see Figure 9.26b).

BUTTONS

Create Activity Log	Opens a new Activity Log document and inserts the job requisition information into the form.
Edit	Places the document in edit mode so that the user can change the document. It is visible only when the document is being read.
Find Job Posting	Assists users in bringing job posting information from the Job Posting database. The button opens a view in the Job Posting database. The user selects a document and presses an Add Link to Candidates button in the form to return to

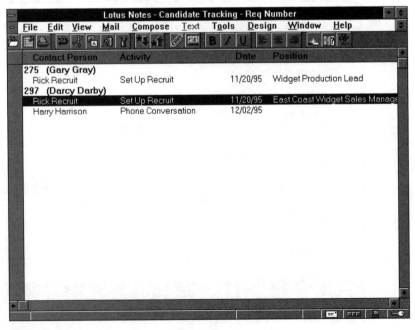

FIGURE 9.26b Job Candidates by Req Number view.

the Candidates form and paste in the position ID and title to the Candidate Tracking database.

Mail to Mgr	Forwards the entire Candidate form to the hiring manager.
Save	Saves the document and exits to the last open view. The button is visible only when the document is being edited.

ACCESS CONTROL

The default access control should be set to Editor for all Personnel users. No other users should have access to the database.

ENHANCE IT!

You can make this database even more powerful by:

1. Changing the database to a mail-in database and creating a custom form accessible from the Mail Compose menu that allows interviewers to send activity logs to the database.

USING CANDIDATE TRACKING

The database is intended for use by all **Personnel Users.** To track a candidate:

1. The **Personnel User** adds a document using the Candidates form.
2. The **Personnel User** links the candidate to the Job Posting database.
3. The **Personnel User** mails a copy of the information to the hiring manager.
4. The **Personnel User** logs activities as the candidate moves through the hiring process.

Job Postings and Descriptions (27)

PURPOSE

Growing companies offer many employment opportunities for current and potential employees. The entire employment process is time-consuming for both the manager who is requesting a new employee and for the Personnel department employee who is coordinating the search. The Job Posting and Descriptions database allows managers to create job descriptions, submit requests for positions to be filled, and create job postings.

FORMS USED

Job Descriptions Captures job descriptions for every position available at ABC Company. This form must be completed before a job requisition can be created (see Figure 9.27a).

Job Postings Created by the Job Requisition form once a requisition has been approved.

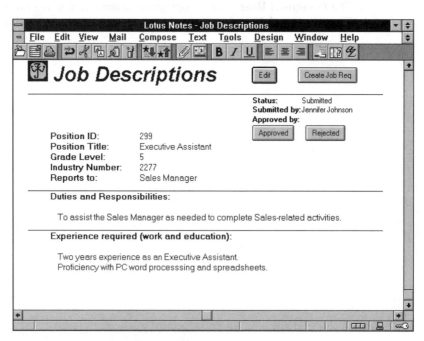

FIGURE 9.27a Job Descriptions form.

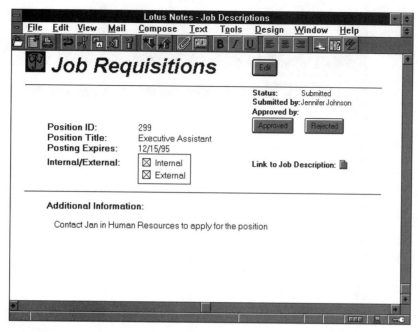

FIGURE 9.27b   Job Requisitions form.

Job Requisitions   Captures the information needed to schedule the move of employees from one building to the next (see Figure 9.27b).

VIEWS

Job Descriptions Industry ID	Displays the job descriptions by an industry standard ID.
Job Descriptions Position	Displays the job descriptions by the position description (see Figure 9.27c).
Job Descriptions Position ID	Displays the job descriptions by the position ID assigned to it by the Personnel department. The ID can be the same as the Industry ID.
Job Descriptions Report To	Categorizes the job description by the name of the manager to whom the employee would report.
Job Descriptions Status	Categorizes the job descriptions by the status (Submitted, Approved, or Rejected).
Job Postings by Type	Categorizes the job postings by type (Internal or External) and lists the jobs by job description.
Job Requisition Status	Categorizes the job requisitions by status (Submitted, Approved, or Rejected).
Job Requisitions, Type	Categorizes the job requisitions by the posting type (Internal or External) and lists the jobs in job description order.

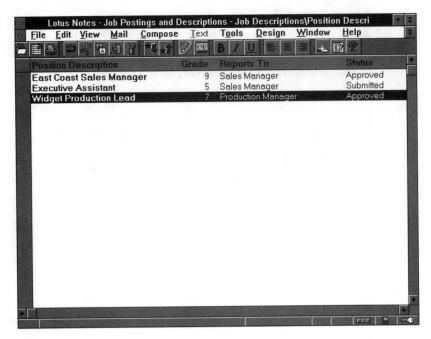

FIGURE 9.27c   Job Descriptions by Position view.

BUTTONS

Add Link, Candidates	Returns the job description and job title to the Candidate Tracking database after the Find Job Posting button has been used.
Approved	Updates the status of a job description or job requisition to Approved, adds the name of the approver to the Approved by field, and mails a message to the manager who requested the position. The button also changes a job requisition into a job posting document.
Create Job Req	Creates a Job Requisition document and copies the position ID and position description into the document.
Edit	Places the document in edit mode so that the user can change the document. It is visible only when the document is being read.
Rejected	Updates the status of a job description or job requisition to Rejected and mails a message to the manager who requested the position.
Save	Saves the document and exits to the last open view. The button is visible only when the document is being edited.
Submit	Sends a mail message to a user called HR (Human Resources) to notify him or her that a job requisition or job description has been submitted for approval.

ACCESS CONTROL

The default access control should be set to Read for all users, Author for managers and supervisors, and Editor for Personnel department employees. The Job Descriptions and Job Requisitions views should be limited to managers and supervisors who can hire employees.

ENHANCE IT!

You can make this database even more powerful by:

1. Adding a button to allow employees to apply for positions and mail the applications to a mail-enabled database.

USING JOB POSTINGS AND DESCRIPTIONS

The database is intended for all **Users, Managers, Supervisors,** and **Personnel Users.**

To create a job description:

1. The **Manager** or **Supervisor** adds a document using the Job Descriptions form.
2. The **Manager** or **Supervisor** pushes the Submit button, which sends a mail message to the **Personnel Users** in the Personnel department.
3. **Personnel Users** review the job description and push Approved or Rejected, notifying the **Manager** or **Supervisor** of the job descriptions status.

To create a job posting:

1. The **Manager** or **Supervisor** adds a document using the Job Requisitions form.
2. The **Manager** or **Supervisor** pushes the Submit button, which sends a mail message to the **Personnel Users** in the Personnel department.
3. **Personnel Users** review the job requisitions and push Approved or Rejected, notifying the **Manager** or **Supervisor** of the job requisition status.
4. Approved requisitions are converted to Job Postings using the Job Requisitions form after the Approved button has been pushed.

Performance Review (28)

PURPOSE

Performance reviews are a valuable method by which a manager can inform employees of their job performance on a regular basis. During reviews, both the manager and employee can agree on goals and review progress on goals from a previous review. The Performance Review database captures the goals for a quarter and allows the manager to update the goals with the results of the reviews.

FORMS USED

Goal Response	Allows the employee to respond to a Performance Review document.
Perform Goals	Captures the information that describes goals and the measurements used to evaluate the goals at review time.
Performance Review	Used to update the Performance Goal documents with the quarterly results (see Figure 9.28a).

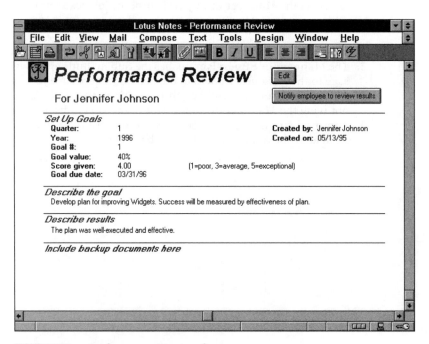

FIGURE 9.28a   Performance Review form.

VIEWS

Goals by Year and Quarter	Categorizes the performance goals by the year and quarter the goals are established and displays them in goal number order.
Goals/Reviews by Year and Quarter	Categorizes the performance goals and reviews by the year and quarter the goals were assigned and displays them in goal number order. Also displays the response documents created by the employee (see Figure 9.28b).
Reviews by Year and Quarter	Categorizes the performance reviews by the year and quarter the goals were assigned and displays them in goal number order.

BUTTONS

Edit	Places the document in edit mode so that the user can change the document. It is visible only when the document is being read.
Notify Employee to Review Results	Sends an electronic mail message to the employee asking him or her to review the performance goals or reviews.
Respond to Review	Creates a response document that allows an employee to add comments to a review given by supervisor.

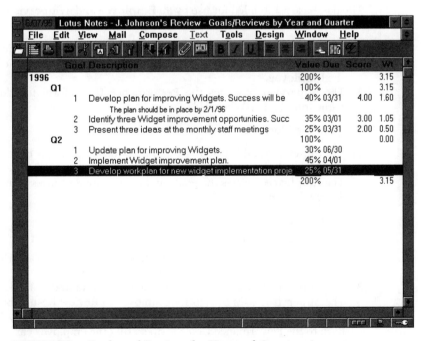

FIGURE 9.28b   Goals and Reviews by Year and Quarter view.

Save	Saves the document and exits to the last open view. The button is visible only when the document is being edited.
Save and Compose	Saves the document but also opens a new form so that a user can enter another document. The button is visible only when the document is being edited.

ACCESS CONTROL

The database should be accessible only by the employee and his or her supervisor. The default access control should be set to Author for the user, and Editor for the supervisor. The employee should not have access to the Performance Review form. The employee's access should be turned off while the supervisor is preparing the review so that misunderstandings do not occur while the supervisor is writing the review.

ENHANCE IT!

You can make this database even more powerful by:

1. Integrating the database with the Company goals database.

USING PERFORMANCE REVIEW

The database is intended for use by an **Employee** and a **Supervisor.** To create a performance review database:

1. The **Supervisor** creates the database from a Performance Review template.
2. The **Supervisor** changes the access control to give access to the **Supervisor** and the **Employee.**
3. The **Supervisor** changes the Performance Goals form to add the **Employee** name into the PerfWho field.

To create a performance goal:

1. The **Supervisor** adds a goal using the Performance Goals form.
2. The **Supervisor** sends a mail message to the Employee to review the goals.
3. The **Employee** reviews the goals and enters any responses using the Respond to Review button.

To complete a review:

1. The **Supervisor** selects a goal from a view.
2. The **Supervisor** uses the View menu to switch the form to a Performance Review form.
3. The **Supervisor** adds the results of the review and updates the score.
4. The **Supervisor** uses the Notify Employee to Review Results button to send the employee an electronic mail message to review the additions. The form reverts back to the Performance Goals form so that the employee can't edit it.
5. The **Employee** checks the review and enters any responses using the Respond to Review button.

Employee Handbook (29)

PURPOSE

The Employee Handbook is an essential tool to help employees understand company policies and procedures, as well as their employee benefits. In most cases, companies are required by law to provide their employees with a booklet about their benefits. However, these booklets are often taken home so employees need another source for the information when questions arise during the workday.

The Employee Handbook database provides an online source for the information that is also found in the printed handbook. The database should be identical in content to the printed handbook and accessible to all employees. When questions are sent to the Personnel department via e-mail, the Personnel employees can find the answer in this database, create a doclink to the proper document, and include the doclink in a mail message back to the employee. The message should also include a suggestion that the employee check the Employee Handbook database before calling Personnel.

FORMS USED

Employee Handbook   Captures the section numbers and topics for each document in the database. The first four fields gather the section numbers and are shown only during edits. The EmpHandbookHeading field combines the previous fields and builds a more attractive section title on the screen (see Figure 9.29a).

VIEWS

Handbook   Displays the documents in sections to resemble the table of contents of a book. The documents are sorted by section number, and each subtopic is indented. This view is the only one available, which means that users are always viewing the table of contents (see Figure 9.29b).

BUTTONS

Edit   Places the document in edit mode so that the user can change the document. It is visible only when the document is being read.

Save   Saves the document and exits to the last open view. The button is visible only when the document is being edited.

Save and Compose   Saves the document but also opens a new form so that a user can enter another document. The button is visible only when the document is being edited.

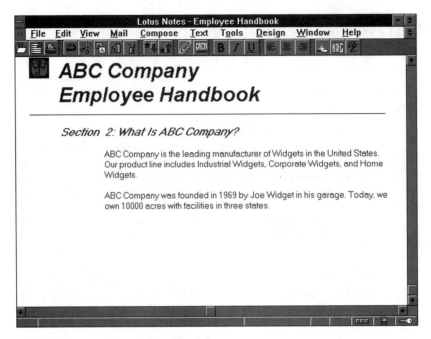

FIGURE 9.29a   Employee Handbook form.

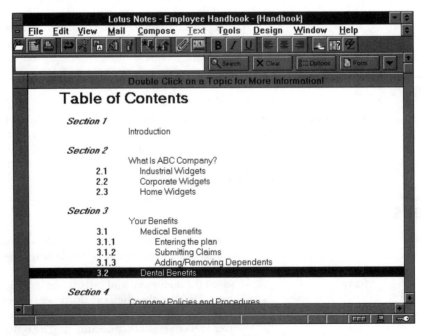

FIGURE 9.29b   Employee Handbook Table of Contents view.

ACCESS CONTROL

The default access control should be set to Reader for all users. The Personnel department should have Editor access.

ENHANCE IT!

You can make this database even more powerful by:

1. Including doclinks in those documents that refer to other documents in the Employee Handbook.
2. Adding a section for questions, and including a button that, when pushed, automatically mails the question to someone in the Personnel department.

USING EMPLOYEE HANDBOOK

The database is intended for all **Users** and the **Personnel department.** To review the handbook:

1. The **User** opens the database and selects an item from the view.
2. **Personnel** adds and modifies handbook documents as needed.

Timecards (30)

PURPOSE

All employees at ABC Company are required to submit timecards weekly to provide the Personnel department with the information needed to process the payroll and to provide Accounting with project information required to assign costs to a project. The Timecards database allows users to electronically submit timecards.

FORMS USED

Projects Captures the project IDs and descriptions for those projects that are to be tracked by the Timecards database.

Timecards Captures the timecard hours and project IDs for employees for one week. One document should be created for each project. Time not allotted to a project should go under an Administration project or a Paid Time Off project (see Figure 9.30a).

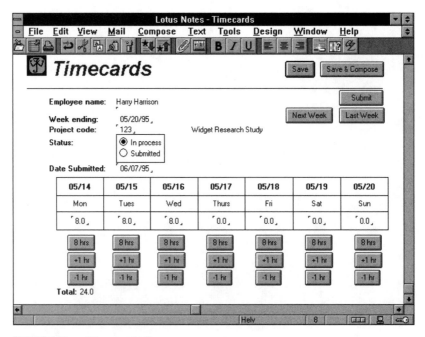

FIGURE 9.30a   Timecards form.

VIEWS

Export by Employee	Displays the timecards by the week ending date and employee so that they can be exported to a spreadsheet.
Export by Project	Displays the timecards by the week ending date and project ID so that they can be exported to a spreadsheet.
Projects	Displays the list of projects being tracked by the Timecards database.
Time Not Submitted	Categorizes the timecard information that has been entered, but not submitted, by the week ending date and by the employee name.
Timecards by Employee	Categorizes the timecards by the employee names and by the week ending date.
Timecards by Project	Categorizes the timecards by the project listed in the timecard, and lists the documents in reverse chronological order.
Timecards by Week Ending Date	Categorizes the timecards by the week ending date and by the employee name. Timecards not submitted are shown with an asterisk next to the project code (see Figure 9.30b).

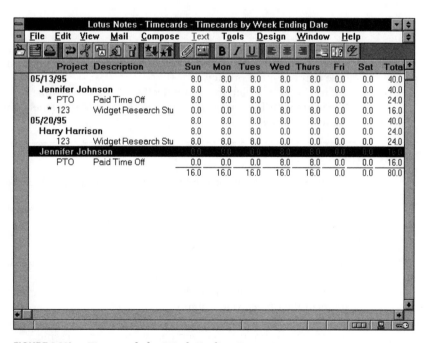

FIGURE 9.30b Timecards by Week Ending Date view.

BUTTONS

8 hrs, +1 hr, −1 hr	Stores eight hours in the field above the button, or adds or subtracts one hour from the value in that field.
Edit	Places the document in edit mode so that the user can change the document. It is visible only when the document is being read.
Last Week	Subtracts seven days from the week ending date.
Next Week	Adds seven days to the week ending date.
Save	Saves the document and exits to the last open view. The button is visible only when the document is being edited.
Save and Compose	Saves the document but also opens a new form so that a user can enter another document. The button is visible only when the document is being edited.
Submit	Saves the document and changes the timecard status from In Process to Submitted.

ACCESS CONTROL

The default access control should be set to Author for all users for the Timecards form. The Personnel and Accounting departments should have Editor access so that they can correct any mistakes found in the database.

ENHANCE IT!

You can make this database even more powerful by:

1. Using the Timecards form as a custom form in the electronic mail system so that the user can complete a timecard and send it to a mail-enabled timecards database that has more privacy.
2. Adding fields in which to automatically calculate overtime.
3. Integrating the Timecards database and Project Management database to reduce duplicate entries.

USING TIMECARDS

The database is intended for use by **Accounting, Personnel,** and all **Users.** To create a project:

1. **Accounting** adds a document using the Projects form.

To create a timecard:

1. The **User** adds one document for each project, including Paid Time Off and Admin time, using the Timecards form.
2. The **User** reviews the timecard entries and uses the Submit button to change the status of the timecard to Submitted.
3. **Accounting** uses the Export View by Project to export the weekly timecards to a spreadsheet or project management system for processing.
4. **Personnel** uses the Export View by Employee to export the weekly timecards to the payroll system or a spreadsheet for processing.

Benefits Requests (31)

PURPOSE

People change their addresses and personal information regularly. Medical, dental, and retirement benefits change at least once a year and, in some cases, quarterly. These changes often have to be implemented manually and generate a lot of paperwork.

The Benefits Requests database allows users to enter a request to change their benefits without paperwork. The Personnel department simply reviews the changes and updates its systems.

FORMS USED

401K Changes	Displays the current values for each of the 401K benefit options, and allows users to make their changes.
Address Changes	Displays the users' name and addresses, and allows them to make their changes.
Benefits Master Records	Displays the values stored in the documents shown in the Benefits Import view (see Figure 9.31a).
Change Document	Displays the buttons that allow users to select the type of change they want to make. Only one record in the database, the Instructions document, uses this form.
Status/Insurance Change	Displays the current values for each of the insurance options, for marital status, and number of dependents. The form allows users to make their changes (see Figure 9.31b).

VIEWS

401K Changes	Displays the new values on the 401K benefits requests.
Address Changes	Displays the new name and address information on the address change requests.
Benefits Import	Used by all forms in the database as a lookup table for all the beginning benefits' values, prior to changes. Also used to import benefits information into Notes.
Instructions	Displays one record that instructs the user on how to use the database. It includes three buttons that activate three different change forms (see Figure 9.31c).
Status/Insurance Change	Displays the new status changes on the benefits requests.

BUTTONS

401K Changes	Creates a document that allows users to log changes to their 401K selections.

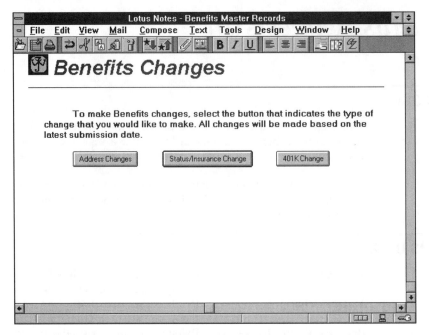

FIGURE 9.31a Benefits Master Records form.

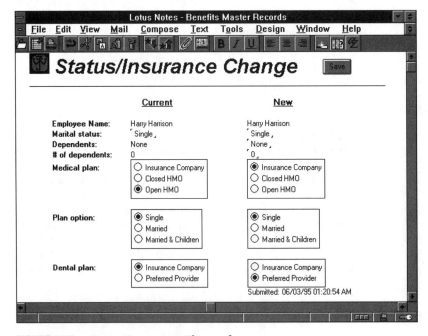

FIGURE 9.31b Status/Insurance Change form.

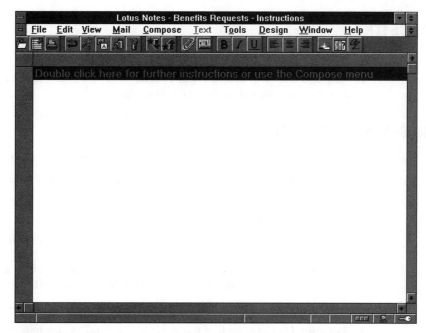

FIGURE 9.31c   Benefit Requests Instructions view.

Address Changes	Creates a document that allows users to log address changes to their database.
Edit	Places the document in edit mode so that the user can change the document. It is visible only when the document is being read.
Save	Saves the document and exits to the last open view. The button is visible only when the document is being edited.
Save and Compose	Saves the document but also opens a new form so that a user can enter another document. The button is visible only when the document is being edited.
Status/Insurance Change	Creates a document that allows users to change insurance and status information.

ACCESS CONTROL

The default access control should be set to Author for all users. The Personnel Users should have Editor access in case changes are necessary after a request is submitted. All views except Instructions should be accessible only by a group called Personnel Department.

ENHANCE IT!

You can make this database even more powerful by:

1. Adding a button enabling a user to send comments back to the requester or send an e-mail message that the task is complete.

USING BENEFIT REQUESTS

The database is intended for all **Users** and **Personnel.** To set up the database:

1. **Personnel** imports a list of benefits from the personnel system into the View called Benefits Import.

To create a Benefit Request:

1. The **User** selects the Instructions document or selects a form from the Compose menu.
2. The **User** selects the appropriate button to call up a form that allows him or her to change addresses, medical and dental selections, or 401K features.

To monitor the database and make the changes to the personnel system:

1. **Personnel** reviews each of the views in the database for new documents.
2. **Personnel** enters the changes manually into a personnel system or uses the view to create a file that can be imported into a personnel system.
3. **Personnel** deletes those records that have been exported or updated.

Training Schedules (32)

PURPOSE

Training provides employees with the latest skills needed to perform in today's high-tech business environment. New ABC Company employees receive training in the standard company word processing and spreadsheet applications, along with an intensive general orientation. All employees have access to a wealth of classes that will help them keep their skills up to date.

The Training Schedules database provides employees with a list of classes, a schedule of those classes, and the opportunity to sign up for classes. A complete outline or manual for the class is included in the Classes document.

FORMS USED

Classes	Captures the information about a class that is being offered so that a class schedule can be created (see Figure 9.32a).
Class Schedules	Contains the class name, its instructor, the time it's offered, and the location of the class, and allows the potential student to sign up for the class that is displayed (see Figure 9.32b).
Class Signup	Uses the information from the Class Schedules form to create a signup document with the user's name. Allows the user to confirm the signup before being added to the class list (see Figure 9.32c).

VIEWS

Class Roster	Categorizes the students signed up for a class by the date of the class, the class category, and the class title (see Figure 9.32d).
Classes by Category	Categorizes the classes offered by a user-defined category (see Figure 9.32e).
Schedule by Class	Categorizes the class offered by a user-defined class category and by the date that the class is being offered.
Schedule by Date	Categorizes the class offered by the date that the class is being offered and by a user-defined class category.
Schedule by Facility	Categorizes the class offered by the facility where the training will be given and by the date that the class is being offered.

BUTTONS

Confirm Class Signup	Saves the document and signs the user up for the class. The user can also use File Save to accomplish the same task.

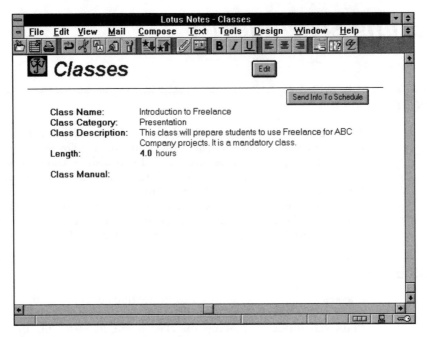

FIGURE 9.32a   Training Classes form.

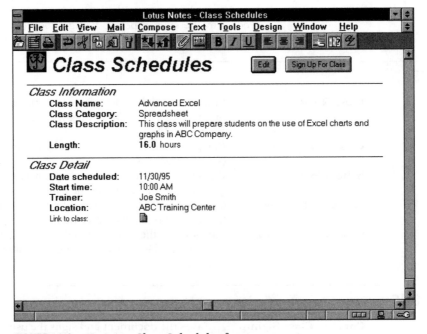

FIGURE 9.32b   Training Class Schedules form.

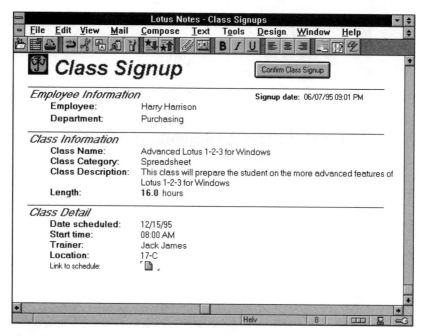

FIGURE 9.32c   Training Class Signup form.

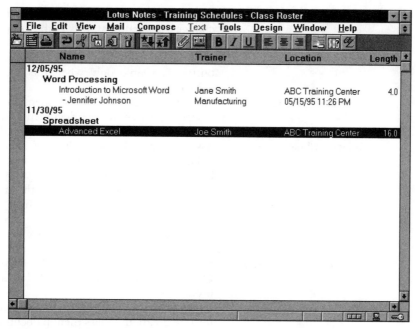

FIGURE 9.32d   Class Roster view.

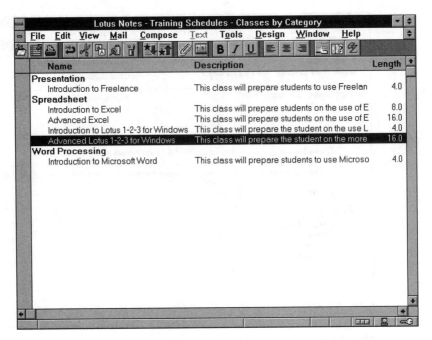

FIGURE 9.32e   Classes by Category view.

Edit	Places the document in edit mode so that the user can change the document. It is visible only when the document is being read.
Save	Saves the document and exits to the last open view. The button is visible only when the document is being edited.
Save and Compose	Saves the document but also opens a new form so that a user can enter another document. The button is visible only when the document is being edited.
Select a Class	Assists users in bringing class information into a Class Schedules form and creating a doclink to the class. The button opens the Class Category view from which the user selects a document. After the document is displayed, the user presses the Send Info To Schedule button to return to the Classes form, then pastes in the class information and a doclink to the class being scheduled.
Send Info To Schedule	Sends the information from the Classes form to the Class Schedules form after the Select a Class button is used.
Sign Up for a Class	Uses the information for a class on a Class Schedules form to create the Class Signup document.

ACCESS CONTROL

The default access control for the Class Signup form should be set to Author; it should be set to Read for all other forms. The Training department should have Editor access to make changes to any of the documents.

ENHANCE IT!

You can make this database even more powerful by:

1. Adding a field that holds a class size limit; using @ functions to calculate how many students are signed up for a class, and to tell users when the class is full.
2. Adding fields for off-site training, with address information and buttons to allow a third-party vendor to use Notes to notify students of approvals.
3. Including a manager's approval section.
4. Including a macro that automatically notifies students by mail that a class was cancelled or rescheduled.

USING TRAINING SCHEDULES

The database is intended for use by **Training Personnel** and all **Users.** To create a class:

1. **Training Personnel** adds a document using the Classes form.

To create a class schedule:

1. **Training Personnel** adds a document using the Class Schedules form.
2. **Training Personnel** uses the Select a Class button to link the Class Schedule to the class information.

To sign up for a class:

1. **Users** open the Classes by Category view and select a class document.
2. **Users** press the Signup for Class button to send a completed Class Signup document.
3. **Users** press the Confirm Class Signup button to complete the signup process.

Proposal Planning (33)

PURPOSE

Proposals from state and federal government agencies can often result in lucrative contracts and significant sales. A major proposal to generate those contracts and sales requires planning and teamwork to ensure that it is completed and delivered on time. The Proposal Planning database allows the Proposal team to log in the proposal and build an outline as a guide for developing a complete proposal.

FORMS USED

Proposal Check-in   Captures the information about the proposal, including the addresses and the names of the people assigned to the proposal team (see Figure 9.33a).

Proposal Outline   Adds an outline document for each topic in the proposal. The form can be accessed only from the Proposal Check-in form.

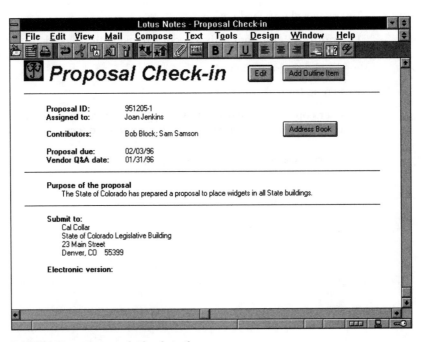

FIGURE 9.33a   Proposal Check-in form.

VIEWS

Proposal Number	Categorizes the proposals by number and lists the outline items in outline number order (see Figure 9.33b).

BUTTONS

Address Book	Displays the Name and Address Book so that team members can be added to the Contributors field.
Add Outline Item	Creates a proposal outline document and copies the proposal ID into the document.
Edit	Places the document in edit mode so that the user can change the document. It is visible only when the document is being read.
Save	Saves the document and exits to the last open view. The button is visible only when the document is being edited.

ACCESS CONTROL

The default access control should be set to Author for all Proposal writers and Editor for Proposal managers.

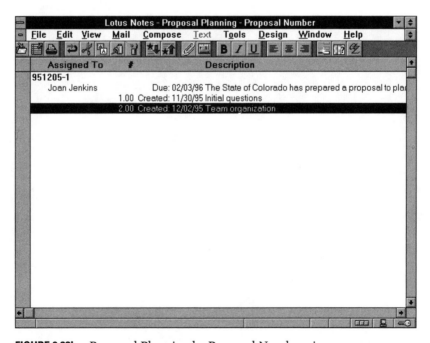

FIGURE 9.33b   Proposal Planning by Proposal Number view.

ENHANCE IT!

You can make this database even more powerful by:

1. Adding a button to notify the proposal team that a proposal has been received.
2. Adding mail-enabled fields in the Outline form so that a user can send comments to the person who created the outline item.

USING PROPOSAL PLANNING

The database is intended for use by all **Proposal Writers** and **Proposal Managers.** To create a Proposal:

1. The **Proposal Manager** adds a proposal document using the Proposal Check-in form.
2. The **Proposal Writer** adds to the outline by adding a document using the Proposal Outline document.

Project Tracking (34)

PURPOSE

At any given time, ABC Company has a number of active projects with 2 to 20 people working on them. Tracking them requires a coordinated effort from all employees and someone to manage the projects to make sure that each task is completed on time and within budget. The Project Tracking database holds the details of a project from the initial setup to daily time entries from employees. Using the many views, the project manager can monitor the people involved, the status of the project, and the time spent on each item.

FORMS

Project Cost	Captures nonlabor cost information for a project.
Project Document	Captures the information needed to set up a new project, including the project name, project managers, hourly estimates, and time line (see Figure 9.34a).
Task Assignment	Creates a task item for a person working on the project, including due dates and actual hours worked on the task. The project manager can mail the assignment to that user's Notes mailbox. The item will show up in the user's action item list in the mail database (see Figure 9.34b).
Time Entry	Captures time information by employee for tasks in the project. Employees can add time entries daily or even several times a day (see Figure 9.34c).

VIEWS

Enter Time	Displays the time entry form and allows a time document to be entered.
Lookup Dept Manager	Checks the contents of the department manager field to determine if the manager is still active.
Mail Assignment	Sends an action item to another user's Notes Mail database.
Persons, Customer Lead	Categorizes all the projects by the name of the customer person leading the project and by project name. Displays the project document, all the tasks, and all time entries for the project.
Persons, Direct Report	Categorizes all the projects by direct report (person reporting to the president of the company) and by project name. Displays the project document, all the tasks, and all time entries for the project.
Persons, Manager	Categorizes all the projects by manager name and by project name. Displays the project document, all the tasks, and all time entries for the project.

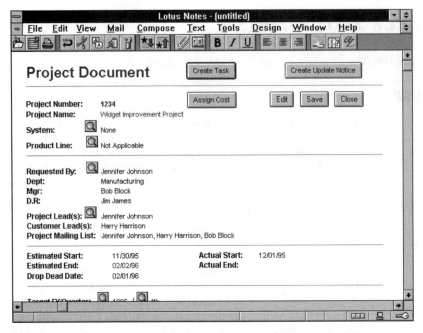

FIGURE 9.34a Project Tracking Project Document form.

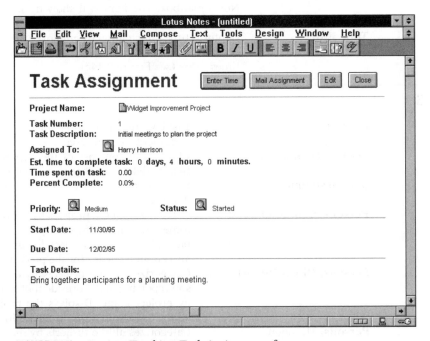

FIGURE 9.34b Project Tracking Task Assignment form.

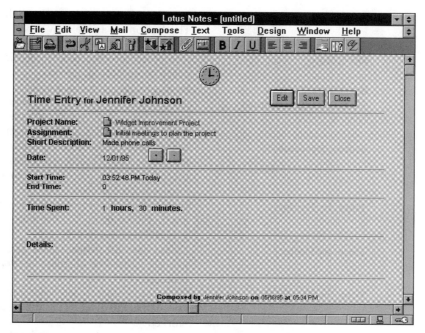

FIGURE 9.34c   Project Tracking Time Entry form.

Persons, Project Lead	Categorizes all the projects by the project manager name and by project name. Displays the project document, all the tasks, and all time entries for the project.
Persons, Requested by, All	Categorizes all the projects by the name of the person requesting the project and by project name. Displays the project document, all the tasks, and all time entries for the project.
Persons, Requested by, IP	Categorizes the projects that are in progress by the name of the person requesting the project and by project name. Displays the project document, all the tasks, and all time entries for the project.
Projects, All Projects	Categorizes all the projects by project name and displays the project document, all the tasks, and all time entries for the project.
Projects, Completion Approved	Categorizes the projects by project name and displays only those projects that are completed. Displays the project document, all the tasks, and all time entries for the project.
Projects, In Progress	Categorizes the projects by project name and displays only those projects that are incomplete. Displays the project document, all the tasks, and all time entries for the project (see Figure 9.34d).

Save	Saves the document and exits to the last open view. The button is visible only when the document is being edited.
Set Billing	Composes an electronic mail message using the user's Notes Mail database.
Start Time Now	Begins logging time on a task.
Status, Project Names	Categorizes the projects by status and by project name. Displays the project document, all the tasks, and all time entries for the project.
Status, Systems	Categorizes the projects by status and by the system name stored in the project document. Displays the project document, all the tasks, and all time entries for the project.
Time, by Person	Categorizes all time entries by the person who entered the time and by the date of the entry for all projects that are in progress.
Time, by Project	Categorizes all project tasks and time entries by project name and displays estimated and actual hours worked.
Time, by Status	Categorizes all project tasks and time entries by task name and displays estimated and actual hours worked.
Time, by Week	Categorizes all the projects by the week in which time was logged, by the name of the person performing the task, and by project name. Displays the project document, all the tasks, and all time entries for the project.

MACROS

Change Project Name	Changes the name of the project in each Project document.
Create Billing	Displays the Billing view and stores the direct report and department values in each of the project fields so that the Cost views will have the information needed to display cost by direct report and department.
Cost and Time by Project	Categorizes all project tasks and time entries by project name and displays actual hours and costs.
Costs, Variable Costs by Project	Categorizes all project tasks and time entries by project name and displays variable costs only.
Billing	Categorizes all the projects by the month of activity, by direct report, and by project name. Displays the project document, all the tasks, and all time entries for the project, with total hours calculated for internal billing purposes.

BUTTONS

 Indicates that the field next to the icon is a lookup field. The user must hit the Enter key to bring up the list.

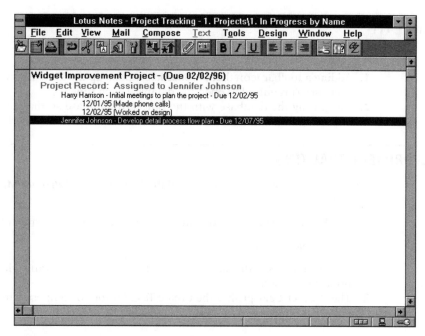

FIGURE 9.34d   Projects in Progress view.

+, −, and Date Buttons	Adjusts the due date in the Task Assignment form by one day (+, −) and by the values listed on each button.
+5, −5, to +4 hrs, −4 hrs	Adjusts the time spent on a task in a range of five minutes (+5, −5) to four hours (+4, −4).
Assign Cost	Assigns a cost to the project.
Change Department	Changes the department name for the project.
Change Direct Report	Changes the name of the Direct Report person for the project.
Change Manager	Change the name of the manager for the project.
Close	Exits the form and returns to the active view.
Compute Time Spent	Calculate the time spent on a task.
Create Task	Displays the Task Assignment form so that a task can be created.
Create Update Notice	Creates a mail message to all project participants that notifies them of the progress of the project.
Edit	Places the document in edit mode so that the user can change the document. It is visible only when the document is being read.
End Time Now	Stops logging time for a task.

ACCESS CONTROL

The default access control should be set to Author for all users. Project Managers and database administrators should be given Editor access.

ENHANCE IT!

You can make this database even more powerful by:

1. Adding a toolbar icon that automatically pops up the Time Entry window so that users aren't required to open the database each time.
2. Integrating the database with the timecard database so that employees are not required to enter their time twice.

USING PROJECT TRACKING

The database is intended for use by all **Project Users** and **Project Managers.** To add a project:

1. The **Project User** adds a document using the Project Document form.

To add a project task:

1. The **Project User** displays the Projects in Progress by Name view and selects a project document.
2. The **Project User** pushes the Create Task button to compose a task document.

To create time entries:

1. The **Project User** displays the Projects in Progress by Name view and selects a task document.
2. The **Project User** pushes the Enter Time button to compose a time entry document.

To update all documents when a project name changes:

1. The **User** executes the Change Project Name macro.

To update the billing hours for all projects:

1. The **User** executes the Create Billing macro.

To update the project as it progresses:

1. The **Project User** displays the Projects in Progress by Name view and selects a project document.
2. The **Project User** changes the status as needed.
3. The **Project User** displays the Projects in Progress by Name view and selects a task document.
4. The **Project User** changes the estimated time to complete as needed.

To mark a project as complete:

1. The **Project User** displays the Projects in Progress by Name view and selects a project document.
2. The **Project User** changes the status to Completion Approved and updates the actual completion date.

Capital Planning (35)

PURPOSE

Capital expenditures are vital to the long-term growth of a company. Capital spent wisely ensures that facilities, equipment, and computer systems are maintained, enhanced, and improved to keep the company running at its peak efficiency. The Capital Planning database brings together the capital plans for all departments so that the financial planners at the company can analyze the requests and approve the projects that will provide the highest return on the capital investment. Once the projects are approved, the database can be used to generate purchase requisitions against the projects so that expenditures can be tracked against the capital budget.

FORMS USED

Add Detail Items
Captures the line items of a purchase requisition, communicates with the requester, and manages the purchase approval process. The form can be accessed only from the Purchase Requisition form.

Capital Projects
Captures the details of the capital request, including the expected cash flow dates, a full description of the project, and return-on-investment calculations. The bottom of the form is used for the financial planners to communicate with the requester and approve or deny the request (see Figure 9.35a).

Purchase Request
Creates a purchase requisition using the capital project ID and captures the accounting information needed to process the requisition. The form also controls the approval process for the requestor and his or her supervisor (see Figures 9.35b and c).

VIEWS

Priority 1 by Department
Displays only priority 1 items and categorizes them by a secondary priority assigned by Accounting. The multiple priorities eliminate all items that do not have a priority 1 while allowing the user to further prioritize the items in the priority 1 category.

Projects by Department
Categorizes and totals the capital projects by the department that submitted the projects (see Figure 9.35d).

Projects by Project ID
Displays the projects by a project ID assigned by the Accounting department.

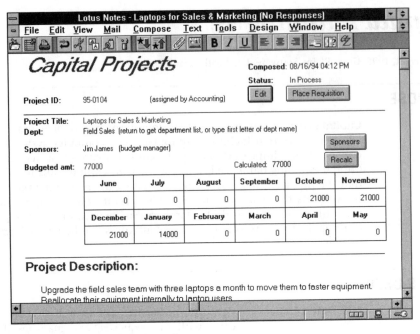

FIGURE 9.35a   Capital Projects form.

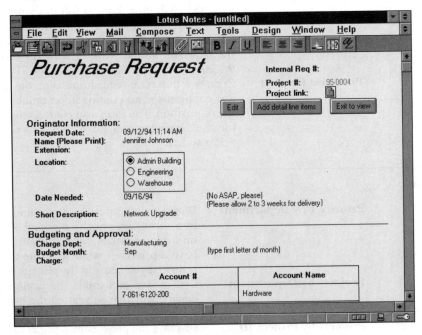

FIGURE 9.35b   Capital Purchase Request form.

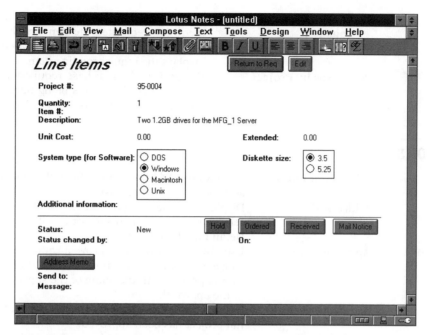

FIGURE 9.35c   Capital Purchase Request Line Items form.

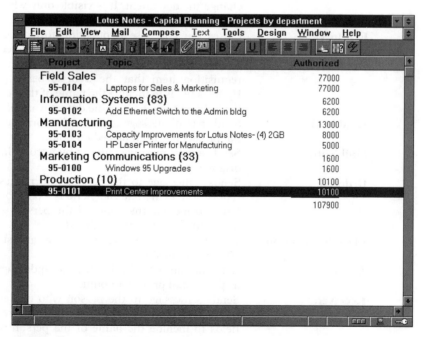

FIGURE 9.35d   Capital Projects by Department view.

Purchases, Department/ Project	Categorizes the purchase requisition by the department that requested the item and by the project ID for which the item is being purchased. The view also displays the requisition line items.
Purchases by Project	Categorizes the purchase requisition by the project ID for which the item is being purchased. The view also displays the requisition line items.

BUTTONS

Add Detail Lines	Displays the Add Detail Line Items form so that a user can add a line item to a requisition.
Address Memo	Displays the Name and Address Book so that a user can select a person to whom a message will be sent from the Add Detail Line Item form.
Approve	Used by supervisors to approve a capital project before it is considered available for review by Accounting. Updates the capital project with the name of the supervisor and the date of the approval.
Approval Notice	Sends a mail message to the project originator that the capital project has been approved.
Denied Notice	Sends a mail message to the project originator that the capital project has been denied.
Edit	Places the document in edit mode so that the user can change the document. It is visible only when the document is being read.
Exit to View	Closes the Purchase Requisition form and returns to the view from which the requisition was selected or composed.
Hold	Sends a message to the person who requested a purchase requisition item that the item is being placed on hold. Updates fields to include the name of the person who placed the hold on the item and the date it was held.
Hold Notice	Sends a mail message to the project originator that the capital project has been placed on hold.
Mail Notice	Sends a mail message entered by Accounting to the project originator.
Ordered	Sends a message to the person who requested a purchase requisition item that the item is being ordered. Updates fields to include the name of the person who ordered the item and the date it was ordered.
Place Requisition	Creates a purchase requisition form and stores the project ID in the requisition.
Recalc	Refreshes all fields in the form to update calculations such as the capital project amount.
Received	Sends a message to the person who requested a purchase requisition item that the item has been received. Updates fields to include the name of the person who marked the item received and the date it was marked.

Return to Req	Saves the requisition line item document and returns to the requisition screen.
Rework Notice	Sends a mail message to the project originator that the capital project requires rework. The person sending the message can add comments in the form that will be sent as a mail message.
Save	Saves the document and exits to the last open view. The button is visible only when the document is being edited.
Sponsors	Displays the Name and Address Book so that the originator can select the person who is sponsoring the project, usually a department manager.

ACCESS CONTROL

The default access control should be set to Author for all forms. The access should be limited to users who are approved for entering capital projects. All Accounting users should be given Editor access to all forms. No other users should have access to the database.

ENHANCE IT!

You can make this database even more powerful by:

1. Integrating the purchase requisitions into an Accounting package using third-party software.

USING CAPITAL PLANNING

The database is intended for use by all **Capital Project Users** and **Accounting Users.** To create and process a capital project:

1. **Capital Project Users** use the Capital Projects form to create a capital project.
2. The **Supervisor** of the **Capital Project Users** selects a capital project and pushes the Approved button to mark the project as approved by the department.
3. **Accounting Users** review the project and send notices for rework, denial, or approval.
4. **Accounting Users** assign a project ID to the capital project.

To create a purchase requisition:

1. The **Capital Project User** displays the Projects by Department view to display a capital project.
2. The **Capital Project User** pushes the Place Requisition button to display the Purchase Requisition form.
3. The **Capital Project User** enters the requisition information and pushes the Add Detail Line Items button to add line items.
4. The **Capital Project User** enters the line item information.
5. The **Supervisor** of the **Capital Project Users** approves the requisition.

To process a purchase requisition:

1. The **Accounting User** reviews the capital project and determines whether the requisition is valid.
2. The **Accounting User** approves the requisition.
3. The **Accounting User** reviews the detail line items and approves each line item.
4. The **Accounting User** orders the line items and pushes the Ordered button.
5. The **Accounting User** receives the items and pushes the Received button.

Meetings (36)

PURPOSE

It's often difficult to find a meeting room that is big enough, has the proper equipment, and is not being used. Once you've found the room, it's even more difficult to find a time convenient for everyone. The Meeting Database holds the configuration of each meeting room and provides users with a place to schedule the use of the rooms. The database also allows users to schedule meetings and view the schedules of attendees.

FORMS USED

Meeting Confirmation   Allows users to confirm that they will be attending a meeting.

Meeting Rooms   Captures the room information, including features and size, and allows the storage of a room diagram (see Figure 9.36a).

Schedule Meeting   Captures the information needed to schedule a meeting (see Figure 9.36b).

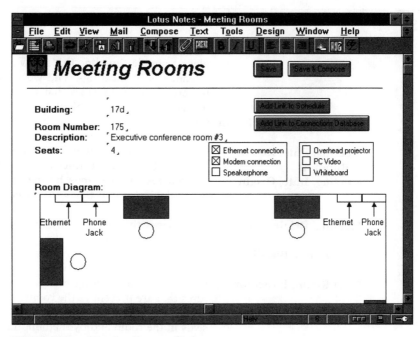

FIGURE 9.36a   Meeting Rooms form.

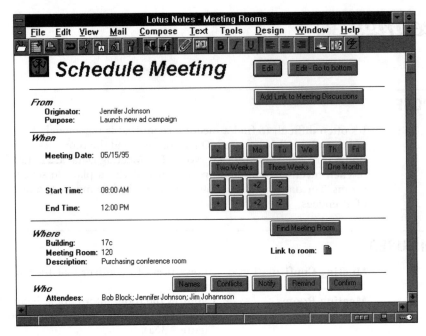

FIGURE 9.36b   Schedule Meeting form.

VIEWS

Attendee Time by Date	Categorizes the schedules by attendee names and displays a simple time line that shows the times that the attendee is in meetings. The view font is Courier (a nonproportional font) so that the space for the time line characters can be calculated.
Meeting, Building, Room	Categorizes the meetings by building, room, and date of the meeting. Sorts the meetings by start time.
Meeting, Date, Room, Building	Categorizes the meetings by meeting date, room, and building. Sorts the meetings by start time.
Meeting, Date, Origin	Categorizes the meetings by meeting date in reverse chronological order. Sorts the meetings by originator and start time.
Meeting, Originator	Categorizes the meetings by originator and sorts the meetings by start time.
Meet Room, Building	Categorizes the meeting rooms by building and sorts the rooms by room number.
Meet Room, Projector	Categorizes the meeting rooms by the projection features that are present in the room.
Meet Room, Seats	Categorizes the meeting rooms by the number of the seats in the room and by the building. Sorts the rooms by room number.

Meet Room, Telecom	Categorizes the meeting rooms by the type of telecommunications features in them. Sorts the rooms by building and room number.
Time line, Date, Building, Room	Categorizes the meetings by meeting date, building, and room number. Sorts the meetings by start time and displays a simple time line that shows the times that the room is busy. The view font is Courier (a nonproportional font) so that the space needed for the time line characters can be calculated (see Figures 9.36c and d).

BUTTONS

+, −, Mo, Tu, We, etc.	Modifies the meeting date by adding one day (+), subtracting one day (−), changing the day of the week (Mo, Tu, etc.), or changing it by one, two, or three weeks.
+, −, +2, −2	Modifies the start or end time by adding one hour (+) or two hours (+2) or by subtracting one hour (−) or two hours (−2).
Add Link to Schedule	Sends the room number, room description, and building for the meeting room that was selected in the Schedule Meeting form in this database. A user must push the Find Meeting button in the Schedule Meeting form before this button is used.

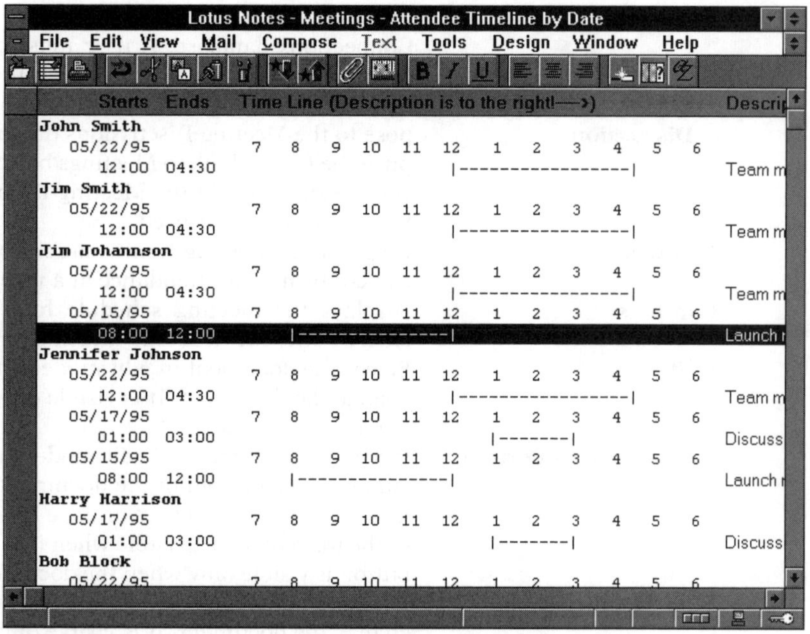

FIGURE 9.36c Meetings Time Line by Date view.

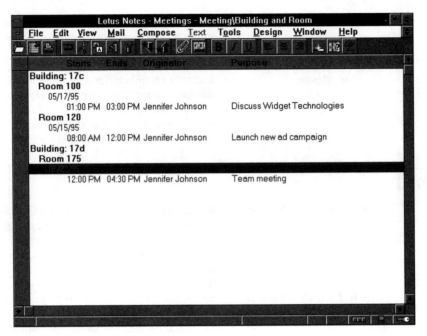

FIGURE 9.36d Meetings by Building and Room view.

Add Link to Connection Database	Sends the meeting room description and a doclink for the meeting room that was selected in the Telecom Connections database. A user must push the Link to Meeting Room button before this button is used.
Add Link to Meeting Discussions	Sends the meeting date, originator, and meeting purpose to the Meeting Discussions database. A user must push the Create Link to Meetings button in the Meeting Discussions form in the Meeting Discussions database before this button is used.
Confirm	Displays the Meeting Confirmation form so that users can confirm their attendance at a meeting.
Conflicts	Displays the meeting schedule for the last attendee entered onto the Schedule Meeting form.
Edit	Places the document in edit mode so that the user can change the document. It is visible only when the document is being read.
Edit—Move to Bottom	Places the document in edit mode but also moves the cursor to the bottom of the document. This eliminates have to use the scroll bars or Page Down to see the part of the form that isn't visible when it is first opened. The button is visible only when the document is being read.
Find Meeting Room	Places the document in edit mode so that the user can change the document. It is visible only when the document is being read.

Names	Displays the Name and Address Book so that potential attendees can be added to the meeting schedule.
Notify	Sends an electronic mail message to all attendees to inform them about the meeting time, location, and purpose.
Remind	Sends an electronic mail message to all attendees to remind them about the meeting time, location, and purpose.
Save	Saves the document and exits to the last open view. The button is visible only when the document is being edited.
Save and Compose	Saves the document but also opens a new form so that a user can enter another document. The button is visible only when the document is being edited.

ACCESS CONTROL

The default access control should be set to Author for all users.

ENHANCE IT!

You can make this database even more powerful by:

1. Adding a button to interface with scanning software to automatically save the scanned image of a meeting room diagram.

USING MEETINGS

The database is intended for all **Users.** To create a meeting room entry:

1. The **User** adds a document using the Meeting Rooms form.

To create a meeting schedule entry:

1. The **User** adds a document using the Schedule Meeting form.
2. The **User** pushes the Find Meeting Room button to create a doclink to the Meeting Room documents.
3. The **User** pushes the Names button to add an attendee, the Conflicts button to view an attendee's schedule, the Notify button to notify attendees of the meeting, or the Remind button to remind users of the meeting.

To confirm a meeting schedule entry:

1. The **User** recalls the schedule meeting document using the doclink in the mail message.
2. The **User** presses the Confirm button to create a document that shows the originator the date and time that the **User** confirmed attendance at the meeting.

Meeting Discussions (37)

PURPOSE

The minutes of every meeting provide attendees with a confirmation of what was discussed, what steps were agreed upon, and when the next meeting should take place. The Meeting Discussion Database holds the meeting minutes and provides all users with a forum for adding follow-up information or comments to support the results of the meeting.

FORMS USED

Meeting Discussions	Captures the meeting attendees, the date and purpose of the meeting, and the meeting minutes (see Figure 9.37a).
Meeting Responses	Allows users to create a response document for a meeting so that they can add their comments.
Meeting Response to Response	Allows users to create a response to a response document for a meeting so that they can add their comments.

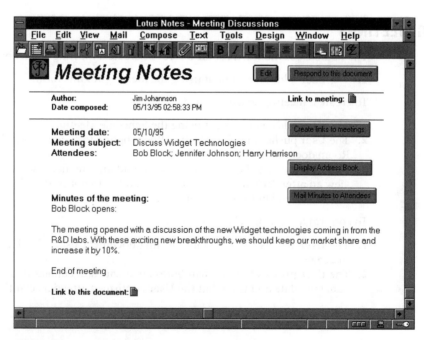

FIGURE 9.37a   Meeting Notes form.

VIEWS

Attendee	Categorizes the meeting discussions by attendee and meeting date. Displays the meeting topic and the subject of each response.
Author of Minutes	Categorizes the meeting discussions by the author of the minutes and by meeting date. Displays the meeting topic and the subject of each response.
Meeting Date	Categorizes the meeting discussions by meeting date, and displays the meeting topic and the subject of each response (see Figure 9.37b).

BUTTONS

Create Link to Meeting	Assists users in bringing meeting information from the Meetings database. When pressed, the button opens a view in the Meetings database, the user selects a document and presses the Add Links to Meeting button in the form to return to the Meetings Discussion form. The Add Link button pastes the attendees, meeting purpose, and meeting date into the Meeting Discussions form.
Display Address Book	Displays the Name and Address Book so that the user can add attendees to the meeting.

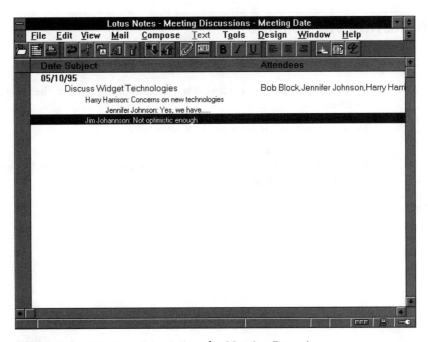

FIGURE 9.37b   Meetings Discussions by Meeting Date view.

Mail Minutes to Attendees	Creates a doclink to the meeting minutes document and sends it to all attendees, notifying them that they can use it to review the meeting minutes.
Respond to Document	Creates a response document so that a user can add comments about the meeting.
Save	Saves the document and exits to the last open view. The button is visible only when the document is being edited.

ACCESS CONTROL

The default access control should be set to Author for the users who will be adding the process improvement documents. The managers of the process improvement activity should have Editor access so that they can add comments in the documents when a further explanation may be required. The managers will also need to add the methodology steps.

ENHANCE IT!

You can make this database even more powerful by:

1. Adding buttons to create a doclink to any presentations in the Presentation database used during the meeting.
2. Adding buttons to create to-do items in the Notes Mail system and link them to the meeting minutes.

USING MEETING DISCUSSIONS

The database is intended for all **Users.** To create a meeting discussion and store the minutes:

1. The **User** creates a meeting discussion document using the Meeting Discussions form.

To add a response or response to a response:

1. The **User** selects a document from a view and displays it.
2. The **User** pushes the Respond to This Document button and saves the completed response document.

Status Reports (38)

PURPOSE

Status reports are often an effective tool to help employees notify their managers of the progress of their ongoing tasks and key issues that may need to be addressed. The Status Reports database consolidates all the status reports into a single database so that a manager can review all the information in one place. It also eliminates the piles of electronic mail messages that staff members may have used previously to keep managers up to date.

FORMS

Confidential Issue	Captures in the status report information about a confidential issue that must be addressed. Confidentiality is maintained using a ReaderNames field. The form is accessible only from the Status Report form.
Confidential Response to a Response	Captures a confidential response to a response document. Confidentiality is maintained using a ReaderNames field. The form is accessible only from the Status Report form.
Confidential Status	Captures a confidential status item. Confidentiality is maintained using a ReaderNames field. The form is accessible only from the Status Report form.
Defaults	Builds a list of employees who can add status reports to the database. The form is accessible only from the Set Default macro.
Non-Secure Discussion	Captures discussions about a status report. The form is accessible only from the Status Report form (see Figure 9.38a).
Non-Secure Issue	Captures information about an issue that is not confidential but must be addressed in the status report. The form is accessible only from the Status Report form.
Response to Response	Captures a response to a response document. The form is accessible only from the Status Report form.
Status Report	Creates a status report document and allows users to create other documents using the Respond button (see Figure 9.38b).

VIEWS

Defaults	Displays a list of the employees who can add status reports to the database.
Status Reports by Person	Categorizes a status report by the person who submitted it.

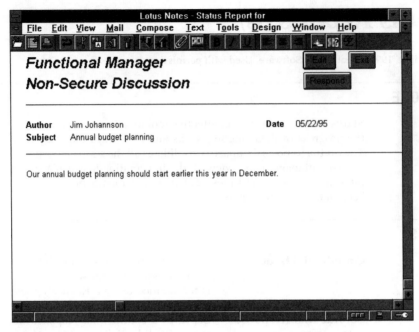

FIGURE 9.38a   Status Report Discussion form.

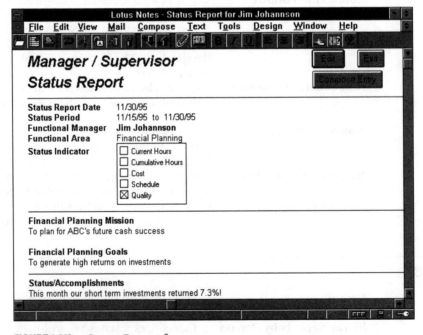

FIGURE 9.38b   Status Report form.

Status Reports by Week   Categorizes a status report by the week covered by the status report and by the person who submitted the report (see Figure 9.38c).

BUTTONS

Compose Entry	Lists the forms that are available for entering confidential and non-secure issues and discussions.
Edit	Places the document in edit mode so that the user can change the document. It is visible only when the document is being read.
Exit	Closes the windows and returns to the active view.
Respond	Creates a response to the current document.
Save	Saves the document and exits to the last open view. The button is visible only when the document is being edited.

MACROS

Set Defaults	Accesses a hidden form to add the current user to the list of people who can add status reports to the database.

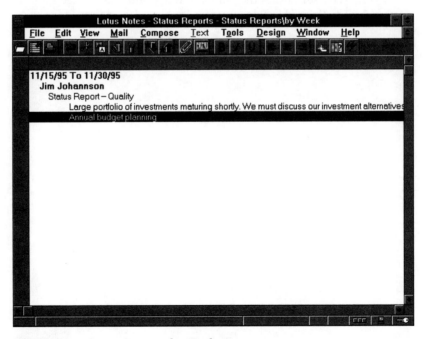

FIGURE 9.38c   Status Reports by Week view.

ACCESS CONTROL

The default access control should be set to Author for all users. Only users listed in the Defaults view can add information. The department manager should be given Editor access. All supervisors who are allowed to view confidential information should be added to a group list, and the group should be included in the Reader-Names fields of the confidential forms.

ENHANCE IT!

You can make this database even more powerful by:

1. Integrating the database with the Company Goals database to automatically bring goals in for each manager and supervisor.

USING STATUS REPORTS

The database is intended for all **Users** and **Managers.** To create a default document:

1. The **User** executes the Set Defaults macro and adds a document using the Defaults form.

To create a status report:

1. The **User** adds a document using the Status Reports form.
2. The **User** pushes the Compose Entry button and selects a form to complete.
3. The **User** adds a document using the selected form.

Sales Data Warehouse (39)

PURPOSE

Sales management is critical to the success of a company, because sales generate the revenue that pays the bills. Sales and marketing managers need up-to-date information about the sales of their products to help them make decisions on marketing campaigns, product strategies, and customer satisfaction. The Sales Data Warehouse meets these needs by providing the sales and marketing managers with detail information from the accounting system in a format that is easy to review and summarize.

FORMS USED

Sales Data Warehouse   Captures detailed sales-transaction information, including customer, inventory, and salesperson details (see Figure 9.39a).

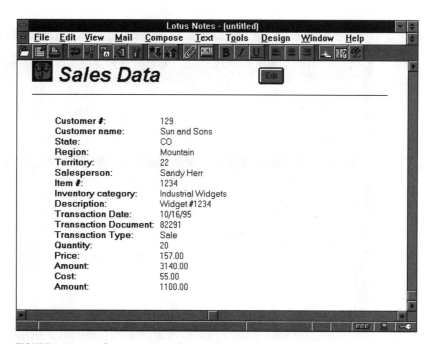

FIGURE 9.39a   Sales Data Warehouse form.

VIEWS

Import View	Contains all of the fields in the Sales Data Warehouse form and accepts a text file or spreadsheet information to load the database.
Item, Customer, Date	Categorizes and totals sales by inventory item number and customer. Sorts the transactions by date.
Item, Date, Document	Categorizes and totals sales by inventory item and transaction date. Sorts the transactions by document number.
Item, Region, Date	Categorizes and totals sales by inventory item and sales region. Sorts the transactions by date.
Product Line, Item, Region	Categorizes and totals sales by product line, inventory item, and sales region. Sorts the transactions by date.
Product Line, Region, Item	Categorizes and totals sales by product line, sales region, and inventory item. Sorts the transactions by date (see Figure 9.39b).
Region, Territory, Salesperson	Categorizes and totals sales by sales region, territory, and salesperson. Sorts the transactions by date.
Salesperson, Customer	Categorizes and totals sales by salesperson and customer. Sorts the transactions by document number.
Sales, Customer	Categorizes and totals sales by customer and sorts the transactions by document number.

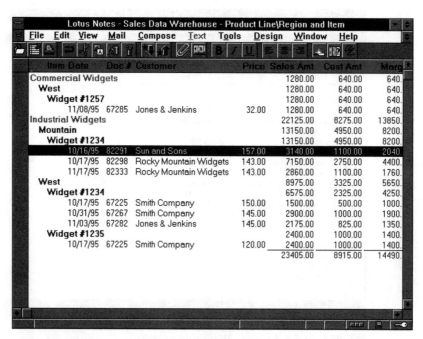

FIGURE 9.39b Sales by Product Line, Region, and Item view.

Sales, Date, Document	Categorizes and totals sales by transaction date and sorts the transactions by document number.
Sales, Document	Displays and totals sales by document number.

BUTTONS

Edit	Places the document in edit mode so that the user can change the document. It is visible only when the document is being read.
Save	Saves the document and exits to the last open view. The button is visible only when the document is being edited.
Save and Compose	Saves the document but also opens a new form so that a user can enter another document. The button is visible only when the document is being edited.

ACCESS CONTROL

The default access control should be set to Read for all sales managers. The employees responsible for updating this database should be given Editor access so that they can perform the imports and clean up any problems with the database.

ENHANCE IT!

You can make this database even more powerful by:

1. Using development tools to automate the import of information into this database.

USING SALES DATA WAREHOUSE

The database is intended for use by all **Sales Managers** and the **Sales Database Administrator.** To create the sales documents in the Sales Data Warehouse:

1. The **Sales Database Administrator** transfers the new sales transactions from the accounting system into a text file or spreadsheet.
2. The **Sales Database Administrator** imports the transactions into the Sales Data Warehouse using the Imports view.

General Ledger Data Warehouse (40)

PURPOSE

The accounting system in any company holds a wealth of financial information that can help financial managers make better decisions. These systems often give users the capability to perform inquiries on only one account at a time or create financial reports that can take a long time. In addition, accounting software is often limited to a certain number of users, restricting the number of budget managers who can be on the system at any one time.

With a General Ledger (G/L) Data Warehouse, budget managers can review all the G/L transactions without inquiries or reports. They can research budget concerns or anomalies instead of calling Accounting and asking questions.

FORMS USED

G/L Accounts	Captures information about a G/L account and the balances by month, quarter, and year (see Figure 9.40a).
G/L Transactions	Captures detailed transaction information. The import should also place the transaction amount in the proper time period (see Figure 9.40b).

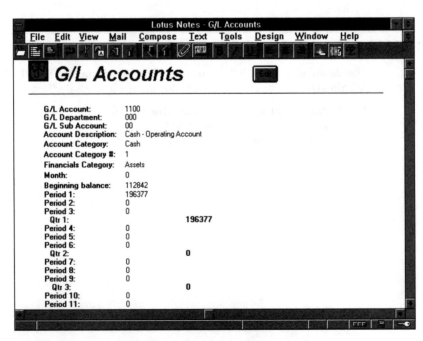

FIGURE 9.40a   General Ledger Data Warehouse Accounts form.

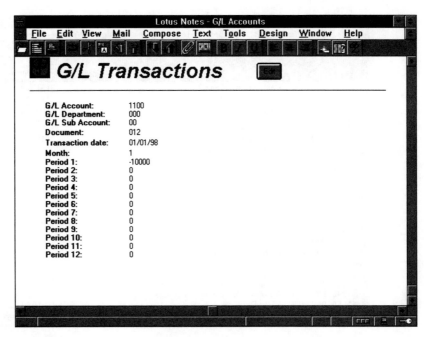

FIGURE 9.40b   General Ledger Data Warehouse Transactions form.

VIEWS

Account Category Categorizes the G/L accounts and transactions by an account category. Most accounts systems have a category to help build automatic financial statements.

Expenses—High Dollar Amount Sorts the G/L accounts by the highest year-to-date dollar amount.

Financial Statement Category Categorizes the G/L accounts and transactions by the five standard financial categories. A hidden column is included so that the documents can be sorted by Assets, Liabilities, Equity, Revenues, and Expenses.

G/L Account Sorts the G/L accounts by account number (see Figure 9.40c).

G/L Account with Transactions Categorizes the G/L accounts by account number, displaying the account balance as the first item in the list of transactions for that account. A hidden field sorts the transactions so that the balances show first, followed by the transactions in chronological order.

G/L Account Import Used for importing G/L accounts into the G/L Data Warehouse.

G/L Transaction Import Used for importing G/L transactions into the G/L Data Warehouse.

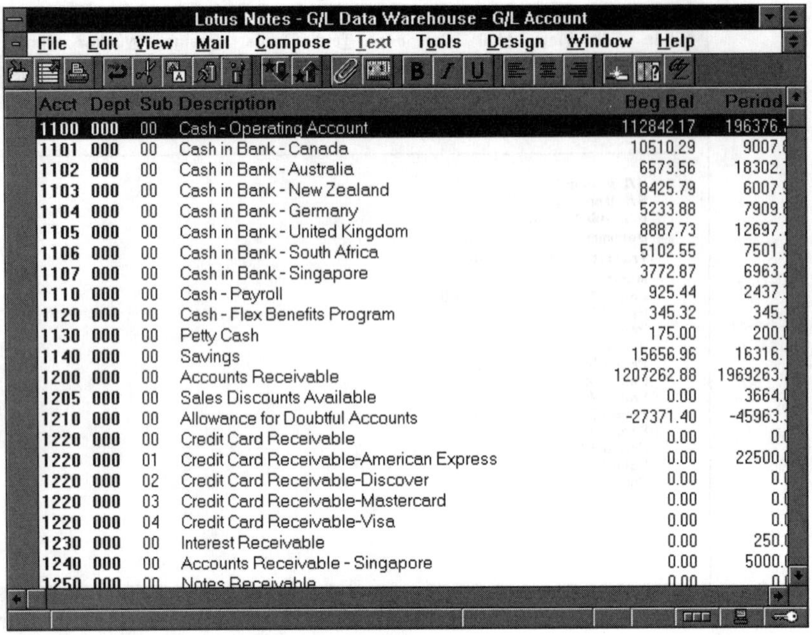

Acct	Dept	Sub	Description	Beg Bal	Period
1100	000	00	Cash - Operating Account	112842.17	196376.
1101	000	00	Cash in Bank - Canada	10510.29	9007.
1102	000	00	Cash in Bank - Australia	6573.56	18302.
1103	000	00	Cash in Bank - New Zealand	8425.79	6007.
1104	000	00	Cash in Bank - Germany	5233.88	7909.
1105	000	00	Cash in Bank - United Kingdom	8887.73	12697.
1106	000	00	Cash in Bank - South Africa	5102.55	7501.
1107	000	00	Cash in Bank - Singapore	3772.87	6963.
1110	000	00	Cash - Payroll	925.44	2437.
1120	000	00	Cash - Flex Benefits Program	345.32	345.
1130	000	00	Petty Cash	175.00	200.
1140	000	00	Savings	15656.96	16316.
1200	000	00	Accounts Receivable	1207262.88	1969263.
1205	000	00	Sales Discounts Available	0.00	3664.
1210	000	00	Allowance for Doubtful Accounts	-27371.40	-45963.
1220	000	00	Credit Card Receivable	0.00	0.
1220	000	01	Credit Card Receivable-American Express	0.00	22500.
1220	000	02	Credit Card Receivable-Discover	0.00	0.
1220	000	03	Credit Card Receivable-Mastercard	0.00	0.
1220	000	04	Credit Card Receivable-Visa	0.00	0.
1230	000	00	Interest Receivable	0.00	250.
1240	000	00	Accounts Receivable - Singapore	0.00	5000.
1250	000	00	Notes Receivable	0.00	0.

FIGURE 9.40c General Ledger Account view.

BUTTONS

Edit Places the document in edit mode so that the user can change the document. It is visible only when the document is being read.

Save Saves the document and exits to the last open view. The button is visible only when the document is being edited.

Save and Compose Saves the document but also opens a new form so that a user can enter another document. The button is visible only when the document is being edited.

ACCESS CONTROL

The default access control should be set to Read for all budget managers. The Accounting employee who is responsible for updating this database should be given Editor access so that he or she can perform the imports and clean up any problems with the database.

ENHANCE IT!

You can make this database even more powerful by:

1. Creating a view that sorts the transactions by whatever part of the account number represents the department number.
2. Using development tools to automate the import of information into this database.

USING G/L DATA WAREHOUSE

The database is intended for use by all **Budget Managers** and **Accounting. Budget Managers** should have Read access and **Accounting** should have Editor access. To create the G/L Accounts documents in the G/L Data Warehouse:

1. **Accounting** transfers the chart of accounts and balances from the accounting system into a text file or spreadsheet.
2. **Accounting** imports the chart of accounts and balances into the G/L Data Warehouse using the Imports\G/L Accounts Import view.

To create the G/L Transactions documents in the G/L Data Warehouse:

1. **Accounting** transfers the new transactions from the accounting system into a text file or spreadsheet.
2. **Accounting** imports the transactions into the G/L Data Warehouse using the Imports\G/L Transactions Import view.

Phone/Fax Usage Summary (41)

PURPOSE

Accounting calculates the phone bills for each department based on the amount of usage measured by software running on the telecommunications equipment. The allocations appear on budget reports at month's end, and the department managers often call Accounting to find out the details behind their bills. The Phone Charges/ Fax Usage Summary database is a data warehouse that contains the details behind the amounts that were allocated. Budget managers can review the database when they have questions instead of calling the Accounting department.

FORMS USED

Fax Usage Summary	Displays the fax usage amounts imported into the database (see Figure 9.41a).
Telephone Allocation Summary	Displays the telephone allocation summaries imported into the database.

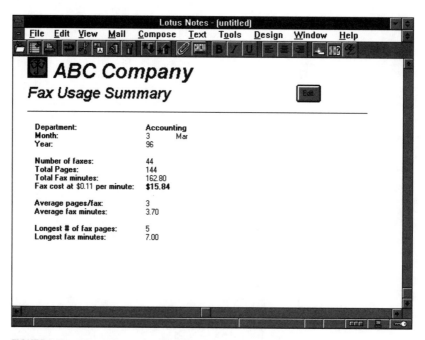

FIGURE 9.41a Fax Usage Import form.

VIEWS

Fax Summary, Date and Department Categorizes the fax usage summaries in reverse chronological order by the month in which the charges were incurred and displays them in department order.

Fax Summary, Department and Date Categorizes the fax usage summaries in department order and displays them in reverse chronological order by the month in which the charges were incurred (see Figure 9.41b).

Import, Fax Usage Used for importing a spreadsheet or text file that contains fax usage summaries generated from the software that controls automatic fax capabilities on the network.

Import, Phone Usage Used for importing a spreadsheet or text file that contains fax usage summaries generated from the software running on the telecommunications equipment.

Phone Use, Date and Department Categorizes the phone usage summaries in reverse chronological order by the month in which the charges were incurred and displays them in department order.

Phone Use, Department and Date Categorizes the phone usage summaries in department order and displays them in reverse chronological order by the month in which the charges were incurred.

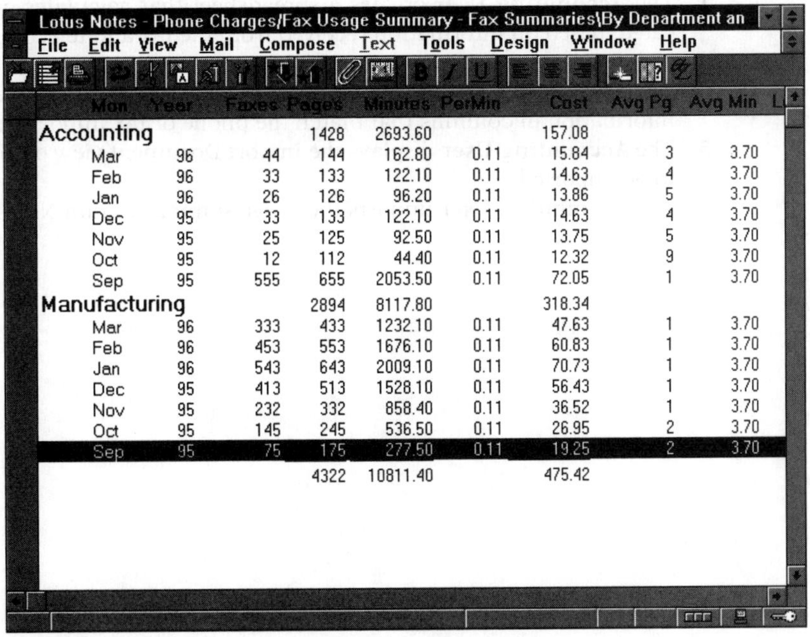
Lotus Notes - Phone Charges/Fax Usage Summary - Fax Summaries\By Department an
File Edit View Mail Compose Text Tools Design Window Help
Mon Year Faxes Pages Minutes PerMin Cost Avg Pg Avg Min
Accounting 1428 2693.60 157.08
Mar 96 44 144 162.80 0.11 15.84 3 3.70
Feb 96 33 133 122.10 0.11 14.63 4 3.70
Jan 96 26 126 96.20 0.11 13.86 5 3.70
Dec 95 33 133 122.10 0.11 14.63 4 3.70
Nov 95 25 125 92.50 0.11 13.75 5 3.70
Oct 95 12 112 44.40 0.11 12.32 9 3.70
Sep 95 555 655 2053.50 0.11 72.05 1 3.70
Manufacturing 2894 8117.80 318.34
Mar 96 333 433 1232.10 0.11 47.63 1 3.70
Feb 96 453 553 1676.10 0.11 60.83 1 3.70
Jan 96 543 643 2009.10 0.11 70.73 1 3.70
Dec 95 413 513 1528.10 0.11 56.43 1 3.70
Nov 95 232 332 858.40 0.11 36.52 1 3.70
Oct 95 145 245 536.50 0.11 26.95 2 3.70
Sep 95 75 175 277.50 0.11 19.25 2 3.70
4322 10811.40 475.42

FIGURE 9.41b Fax Summary by Department view.

BUTTONS

Edit   Places the document in edit mode so that the user can change the document. It is visible only when the document is being read.

Save   Saves the document and exits to the last open view. The button is visible only when the document is being edited.

ACCESS CONTROL

The default access control should be set to Read for all users. Accounting users should be given Editor access so that they can import the usage information into the database.

ENHANCE IT!

You can make this database even more powerful by:

1. Using the API or a third-party package to interface with the telecommunications equipment to import the information automatically into Notes.

USING PHONE/FAX USAGE SUMMARY

The database is intended for all **Users** and **Accounting Users.** To create usage summaries:

1. The **Accounting User** creates a spreadsheet that calculates charges to be allocated, based on information received from the fax and telecommunications software.
2. The **Accounting User** formats and saves a version of the spreadsheet with the information in columns that match the phone or fax import view in Notes.
3. The **Accounting User** displays the Import Document view of the usage summary to be imported.
4. The **Accounting User** imports the usage summaries into Notes.

Phone Messages (42)

PURPOSE

The phone messages of many busy executives and managers are screened each day by assistants who make sure the intended recipient gets them. Unfortunately, the familiar pink slips can be misplaced, ignored, or misunderstood, possibly jeopardizing a business relationship or important business deal.

The Phone Messages database lets the assistant enter the phone messages into a database, format them into a more complete format, and send the phone messages into the executive's electronic mail box. The executive can then deal with phone messages and electronic mail messages in the same Notes Mail database.

FORMS USED

Mail Message Displays phone messages in a more readable manner, and allows the recipient to log the outcome of the return phone call (see Figure 9.42a).

Phone Message Captures phone message information and the actions required, and allows the user to mail the phone message to the intended recipient. The document is assigned to the Inbox Phone Message as soon as the user saves the document (see Figure 9.42b).

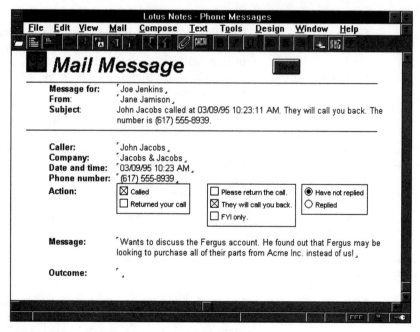

FIGURE 9.42a Mail Message form.

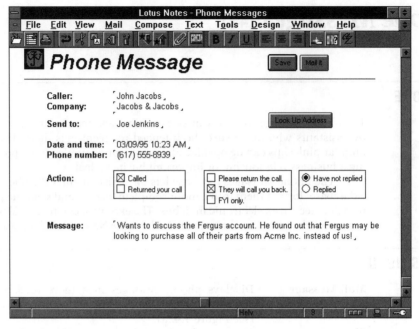

FIGURE 9.42b   Phone Message form.

VIEWS

Caller	Categorizes the phone messages by the name of the caller. Displays the caller's company name and sorts the messages in reverse chronological order.
Company Calling	Categorizes the phone messages by the caller's company name and sorts the messages in reverse chronological order.
Person Called	Categorizes the phone messages by the person called and sorts the messages in reverse chronological order.
Person Called/No Answer	Categorizes the phone messages by the person called, sorts the messages in reverse chronological order, and displays only those messages that have a status of Have Not Replied.
Time Called	Categorizes the phone messages in reverse chronological order by the date and time of the call (see Figure 9.42c).

Note: The database is indexed for a full-text search so that a user can search for any text information in any view.

BUTTONS

Edit	Places the document in edit mode so that the user can change the document. It is visible only when the document is being read.

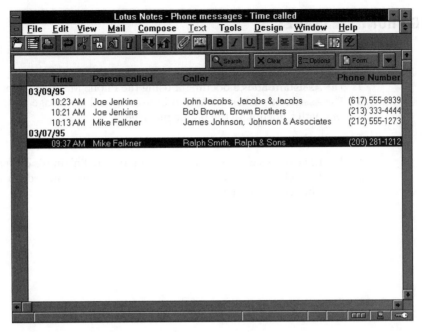

FIGURE 9.42c Phone Messages by Time Called view.

Look Up Address	Displays the Name and Address Book so that the user can search for the name of the person who will be receiving the message.
Mail It	Sends an electronic mail message that notifies the recipient that he or she received a phone message, and includes caller, time, and subject.
Save	Saves the document and exits to the last open view. The button is visible only when the document is being edited. New documents will be assigned to the Inbox Phone Messages form as they are saved.

ACCESS CONTROL

The default access control should be set to Editor for the executive and assistant who will use the database. No other users should be given access to this database.

ENHANCE IT!

You can make this database even more powerful by:

1. Adding a button to create to-do's and assign them using the electronic mail system.

USING PHONE MESSAGES

The database is intended for use by one or more **Users** supported by an **Assistant.** To create a phone message:

1. The **Assistant** adds a document using the Phone Message form.
2. The **Assistant** pushes the Mail It button to send a message to the intended recipient with a doclink to the phone message.

To respond to a message:

1. The **User** recalls a phone message using the doclink in his or her mail message.
2. The **User** clicks the check box marked Have Replied and edits the Outcome field with the results of the phone call.

Executive Phone Book (43)

PURPOSE

It isn't enough to just keep a list of names and contacts if you want to make a good impression in the business world. Successful entrepreneurs gather both personal and professional information about their contacts, and they send cards, gifts, or other personal acknowledgments that make the contacts feel important and valued. The Executive Phone Book database stores the extra information about a contact that can help an executive add the personal touch to business relationships.

FORMS USED

Phone Book   Captures information about a personal or business contact, including business and home addresses, e-mail addresses, family information, hobbies, and miscellaneous important facts (see Figures 9.43a and b).

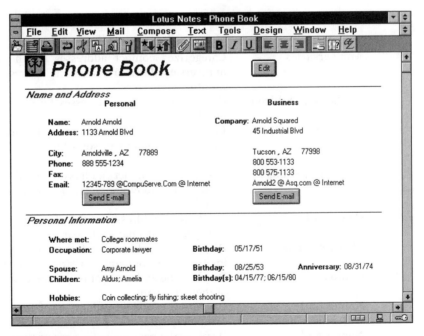

FIGURE 9.43a   Executive Phone Book form.

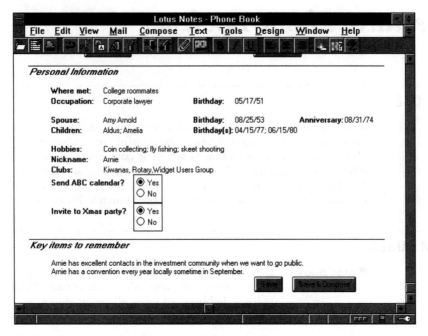

FIGURE 9.43b   Executive Phone Book form, bottom half.

VIEWS

Anniversaries	Categorizes contact addresses by the month of their anniversary dates and sorts the addresses by day of the month.
Birthdays, Children	Categorizes contact addresses by the birthdays of their children.
Birthdays, Contact	Categorizes contact addresses by the month of the main contact's birthday and sorts the addresses by day of the month.
Birthdays, Spouse	Categorizes contact addresses by the month of the spouse's birthday and sorts the addresses by day of the month.
Calendars	Displays the addresses of the contacts who should receive a company calendar each year.
Christmas Party	Displays the addresses of the contacts who should be invited to the company Christmas party each year.
Company	Displays the addresses of the contacts sorted by the name of their company.
Names and Business Info	Displays the business addresses of the contacts sorted by company name.
Names and Personal Info	Displays the personal addresses of the contacts sorted by company name (see Figure 9.43c).

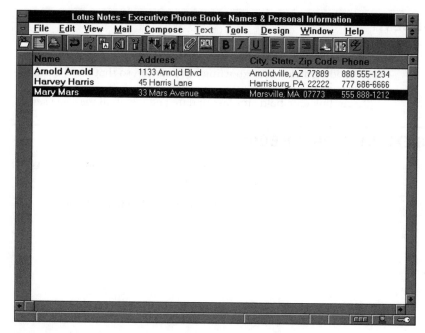

FIGURE 9.43c   Phone Book by Names and Personal Information view.

BUTTONS

Edit   Places the document in edit mode so that the user can change the document. It is visible only when the document is being read.

Save   Saves the document and exits to the last open view. The button is visible only when the document is being edited. A second button is placed at the bottom of the screen to make it easier to save a document once it is complete.

Save and Compose   Saves the document but also opens a new form so that a user can enter another document. The button is visible only when the document is being edited. A second button is placed at the bottom of the screen to make it easier to save a document once it is complete.

Send E-mail   Composes a mail message using the form in the user's electronic mail database and automatically inserts the electronic mail address of the contact. It assumes that the user is using the Notes Mail database included in this book.

ACCESS CONTROL

The default access control should be set to Editor for the phone book user and his or her assistants. No other users should be given access to this database.

ENHANCE IT!

You can make this database even more powerful by:

1. Adding a view for exporting information so that a word processor can be used to send letters or labels.
2. Adding date fields for last update and last mail message sent.

USING EXECUTIVE PHONE BOOK

The database is intended for use by one **User** and his or her **Assistant.** To create an entry in the Executive Phone Book:

1. The **User** adds a document using the Phone Book form.

People Database (44)

PURPOSE

As a company grows, it becomes more difficult to meet all the employees and find out more about them. It's also good business to foster a closeness with the people who resell the company's products so that they remain loyal representatives and feel like more than just vendors. The People Database provides users and resellers with a forum for sharing information about employees and resellers. If one person spends hours on the phone with someone he or she has never met, the People Database can provide a picture of that person and some information about his or her background. Note: This information was not incorporated into the Name and Address Book because the pictures greatly increase the size of the file, requiring remote users to do large replications regularly, which eat up disk space, when all they need is a name to which they can send mail.

FORMS USED

People Base-Employees   Captures personal information about employees and provides a place to store their pictures (see Figure 9.44a).

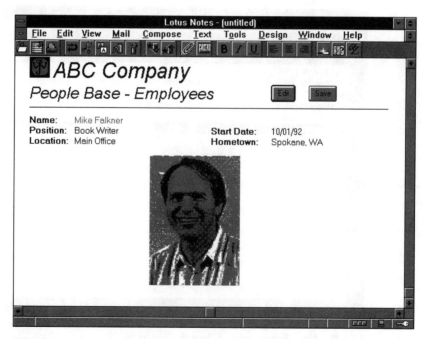

FIGURE 9.44a   People Database Employee form.

People Base-Resellers	Captures personal information about resellers, including the awards that they have won, and it provides a place to store their pictures.

VIEWS

All Records by First Name	Displays all documents by the first name of the person represented in the document.
Employees by Home City	Categorizes employees by their home city and sorts them by first name (see Figure 9.44b).
Employees by Home State	Categorizes employees by their home state and sorts them by first name.
Employees by Position	Categorizes employees by their positions within the company and sorts them by first name.
Resellers by City	Categorizes resellers by the location of their company and sorts them by first name.
Resellers by Relationship	Categorizes resellers by their relationship with the company and sorts them by first name.
Resellers by State	Categorizes resellers by the state in which their company resides and sorts them by first name.

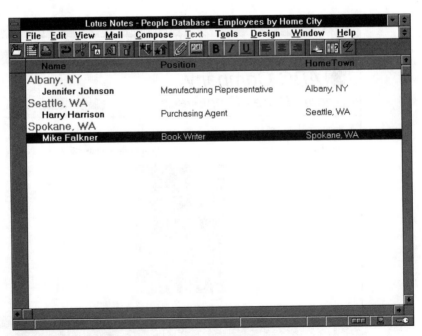

FIGURE 9.44b   Employees by Home City form.

BUTTONS

Edit   Places the document in edit mode so that the user can change the document. It is visible only when the document is being read.

Save   Saves the document and exits to the last open view. The button is visible only when the document is being edited.

ACCESS CONTROL

The default access control should be set to Editor for all Personnel users. All other users should be given Read access to this database.

ENHANCE IT!

You can make this database even more powerful by:

1. Integrating the database with the Personnel system so that the information can be updated automatically at regular intervals.
2. Allowing optional fields for birthdays, hobbies, and other personal information that people might want to share.

USING PEOPLE DATABASE

The database is intended for all **Users** and **Personnel Users.** To create an employee document:

1. The **Personnel User** adds a document using the Add Employee form.

To create a reseller document:

1. The **Personnel User** adds a document using the Add Reseller form.

Newsletters (45)

PURPOSE

Newsletters are an excellent source of information for users and customers alike, focusing on a key area that brings the reader up to date in a short period of time. However, creation, printing, and distribution of the newsletter can be costly and labor-intensive, and sending newsletters via electronic mail can clog the system.

The Newsletter database gives readers a central repository for all the company newsletters. At their leisure, employees and customers can view new titles and review information from earlier issues.

FORMS USED

Newsletters   Captures the title, author, and publication date of the newsletter and allows the storage of the newsletter text or word processing document in a rich text field (see Figure 9.45a).

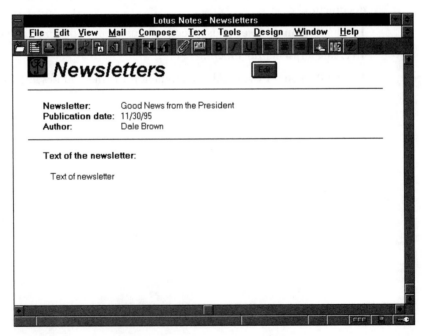

FIGURE 9.45a   Newsletter form.

VIEWS

Author	Categorizes the publications by author.
Publication	Categorizes the publications by their name (see Figure 9.45b).
Publication Date	Categorizes the publications by the publishing date.

BUTTONS

Edit	Places the document in edit mode so that the user can change the document. It is visible only when the document is being read.
Save	Saves the document and exits to the last open view. The button is visible only when the document is being edited.
Save and Compose	Saves the document but also opens a new form so that a user can enter another document. The button is visible only when the document is being edited.

ACCESS CONTROL

The default access control should be set to Read for all users. The authors of the newsletters should be given Author access, and the employees of the department responsible for publishing the information should be given Editor access so that they can add and remove information if necessary.

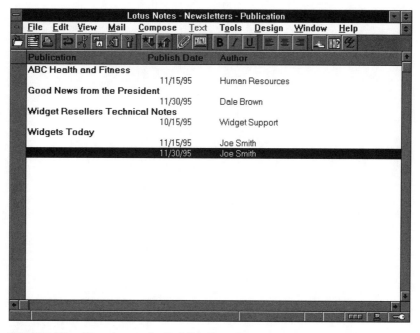

FIGURE 9.45b   Newsletters by Publication view.

ENHANCE IT!

You can make this database even more powerful by:

1. Adding a field for an expiration date, or for automatically removing issues over a certain period of time.
2. Creating a field marked Internal/External. Creating a replica for external customers that replicates only those items marked for External Use Only.

USING NEWSLETTERS

The database is intended for all **Users, Authors,** and **Publishers.** To create a newsletter entry:

1. The **Author** or **Publisher** adds a document using the Newsletter form.
2. **Users** access documents as needed.

Want Ads (46)

PURPOSE

A company is not only a place to work but also a social environment. Bulletin boards become the center of commerce, filled with services and items for sale. At times, employees even send out "junk" mail via the electronic mail system as they discover the power of a captive audience.

An enlightened company will control this unsolicited electronic mail and provide a better outlet for their employees. A Want Ads database gives employees a forum for placing ads, and uses electronic mail for discreet responses and replies.

FORMS USED

Want Ad	Captures the information needed to create a Want Ad. The form includes a disclaimer, which allows company representatives to monitor the database. The form displays the document in a more concise form than when it is being read (see Figures 9.46a and b).
Reply to Want Ads	Allows a reader to send an electronic offer to an ad originator.

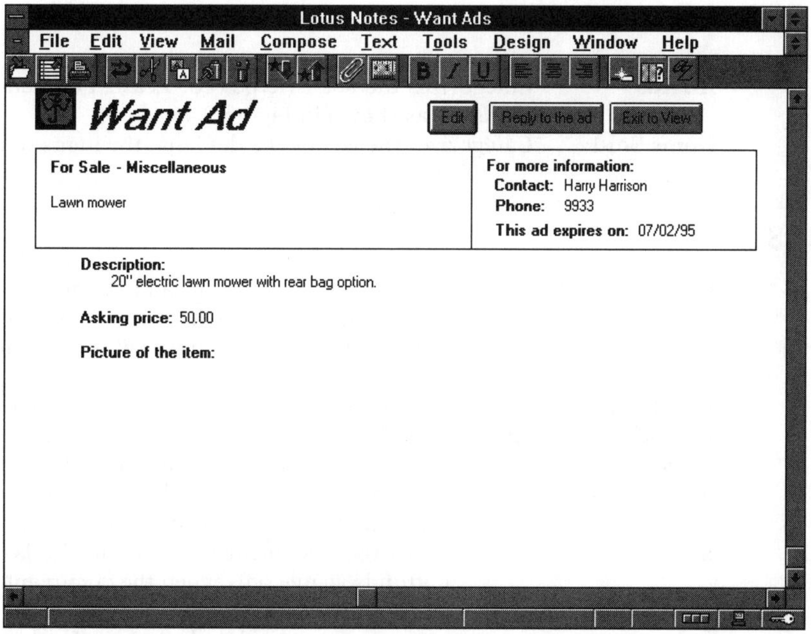

FIGURE 9.46a   Want Ad display form.

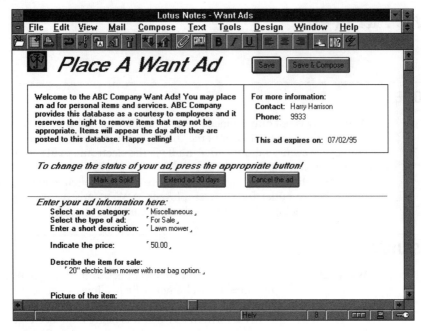

FIGURE 9.46b   Place a Want Ad form.

VIEWS

All Ads	Categorizes the ads by type (For Lease, For Rent, For Sale, Free!, Wanted), as shown in Figure 9.46c.
Items Sold	Categorizes the ads by the date that the items were sold.

BUTTONS

Cancel the Ad	Changes the status of the ad to Cancel.
Edit	Places the document in edit mode so that the user can change the document. It is visible only when the document is being read.
Exit to View	Closes the document and returns to the view.
Extend Ad 30 Days	Adds 30 days to the ad's expiration date.
Mark as Sold	Changes the status of the ad to Sold.
Reply to the Ad	Creates a document that allows the user to create a reply to the ad and send it to the originator via Notes Mail.
Save	Saves the document and exits to the last open view. The button is visible only when the document is being edited.
Save and Compose	Saves the document but also opens a new form so that a user can enter another document. The button is visible only when the document is being edited.

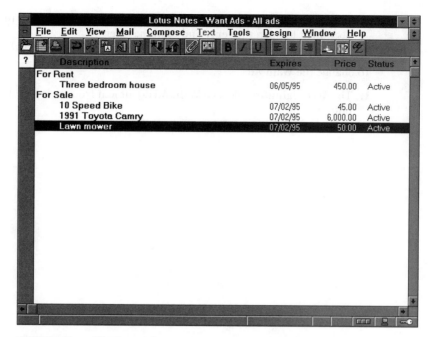

FIGURE 9.46c All Want Ads view.

ACCESS CONTROL

The default access control should be set to Author for all users. This allows users to edit their ads while other users can only read them.

ENHANCE IT!

You can make this database even more powerful by:

1. Adding a button that taps into scanner software that allows users to scan pictures of the items for sale.

USING WANT ADS

The database is intended for all **Users.** To create a Want Ad:

1. The **User** adds a document using the Want Ad form.

To reply to a Want Ad:

1. **Users** select Want Ads from the view.
2. **Users** push the Reply to Ad button and complete a Reply to Ad form.
3. **Users** push the Send Offer to Originator button and send the **Ad Originator** the comments entered on the screen.

4. The **Ad Originator** finds an e-mail in his or her inbox and uses the doclink in the document to open the reply and read the offer.

5. The **Ad Originator** replies in a similar manner and continues the cycle.

To change the Want Ad:

1. The **Ad Originator** selects a Want Ad document from a view and presses the Edit button.

Vacations/Time Off (47)

PURPOSE

In today's companies, everyone is doing two jobs and working long hours. Vacations are vital to recharge an employee's batteries, but it means that others must cover that person's duties while he or she is gone. Managers need help scheduling vacations and time off so that they can minimize the effects of having people out of the office. The Vacations/Time Off database gives managers and employees an effective tool to communicate time-off needs to each other.

FORMS USED

Vacations/Time Off   Captures vacations and time-off requests, submits them electronically to the supervisor, and allows the supervisor to approve them online (see Figure 9.47a).

VIEWS

Department   Categorizes time off by the employee's department and lists the documents in employee order.

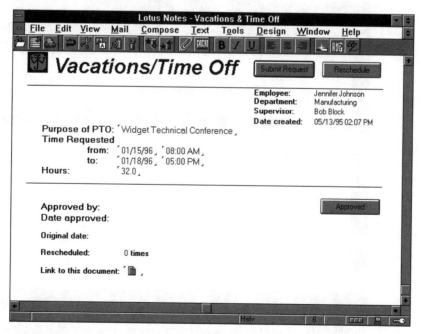

FIGURE 9.47a   Vacations and Time Off form.

Department/ Supervisor	Categorizes time off by the employee's department and by supervisor. Lists the documents in employee order.
Department/ Supervisor/ Month	Categorizes time off by the employee's department, by his or her supervisor, and by the month in which the time off starts. Lists the documents in employee order (see Figure 9.47b).
Start Date	Categorizes time off by the date that the time off begins and lists the documents in employee order.

BUTTONS

Approved	Changes the approved date to the day that the button was pushed and changes the Approved by field to the name of the user pushing the button.
Edit	Places the document in edit mode so that the user can change the document. It is visible only when the document is being read.
Reschedule	Saves the vacation document after it has been edited and sends a new request to the supervisor asking for the rescheduled date be approved. The information about the previously requested time off is saved, the approval information is removed, and the reschedule counter is incremented by one. The button is visible only when the document is being edited.

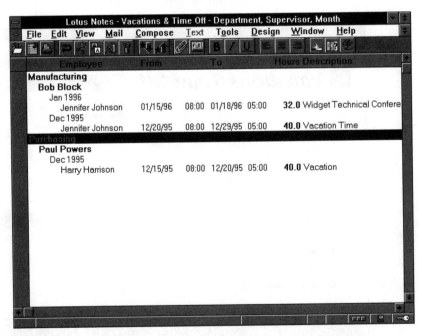

FIGURE 9.47b   Time Off by Department, Supervisor, and Month view.

Submit Request   Saves the document and sends a message to the supervisor requesting approval. The message includes a doclink to the vacation request. The button is visible only when the document is being edited.

ACCESS CONTROL

The default access control should be set to Author for all users and Editor for all supervisors who can approve vacation time.

ENHANCE IT!

You can make this database even more powerful by:

1. Adding a section to restrict the approval area to the department manager.
2. Adding the form to the mail system as a custom form so that vacation requests can be sent to a mail-enabled database that only the supervisor can look at, to maintain more privacy.

USING VACATIONS/TIME OFF

The database is intended for all **Users** and **Supervisors.** To create a time-off entry:

1. The **User** adds a document using the Vacations/Time Off form.
2. The **User** presses the Submit Request button, which sends a mail message to the supervisor asking that the request be approved.
3. The **Supervisor** uses the doclink in the mail message to recall the request and press the Approved button.

To reschedule a time-off entry:

1. The **User** modifies the document using the Vacations/Time Off form.
2. The **User** presses the Submit Request button, which sends a mail message to the supervisor asking that the request be approved. The reschedule counter is incremented and all the approvals are removed.
3. The **Supervisor** uses the doclink in the mail message to recall the request and press the Approved button.

Process Improvements (48)

PURPOSE

Process improvement has become commonplace in most companies. Managers and their staffs are working together to find more efficient ways to do business. When properly organized, these process improvement activities follow a methodology developed to help all employees follow the same steps as they work through an improvement project.

The Process Improvements database allows users to store the process improvement steps of their methodology. It also holds documents that relate to process improvement activities, and these documents can be related to the steps of the methodology. The document can also hold word processing documents and spreadsheets from process improvement activities.

FORMS USED

Process Improvement Steps	Allows the storage of the steps that a company defines for its process improvement methodology.
Improvement Activity	Stores the information about a process activity, categorizes the document by the improvement step, and allows users to store documents created during the process improvement activity (see Figure 9.48a).
Comments	Captures comments as a response document and allows the user to attach documents generated by the process improvement activity.

VIEWS

Activity Date	Displays the documents by activity date in reverse chronological order.
Activity Step	Categorizes the process improvement activities using the process improvement steps assigned to each activity (see Figure 9.48b).
Author	Displays a document by the name of the author who created the document.
Category	Shows a document by a user-defined category added to each document. Examples of these categories are meetings, implementation, and presentations.
Improvement Steps	Lists the improvement steps assigned in the methodology. These steps are used as a lookup table in the improvement activities forms.

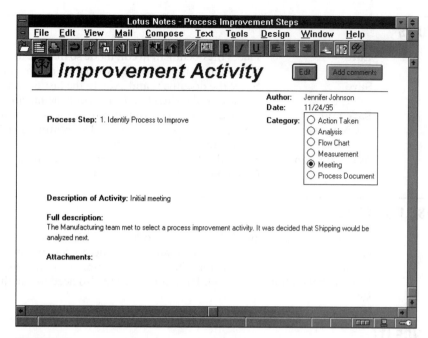

FIGURE 9.48a   Process Improvement form.

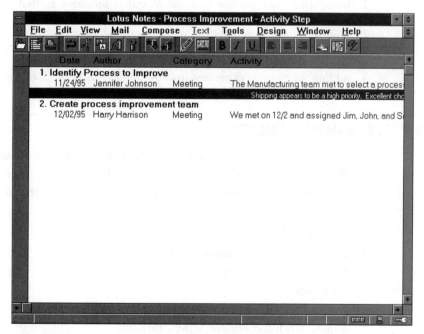

FIGURE 9.48b   Process Improvement by Activity view.

BUTTONS

Edit	Places the document in edit mode so that the user can change the document. It is visible only when the document is being read.
Save	Saves the document and exits to the last open view. The button is visible only when the document is being edited.
Save and Compose	Saves the document but also opens a new form so that a user can enter another document. The button is visible only when the document is being edited.
Add Comments	Saves the Improvements Activity document and composes a Comments response document.

ACCESS CONTROL

The default access control should be set to Author for users who will be adding process improvement documents. The managers of the process improvement activities should have Editor access so that they can add comments in the documents when a further explanation is required. The managers will also need to add the methodology steps.

ENHANCE IT!

You can make this database even more powerful by:

1. Integrating the database with the Meetings database so that you can use it to schedule process improvement meetings.
2. Adding a form on which to store the list of team members.
3. Adding a button to automatically forward a doclink to the improvement activity via e-mail.
4. Adding the company's process improvement steps to the database and publishing it as a template for others to use.

USING PROCESS IMPROVEMENTS

The database is intended for use by all **Process Improvement Team Members** and the **Team Leader.** To add the methodology steps:

1. The **Team Leader** adds the process improvement steps to the database using the Process Improvement Steps form.

To add an activity:

1. The **Process Improvement Team Member** composes a document using the Improvement Activity form.

To add a comment:

1. A **Process Improvement Team Member** selects a document for viewing and displays the Improvement Activity form.
2. The **Process Improvement Team Member** selects the Add Comments button and completes the Comments form.

Company Goals (49)

PURPOSE

Companies and individuals need goals to stay focused on common objectives. The Company Goals database allows management to enter goals at multiple levels so that all employees can see how the goals for their department support the goals of other departments, divisions, and the company at large.

FORMS USED

Add Goals (1)	Captures goals for the level immediately below the company level. The form can be accessed only from the Company Goals form (see Figure 9.49a).
Add Goals (2)	Captures goals for all levels below the first two goal levels. The form can be accessed only from the Add Goals form.
Company Goals	Captures the top-level goals for the company (see Figure 9.49b).
Goal Levels	Captures the organization units and level numbers that will be assigned to each unit.

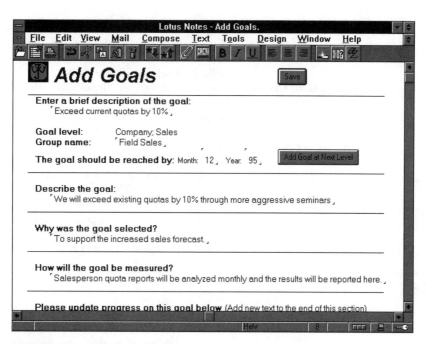

FIGURE 9.49a   Add Goals form.

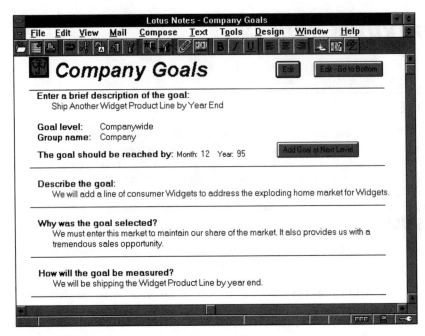

FIGURE 9.49b Company Goals form.

VIEWS

Company Goals	Displays company goals and all the subsidiary goals associated with them. Each level below the company goal is indented and includes the organizational unit associated with the goal (see Figure 9.49c).
Goals by Goal Group	Displays the goals by the organizational unit responsible for the goal.
Goals Levels	Displays the organization units that represent each goal group.
Goals, Select Macro	Displays all goals starting at a level specified in the Choose a Reporting Level macro. The view is set to rebuild the index each time it is used so that it will interrogate the environment variable that defines the reporting level.
Goals, All	Categorizes all goals by any of the organizational units that are affected by it. A goal entered for the Sales department in the Widget Division of ABC Company will appear in all three organizational units.

MACROS

Choose Report Level	Prompts the user for the reporting level that will be used for the view entitled Goals, by Level Selected in the macro. The macro saves the value in an environment variable that the view uses in its selection formula.

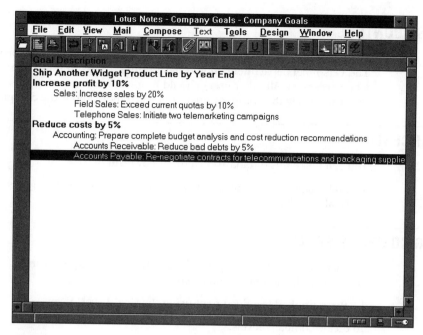

FIGURE 9.49c   Company Goals view.

Reset Level to 1	Resets the environment variable to level 1. The Choose Reporting Level macro will not execute when no goals are displayed, necessitating this macro to reset the variable.

BUTTONS

Add Goal, Next Level	Creates a goal document and creates the relationships to the previous level.
Edit	Places the document in edit mode so that the user can change the document. It is visible only when the document is being read.
Edit—Move to Bottom	Places the document in edit mode but also moves the cursor to the bottom of the document. This eliminates having to use the scroll bars or Page Down to see the part of the form that isn't visible when it is first opened. The button is visible only when the document is being read.
Save	Saves the document and exits to the last open view. The button is visible only when the document is being edited.
Save and Compose	Saves the document but also opens a new form so that a user can enter another document. The button is visible only when the document is being edited.

ACCESS CONTROL

The default access control should be set to Author for all Supervisors and Managers. The Personnel department should have Editor access to make changes to the goals when necessary. All other users should be given Read access to this database so that they can review the company goals and learn more about the company.

ENHANCE IT!

You can make this database even more powerful by:

1. Linking the Performance Review database and individual goals to the Company Goals database.

USING COMPANY GOALS

The database is intended for use by all **Managers, Supervisors,** and **Personnel.** To create organization units and levels:

1. **Personnel** adds a document using the Goal Levels form.

To create company levels:

1. **Personnel** adds a document using the Company Goals form.

To create levels below the company level:

1. **Managers** and **Supervisors** select a company goal from the Company Goals view.
2. **Managers** and **Supervisors** push the Add Goal at Next Level button and add a document using the Add Goals form.

Surveys (50)

PURPOSE

Everyone serves a customer of some kind. Even an employee at a company has internal customers. Surveys are one popular method used to assess the satisfaction levels of all customers. Using embedded forms, the mail-enabled Survey database facilitates the distribution, return, and tabulation of surveys.

FORMS USED

Survey Descriptions	Captures the name of the survey and an ID number assigned to the survey.
Survey #0001, etc.	Customized survey form that is mailed to an audience and captures the answers to the survey (see Figure 9.50a).

VIEWS

Surveys	Lists the survey description and the ID number assigned by the survey creator.

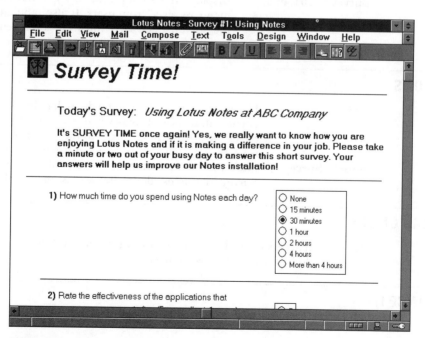

FIGURE 9.50a   Survey Form.

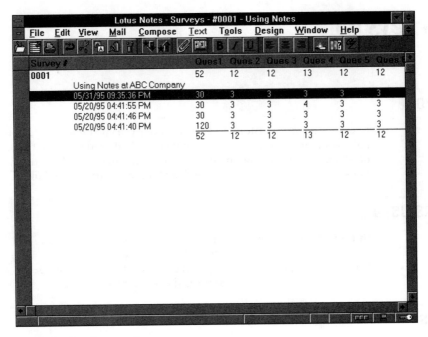

FIGURE 9.50b   Survey view.

Survey #0001, etc.	Displays the survey description followed by the documents received from users. It also tabulates the values in the survey. Each view must be developed by the survey creator (see Figure 9.50b).

BUTTONS

Edit	Places the document in edit mode so that the user can change the document. It is visible only when the document is being read.
Save	Saves the document and exits to the last open view. The button is visible only when the document is being edited.
Submit Survey	Mails the survey document to the mail-enabled database called Survey. The Notes administrator must mail-enable this database.

ACCESS CONTROL

The default access control should be set to Editor for all Survey creators. No other users should have access to this database.

ENHANCE IT!

You can make this database even more powerful by:

1. Creating one database per survey when you expect a large number of submissions.

USING SURVEYS

The database is intended for all **Users** and by **Survey Creators.** To create a survey:

1. **Survey Creators** add a title document using the Survey descriptions form.
2. **Survey Creators** create a survey form along with a survey form that adds up the values in the form.
3. **Survey Creators** mail the Survey form to all **Users** who should complete the survey.
4. **Users** complete the survey and select the Submit Survey button to mail the survey to the Survey database.
5. **Survey Creators** display a view that adds up the survey values.

10

Developing a Notes Application

The best way to try out the Lotus Notes development standards and principles is to create an application. And because we've spent a lot of time talking about the Purchase Requisition database, let's create one of those. We'll assume that the Notes infrastructure and standards are in place and that we have users ready and eager to get started.

By the time this chapter is completed, we will have created a functional Purchase Requisition database in Notes. You will be able to experience the power of Notes—and some of its limitations. The actual database is on the CD-ROM included with this book.

As in previous chapters, the examples that follow use the Notes 3.x commands to build the application. Appendix A describes many of the dramatic changes in the way that the properties of forms and views are created in an application; however, the concepts used to develop the application remain the same.

In Chapter 8, we discussed the steps that we should follow to plan and develop an application. Those steps are listed here again to remind us how to approach a development project:

- ♦ Develop a process flow
- ♦ Identify data elements and data types
- ♦ Define the databases
- ♦ Define the forms and their relationships
- ♦ Define views
- ♦ Develop a prototype
- ♦ Finalize requirements
- ♦ Implement the prototype and enhance the product

We performed some of these tasks in previous chapters, which will help us to complete the project. In doing so, we are, in effect, building a prototype in the same way as if we were both working together in the same company. Although we can't interactively alter the application, certainly you can modify it to suit your own needs as we move forward.

Develop a Process Flow

We developed a simple process flow in Chapter 3 for the Purchase Requisition database. If necessary, reread the discussion there to refresh your memory with the details of our project. We are going to focus on the flow of information from the originator to the point at which the Purchasing agent sends a fax to the vendor.

In Chapter 3, we developed three simple flowcharts to define the purchase requisition process. Figure 10.1 shows that the originator enters a requisition into a Notes database and sends it to the appropriate managers for approval. Figure 10.2 illustrates the ongoing task of testing for overdue approvals that require attention. It also shows that once a manager approves a requisition, it appears automatically in a view accessible by Purchasing.

Figure 10.3 completes the process: Purchasing performs its reviews and prepares the requisition for placement with a vendor. When all Purchasing approvals are complete, Notes faxes the order to the vendor. The process is fairly straightforward. We are going to enter information into a Notes database, use the mail system to coordinate approvals, and send the completed requisition to a vendor as a purchase order.

Identify Data Elements and Data Types

Now that we understand how the purchase requisition will flow through the system, we can begin to gather the data elements that we need to support

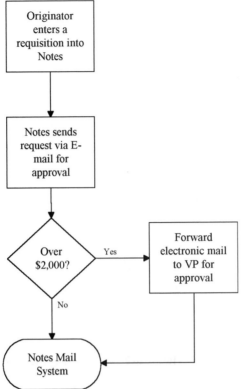

FIGURE 10.1 Initiation of the Purchase Requisition process.

the application. In the previous chapter, we saw that operations where a user enters information are good places to look for data elements. Looking at the process flow, we see several boxes where the user enters information:

- Originator enters information into Notes
- Approver electronically signs the requisition
- Purchasing agent completes purchase requisition
- Purchasing manager electronically approves requisition

We should interview one or two people who originate purchase requisitions to find out what they want to place on the purchase requisition. We can then talk to a few managers who probably have strong feelings about the requisition process and would like to see it simplified. Next, we'll touch base with a few Purchasing agents who have to process the purchase requisitions and correct them. Finally, we should talk with the Purchasing manager about the approval process. We should also gather a copy of the existing forms, which are being replaced by the system, to help us discover any data elements that someone may have forgotten.

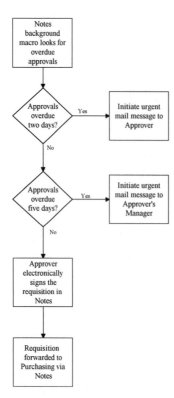

FIGURE 10.2 Approval of the requisition.

After our interviews with the originators of requisitions and their managers, we gathered the data elements shown in Table 10.1.

The data types were added to the checklist based on the characteristics of the data element. For example, in talking with the originator, we found that the purchase requisition number uses six alphanumeric characters, which means we need to use a text field. We also found that the inventory item number is alphanumeric, as is the budget account. We use a names field for elements containing a person's name so that we can take advantage of the Notes @ functions for user names.

Our interviews with the Purchasing agents generated most of the same elements with a few more additions (see Table 10.2). Both the shipping method field and the terms fields have definable values, so we'll make them keywords. However, the users indicated that they may have other values periodically; therefore we must allow them to override the keywords and add their own values.

Our interviews have been fruitful, and we have all the information from the users that we need to work on our database design. But because, we know that the application will be mail-enabled, we need to include some additional data elements so that Notes can mail messages for us (see Table

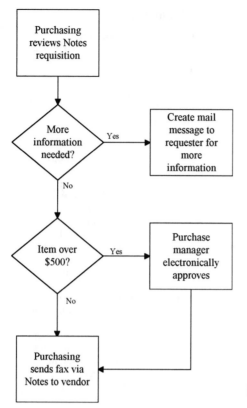

FIGURE 10.3   Placing the order.

10.3). These fields will be invisible to the user, and we will fill them in automatically before sending a message.

Define the Databases

In reviewing our data elements, we find that there are four categories of information that we need to manage: 1. purchase requisitions, 2. inventory items, 3. vendors, and 4. employees. For items 2, 3, and 4, we would expect the information to exist in some kind of master database that is used by other Notes applications for the same reasons that we need it. In other words, there should be an existing application that creates inventory items, vendors, and employee records, which we can access on a server. If, however, the information doesn't exist somewhere else, then we need to create forms and views for it in this application.

Although Notes is capable of handling all of this information in one database, the views would have to process all of the inventory, vendor, and

TABLE 10.1 Data Elements from Originators and Managers

Data Element	Full Description	Data Type	Restrictions (Range or List of Values)	Access Limits
Purchase Requisition	Purchase requisition number	Text	6 letters	
Requisition Date	Date that the requisition was issued	Time	None	
Requisition Status	The status of the requisition	Keyword	A List: New Submitted to Mgr Approved by Dept Submitted to VP Approved by VP Submitted to Purch Approved by Purch Order Placed Order Received	Users can only change this using buttons—no editing allowed
Originator	The person who created the requisition	Name	User who created the requisition	
Department	The originator's department	Text	Use dept lookup table	
Department Manager	The originator's manager	Names	Use dept lookup table	
Department VP	The vice president in charge of the department	Names	Use dept lookup table	
G/L Budget Account	The budget account that will be charged for the items on the requisition	Text	Default to department number, 5120, and 200 for the three segments of the account	
Date manager approved	The date that the department manager approved the req	Time	Default to today	
Date VP approved	The date that the department VP approved the requisition	Time	Default to today	
Vendor name	The name of the vendor	Text	Use vendor lookup table	
Vendor address	The vendor address	Text	Use vendor lookup table	
Vendor city	The vendor city	Text	Use vendor lookup table	
Vendor state	The vendor state	Text	Use vendor lookup table	
Vendor zip	The vendor zip code	Text	Use vendor lookup table	
Vendor phone	The vendor phone number	Text	Use vendor lookup table	
Vendor fax	The vendor fax number	Text	Use vendor lookup table	
Item #	The internal item # for the goods to be ordered	Text	Use inventory lookup table	
Quantity	The quantity ordered	Number	No decimals	
Description	The description of the item to be ordered	Text	Use inventory lookup table and allow additions	
Unit Price	The cost of each item	Number	Use inventory lookup table. Use two decimal places.	
Extended Price	The total cost for the item on this line of the requisition	Number	Quantity times price	
Freight	Freight costs	Number	Two decimal places	

TABLE 10.2 Data Elements from Purchasing Agents

Data Element	Full Description	Data Type	Restrictions (Range or List of Values)	Access Limits
Date assigned	The date that the Purchasing Agent was assigned the requisition	Time	Default to today	
Data reviewed	The date that the Purchasing Agent reviewed the approved requisition	Time	Default to today	
Date Purchasing manager approved	The date that the Purchasing manager approved the req	Time	Default to today	
Date Faxed	The date that requisition was faxed to the vendor	Time	Default to today	
Date item received	The date that a line item was received in Shipping	Time	Default to today	
Shipping method	The shipping method to request from the vendor	Keyword	Ground 2nd day air Overnight	Others can be used
Needed by	The date that the originator needs to receive the goods	Date	None	
Terms	Payment terms from the vendor	Keyword	Net 30 2% 10 days, net 30	Others can be used
Purchasing Agent	Name of the agent who will be processing the requisition	Names	Use the user name	

employee documents every time they were updated. It makes more sense to store the four categories in separate databases and perform lookups into them to retrieve our information. Our purchase requisition database would grow only because of new purchase requisitions, not because of all the lookup items.

Our focus in this chapter is to develop the Purchase Requisition database, therefore we'll assume that the other databases have already been created for other applications and they exist on a Notes server. We'll use the following names and file names for our databases:

TABLE 10.3 Data Elements for Mail Messages

Data Element	Full Description	Data Type	Restrictions (Range or List of Values)	Access Limits
Send to	The name of the person who will receive the mail message	Names	None	
Subject	The subject of the mail message	Text	None	
Body	The body of the mail message	Text	None	

Purchase Requisitions	PURCH.NSF
Inventory Items	INVENTRY.NSF
Vendors	VENDORS.NSF
Employees/Departments	DEPT.NSF

These databases can be found on the CD-ROM included with this book.

Define the Forms and Their Relationships

Now that we have a list of data elements, let's look for the one-to-one and one-to-many relationships to help us define the number of forms we need; that is, let's identify those data elements that are required only once on a purchase requisition and those that are required many times for the requisition to determine how many forms we need.

A requisition such as the one shown in Figure 10.4 usually has basic information about the vendor and originator at the top (or header) and multiple lines at the bottom (or detail) showing the items that need to be ordered. One occurrence of the fields in the header of the form is required for a requisition (one-to-one), and many occurrences of the fields in the detail of the form are required for a requisition (one-to-many). Based on our analysis, we should have one form for the header information and one form for the detail.

Let's separate our data elements worksheet into two groups of data elements. Table 10.4 will hold the data elements for our purchase requisition

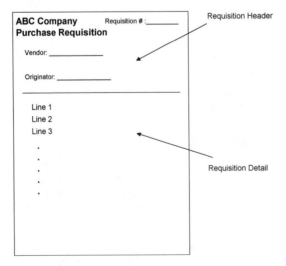

FIGURE 10.4 The layout of a typical purchase requisition.

header form and Table 10.5 will hold the data elements for our purchase requisition detail form. Note that both tables include the purchase requisition number so that all the documents associated with the purchase requisition have a common field. Otherwise, we would not be able to match the detail items to the header document that goes with them.

Although we now have two forms, we don't want the users to be able to add detail items without creating a requisition header document, nor do we want to require them to remember the requisition number when they add detail items. We want users to enter the header information in one form and then request the second form, which automatically copies the requisition number in the form as they create detail items. We accomplish this task by creating the header requisition form with a button that, when pressed, brings up the detail requisition form. We prevent the use of the detail requisition form by itself by changing the form attributes so that it does not appear in the Compose menu. We then set the form to all inherit default values, and the requisition number will appear in each detail item.

Based on our new worksheets and form analysis, we can begin to develop our purchase requisition forms. First, however, let's define the views that we need to help us determine whether there are any additional fields that we should use in either form to help us build the views.

Define Views

In the interviews with the originators, managers, purchasing agents, and purchasing managers, we were able to come up with a list of views to help them manage their information. When we asked them why they needed the views, they indicated that it would be helpful if they could locate documents by:

- ♦ Purchase requisition number
- ♦ Originator department
- ♦ Originator manager
- ♦ Purchasing agent
- ♦ Vendor

In addition, they wanted a view that summarized the purchase requisitions by total dollar value. Of course, they wanted to be able to print the requisition and send it to the vendor. As we talked to them about their views, they provided us with details about how they wanted the view to work and which elements they wanted to display.

TABLE 10.4 Purchase Requisition Header Information

Data Element	Full Description	Data Type	Restrictions (Range or List of Values)	Access Limits
Purchase Requisition	Purchase requisition number	Text	6 letters	
Requisition Date	Date that the requisition was issued	Time	None	
Requisition Status	The status of the requisition	Keyword	A List: New Submitted to Mgr Approved by Dept Submitted to VP Approved by VP Submitted to Purch Approved by Purch Order Placed Order Received	Users can only change this using buttons— no editing allowed
Originator	The person who created the requisition	Name	User who created the requisition	
Department	The originator's department	Text	Use dept lookup table	
Department Manager	The originator's manager	Names	Use dept lookup table	
Department VP	The vice president in charge of the department	Names	Use dept lookup table	
G/L Budget Account	The budget account that will be charged for the items on the requisition	Text	Default to department number, 5120, and 200 for the three segments of the account	
Date manager approved	The date that the department manager approved the req	Time	Default to today	
Date VP approved	The date that the department VP approved the requisition	Time	Default to today	
Vendor name	The name of the vendor	Text	Use vendor lookup table	
Vendor address	The vendor address	Text	Use vendor lookup table	
Vendor city	The vendor city	Text	Use vendor lookup table	
Vendor state	The vendor state	Text	Use vendor lookup table	
Vendor zip	The vendor zip code	Text	Use vendor lookup table	
Vendor phone	The vendor phone number	Text	Use vendor lookup table	
Vendor fax	The vendor fax number	Text	Use vendor lookup table	
Freight	Freight costs	Number	Two decimal places	

TABLE 10.4 Purchase Requisition Header Information (*Continued*)

Data Element	Full Description	Data Type	Restrictions (Range or List of Values)	Access Limits
Date assigned	The date that the Purchasing Agent was assigned the requisition	Time	Default to today	
Date reviewed	The date that the Purchasing Agent reviewed the approved requisition	Time	Default to today	
Date Purchasing manager approved	The date that the Purchasing manager approved the req	Time	Default to today	
Date Faxed	The date that the requisition was faxed to the vendor	Time	Default to today	
Shipping method	The shipping method to request from the vendor	Keyword	Ground 2nd day air Overnight	Others can be used
Needed by	The date that the originator needs to receive the goods	Date	None	
Terms	Payment terms from the vendor	Keyword	Net 30 2% 10 days, net 30	Others can be used
Purchasing Agent	Name of the agent who will be processing the requisition	Names	Use the user name	
Send to	The name of the person who will receive the mail message	Names	None	
Subject	The subject of the mail message	Text	None	
Body	The body of the mail message	Text	None	

Purchase Requisition Number

Sort on requisition number.

Show only the requisition header at first.

Allow users to expand the requisition to show all items.

Include the following fields for the header line:

- ◆ Requisition number
- ◆ Needed-by date
- ◆ Originator department
- ◆ Status

TABLE 10.5 Purchase Requisition Detail Information

Data Element	Full Description	Data Type	Restrictions Range or List (of Values)	Access Limits
Purchase Requisition	Purchase requisition number	Text	6 letters	
Item #	The internal item for the goods to be ordered	Text	Use inventory lookup table	
Quantity	The quantity ordered	Number	No decimals	
Description	The description of the item to be ordered	Text	Use inventory lookup table and allow additions	
Unit Price	The cost of each item	Number	Use inventory lookup table. Use two decimal places.	
Extended Price	The total cost for the item on this line of the requisition	Number	Quantity times price	
Date item received	The date that a line item is received in Shipping	Time	Default to today	

Include the following fields for the detail lines:
- ♦ Item number
- ♦ Quantity
- ♦ Description
- ♦ Unit price
- ♦ Extended price
- ♦ Total amount

Originator

Sort on originator, then requisition number.

Allow the view to expand and collapse on originator.

Use the same specification as listed for the requisition view.

Originator's Manager

Sort on originator manager, then requisition number.

Allow the view to expand and collapse on manager.

Use the same specification as listed for the requisition view.

Create a second view sorted by manager, status, and requisition.

Allow the view to expand and collapse on manager and on status.

Use the same specification as listed for the requisition view.

Purchasing Agent

Sort on purchasing agent, then requisition number.

Allow the view to expand and collapse on purchasing agent.

Use the same specification as listed for the requisition view.

Vendor

Sort on vendor name, then requisition number.

Allow the view to expand and collapse on vendor.

Use the same specification as listed for the requisition view.

The users agreed that the view by originator manager would also be good for creating totals by requisition. To accommodate this, we will modify the specification to show only the requisition number and the vendor name on the requisition header line, which will make the document totals more easy to read. Now let's take a look at our views and see what we will need to add to the forms to help us create the views.

The requisition view can be created easily using the fields that will be in each of the forms. The sorts by originator and originator manager, however, cannot be done using the existing forms because the detail item documents do not contain those fields. We must include those fields in the detail requisition form and fill them in automatically from the requisition header form as we add new items so that we can display the documents in the view.

The sorts by originator manager and status, by purchasing agent, and by vendor pose a problem, and reveal a limitation in Notes. The status of the requisition will always be changing and we won't know the Purchasing agent or vendor until the requisition has been created and approved. As a result, there is no easy way for Notes to update the detail documents with the new values from the header document. We can create a macro that uses a lookup function for each detail line item to obtain the latest values for the status, purchasing agent, and vendor from the requisition header. Those lookups will take a lot of time, but we can try it. At this point, we must alert the users to the speed issues and the necessity of running a macro so that their expectations are set properly.

The users also want to print a purchase requisition, another task ill-suited for a Notes view. Notes does not allow a lot of formatting in a view, and it is difficult to come up with an acceptable requisition in any view. And we can't merge two forms into one so that the detail lines appear on the same form as the header lines. Version 4.0 of Notes allows multiple lines of text to appear for each line of a view, but the result still won't print out in a way that can be sent to a vendor.

To work around the problem, we can use a combination of a form and a view to get the requisition. We'll create a hidden view that has two columns, one for the requisition number and one that uses all of the detail line fields to build a text version of the detail item. In the form, we'll use lookup commands to search the view and place the lines on the form for printing.

Develop a Prototype

We're finally ready to create the purchase requisition application. Remember, this isn't a true prototype because we aren't able to interact. However, we'll stop during key steps in the development process and consider what has been completed and what a user might change.

First, we'll create the purchase requisition header form. As a part of our development infrastructure, we'll create a template called Empty Database that has our logo and a few buttons to help us get started. As shown in Figure 10.5, we'll use the template to begin our first form. Notice that the logo and title appear twice at the top of the form. The first line is set up to appear only when the document is being read. The second line

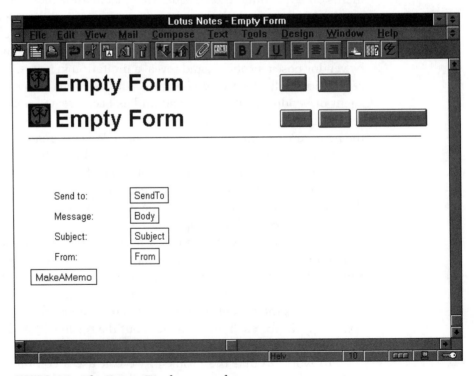

FIGURE 10.5 The Empty Database template.

shows up only when the document is being edited. By using two lines, we can show only the buttons that are required for the document in whatever state it is in.

Using our first worksheet, we'll change the empty form into a requisition header form. At this point, we are more interested in getting the form right than developing the workflow, so we'll just concentrate on building a functional form. After the first pass at the form (shown in Figures 10.6 and 10.7), it's a good time to show it to the users.

Notice how the form automatically calculates departments and managers based on the name of the originator. The vendor name field uses the vendor file to display a list of vendors and then automatically updates the address fields. Shipping methods and terms are keyword fields that can be overridden to add custom entries.

Now we need to modify the prototype to add the form for the detail requisition items. Again, we are interested in just getting the form done, so we'll build the version shown in Figure 10.8. We'll show the users this stage, too, and get some feedback on the look and content of the forms. Let's assume that they told us that they would like a way to call up a requisition header from the detail screen. If we had a doclink in the detail form, the

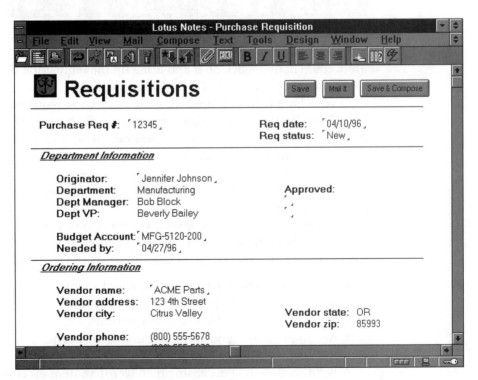

FIGURE 10.6 The Purchase Requisition form, part 1.

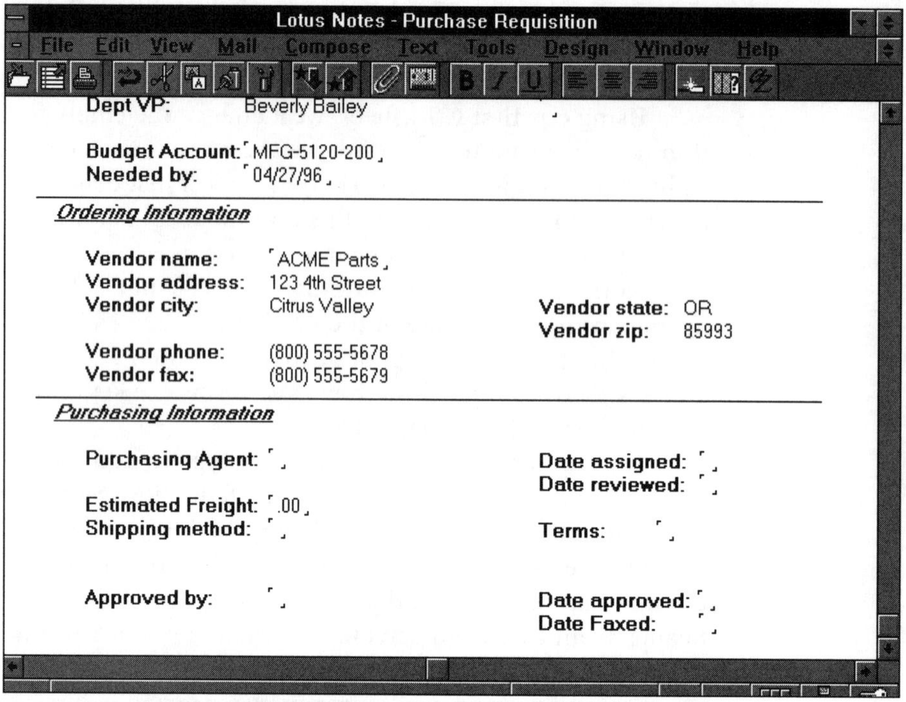

FIGURE 10.7 The Purchase Requisition form, part 2.

users could double-click on it and bring up the requisition header. We'll add a rich text field to the detail form for the doclink.

With both forms completed, we'll modify the requisition header form to call the detail form by using a button. We don't need the Mail It or Save and Compose buttons for this application, so we'll erase them and substitute a Create Detail Lines button. We'll also use the button to store a doclink to the requisition header and to paste it into the rich text field on the detail form. Figure 10.9 shows the button definition and the formula required to call the detail form.

At this stage of development, we can capture information with our forms, so now it's time to add workflow capabilities to them. Looking at our workflow diagram reveals seven workflow tasks to accomplish:

♦ Send mail to the department manager for approval.
♦ Send mail to the vice president if any line item exceeds $2,000.
♦ Test approval cycle for overdue approvals.
♦ Assign purchase requisition to Purchasing agent.
♦ Request more information.
♦ Send mail to the Purchasing manager if an item exceeds $500.
♦ Fax the purchase requisition to a vendor.

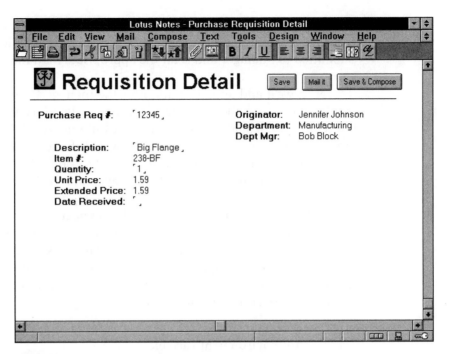

FIGURE 10.8   The Purchase Requisition Detail form.

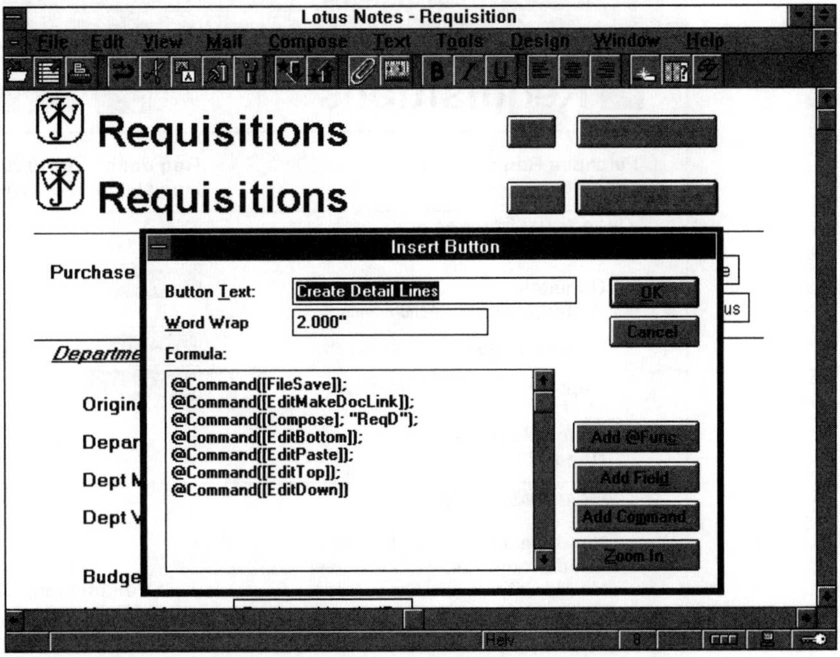

FIGURE 10.9   Creating a button to call the Purchase Requisition Detail form.

We'll also add a button to our form for the originator to push when the requisition is entered. The button will change the requisition status to Submitted to Manager and send the appropriate mail message to the manager.

Next we'll add another button for the manager to use to approve the requisition and set the status to Submitted to Purchasing. If there are any line items over $2,000, the button will use Submitted to VP instead and send the VP a mail message, asking for approval of the requisition.

Finally, we'll add a button for the VP to push that sets the status to Submitted to Purchasing. Both the manager and the VP buttons update the appropriate approval date field, as shown in Figure 10.10.

Before we move on to the rest of the application, let's take a closer look at some of the formulas behind the buttons and in some of the fields. Both the button formulas and the field formulas work together to make the appropriate changes happen. When you push the Submit to Manager button, for example, the formula shown in Figure 10.11 is executed. The formula causes several events to occur:

♦ The originator name, manager name, and requisition status are stored in three environment variables.

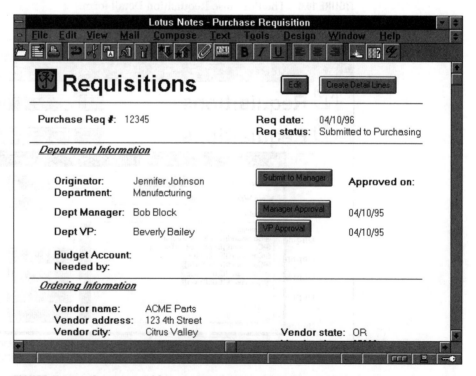

FIGURE 10.10 The approval buttons in the Purchase Requisition form.

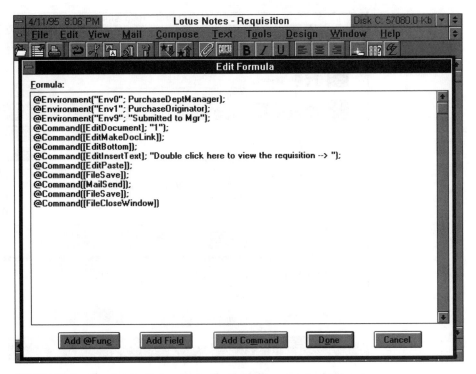

FIGURE 10.11   The formula for the Submit to Manager button.

♦ A doclink is created and stored in the last field on the form.
♦ The document is saved with the changes.
♦ A mail message is sent to the manager.
♦ The document is saved after the mail message is sent and the form is closed.

You may have noticed that there is no place where the Requisition Status field seems to change. In Notes, every field is recalculated when a document is saved. Let's look into the field formula for the Requisition Status to see how the act of pushing the button forces it to change (see Figure 10.12).

The Requisition Status is a calculated field that tests an environment variable for a value. If there is a value, it changes to that value. If there is no value in the environment variable, then it sets itself to a New status if the document is new; otherwise, it uses its current value. A hidden field at the end of the form clears all environment variables preventing the formulas from picking up unintended changes.

Note that, currently, anyone can push the approval buttons. The fields were not set up to limit access to them in the prototype stage so that we

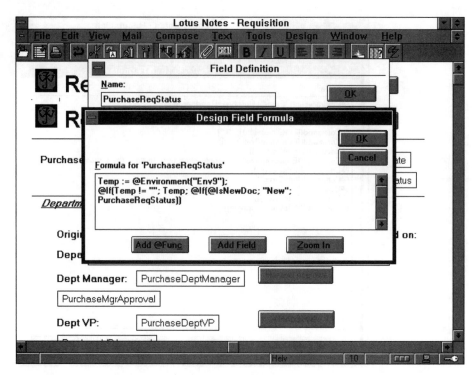

FIGURE 10.12   Changing the Requisition Status field.

could test the application and play with it. When the application is ready for production, a developer must insert formulas that compare the manager name with that of the person pushing the button. If the names don't match, the button won't execute the tasks.

Let's get back to our Purchase Requisition project. Our next workflow task calls for a macro to test for documents that have not been approved in a timely fashion by the manager. We want to test the status and approval dates to make sure that the manager approves requisitions on time. We'll assume that the macro will be run once a day. The macro in Figure 10.13 shows the formula required to perform one of the tests of approval dates. It tests to determine that: 1. the status is set to Submitted to Manager, 2. the requisition has not been approved by the manager (a blank date), 3. the requisition is over two days old, and 4. the document being reviewed is a requisition head, not a detail document. If all four tests are successful, the macro updates the mail-enabling fields (SendTo, Subject, From) and then sends the mail message.

The macro for the vice president would be very similar, checking instead for the Submitted to VP status and waiting for five days after the manager's approval date. We could also enhance any of the macros to notify

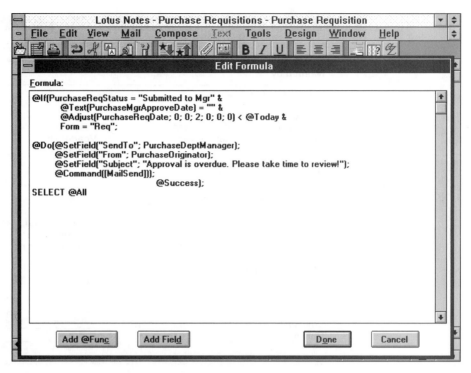

FIGURE 10.13   Macro that looks for overdue approvals.

superiors (assuming the employee database indicates who they are) of late approvals. If we had the right kind of third-party package or an application written with the Notes API, we could even send the message to the offender's beeper!

Now that the macro is reminding everyone to approve the requisitions, we can move on to the workflow for Purchasing. The Purchasing agents review the databases periodically to see if there are any requisitions marked Submitted to Purchasing. When they find one, they call it up and push a button called Assign to Agent that inserts the user name as the Purchasing agent and changes the assignment date to today's date.

The Purchasing agent reviews the requisition for accuracy. If information is missing, the agent wants to be able to send the originator a comment and request more information. We will add a comment field at the bottom of the form and a Need More Information button next to it. When the agent presses the button shown at the bottom of Figure 10.14, the mail message is sent to the originator, with the requisition number and the comment in the subject of the mail message.

Once the Purchasing agent is satisfied that the requisition is complete, he or she pushes a button to mark the requisition as reviewed. If there is a

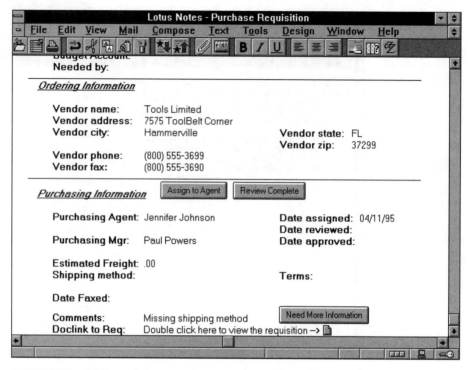

FIGURE 10.14 Adding a button to request more information.

line item over $500, the button also sends a mail message to the manager of Purchasing. Otherwise, the button fills in the approval date for the Purchasing manager and marks the requisition as Approved by Purchasing.

The Purchasing manager needs a button to mark the requisition after it is ready for approval. The button updates the approval date and changes the status of the requisition to Approved by Purchasing.

Finally, we need to send the completed requisition to the vendor. Notice the Fax It button on the form in the Purchasing Information section. We'll use that button to bring up a form that puts both the requisition header and requisition detail on one screen. We'll assume that the user has a fax program such as WinFax or a fax gateway that uses the printer driver to "print" the requisition to the appropriate modem that will send it out. The resulting changes are shown in Figure 10.15.

The Purchase Requisition Fax form is shown in Figure 10.16. It uses fields from the Purchase Requisition form to display the information in a way that mimics a purchase requisition. A field was added at the top of the screen to log the date and time that the fax was sent. The Print Fax button "prints" the fax and saves a copy of the document with the date that the fax was sent.

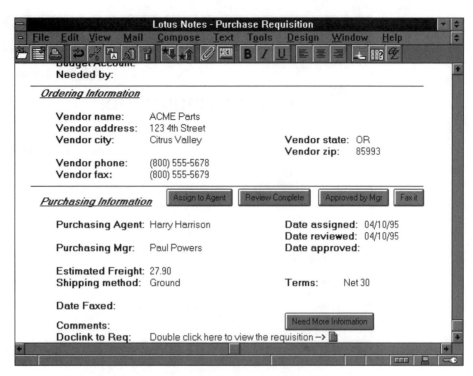

FIGURE 10.15   Completed Purchase Requisition form.

We had to make a few compromises in developing this form because of some other limitations in Notes. The line items at the bottom of the screen did not come from detail requisitions; instead, a hidden view called Purchase Req Fax was created, containing two columns, one for the requisition number and another built from the five fields that make up the detail line. Using a **@DbLookup** command in a text field, the form searches the Purchase Req Fax view and returns all of the text lines that match the requisition number. Unfortunately, the text will not line up if formatted in proportionally spaced fonts such as Helvetica, therefore the text field had to be formatted in a Courier font. In addition, version 3.x of Notes does not include a formula to sum up the line items, which means the requisition doesn't have a total.

The reason that we had to go to so much trouble to print the lines is that Notes does not supply the developer with a method for listing data elements side by side in columns. We could have placed five keyword fields in the detail area, but every element would have been displayed with a radio button or check box. For now, this is about the best we can do to get our requisition out.

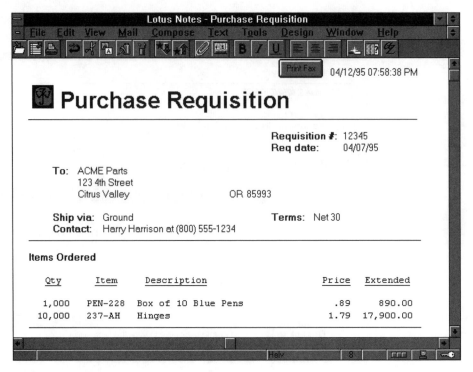

FIGURE 10.16   Purchase Requisition Fax form.

It's time again to take the forms to the users and see how they like them. The workflow features are ready to go, and we could even ask the users to start testing the prototype on some sample applications. The worst that they could do is send a few too many electronic mail messages or fax one or two bogus requisitions to an unsuspecting vendor.

At this juncture, the prototype will also give us more information to work with as we develop the views. Although the users requested several views, they shouldn't take long to develop because they are very similar. We'll start with the view by Purchase Requisition Number, shown in Figure 10.17. The view provides us with a list of documents sorted by requisition number. A hidden column was added to the view to sort the requisition header to the top, followed by fax documents and then detail line items. We modified the requisition header so that it displays the due date, department, and requisition status. The fax document shows the date that the fax was sent.

The view by Originator and Originator's Manager are simply modifications of our Requisition Number view. By adding one more category to the view, as shown in Figures 10.18 and 10.19, we are able to display the

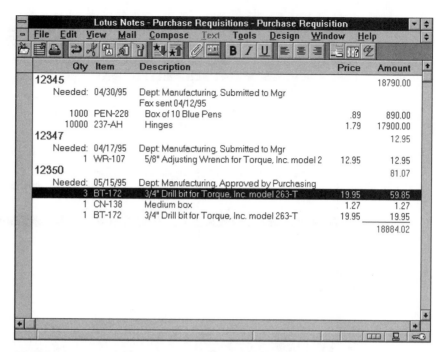

FIGURE 10.17 Purchase Requisitions by Requisition Number.

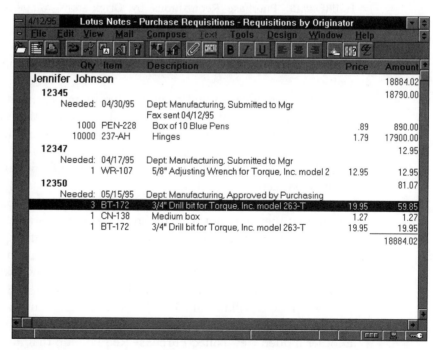

FIGURE 10.18 Purchase Requisitions by Originator and Requisition Number.

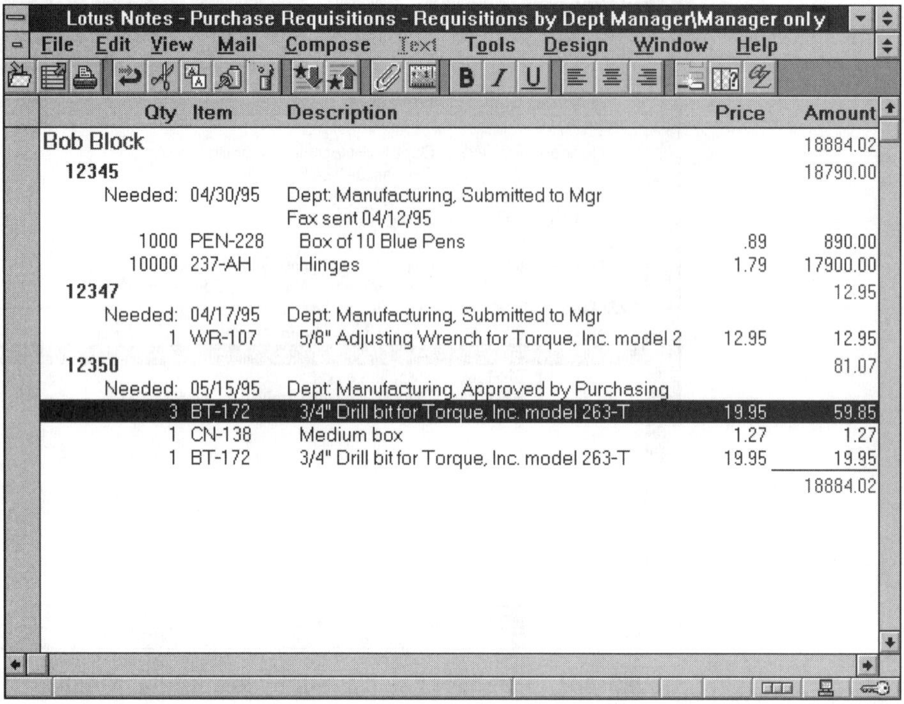

FIGURE 10.19 Purchase Requisitions by Originator's Manager and Requisition Number.

same information, but now sorted by originator or originator's manager as well.

Our users also wanted a view sorted by manager and requisition status, which poses a problem because the detail requisition documents do not contain the latest requisition status. We can choose to print only the requisition headers, or we can create a macro that updates the detail documents with the status. The header information is probably not enough, so we will create the macro.

Our views by Purchasing Agent and Vendor Name pose the same problem in that they may not have the most current information in them. We'll create the macro so that it updates all three fields (status, purchasing agent, and vendor name) at once. The macro must be run each time we want to display the views, and the lookups to update those views will take time. The user should be made aware of these limitations before we move forward.

The macro will be called Update detail documents, and it will contain the formula shown in Figure 10.20. The formula performs a lookup into another hidden view called Purchase Req Lookup that has a sorted column

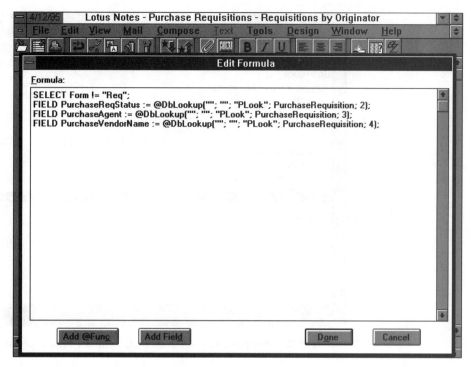

FIGURE 10.20 The Update detail documents macro.

for the requisition number, followed by columns for status, purchasing agent, and vendor name. It searches for documents with a form called ReqD, the detail documents, and replaces all the fields.

With the fields in the detail documents updated, we can create the final views. Figure 10.21 shows the view by Originator's Manager and Status. Figure 10.22 shows the view by Purchasing Agent, and Figure 10.23 shows the view by Vendor Name.

If the users decide that they don't really want to go through the update process, all we can provide them with is the information in the requisition header or the requisition detail document. We can certainly create all the same views without the requisition details, but they wouldn't be as informative. It is possible to automatically paste doclinks in the requisition header that point to each line item, but the existing Requisition by Requisition Number view is probably easier to read. In any case, there will be some compromises, and they can be worked out.

Finally, our prototype is finished. Actually, prototypes are never finished, but we have enough forms and views to give our users something to

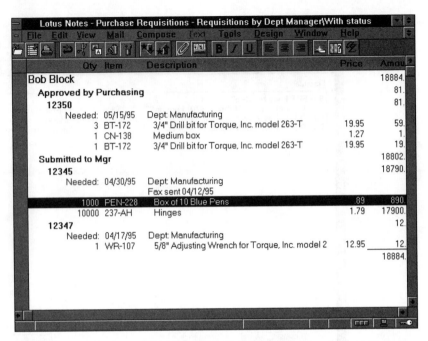

FIGURE 10.21   Purchase Requisitions by Originator's Manager and Status.

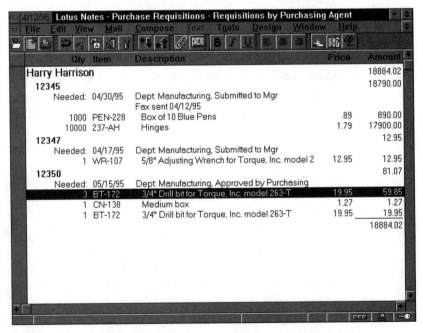

FIGURE 10.22   Purchase Requisitions by Purchasing Agent and Requisition Number.

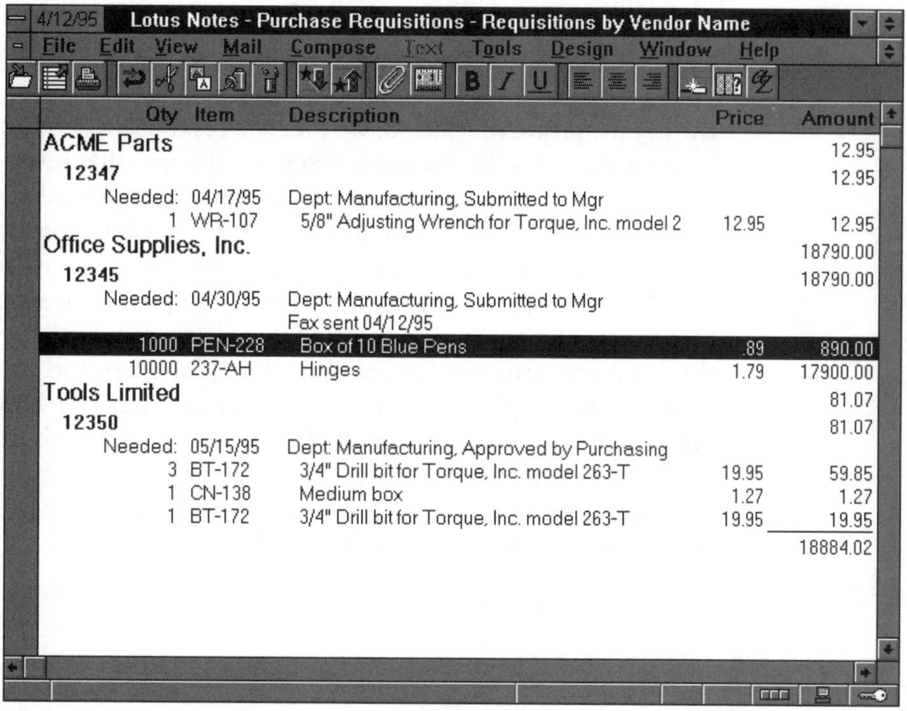
4/12/95 Lotus Notes - Purchase Requisitions - Requisitions by Vendor Name
File Edit View Mail Compose Text Tools Design Window Help
Qty Item Description Price Amount
ACME Parts 12.95
12347 12.95
Needed: 04/17/95 Dept: Manufacturing, Submitted to Mgr
1 WR-107 5/8" Adjusting Wrench for Torque, Inc. model 2 12.95 12.95
Office Supplies, Inc. 18790.00
12345 18790.00
Needed: 04/30/95 Dept: Manufacturing, Submitted to Mgr
Fax sent 04/12/95
1000 PEN-228 Box of 10 Blue Pens .89 890.00
10000 237-AH Hinges 1.79 17900.00
Tools Limited 81.07
12350 81.07
Needed: 05/15/95 Dept: Manufacturing, Approved by Purchasing
3 BT-172 3/4" Drill bit for Torque, Inc. model 263-T 19.95 59.85
1 CN-138 Medium box 1.27 1.27
1 BT-172 3/4" Drill bit for Torque, Inc. model 263-T 19.95 19.95
18884.02

FIGURE 10.23 Purchase Requisitions by Vendor Name and Requisition Number.

test and check out. Any further changes to the database can probably be made with the users sitting next to us as they show us how they use the new requisition application.

Finalize Requirements

If we review our database, form, and view definitions, it looks like we've accomplished everything that the users wanted. At some point, we should draw up a written agreement with the users stating either that we have accomplished the project goal, or that the listed features should have been included but weren't. The users need to understand where the project ends so that we can make the application operational and assign someone to its maintenance.

Finally, we should agree on a time line for testing the prototype and develop a test plan that will show we have satisfied user requirements. We need to check in with the users regularly to make sure that they are using the prototype and adequately testing it. (In most cases, they will be checking in with us frequently, asking questions and requesting changes.)

Implement the Prototype and Enhance the Product

During the prototype period, we must be responsive to fine-tuning the database for the users. We want to encourage changes that result in time savings or efficiencies, but we also want to discourage large-scale design modifications unless the application just doesn't work. With Notes on the network, the changes should be easy to make and distribute to the user.

Once the prototype is considered complete, the database is implemented for the entire organization. We discussed all the requirements for this implementation in Chapter 7: training for users and support people, an implementation plan, hardware upgrades, and ongoing support. The original prototypers may be excited about the application, but the other users still don't have a clue about what it does. They will come to understand how the application works through good training, and they won't fear using it if they know good support is a phone call away.

Summary

Application development in Lotus Notes follows many of the same patterns found in other development environments. The key to success is the mixture of the disciplines of traditional methodologies and the freedom of rapid application development through prototyping. If we take time up front to gather requirements and document what the users want, while actively pursuing prototyping during the development phase, our Notes applications should have an excellent chance of success.

11

The Morning After

It can be difficult to understand how Notes works until you see it in action. Nevertheless, through the printed word and our imaginations let's consider how ABC Company will benefit from a Notes implementation once the entire staff has it on their desktop. The scenario that follows portrays a typical day at ABC Company after Notes has been installed throughout the company. These ideas are practical and well within the capabilities of any company using Notes. You may want to refer back to Chapter 9 as a database that is mentioned here can be better understood by looking at its screen reproductions included in that chapter's samples.

A Day in the Life of ABC Company

Joe arrives, as usual, at 6 A.M. to get a head start before the morning rush. As the facilities engineer, Joe fixes everything and anything at ABC Company. He flips on his PC on the way to the coat rack, grabs a cup of coffee, and returns to log in to Notes Mail. His work life revolves around the mail system. After some initial misgivings about Notes, Joe feels pretty good about using the system now.

Today's mail is typical, with two messages labeled URGENT! and 10 entries that can wait until later. He pops up the urgent messages and finds that he has a busy morning ahead of him. Message 1 requests the connection of phone equipment by 9 A.M. for a vice president and three staff people who moved to the second floor to work on a rush project. Four doclinks are included with the message, pointing to the Move database, which contains the room numbers and the phone extensions involved.

The next message begs for help in setting up a conference room requiring extra network connections for a big demonstration at 1 P.M. The sender forgot to arrange the setup, but has promised Joe a dozen donuts and juice the next morning if he can get it done on time. The message includes the request that Joe try not to interrupt the other meetings in that room. He switches windows in order to open the Meeting Schedule database. He finds that the room is open for 30 minutes at 8:30 A.M., at which time he can easily make the connections and do a quick test of the ports.

Joe wants to add the mail messages to his to-do list, so he selects the To-Do form from the View menu and changes the message. He clicks Priority One for the urgent messages, saves them, and then checks the view to see how he's doing on his other calls. He's in good shape, so he grabs his tools and heads for the wiring closet.

It takes Joe only 30 minutes or so to make the wiring changes on the second floor and update the Telecommunications Punchdown database with those changes. He wants to leave a voice mail message for the VP's administrative assistant saying that the job is finished, so he opens the Name and Address Book, selects a view by last name, finds the assistant's phone number, and makes the call.

Next he sets up the conference room, returns to his desk, and pulls up the priority calls so he can close them out. The to-do document holds a doclink to the Help Desk Call Tracking database and he clicks on the icon, enters the completion time, and closes the call.

Joe isn't the only early riser at ABC Company. Sharon opens up the Help Desk at 7 A.M. for all the early birds who roll into ABC and need her help. She opens the Call Tracking database and reviews the new calls and the status of the open calls. She prioritizes the new calls, answers one or two easy ones, and clicks on the Reply button to forward the answers back to the senders. One call was from a user who was having trouble selecting a network printer in the Windows Control Panel. Sharon thinks she remembers helping someone else with the same problem, and to find out, she opens the

PC Expert System database. Sure enough, there is already a full explanation of the procedure in the database. Sharon creates a doclink, places it in the call, and forwards it to the sender.

The phone rings for the first time that day and it's the technician from the local computer store. A user has called in a bad monitor and the tech needs some warranty information. She opens the Computer Inventory database for him and finds that the PC was purchased six months ago on invoice #12874. In anticipation of receiving a return authorization number, Sharon pushes the RMA button on the inventory form to open the RMA database. She keys in the number as the technician reads it to her.

Another call lights up the phone set, and it's one of the software support specialists. She needs a TCP/IP address for another user who wants to be on the company network. As Sharon pops up the Network Addresses database, the specialist also wants to know if the server called SERVER_MFG was backed up last night, and if so, if a certain file was on the tape. Sharon reads the new network address to the specialists and opens the Tape Backup library database, using the server view to find last night's log. Yes, the file is on Tape 17 and Sharon tells the specialist which drive in the computer room she can use to recall the file.

Sharon next takes time to replenish her office supplies. Having Lotus Notes doesn't mean Sharon doesn't still use a lot of sticky notes, floppies, and other miscellaneous items. Besides, users know she has them so she's always running short. She selects Purchase Office Supplies from the custom forms Mail menu and fills in the form. A new Help Desk person will be starting shortly so she adds business cards on the order for him as well. One click of the Send button and the order heads for Purchasing.

Jim in Purchasing checks the Purchase Requisitions Database several times a day. Today's batch includes the list from Sharon and a requisition from the storeroom clerk in Manufacturing for some cleaning fluid and safety glasses. The clerk forgot to get the necessary supervisor's approval, so Jim adds a message to the document and pushes the More Information Needed button to send the requisition back. Sharon has purchase authority so Jim marks the document approved. He uses suppliers that also have Notes, and the ABC server will replicate with them at noon, sending Sharon's request to one of them.

Around 9 A.M., Jim takes a break and walks next door to see his friend Terri in the Print Shop. Terri is a little busy because the head of Sales sent a big request to her Print Shop Request database this morning—1,000 copies of a 20-page piece created in Microsoft Word, due out tomorrow morning. She had detached the file from the Notes document and was printing the document when Jim walked in.

While she waited for the output, Terri asked Jim if he had heard back about their suggestion on how to reduce the cost of copier paper. Jim hadn't received a response, so, once the document finished printing, they opened the Suggestions database and checked on the status. Their eyes lit up as they read that their idea was approved and was being considered for a monetary reward.

Jim returns to his desk and works on a few more requisitions. He chuckles as he pops up another T-shirt requisition from Bob in Advertising. Jim was warned by Accounting that Bob is over budget and shouldn't buy any unnecessary items. Besides, Jim remembers that he just received 1,000 shirts a couple of weeks ago. He opens the Inventory Data Warehouse and finds that there should be 500 shirts in the warehouse as of last Friday. He adds a comment to the requisition, clicks on the Not Approved button to send Bob the news, and forwards a copy to Susan in Accounting to let her know Bob is up to his old tricks.

Susan keeps a tight rein on the budgets at ABC Company. She worked hard on the project that used Notes to facilitate a yearly budget process that formerly took months to complete. The Budget database now integrates with the managers' budget spreadsheets and the company accounting package, allowing her to integrate changes, track justifications, and compare budgets to actuals on a daily basis.

Tom sits in the cube next to Susan and handles the accounts receivables collections. Susan sold him on Notes, and now he uses a Bad Debt database to track all the sordid details about their slow-paying customers. Every night, the database is updated with all new overdue accounts, along with any transactions that had been posted for them. Tom logs all phone calls and correspondence in the database. He also built a "tickler" view to remind him who should receive a follow-up call when a customer doesn't clear up the account. If a customer pays the balance, Tom clicks a button that notifies the appropriate salesperson via e-mail that the account is clear and they can again accept COD orders. He also checks the Fax database to see if any new faxes have come in for him and, if he finds one, he creates a doclink and pastes it into the customer record of his Bad Debt database.

Remote salespeople like Brenda breathe a sigh of relief when they see Tom's messages, because it means they'll finally get their commission on the sale. Notes has really helped them sell more products now that the entire widget line has been loaded into the Widget Catalog database. Now they can show their clients the product line, print out the specifications, and even enter quotes and orders in the Widget Quotes/Orders database. Periodically, Brenda connects with the home office, opens up the Presentations database, and downloads the slides from the latest regional sales meeting.

Brenda's customers have also been very pleased with the Notes databases that they can now access. For an annual fee, a customer can call ABC Company and download the ABC Information Database and get the latest scoop on widgets. They also can bring up the Widget Technical notes database so that their employees can look up information online as they implement their widgets.

After another long day of selling, Brenda arrives home, kicks off her shoes, and fires up her laptop to update her Notes databases. She calls up the Contacts database and enters all the information off the business cards that she collected that day. She also needs an advance for a big trip to the National Widget Convention, and for that she opens the Advance Requests database and creates a document. One click on the Submit button saves the request and sends a mail message to her supervisor, asking that her request be approved and forwarded to Accounting.

Each Friday, Brenda pulls the pile of receipts out of her briefcase, opens the Expense Reports database, and creates an expense report for the week. The Accounting department processes the Notes expense reports immediately and holds them until they receive the accompanying receipts in the mail. If Brenda can get hers in the mail today, her reimbursement should be direct deposited in the bank by Tuesday.

Once the Notes chores are complete, Brenda uses Notes to dial the 800 number and replicate with the server. Ten minutes pass before Notes finishes the last update, and she refreshes the unread messages indicator on the desktop icons. She sees that three new documents are available in the Sales Leads database, and she can't resist checking them out. Brenda adds some quick thoughts to the lead document and then checks her mail one last time, answers a few more messages, and saves the replication for Monday morning.

Back in Accounting, Suzanne checks her mail and sees Brenda's automatic message telling her that the expense report has been submitted. Suzanne takes advantage of the time difference between many of the salespeople and the home office because it gives her time to process their expense reports before she goes home at 5 P.M. When she opens her mail on Monday, she'll find Brenda's receipts, scan them, store the image in Notes, and authorize a reimbursement check for the Tuesday check run.

Suzanne also handles the Accounts Payables invoices, and she's excited about the new integration with the accounting system. Whenever she receives an invoice, she composes an invoice document in the Invoice Approval database and searches the Requisitions database for the original document. When she finds a requisition, Suzanne pushes a button to add a doclink in the invoice document to the requisition. She scans the invoice and attaches the image to the document.

When she is finished updating the invoice document, Suzanne clicks on the Request Approval button, and Notes sends a message to the supervisor who requested the goods or services. That person also clicks a button to approve the invoice and notify Suzanne. She verifies the Notes electronic signature and pushes Send Invoice to the Accounting Module, uploading the invoice into a batch in the accounting system.

The folks in the Human Resources department used to share Suzanne's scanner but they finally had to buy their own as the pile of resumés grew. First thing in the morning, John, the intern from State College, opens the mail and finds all the resumés. He opens the Candidate Tracking database, enters each candidate's basic information, scans the resumé, and adds it to the Notes document.

Jane is responsible for adding new positions to the Job Posting database and for circulating the new resumés. She checks the database for new candidates regularly, matches them to the appropriate position in the Job Posting database document, and clicks a button to doclink the Job Posting to the resumé. Jane clicks another button that notifies the originator of the job posting that a potential candidate is available and listed in the Candidate Tracking database.

Brad takes over for Jane when a manager wants to hire a candidate. Every time an offer is made, he attaches the Microsoft Word document to a Notes document in the tracking database. When people are hired, Brad uses a template to create a new database called the Performance Review database. Managers will use this database throughout the year to set goals for the employee, to store activities that support the goals, and to help them finish their reviews on time.

Each new employee also receives a welcome message in his or her new electronic mailbox. The message explains that the Employee Handbook database contains an electronic version of the handbook given to them at orientation. It also explains how to use the timecard form, complete a timecard, and update the Timecard database. When new hires need to change an address or apply for the 401K program, the message instructs them on how to use the Benefits Requests database to confidentially make the changes. The message also informs them that they will be shown the Training Schedules database so that they can sign up for the mandatory classes on the company's standard word processing and spreadsheet applications.

The latest addition to ABC Company is a project manager named Diana. She used Notes at her previous job and was excited to see the databases that were created to facilitate project management at this new job. The proposal manager uses a Proposal Planning database to track Requests for Proposal (RFP) that have been received and to store preliminary information gathered about the RFP. The project managers use a Project Management database to keep tabs on each project that is approved, and to store tasks, track hours, and generate to-do's for the members of their team. The team members update the database every night before they go home.

Diana specializes in large government RFPs and, for her proposals, she uses a template to create the Proposal Management database. She doclinks back to the original proposal in the planning database and creates an outline for her response. She adds all the supporting information that will go into the final proposal, and she uses Notes to add text and edit the work of others who assist her.

The latest proposal requires some special equipment so Diana opens the Capital Planning database to see if the funds are available. She submits a request for the equipment, pending approval of her bid, and explains the circumstances in the comments field. She adds a doclink back to the proposal to assist the reviewer in understanding the project.

In the Executive Suite, Rachel is busily preparing for the weekly planning meetings with the president. She checks the Meetings database to see if all the managers have indicated that they will attend. She makes some minor changes to the agenda and pushes a button to send a reminder to every attendee that the meeting is scheduled for 9 A.M. the next morning.

During the meeting, Rachel is responsible for taking notes and updating the Weekly Meetings Discussion database. The discussions are often lively, and the planning team really appreciates how well Rachel captures both the content and the emotion that is exchanged. The managers also check the database sometime during the week and add response documents to clarify what was said at the meeting.

As president of ABC Company, Dale relies on Notes for much of his information. Every Monday morning, he opens the Status Reports database and peruses the messages from each of his direct reports. Each manager summarizes the highlights from the week as responses; subsequently, Dale clicks on a radio button to indicate to Rachel that he wants the item on his weekly Good News messages to employees. The managers also summarize their concerns, which Dale brings to the weekly meeting as discussion items.

Next, Dale opens the Sales Data Warehouse database to check on yesterday's sales figures. The year-end is only two months away and he's been considering a special campaign to boost revenue and end the year on an all-time high. The view by product line shows strong sales for the Industrial and Commercial Widgets, but lackluster numbers for Home Widgets. The view by region shows that the West Coast figures are low for Industrial Widgets, and the Mountain region is even lower. He'll bring up the campaign idea for Industrial Widgets at the weekly meeting and see what may be causing the slow sales for that product line.

Dale is also concerned about the company's spending. Last month, it had record sales but also record expenses. He opens the General Ledger Accounts Data Warehouse and displays the view by month and highest dollar value. The company Telecommunications Expense account has become the highest nonmanufacturing expense, and the Promotional Gifts and Trade Shows accounts appear to be significantly over budget. He selects the view by account and month, and sees that the trend has continued for the last four months, although the last sales campaign ended two months ago. Dale sends a mail message to Rachel to add another topic to the planning meeting agenda. He forwards a copy to the company controller, Janet, for followup.

Notes Mail notifies Janet that new messages have been received just as she opens the Copier/Fax/Phone Usage database. The company implemented automatic fax capability for anyone who wants product literature, and many marketing campaigns for Industrial Widgets are introduced to ABC resellers via fax. Sure enough, fax usage by Marketing is up 400 percent over last month. A quick look in the Sales Data Warehouse shows that Industrial Widgets aren't logging the sales numbers to support the increased activity, information she will bring to the weekly planning meeting.

Janet checks her mail and finds Dale's query. She jumps back to the Copier/Fax/Phone Usage database and uses the view by month and service type to check the numbers. She notes a large increase in the bills for 800 numbers about a month after the new support center came online. There are additional T1 line costs as well, which, coupled with the higher fax usage, has caused the spike. Janet summarizes the costs in a mail message and forwards it to Dale for the weekly meeting.

Like the rest of the executive team, Janet relies on Rachel for many administrative tasks. To keep track of phone calls, Rachel created her own Phone Message database. As she picks up the phone, Rachel switches Notes windows to the Phone Message database and immediately starts composing a phone message. After she fills in the appropriate information, she pushes a button to send it to the intended recipient. If the sometimes absentminded executives lose a message, Rachel can bring up a view by recipient, caller, or date and find it for them.

Dale likes to stay in close contact with key customers, vendors, and community leaders, and for that purpose, Rachel also maintains the Executive Phone Book. In it, Dale and the other executives store names and addresses of key people, their spouses and childrens' names, birthdays, anniversaries, and anything that will help them remember personal information. An intern at the local college comes in every two weeks to send out company calendars and cards that the executives sign before mailing.

The Human Resources employees want the same kind of closeness with their employees, and to that end, they created an ABC People database. In it, they store a scanned image of each employee with his or her department, hometown address, birthday, and college name. Employees have the option not to have their personal information included, but most of them get a kick out of the pictures. The view by college has become the focus of a small rivalry as alumni from the two local colleges check to see who has the most alums at ABC Company.

The Human Resources people also replaced the company newsletters with a Newsletter database. Dale's weekly Good News column is now a document, as are the listings of new hires, upcoming events, and policy changes. They work closely with local hospitals that also use Notes and include tips on wellness, health clinics, and medical services.

ABC Company also has an underground flea market that pre-Notes filled the company bulletin boards with ads for everything under the sun. Human Resources wanted to be able to preapprove the items before posting and monitor the boards for appropriate items. They replaced the bulletin boards with a Want Ads database where people can sell their wares via Notes. An employee composes a Want Ad and indicates when it should expire. The Human Resources people approve the ad so that it will show up on views sorted by category, location, and person. Employees who call up an ad can respond via Notes Mail to the originator. The item will either be erased during the monthly purge, or the originator can click on Sold! to eliminate it.

Supervisors also wanted some help from Human Resources to manage vacations schedules, and for that reason, Brad created a Vacation database template. The database stores vacation requests and approvals for all the employees in every department. The IS group has set up a semimonthly feed to the database that brings in the hours available to each employee. The view by available hours is available only to the supervisors to help them know when to approve vacations.

Human Resources has also started a new process improvement initiative, and to keep everyone informed on the progress of each group, a Process Improvement database was created to store the results of meetings, interviews, and findings, and to hold flowcharts and diagrams created to explain the process. The executive team browses the database regularly to learn more about the company, and the process improvement facilitators can keep track of the amount of time invested in the improvement activities.

When Human Resources queried ABC Company employees about improvement, the employees felt strongly that they must have a better understanding of the company goals to be able to recommend the best areas for improvement. The executives were more than willing to publish their strategic goals, as were the managers of each of the major departments. Brad worked with each of them to create a Company Goals database. It lists the corporate goals and ties the department managers' goals to them. Each document describes the goal, why it has been selected, how it will be measured, and what progress has been made against it. Within a week of publishing the database, hundreds of employees had read the information, and a general rise in morale was evident.

It's almost quitting time, so Joe, our facilities engineer, plops down in his chair to check his mail one last time. In it, he finds a survey about the use of Lotus Notes at ABC Company. There are only 10 questions and he answers them favorably by clicking on the appropriate check boxes and radio buttons. In the comments field, he writes "It sure has helped me do my job better!" Joe pushes the Return the Survey—Thanks! button to send his reply to the Surveys database. He exits Notes and Windows, shuts off his computer, and heads home. Notes will be waiting for him in the morning with another crazy day of activities.

12

The Culture Surrounding Lotus Notes

At first glance, Lotus Notes may look like just another application package to you. Many people are introduced to it at work or as part of an applications suite. Soon, however, Notes power users are telling you "Isn't Notes great! We can do a zillion things with it. You begin to wonder: Are these people serious or in desperate need of deprogramming? If Notes power users seem a little overzealous, it's because Lotus Notes is more than an application to them. In owning Notes, they have joined a culture supported by the resources of Lotus Development and fostered by a growing armada of resellers and consultants who have built thriving businesses on Notes sales and support. These groups actively share information and ideas with each other and customers via the Lotus Notes Network, and they work hard to advance the use of Notes throughout the PC community. The power users know that there is always someone out there in a Lotus discussion forum who will help them out or suggest someone who can.

The power users also regard the culture as a partnership between the people who use and sell Notes and Lotus Development itself. Lotus controls the development of the Notes product, runs the Notes Net discussion forums, and sponsors the LotusSphere trade show. The Notes culture aggressively stretches the product and actively pressures Lotus to move in the directions that it wants Notes to go.

Notes Express is a good example of the Notes culture in action. There has been a demand for a cheaper, run-time version of Notes for some time. Lotus felt that its Notes Express product, the run-time version that would support only a few applications, would fill that void. Users soundly rejected Notes Express because it didn't live up to their expectations, and it wasn't the product they wanted. Lotus responded with Notes Desktop, the run-time version, for $155 and all was soon forgiven.

As you explore Notes, it's important to understand the culture so you will know where you can go to find the sales, support, and training you need to make your Notes installation successful. Let's go a little deeper into the organizations, people, and events that make up the Notes culture:

Lotus Development

Lotus Development Support

Business Partners

Certifications

Training and Trainers

LotusSphere

Notes Information Services

WALNUT

Lotus Development

Anyone who has been involved with PCs since the early '80s has noticed significant changes in Lotus Development. The company has seen substantial growth since its first product, 1-2-3, became the de facto standard for DOS-based spreadsheets. It has had its share of successes, along with a few challenges with products such as Agenda and Jazz for the Macintosh.

When 1-2-3 was first released, no one expected it to be as wildly successful as it was. The product hit the streets during a period when free support was expected, and it wasn't long before the support lines were swamped with user questions. It wasn't unusual for a caller to wait 30 minutes or more to get through to somebody.

During this time, the Lotus organization appeared to become extremely self-confident. As sales continued to climb, sales efforts were focused on demonstrating products in seminars to corporate customers. There wasn't a spreadsheet competitor close in the game for a number of years, and Lotus was able to charge what was considered hefty fees for product upgrades. But several events occurred in the mid '80s that shook the confidence of Lotus customers and threatened Lotus' success. Lotus launched Symphony, an integrated spreadsheet that included the spreadsheet, database, and graphing capabilities of 1-2-3, along with word processing and communications capabilities. Lotus tried to position Symphony as the future direction for 1-2-3, but customers weren't sold. Symphony was mildly successful, but Lotus continued development on 1-2-3 as well.

In 1986, Lotus upgraded 1-2-3 to version 2.01, one of its most stable versions. Soon after the release, Borland introduced Quattro, a 1-2-3 clone that later became the issue of a long, drawn-out lawsuit between the two competitors. Quattro was much cheaper and had more features than 1-2-3. Despite the new competitor, Lotus failed to release a significant upgrade to 1-2-3 for over a year and a half while Borland moved quickly into the market.

In addition, Microsoft had some success with its spreadsheet Multiplan, and it used the Macintosh as its springboard into the spreadsheet market with Excel. Lotus developed a 1-2-3 for the Macintosh called Jazz, but it was plagued with problems and died a quick death. Meanwhile, with Windows becoming a viable desktop platform, Microsoft brought Excel to the PC and patiently rode out speed issues as they went for Lotus' corporate market.

Lotus was no longer the industry darling that it had been. 1-2-3 for Windows was late and not very spectacular. Excel was gaining momentum, and Borland's Quattro Pro for Windows looked promising. Microsoft was building an attractive suite of products for sale as a bundle. Lotus wasn't down for the count, however. It picked up Approach and AmiPro to build its own suite of products, and they did a lot of low-key marketing to corporate customers on its new and promising product, Lotus Notes. The company also purchased cc:Mail, one of the top sellers of electronic mail packages with a large corporate customer base.

The subsequent phenomenal growth of Notes put Lotus in almost the same position they were in with 1-2-3. The release of version 3.0 caused an explosion of new products, new resellers, and interest in the product. And instead of being able to focus on a few dedicated corporate clients and resellers, they were dealing with the entire PC industry, which began evaluating Notes. Currently, there isn't any serious competition for Notes, nor does it appear there will be any for a while.

These struggles through the good and bad times have shaped Lotus Development. The organization has recognized the market opportunity it has with Notes and has restructured its marketing to focus on helping its resellers to sell Notes in big and small businesses. The company is by no means perfect, and it can still be difficult to find the person you need. But, you can usually find a reseller who has a good relationship with Lotus and can help you out.

Lotus has also broken out of the inward focus that resulted in only enhancing products with features. Now the company actively seeks to provide the auxiliary services that its customers want when they purchase Notes. Lotus has an extensive consulting organization to help its customers solve problems, and companies including CompuServe, and AT&T are partnering with Lotus to provide better access to Notes databases. Almost daily, you can read about new partnerships with vendors to extend the functionality of Notes.

Support from Lotus Development

Product support has come a long way since the days when Lotus was shipping only DOS products. Now you can call, fax, e-mail, and even replicate your questions into the Lotus support organization; or, a Lotus representative will come to your company. You can get just about any level of support—as long as you are willing to pay the price for it. Lotus has tailored its support programs to match the size of the company. At the time this book was written, their supports plans included:

Free Support	New Notes users receive 30 days of free telephone support.
Per Incident	If users don't have a service agreement, they can call Lotus and pay $175 per incident. An incident is a single problem that must be resolved, which may result in several calls.
Telephone Support	Users can call for Notes support on up to 10 incidents. It costs $495, which means the per-incident rate is $49.50 instead of $175.
Premium Plan	Users work through their reseller to come up with an annual, customized support agreement with the Lotus Support Center. It describes who can call, when they can call, and how many times they can call. The fees depend on the services chosen.
Premium Plus Plan	Users work through their reseller to obtain an annual support contract with the Lotus Support center for limited or unlimited support calls. The agreement specifies who can call the center and the Lotus Support Knowledge base. The fees depend on the number of users who can call and the number of incidents.

Support Account Management	Users are assigned a senior technical support person who is responsible for any support problems that can't be handled by the Support Center. The fee is $35,000.
On-site Support	A Notes software engineer will travel to the customer site for $1,500/day plus expenses.

As you can see, users can always get their problems fixed through Lotus as long as they have a healthy checkbook.

Lotus also has several forums on CompuServe for users who don't need the heavyweight Notes support but want to stay up-to-date. As with most CompuServe forums, Notes users can post questions for technical support people and other users, and check out the download libraries for interesting utilities. Lotus also stores product demos and templates on the forum. In addition, Lotus has jumped on the Internet bandwagon with a Lotus World Wide Web server, www.lotus.com for technical support. Users can view product information, support program offerings, and frequently asked questions, as well as view a database of technical notes with English language queries using Lotus' Orion information retrieval system. They can also use FTP to download a variety of demos, updates, and other files relating to Lotus products.

Most Notes sites have some kind of agreement with Lotus that includes the Lotus Knowledgebase. The Knowledgebase is a Notes database that started out as a database for the Lotus technical support staff and turned into the repository for all the technotes, press releases, policies and procedures, product information, and almost anything else you need to know about Lotus and the Notes product. The database has exceeded 54MB of information at the time of this writing.

The Notes Knowledgebase is a must for anybody who is serious about installing and maintaining Notes because it practically eliminates the need to contact Lotus for nonsupport issues. For a long time, the Notes Knowledgebase was available only to customers who paid for an annual support plan. As a part of the plan, Lotus would certify its Notes server and then replicate changes to the Knowledgebase on a regular basis. Many companies wanted the Knowledgebase but they didn't need a support plan nor did they require daily updates from Lotus. For these groups, Lotus now provides the Notes Knowledgebase on CD-ROM for an annual subscription fee of $295. Once a month, Lotus sends out the latest version of the Knowledgebase to subscribers. A user can access it from a local CD drive, or the Notes administrator can copy it onto a Notes server to make it available to all Notes users.

Those companies that want to actively communicate with Lotus and other Notes users can use the Lotus Notes Network (LNN). Originally called Notes Net, the network was intended as a forum for developers and resellers (called Business Partners) to communicate with Lotus. Those developers and partners that purchased a developer support contract had access to Notes Net and its databases. One of its key communications vehicles was a Notes discussion database called the Partners Forum. Users would post questions to Lotus concerning problems, product releases, and other Notes issues. Lotus and partners would respond to the questions in a fairly loose and unstructured format.

As Notes grew in popularity, the number of Notes Net users also increased. The forum became a valuable place to place a question and get help from other Notes users. It was the primary place where the sharp developers hung out and the best source for answers to tough questions. However, users began to experience replication problems, poor etiquette from a few Notes users, and some frustration with its unstructured format. In response, in the fall of 1994, Lotus replaced the Partners Forum with a much improved version. The discussion view is a little cleaner, the document screen is clearer, and forum contributors can add a lot more categories to their documents. Lotus also added a special view for announcements that affect its partners, and the discussion can be lively as Lotus explains the contents of the announcements to its partners and the reasoning behind them.

Lotus realized that the growing popularity of Notes Net called for a new generation of communication capabilities between Business Partners, Lotus, and customers. It also saw a business opportunity—it could expand the capabilities of Notes Net and charge its users a fee for using it. The Business Partners weren't excited about paying for a service that had previously been offered at no cost as a part of the service contract, but a more sophisticated network was inevitable. Unlike its predecessor, the Lotus Notes Network is patterned after a commercial service. Users can connect to the service at no cost, but they pay for connect time and the amount of data that they replicate to their service. The service supports electronic mail, forums, and third-party information services, which charge additional fees for accessing their information.

Business Partners (Consultants, Resellers, and Developers)

When Notes was first released, Lotus sold it directly to a few large corporations. As the product evolved and the demand grew, Lotus realized that it could no longer support the direct sales approach, and it switched to using a reseller channel that could effectively handle the demand. These Business Partners now number in the hundreds and their ranks grow daily. Many of the most experienced ones are active participants in the Partners Forum, who survived the weaknesses of earlier Notes versions and have answers to most problems. They converse with each other like old friends while providing concise yet friendly answers to questions, even those posed by novices. The contributors to the forum are often vocal about perceived errors in judgment by Lotus and intolerant of the poor etiquette of other Partners who misuse the forum.

Lotus provides a complete list of Business Partners in a database called the Partners Catalog. The database contains views of all of the active partners by name and company and lists products that the partners offer by category. The documents describe the product and provide information on how to contact the partner.

Most Notes installations will benefit from a good relationship with a Notes consultant or developer. Lotus Notes administration and development skills are more an art than a science, requiring someone who has experienced the quirks and hidden features of Notes to make the installation work. The consultants and developers use Notes at a variety of installations and are able to bring the breadth of experience with them to help any organization avoid the same problems.

Lotus and third-party developers are always adding new enhancement products for Notes and it is impossible for an IS manager or Notes administrator to stay on top of all the latest technologies. It's the job of the Notes consultants and developers to stay informed and translate the latest announcements into solutions for their customers. Many developers already have a close relationship with Lotus or another developer who can help them come up with the answers to tough problems.

As with Notes support, anyone can hire a good consultant but not without a deep dip into the pocketbook. There are several consultants and developers available, but business is brisk and they can charge some pretty hefty fees for their services. Even Lotus charges almost $200 an hour for its consultants, so expect to pay the price if you want a good Notes consultant.

Certification Programs

A professional accreditation adds credibility to its owner, showing that he or she has been tested for competence in a certain subject area. With Notes,

TABLE 12.1 Notes Certification Requirements

Lotus Certification	Expertise Technical Usage	Application Developer, Level 1	Application Developer, Level 2	Systems Admin, Level 1	Systems Admin, Level 2
Notes Consultant	X	X		X	
Notes Specialist	X	X	X	X	X
Notes Systems Administrator	X			X	X
Notes Applications Developer	X	X	X		

that accreditation is called a Certified Lotus Professional (CLP). Within this accreditation, the Notes professional can become a:

Lotus Certified Notes Consultant (LCNC)

Lotus Certified Notes Specialist (LCNS)

Lotus Certified Notes Systems Administrator (LCNSA)

Lotus Certified Notes Applications Developer (LCNAD)

Lotus offers exams in three areas: Notes Technical Usage, Notes Application Development, and Notes Systems Administration. Consultants obtain one or more of the certifications based on the exams that they pass. Table 12.1 shows the exams required to reach each level of certification. As you can see, all professionals must show expertise as a technical Notes user. A consultant can specialize in development or administration, become a generalist, or become certified in all areas to become the Lotus Certified Notes Consultant.

Notes certification exams are given through Drake Training and Technology centers. Anyone can take the Notes exams, and Lotus offers training courses toward that goal. With the hot market for Notes expertise in general, people with a Notes background don't necessarily need the accreditation to land a good position or bring in the clients. However, the CLP designation assures that the consultant has at least gone through the training and should know something about Notes. You should definitely ask prospective consultants if they have the CLP accreditation as a part of your overall evaluation of a Notes consultant.

Training and Trainers

As Notes continues to be installed in more companies, the Notes training market is exploding. Currently, it is next to impossible to find employees with a lot of experience in Notes programming or administrative skills because Notes only recently boomed in popularity, and many of the APIs and tools are fairly new. IS departments are looking internally to fill the Notes positions and scrambling to get their people into training classes. In response to this high demand for training, Lotus created an entire curriculum of Notes classes and developed a program to authorize independent training organizations to become Lotus Authorized Education Centers. Their teachers are required to become Certified Lotus Trainers before they can teach students using the Lotus classes materials. Lotus publishes the list of authorized centers in the Notes Knowledgebase.

Companies that become Lotus Authorized Education Centers often already have on staff Notes developers and consultants. They charge a comparable price for the classes but you receive training from people who have experienced Notes in the field, and, the potential interaction between student and teacher between classes is often more valuable than the class itself.

Lotus also offers training videos as an alternative to off-site training. The videos use computer-based training techniques (CBT) and cover topics on Notes usage, applications development, and systems administration. A large organization can place the materials on its LAN, meter their usage, and make them available to all employees. The videos aren't a perfect substitute for classroom training but they can reach many more students for the same price.

LotusSphere

LotusSphere is the trade show Mecca for Notes users from all over the world. Like many other vendors, Lotus discovered that trade shows such as Comdex did not offer its loyal customers an opportunity to really "get into" its products and learn more about them. Consequently, several years ago, the company previewed LotusSphere as a better forum for introducing new products, training customers on new products, and helping Lotus users to make the best use of its products.

Initially, LotusSphere covered the entire Lotus product line. It was held in late January at Disney World in Orlando, Florida, in order to attract a good crowd. Notes was just one of many attractions at that first show, but in the last two years, Notes has dominated the show as its popularity skyrocketed and eclipsed the other Lotus products. LotusSphere has been a runaway success for Lotus, which now saves all of its big announcements for the show to attract a lot of media attention. The conference sets the stage for Lotus' short- and long-range strategies for Notes, and loyal Notes followers want to be there to hear and see them.

Lotus also showcases the most successful Notes Business Partners in an award ceremony called the Beacon Awards. Vendors are given awards for new products, innovative use of Notes tools, the best solutions to business problems, and customer support. The recipients at the first awards ceremony represented many of the big names in the Notes reseller and consulting community. Attendees also walk away from the conference with a lot of excellent materials. All the conference slides are published in books for each day of the conference. Attendees also receive a CD with most of the conference slides and product demos of Lotus products. If the attendees stay a few extra days, they can also pick up a Goofy hat and get a picture of Mickey doing a full-text search as well.

Notes Information Services

Notes is the next step in the evolution of information services. Notes brings a graphical interface and powerful text-searching capabilities to a distributed, nonstructured data environment. Any organization that wants to sell information can replace its newsletters and faxes with Notes documents and views and download them automatically.

For example, the Gartner Group is a highly respected research and consulting firm that has sold its findings and opinions to corporations for years. Clients sign up for various subject areas and Gartner sends them newsletters, news briefs, and studies that keep them up to date on the issues. Normally, the clients would then have to route it around their office so that all interested parties receive the information. With Notes, the Gartner Group can simply place that information into documents. Instead, the information that the client has purchased comes automatically to their server via replication with the Gartner Group databases. When the client reviews the database, the latest information is there. No one has to open the mail or set up a routing slip.

The huge demand for interstate and global movement of Notes information has attracted some big players into the marketplace. When faced with moving Notes databases to remote sites or connecting hundreds of users to their databases, companies quickly realize that a third-party service eliminates the need to create and maintain a huge network of communications equipment and Notes servers. The price of the services may add up to a substantial sum, but they eliminate the headaches of supporting the network, the users, and the replications of databases.

Let's take a look at the companies lining up to offer Notes network services:

- ♦ **WorldCom** was one of the pioneers of information movement using Lotus Notes. Before companies such as AT&T and CompuServe became

Notes providers, WorldCom built a global network of Notes servers to provide international communications for those subscribing to the service. They provide their customers with electronic mail connections and gateways to a variety of e-mail services, online news services, Internet mail access, private database storage, discussion forums, and consulting on Notes communications projects.

♦ **AT&T** offers a service for this market called AT&T Network Notes. Its product replaces homegrown corporate communications networks and servers with AT&T communications equipment and servers. For a fee, a company contracts with AT&T to place its databases on AT&T servers, which allows the company to replicate with AT&T on a regular basis. AT&T, in turn, replicates the databases to the geographical areas where the company would like people to have access.

Users of this service make a local call into the AT&T service to connect to the company databases. AT&T manages the replication and security of the databases and provides the company with billing information on the amount of connect time and database usage. If needed, AT&T will also sell Help Desk services to a company's customers.

♦ **CompuServe** joined the fray with its CompuServe Notes Information Services. Well known over the years as the place to look for almost any kind of information, CompuServe provides its subscribers with access to hundreds of Notes databases covering many of the forums that they already use. Subscribers can also take advantage of CompuServe's extensive electronic mail gateways and Internet mail and news services.

CompuServe also offers private database services similar to those of AT&T. CompuServe manages the servers, the distribution of the information, and the access to the databases. It also has a Help Desk service for subscribers.

♦ **IBM** announced that it will be developing a public Notes network using its **IBM Global Network**. IBM has already set up its own network to service its huge internal communications needs, and it will be competing head-on with AT&T.

It's obvious by the names of the companies listed here that Notes networking and connectivity is big business. To compete, each service will have its own flavor of support and hardware offerings. CompuServe and WorldCom make their revenues through connect charges, while AT&T will charge less for connections but more for the hardware and support services. Users will benefit from all the competition and have a much easier time moving information.

WALNUT

WALNUT stands for the Worldwide Association of Lotus Notes Users and Technologists—another name for the Notes User Group. The group is head-quartered in Andover, Massachusetts, and is made up of users from several hundred national and international companies that use Notes. In addition, it sponsors regional interest groups (RIGs), which meet regularly, and special interest groups (SIGs), which communicate via Notes databases accessible to members with an electronic membership.

WALNUT has a number of active discussion databases located on the CompuServe Notes service, and it offers electronic mail connections through CompuServe links. WALNUT has developed a process by which members can regularly submit suggestions that are reviewed and prioritized by the WALNUT membership and sent to Lotus Development. Lotus has committed to a program that provides responses to these suggestions.

Tapping into the Culture

The Notes culture started with Lotus and a small group of Business Partners dedicated to a belief in the potential of Notes. Today, it has become a thriving marketplace of consultants, developers, and trainers who are fueling the tremendous growth of Lotus Notes. What this means to you is that there will always be someone out there with an answer to your questions and a solution to your latest challenge.

13

Notes Add-Ons and Third-Party Products

No matter how robust a product is, somebody always wants to extend its functionality or connect it to other products. One company would like its Notes mail system to automatically send messages to a pager, while another wants to download information from its mainframe and tie Notes to its accounting package. Each scenario is a valid extension of Notes and a market opportunity for Lotus or a third-party developer.

Although Lotus has been the largest developer of programming tools and add-on products for Notes since its implementation, the number of third-party developers has grown steadily over the years, and they offer some impressive Notes connectivity options and productivity solutions. We can expect further product development in the future as Notes 4.0 generates more opportunities for third-party vendors to enhance Notes.

A list of all of the third-party products available for Notes would require a lot more pages than are available for this book. Nevertheless, a look at a representative sample of these add-ons and third-party products will help you to see how robust the market has become and how much flexibility you have in expanding your Notes installation.

Lotus Applications

As just stated, Lotus Development is the most prolific developer of applications that enhance Notes. Obviously, Lotus has a vested interest in making Notes successful, and it has pulled together an impressive list of applications through internal development and acquisition of existing products.

Notes Suite

Notes Suite is a group of applications bundled with Notes as a complete office automation solution. The product includes Notes, 1-2-3 for Windows, WordPro, Approach, Freelance, Organizer, and ScreenCam. Lotus has enabled each of the applications with the Notes/FX technology, which makes it possible to integrate their information easily into Notes.

Lotus Approach

Approach is the database application package that is included with Lotus SmartSuite. It is a powerful database product that can also read Notes databases. Users can overcome the poor reporting capabilities of Notes by designing reports in Approach, then using it to access Notes databases and print reports. Approach also supports the Notes/FX file exchange enabling it to be integrated with Notes.

Lotus Fax Server

Lotus Fax Server allows Notes users to send and receive faxes from within Notes Mail. Fax numbers can be stored in a common Notes Name and Address Book, or they can be entered manually into the address field in the mail message. The product includes a fax viewer that lets users view and edit the faxes.

Lotus Notes: Document Imaging (LN:DI)

Lotus Notes: Document Imaging gives users the capability to create and manage large scanned images using Notes. Images are kept on a storage server, and a pointer to the image is kept in the Notes document. LN:DI also integrates Notes and sophisticated third-party document imaging systems, which may be better suited for very large scanned image applications, including those developed by FileNet, IBM, ViewStar, and Wang.

Lotus Notes Pager Gateway

Lotus Notes Pager Gateway sends up to 240 characters from a Notes mail message to any pager device that accepts the Telocator Alphanumeric Paging (TAP) protocol. The gateway runs on the server and, in addition to mail messages, it can also send a message when the database is changed. The product supports paging through McCaw Cellular, MobileComm, PageMar, PageNet, SkyTel, and U.S. Paging.

Lotus Organizer

Organizer is a personal information manager that manages a calendar, to-do lists, addresses, events, and other personal information. It can store individual appointments and perform group scheduling for Notes Mail and cc:Mail users. Organizer uses the Notes Name and Address Book for its list of potential meeting attendees, and it can notify non-Organizer users via e-mail that a meeting will be taking place.

Lotus Video for Notes

Video for Notes allows users to store video recordings in Notes databases on Notes servers. Each document that holds a video recording contains a pointer to the server that holds the recording. When a user requests a video, Notes locates it on the appropriate server and displays it on the PC screen. Users can record, edit, and play video recordings and access video recordings on CD-ROMs.

NotesView

NotesView is an enterprise administration tool for managing Notes servers from a central location. The administrator can monitor Notes servers and reroute Notes traffic in the case of failures. It is based on Hewlett-Packard's OpenView network management product, supporting SNMP (simple network management protocol) and providing statistics on replications, mail traffic, and server status. It can also trigger alarms to network administrators in case of a failure and provide administrators with usage and performance statistics.

SmartSwitcher

With SmartSwitcher, Notes users can store and maintain several setup configurations for their Notes environment. The product eliminates the need to change communications ports, user IDs, mail parameters, and other set-tings in the tool menu every time a user shares a PC with someone else or when a laptop user switches from remote calling to a network-enabled docking bay. The product was developed by a Lotus employee and is dis-tributed as freeware to all Notes users.

Soft-Switch Central and EMX

Soft-Switch Central is a mainframe-based product that links the electronic mail systems from a variety of vendors. EMX is a Unix-based product that provides similar message-switching capabilities and wide area management of messaging systems. Notes Mail is one of the many mail systems that these products support.

Integration Tools

Many third-party vendors have created applications that exchange informa-tion between external information sources and Lotus Notes databases. These tools offer developers and end users with a way to leverage the work-group capabilities of Notes with the structured, transaction-oriented sys-tems that also support business processes.

Common Ground from Common Ground Software

Common Ground captures the output from any application and creates a file that can be viewed without the original application. Users can create flowcharts, presentations, or word processing documents, "print" them to a Common Ground file, and mail them to a database where anyone can view the documents. Using Notes/FX, information stored in the documents by Common Ground can be extracted and placed into a Notes database. Users can then build views to manage the stored documents.

DataLink from Brainstorm Technologies

DataLink allows users to move information between Notes databases and ASCII text files or relational databases that are ODBC (open database con-nectivity) compliant. The product runs on the user's personal computer and accesses products from Borland, Gupta, IBM, Informix, Ingres, Microsoft, Oracle, Sybase, and several others. Users define the fields that they want moved and set restrictions on the information to be moved; information can go to or from Notes.

InfoPump from Trinzic Corporation

InfoPump is a server-based product that moves information between database products from Gupta, IBM, Microsoft, Oracle, Sybase, and several other vendors. The product has a sophisticated scripting language that it uses to transfer and manipulate information from one or several of the databases at once. An administrator uses the InfoPump Manager to schedule and monitor the product's activities.

Notes Integration Manager from Great Plains Software

The Notes Integration Manager is a tool that integrates Lotus Notes with Great Plains Dynamics, an accounting package from Great Plains Software. Developers can link their accounting systems with Notes databases and use the workflow capabilities of Notes to automate their business processes.

VB/Link from Brainstorm Technologies

With VB/Link, developers can create custom applications in Visual Basic that can read and write information in Notes databases. The product can also access SQL databases, allowing developers to integrate them with Notes databases. The tool can also generate Notes Mail, start up Notes macros, and execute full-text searches.

Languages/Development

Some applications are too complex for LotusScript and the capabilities of Notes. To accommodate these apps, Lotus and several third-party developers have created tools that give programmers the capability to create custom applications that access Notes databases.

Notes/FX from Lotus Development

Notes/FX or Notes Field Exchange is a development technology that allows applications that are OLE (Object Linking and Embedding) servers to exchange information with Notes fields. Information can be passed in both directions between Notes and the application that supports Notes/FX. Lotus SmartSuite uses Notes/FX in each application to communicate with Notes.

Notes HiTest C API, HiTest Basic API, and HiTest Tools for Visual Basic from Lotus Development

These APIs provide developers with C language, Basic, and Visual Basic library routines that can be used to develop custom applications for Notes. These APIs access Lotus Notes internal functions and allow developers to build applications that cannot be created using LotusScript or native Notes functions.

NotesSQL from Lotus Development

NotesSQL is an ODBC (open database connectivity) driver that allows applications that support the ODBC standard to access Notes databases using ANSI SQL commands. The driver enables many products that are already on the market to read Notes databases through the ODBC drivers.

Notes ViP from Revelation (formerly from Lotus Development)

Notes ViP is a tool that helps developers build Notes applications without writing a lot of code. Using editors for forms, menus, and reports, a developer can use objects to build applications that tie together Notes databases with ODBC-compliant databases and those that can be read through Lotus' DataLens product. As the application is built, these tools automatically generate scripts for the objects using Lotus' LotusScript language. Developers can then customize the application by modifying the scripts and changing the attributes of the objects.

PowerBuilder Library for Notes from PowerSoft Corporation

This library gives programmers who use the PowerBuilder development environment access to Notes databases. The product includes Notes DLLs (data link libraries) for PowerBuilder, a DLL for VIM (vendor independent messaging) support for cc:Mail and Notes Mail, and a PowerBuilder application called PLAN. With PLAN, the developer can access forms, views, and queries without writing Notes integration code.

SQLWindows from Gupta Corporation

SQLWindows is an application development environment that supports integration with Lotus Notes. Using a technology called QuickObjects, Notes users can drag a Notes object into an SQLWindows application, which will display a Notes view.

Applications in Notes

Notes consultants have developed many applications to solve the business problems of their customers. At the time this book was written, the Partners Catalog contained the following categories for products developed by these Business Partners:

By Vertical Market	*By Industry*
Customer Service	Commercial Banks
Executive Management	Defense
Financial and Strategic Planning	Education
Information Services	Financial
Manufacturing	Government
Marketing	Healthcare
Product Development	High Technology
Quality Management	Hotel Services
Sales Automation	Insurance
Training	Legal
	Oil and Gas Manufacturing
	Real Estate
	Strategic Management

The Future

AT&T Integrated Messaging from AT&T

AT&T plans to integrate its Audix voice mail system with Lotus Notes. Voice mail messages will be stored along with other electronic documents in the Notes Mail system. In addition, users will be able to check their Notes Mail using a telephone, because the AT&T product converts the text message into a voice message.

InterNotes from Lotus Development

Lotus is developing several products for use on the World Wide Web (WWW). The InterNotes Web Publisher will allow users to publish information from Notes databases in a format accessible by WWW users. InterNotes will provide users with access to the Internet Usenet News service. The InterNotes software will be used to manage Lotus' own Web site. By the time this book is published, many of the components of InterNotes will be almost complete or in beta test.

Oracle Integration with Notes from Oracle

Oracle and Lotus plan to develop products that will tightly integrate Oracle and Notes databases. The products will allow users to build oracle applications that access both Notes and Oracle databases. In addition, the developers expect Notes applications to be able to access Oracle databases. They will develop software that will update Notes databases automatically from Oracle servers at scheduled intervals and later in real time.

Proshare from Intel Corporation and Lotus Development

Intel will create a version of its videoconferencing software, Proshare for Lotus Notes. The software is expected to add document sharing in real time and videoconferencing to Notes, as well as to allow users to bring information from a Notes database into a videoteleconference.

SkyNotes from SkyNotes, Inc.

SkyNotes is a combination of server software and client applications for PDAs (personal digital assistants). Users will be able to access a SkyNotes server that works with a Notes server to communicate with the PDA. Applications for workflow management, personal information management, and contact management are planned.

XPump from Trinzic Corporation

XPump is actually an interim name for a new product announced by Trinzic Corporation that will allow users to access SQL databases from Oracle, Sybase, and Microsoft from within Notes. Users will be able to use SQL to make the requests, and Query by example to perform searches.

14

The Lotus Notes Future

If history is any indication of future performance, then there may be some cause for concern for the future of Notes. After all, the huge lead Lotus had in the spreadsheet market with 1-2-3 has steadily dwindled over the years because the company was late in anticipating market demand and released a solid version of 1-2-3 for Windows many months *after* Microsoft Excel gained a stronghold in the market. So what is Lotus doing today that would make us think that Notes won't suffer the same fate?

- Lotus did stumble initially as it began to market Notes. Companies wanted it, but Lotus had to struggle to effectively deliver the product and support it. However, the strength of the product carried it until Lotus solidified its support and Business Partners programs. It is now able to use the partners effectively to move Notes licenses, and the channel is strong and dedicated to the success of Notes.
- Once again, Lotus has no real competition and a huge lead in the market. At the time of this writing, Microsoft Exchange is still months away from shipping, and it isn't perceived as a replacement for Notes.

Hundreds of applications have already been written for Notes, and almost every major corporation has Notes or is considering it.

♦ It will take significant effort for a competitor to dislodge an operational Notes installation at any company, whereas with 1-2-3, the competition simply converted the spreadsheets on the fly, and the user was ready to use the alternate package. None of the competition is building a Notes clone, which means a Notes shop would have to rewrite all of its applications before it could convert to the new software. In addition, the company would be faced with a huge conversion effort to move Notes information into the new format.

♦ Lotus Business Partners can generate more consulting fees with Notes in comparison to 1-2-3, which offered some minor consulting opportunities, but generated most of its revenue on the margin earned from selling a package. With Notes, the partners earn fees on the product but they also have much greater potential for earning additional income from consulting, development, and implementation. As a result, they have to invest a lot more in building product knowledge, and they often can't afford to stretch themselves to cover competing products. Their loyalty will generate a steady stream of Notes sales.

♦ Whereas 1-2-3 is primarily a commodity product that can be marketed against with price and features, Notes' value lies in the applications that are developed in it and the information stored by it. Therefore, corporations must make a longer-term commitment to justify the costs of implementation.

♦ It will take a major paradigm shift to dislodge Notes from its leadership position. Windows gave Microsoft an opportunity to gain market share when users were faced with switching to Windows-based products and learn a whole new interface. Notes already resides in the new user interface paradigm, and there don't appear to be any changes in the near future as significant as the move from DOS to Windows. Microsoft Exchange may offer a new paradigm for organizing and mailing information, but it doesn't appear to be enough of a leap above Notes that would cause a mass migration to it. Internet groupware is starting to become popular but it has a ways to go to match the functionality of Notes.

♦ With IBM behind Notes, Lotus finally has the power to gain the market share it needs to maintain a stronghold in the groupware market.

By all indications, Lotus is not repeating history with Notes. Its marketing efforts are aggressive; it is forming key alliances with heavyweights in the PC market; and its resellers channel shows no sign of diminishing sales efforts. The third-party market is exploding with products, and interest in Notes is keener than ever.

Bright Future

The future of Notes is definitely bright. Ask any major vendor of application software and he or she will no doubt have some kind of plan for Notes integration. Notes is featured almost weekly on the front pages of trade magazines, announcing some new alliance with a major vendor. Lotus has its marketing support organization in place, and no major workgroup software vendors are in their way.

Notes gives software vendors a tool with which to extend their packages into the business processes that they support. Vendors of accounting software and the vertical applications that integrate with them need a mechanism by which to store images of accounting documents and to route approval requests to the appropriate people. Custom applications developed in-house also need tools to integrate with Notes, and companies now expect their database vendors to supply them.

Process improvement has taken hold in corporate America, and it takes more than traditional applications to support those processes. Systems must proactively notify participants to take action via mail applications integrated with measurement systems, and forms must be eliminated and replaced with online versions. These are all tasks well suited for a Notes application.

Notes is also viewed by application vendors and companies alike as the repository for all the unstructured information that they need to distribute. There are plenty of technologies available for storing huge video files, images, and documents, but not many solutions for distributing them like groupware can. By integrating with Notes, vendors can concentrate on creating the hottest package in the market instead of pouring resources into workgroup software.

Crystal Ball Predictions

What if we had a Notes crystal ball? In the future, what would we see on the front pages of trade magazines? There's a good chance we will see headlines like these:

All Software Vendors Integrated with Notes: SlothWare Announces Version 17.0 Has Hooks to Notes Mail

Vendors will inevitably integrate Notes into their applications as more customers discover the value of connecting with Notes groupware. Many File menus already include a choice for sending mail, and one of the options will probably include sending mail via Notes. There will be more options for importing and exporting information into and out of Notes. The more aggressive vendors will write information directly to Notes databases and read directly from them.

Major DBMS Vendors Announce Notes Integration Tools for Developers: Programmers Embrace Notes as a "Real" Database

The large database management systems (DBMS) vendors such as Oracle, Sybase, Microsoft, and Informix realize that users will create most transaction-based systems with their products. However, companies are demanding that these systems tap into internal mail systems and data warehouses without tricky programming techniques or kludgy solutions. All of these vendors, including Microsoft, will need more seamless tools for connection to Notes databases.

Work in this regard has already started. For example, Oracle announced that it will be building extensions into its common desktop environment (CDE) tools so that developers can create applications that use a PL/Sequel exchange to access Oracle and Network Notes databases. It plans to allow Notes clients to access Oracle servers with OLE 2.0 and via Notes FX; in later versions, it hopes to automatically update Notes-rich text fields automatically with information from an Oracle database.

No matter how far these vendors have gone in creating their own workgroup software and links, they will be faced with many customers who have already invested in Notes, and therefore, Notes integration will be necessary to maintain their client base and keep their customers happy.

News from Antarctica: "Last outpost finally connects to public Notes server"

Database applications will proliferate on Notes networks much as Web sites have on the Internet. In less than two years, the industry has gone from one global Notes network vendor to several. The demand for distributed Notes databases and an infrastructure to support it is huge, and it is attracting the big players in the telecommunications industry. But users won't be able to connect to Notes databases as they do on the Web for quite a while, so vendors will use the Web to publish catalogs of Notes servers and the names of their Notes databases. Starter databases will show up on Internet sites so that users can download them, contact a Notes network server, and then begin replicating the rest of the database.

Notes Becomes the De Facto Standard for Connecting to Information Services: Notes Mandatory to Download Information

People do one of two things when they connect to an information service such as CompuServe or the World Wide Web: They either randomly browse through a lot of information, or they review the same database and move information from it to their personal computer on a regular basis. Browsing will always be done with products such as Netscape or vendor-specific interfaces such as Prodigy and America Online. These packages will tap the unique features of the service and make it easy to navigate through the service offerings. They will continue to be valuable as users search for individual documents and specific files that they may need.

Notes will become the method for users of these services to download information that they want to receive on a regular basis. Notes will be shipped with a Name and Address Book containing the connection information needed for all the information services. Users will be able to set their modems to dial late at night and update the Notes databases on their personal computers with a smorgasbord of forums. Notes Mail will become the front end for the myriad mail services that exist, and users will be able to reach their friends anywhere as long as they belong to a service.

Connectlt Software Announces Microsoft Exchange and Lotus Notes Gateways: It Doesn't Matter Which One You Use Now

Microsoft may be behind in the groupware race but it will doubtless be a player in the future. Like Novell's Netware and Microsoft's NT Server, Lotus Notes and Microsoft Exchange will coexist in many companies as internal IS staffs discover the strengths of both Notes and Exchange, and find ways to tap both products to solve internal problems. Inevitably, they will want to share information between the two products using whatever industry standards are built into both of them. Third-party vendors will come up with a solution and marry the two products.

Notes Run-Time Version Ships with Every New PC: "Lotus Inside" Label Prominently Shown

Notes will become as valuable a tool as Windows. It will provide users with a standard interface through which they can access a public network with hundreds of databases targeted at home and business users. Instead of loading proprietary software packages for every vendor who has something to sell, a user can use a single package—Notes—to simply replicate a vendor's database from the network. Vendors could send out CDs to prospective customers with most of the information, and the users could then replicate the updates after they load the database on their PC.

Lotus Announces Pocket Organizer Version of Notes: A Perfect Personal Information Manager for the Busy Executive

Notes will finally complete the workgroup tools that support the daily activities of users. Notes supports their process improvement activities, and they demanded administrative functions like calendars, appointment scheduling, to-do lists, meeting room coordination, and personal goal setting. Lotus Organizer will either be integrated into Notes or an entirely new Notes-based PIM will be developed.

District 47 Publishes Class Schedules for Next School Year: Online Registration Begins Next Friday

Public Notes network services will be affordable for most people. For example, a school district today could do business over a Notes network using applications for registering students, collecting fees via credit cards, sending report cards home, and publishing regular newsletters. Teachers could post homework assignments, and students could even submit their work electronically.

As the cost of being online goes down and Notes client software drops in price, anyone with a newsletter or need to survey the public could tap the public networks. Imagine the minutes of the local town council meeting posted on a server, or public opinion polls on local issues conducted via Notes. Public groups want (*and need*) to disseminate information but they usually don't have the resources to maintain the necessary infrastructure. Public networks would allow them to simply create databases, publish them, and let users pay the service provider for access time.

Reality Check

The future just painted admittedly used too much rose color. Notes will probably not gain that level of popularity, but it does offer the world an opportunity similar to Windows. Before Windows, people were tired of or intimidated by DOS. They needed a friendlier front end that helped them access their applications and manage their files. Thus, Windows became the dominant player and readily available with every new machine purchased. Today, users are faced with a proprietary interface for every information service that they deal with. No database package has achieved industry dominance, nor is there one that provides users with good tools for storing and reviewing unstructured information. Vendors want to distribute information to prospective customers, but few can afford to develop their own package or multiple CDs to handle a variety of software packages. As Notes gains wide acceptance with many companies, it isn't farfetched to think that Notes could become not just a valuable tool, but even a standard for all levels of home and office workers. Imagine the applications that would be available to everyone if developers could assume that Notes existed on most of the computers in use.

Public Notes networks are already in place and growing rapidly to handle the demands of corporate America. When they recoup their setup costs and begin to lower access costs to their services, these network providers will be positioned to tap the home market. Case in point: CompuServe already has a huge user base that would probably welcome the capability to automatically download forum updates then tap the power of Notes to review that forum.

At the office, Notes gives internal developers that long-awaited solution to storing unstructured information. These developers are already stretching Notes as far as it goes. It isn't unreasonable to expect that they will pressure the providers of their applications, tools, and databases to give them more tools with which to access Notes and integrate Notes in their applications.

In the short term, the phenomenal growth of Notes and its services indicates that it will continue to become more entrenched in corporate America. It's safe to say that companies will continue to purchase Notes as long as there are workgroups. We can also assume that third-party developers will continue to offer integration solutions and add-on tools as long as the Notes market is robust. And consultants and resellers will continue to sell Notes vigorously as long as it remains profitable to do so.

But the World Wide Web is still the ideal place to browse for information on demand, and it is much better suited than Notes for the task. Once people lock onto an information source, they often check it regularly, and the Internet offers them the capability at a low cost and with little hassle. Thus, there is no reason to spend excessive amounts of money publishing simple information on Notes servers or Notes services such as CompuServe when you can do it for a lot less on a Web server.

Web servers also allow users to fill out simple forms and submit them to the owner of the Web site. In most cases, the applications for the masses (surveys, sign-ups, simple ordering) can be better accomplished via the Internet. In reality, a process such as students registering for classes is far more likely to take place on a Web server and not on Notes, because more people have access to the Internet. The explosive growth of the World Wide Web will slow the growth of Notes simply because it offers a simpler, less expensive alternative to some applications that would have required something like Notes only one or two years ago.

Probably, Notes will continue to be a popular tool for corporate workgroup computing, but we will continue to see more tools that integrate it seamlessly into Internet applications, enabling developers to use the strengths of both products to build powerful workgroup applications.

A

Summary of Notes 4.0 Features

Following two years of speculation, rumor, sneak peeks, delays, and media hype, Notes 4.0 finally arrived. The upgrade addresses many of the concerns of anxious developers who, although they swear by Notes, have been tempted to swear at it as they faced its limitations in the interface or development language.

At first glance, there may not appear to be significant differences between Notes 3.x and Notes 4.0. The 4.0 desktop with its tabs and SmartIcons looks almost identical to Notes 3.x. However, the differences will quickly become apparent when you use the drastically modified menu tree and open a database to discover not one but three windows for the view. Dig deeper and you will see still more changes, benefiting both users and administrators. None is difficult to learn, although most require some kind of training to assimilate. Let's take a look at the changes and see how they improve the product. Please note that, at the time this book was written, Lotus was just releasing test build 2. It is possible that Notes 4.0 will appear slightly different than it is shown in the Figures.

The Desktop

The desktop still uses tabbed pages to divide the desktop into work areas, and each work area still contains icons that represent databases on a local or remote server. The SmartIcon toolbar looks much the same, as does the status bar at the bottom of the screen. However, you'll find the content and capabilities of the desktop significantly improved.

Replication

In Notes 3.x, replication is one of the most powerful and most complicated features. In the new version, replication has been greatly simplified through the new Replicator and location records in the Name and Address Book. The Replicator shows up as the seventh tab on the workspace (see Figure A.1). On it, you can define your replication process and either execute it with a push of a button or let Notes start it automatically at a scheduled time. You can define the different servers to call, when to call them, and which databases to replicate. If you are in a hurry, there is a button for simply sending and receiving mail immediately.

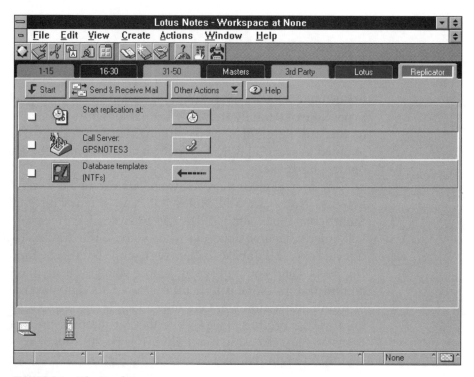

FIGURE A.1   The Replicator.

The new location records replace the connection records stored in the old Name and Address Book. It eliminates the clumsiness users felt when they tried to change all of their mail and replication settings each time they called in from a different location. In effect, these records replace the functionality of the Lotus freeware product SmartSwitcher. With Notes 4.0, you can create any number of location records that define your server, replication schedule, phone numbers, time zone, and mail type. Using the File Mobile menu choice, you can then easily switch between locations. The Replicator also uses these location records to execute a replication session and schedule automatic replications.

Menus

The Notes 4.0 menus are much different than their 3.x predecessors (see Figure A.2). Most of the Tools menu choices have been dispersed to other menus, including the File menu (replication, locations, preferences), the Edit menu (unread marks), and the new Action menu (macros). The Compose menu is now called the Create menu. The Design menu now appears on both the View and Create menus, and it is also available in the

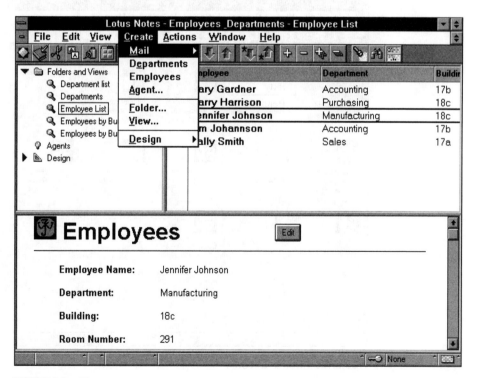

FIGURE A.2   New menus.

view navigator for every database. And to help the user with the new setups, Lotus has provided a Release 3 Menu Finder in the Help menu.

Stacked Icons

Most desktops have two copies of many database icons, one for the local copy of the database and one for its replica on the server. Unfortunately, the multiple icons eat up space on the desktop and require users to turn on server names so that they can figure out which database they are accessing. With 4.0, Lotus implemented stacked icons, as shown in Figure A.3. Whenever more than one replica is added to a desktop, Notes displays only one icon on the workspace page but displays a small arrow in the upper right-hand corner of the icon to indicate that it represents multiple replicas of the same database. Click on the arrow and Notes lists all of the server locations where replicas have been opened by the user. The user selects a server, and Notes opens the appropriate replica of the database.

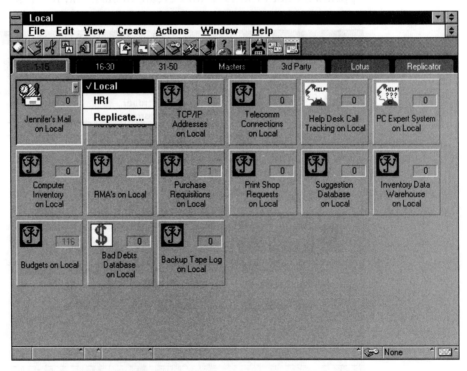

FIGURE A.3 Stacked icons.

Database Properties

In version 3.x, developers had very little control of what a database displayed when a user opened it. If the database had never been opened before, the user automatically viewed a help message about the database. Otherwise, the database remembered the last view displayed and the user was presented with that view. In Notes 4.0, the developer can choose between several displays when a database is opened, including the last open view, a navigator, or the About Database help message.

Notes 4.0 also eliminates a few minor irritations that plagued Notes 3.x databases. Databases can now be assigned a header and footer that appear on documents printed from the database. You can also check a flag that instructs a database not to mark modified documents as unread, saving users the drudgery of looking at documents that have had only insignificant changes made to them. Databases can also be tagged as unlisted so that they do not appear in the Open Database dialog box (see Figure A.4).

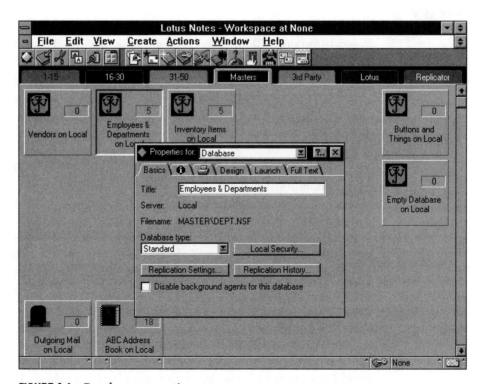

FIGURE A.4   Database properties.

Pass-Through Servers

Pass-through servers allow Notes users to replicate more than one local database by contacting a single server. With Notes 3.x, a user could replicate a database only if the server that contained the replica was contacted by the user, which meant if the user had four databases on four different servers, for example, the user had to make four phone calls. With Notes 4.0, a Notes server can act as a replication router, which simplifies the process and the user has to make only one phone call.

More Tabs

The workspace in Notes 3.x contains six tabbed pages that can be used to organize your databases. The tabs can have names but only six are allowed. In Notes 4.0, you can add additional workspace tabs to your desktop. Notes 4.0 shrinks the size of the tabs so that more will fit at the top of the screen.

Views

Views in version 4.0 have received a major face-lift. The familiar view window has been split into three windows, and a Navigator and a Preview window have been added to the original view. In addition, a number of new properties have been added to enhance the look of the view.

The New View Windows

The new view windows make it much easier to browse a database (see Figure A.5). The leftmost view, called a navigator, helps you move through all the views and design elements in a database (see the next section on navigators). In the rightmost windows, Notes 4.0 displays the view that you had in version 3.x. Underneath both views, in a window called the preview window, you can display the contents of the document that is highlighted in the view. To browse through records, you select the view in the navigator, select a document in the view, and Notes displays the record in the preview window.

Navigators

The navigators provide a snapshot of all the elements contained in a database. They begin by listing all of the views in the database. Tiered menus are also listed, tier name first, followed by the view name indented underneath

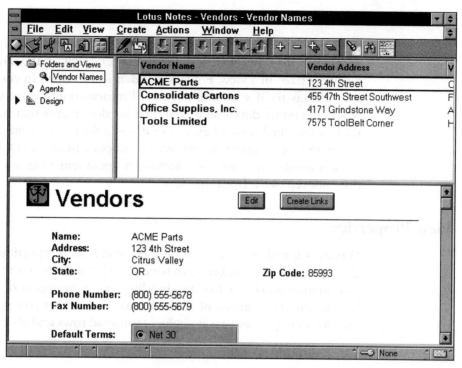

FIGURE A.5   New Notes 4.0 window.

it. Click on a view name and the view appears in a window to the right of the navigator.

Under the views is an icon that displays the agents (formerly macros in version 3.x) available in the database as a view. Another icon, Design, displays all of the design functions (forms, views, and so on) available to the developer. Click on one of the design functions, forms for example, and Notes displays all of the forms in the database in the view window. Click on a form and you can edit it.

Notes 4.0 also gives you the capability to design your own navigator to help your audience more efficiently use the database in the way you intended. Using any bitmap as a backdrop, you can design sophisticated navigators with buttons or hotspots (areas that act like buttons without the picture of a button) that open a view, open a document, display another navigator, or execute formulas or scripts. Launch the navigator automatically when the database is opened and it can become a menu that guides the users quickly to important views or forms without using Notes menus.

Folders

Folders are a simple way in Notes 4.0 to categorize information without requiring a user to create and fill in a special field in the database that can be categorized in a view. Folders are identical to views in design and in how they display the documents as rows of information. Unlike views, however, where the entire database is searched for documents that match a criteria, folders are filled only when a user drags a document from a view into the folder, or when a macro/agent moves a document into the folder based on a certain condition being met. Moving a document from a view to a folder does not remove it from the view.

View Properties

Version 4.0 makes a view a little more viable as a reporting tool. Both the document and the database can have a header and a footer that appear when information is printed. Column headings can now appear on more than one line, as can the contents of the columns. You can set row spacing (1.5" per line, for example) and assign colors to unread rows and alternate rows.

Forms

In appearance, forms are little changed from Notes 3.x, but the new version improves the way they work. Like views, forms now have a number of new properties to provide better control. During forms design, Notes splits the screen into a form layout window and a definitions window where you can quickly update fields and buttons. In short, it's much easier to create forms than it ever has been (see Figure A.6).

New Forms Properties

Properties are now modified in a Properties window, a huge improvement over the myriad menu choices formerly required to define databases, fields, and buttons. Hit the right mouse button on the workspace, select Properties, and a window appears showing several tabs that represent a group of properties including fonts, printer settings, and defaults. You can switch between text, form, and database properties simply by using a pull-down menu at the top of the window.

Database properties have been subtly enhanced in several ways. You can turn off unread marks for modified documents, and you have more control of the screens that appear when you open a database. Each database

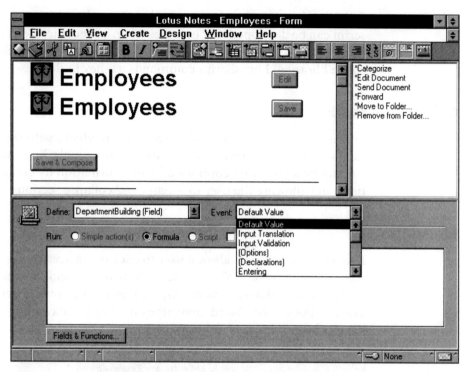

FIGURE A.6 Designing forms.

has its own default settings for fonts, and each can have a header and a footer. You can also disable agents for the database.

Forms properties give you much more flexibility when performing a task on a form. You can automatically launch an application, an OLE object, an attachment, or a doclink when the form is opened. The form can be displayed in the Create menu or in a Create Other dialog box. You can now even make it impossible to move information to the clipboard if you need to keep database information secure.

The biggest change to text properties is in the addition of styles, a feature that enables you to apply the same characteristics, or attributes, to items on a form. In addition, Notes 4.0 can hide paragraphs in the preview area below the navigator based on a formula. A list can also be formatted with bullets or sequential numbers.

Field Definitions

Notes 4.0 gives the developer much more control over the actions that a user can take before, during, and after a field is entered. In addition to values and formulas for defaults, input translation, and verification, a LotusScript script can be developed that executes when a user enters, exits, initializes, or recalculates a field. A browser is also available to help developers view the entire library of LotusScript commands as they build these scripts.

Collapsible Sections

Forms can now have collapsible sections, in which, with the click of a button, sections of a form can be reduced to a single line. A developer can streamline a form that contains a lot of information by breaking it into sections and allowing the user to expand and collapse sections at will.

Hotspots

Like buttons, hotspots allow a user to click on an area of the screen and initiate a task in Notes. When a user selects the hotspot, Notes can execute a doclink and load a document, display pop-up windows, or execute a script. The hotspot can be placed anywhere on a form or navigator, and it does not have to be visible (see Figure A.7).

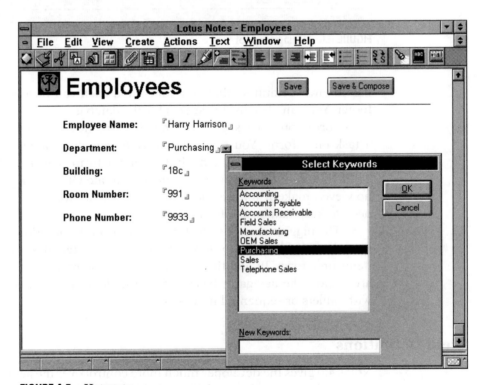

FIGURE A.7   Hotspots.

Viewlinks

Doclinks have been one of the most powerful features of Notes, allowing users to store a link in a document to any other document in a Notes database. Notes 4.0 adds a nuance called a viewlink, which is similar to a doclink except the link displays a view in another database when selected instead of a document. The viewlink gives the user the flexibility to browse an entire database instead of just moving to a single document and not be able to view other documents in the linked database.

Agents

Agents are more than just Notes macros with a new name. Lotus has added significant functionality to the agents and has made it much easier to create and modify them. Agents can be private to a database or shared by other databases; they can be scheduled to operate automatically by the hour, day, week, or month, or they can be kicked off by an event such as mail arriving or a document being modified.

You no longer need to be a Notes programmer to set up an agent. The agent can be defined by selecting from a list of predefined actions, such as modify a field, move to a folder, or send mail. You can still use the same formulas that you wrote for Notes 3.x macros or you can use the new LotusScript language to create them. Agents set to run manually can be executed using the new Action menu, and agents can have an action that starts up another agent.

The setup of agents has been smoothed thanks to the new interface called the Agent Builder, which makes liberal use of pull-down menus and dialog boxes to help you select when and on which documents the agents should act. It also uses a sophisticated dialog box to help you incorporate conditions that limit the actions of the agents, such as searching for a certain form or taking action based on a value. In most cases, you won't need to pull out the language manual to develop your agents.

Electronic Mail

Electronic mail is a cornerstone of workgroup computing, and Notes 4.0 brings a much improved interface to the Notes mail template, as shown in Figure A.8. Patterned after cc:Mail, Lotus' standalone mail product, the new mail template comes with folders for items received (Inbox), items sent (Sent), mail in progress (Drafts), deleted mail (Trash), and all items (All

Documents). Mail arrives in the Inbox, and you can drag documents from any view into any of the folders. You can also create your own folders and move documents to them as well.

When you use the standard folders such as Inbox, Notes adds a button bar below the SmartIcons to handle common mail functions including delete, forward, reply, reply with history, and move to a folder. New mail forms, such as a Phone Message and a Serial Routing form, have been added, and all the mail forms can still be customized to match the needs of your workgroup.

Please note that the mail template has changed significantly throughout the beta cycle. There is a good possibility that it will be different than the picture shown in Figure A.8.

Development Environment

Notes 4.0 has come a long way in making it easier to develop an application. A design icon is now available on the navigator screen, allowing a developer to list all the design components in a database and quickly access one to

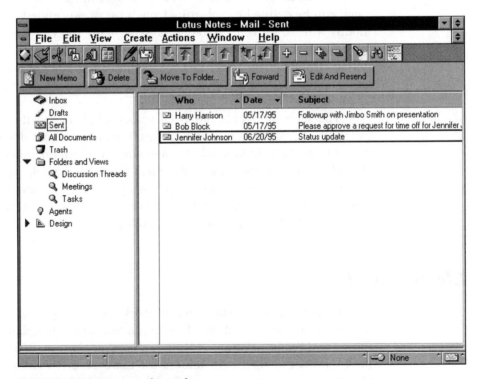

FIGURE A.8 The new mail interface.

make changes. Design screens are split so that the screen itself shows in the upper half of the window and the field definitions show at the bottom of the screen. To edit a button, for example, you simply click on the button and the bottom half of the screen displays the formulas assigned to the button.

Lotus makes liberal use of properties screens in this new development environment. Click on the right mouse button and Notes displays a small window with tabbed pages for editing all the properties of the design elements. You can quickly move between properties of the item that you are changing to the properties for the database, form, or the text of the object. Click on a tab to access properties for fonts, alignment, pagination, and those unique to the design elements being changed.

Version 4.0 also brings LotusScript to Notes. LotusScript is a programming language that closely matches Visual Basic and gives developers a lot more flexibility in developing more powerful applications in Notes. LotusScript can be used in almost all the same places the macro language was found, and it can be used to make calls to the Notes API and external DLLs.

Other Enhancements

You'll find additional enhancements in almost every area of Notes. The properties for almost all design elements have been expanded to give you greater flexibility in developing applications. Menus are better organized (in most cases), making access much easier. The best advice with Notes 4.0 is to explore all the nooks and crannies, and you'll find improvements in most every corner.

Your Training Needs

Upgrading to Notes 4.0 does mean more training—there's no way around it. The menus have changed, the views are different, and the programming environment is more powerful. It doesn't mean, however, that you have to start over. At least four classes should be offered to help users get up to speed on Notes 4.0.

An Overview of Notes 4.0

Most casual users will need only a basic class to help them learn the new interface. They should be given a chance to practice all of the new menus, experience the power of the new agents, and try out familiar applications in the new environment. Once they find that Notes 4.0 works much like Notes 3.x, they will feel better about moving forward with the upgrade.

Writing Simple Applications in Notes 4.0

This class will help the nonprofessional user develop applications using the new properties windows, agents, and LotusScript. These students typically develop small applications or custom forms to simplify their jobs and were probably active with Notes 3.x. The instructor should compare the new way that forms and views are developed with the Notes 3.x method. The students should also receive training on the best way to use the new navigators and how to write a simple LotusScript formula.

Locations and Replication in Notes 4.0

Replication and remote access to servers have been changed for the better in 4.0, and remote users need to learn how to use the new services to their advantage. Students should replicate via a single server, create several locations that match their work and travel schedules, and they create stacked icons on their desktop.

Using New Development Techniques and LotusScript to Enhance an Application

Geared toward the professional developer, this class should explore the changes in the Notes development environment and instruct students how to develop Notes applications in LotusScript. The students should be taught how to modify properties, create agents, and develop an application using LotusScript.

Upgrading Your Systems

Without a doubt, you should upgrade to Lotus Notes 4.0. It addresses many of the weaknesses in Notes 3.x, fixes a lot of the quirks that frustrated developers, and it adds new power that can only make your workgroup applications better. Besides, you'll have to upgrade to Notes 4.0 anyway as it quickly becomes the new standard. That's not to say you have to rush into an upgrade just because it's available. Notes 4.0 can read and use Notes 3.x databases, and you can get by as you migrate users to Notes 4.0. Your current applications will still work, giving users time for training and assimilating the differences.

Implementing Notes 4.0

The best way to introduce Notes 4.0 is to test it on a pilot group and then expand it quickly throughout the company. The pilot would allow your company to upgrade a server, test the compatibility of the existing applications under Notes 4.0, and determine how much work it will take to execute the conversion.

With the successful completion of the pilot, move Notes 4.0 out to the masses as quickly as possible. Schedule training in waves so that trained users are upgraded immediately after their classes, while another group is entering training. Place a hold on all new development and changes until the upgrade is complete. Turn all available support people and developers into evangelists until Notes 4.0 has a positive momentum of its own.

The task plan is simple: plan, test, train, upgrade, train, upgrade, and train some more until everyone has been converted. Unfortunately, this plan may be a little tough to sell to the bean counters, so we'll include a more detailed task plan here to assuage their concerns:

Phase I: Planning

Obtain Notes 4.0 for the server and client equipment.

Schedule Notes administrator training for the internal support staff.

Schedule developers for LotusScript training.

Identify the pilot group for the test.

Obtain or develop training classes for the pilot group.

Schedule the training classes for the pilot group.

Schedule conversion for pilot.

Phase II: Implement Pilot

Train pilot group.

Convert Notes server to Notes 4.0.

Upgrade client machines to Notes 4.0.

Schedule weekly feedback sessions throughout test period.

Phase III: Plan Company-Wide Conversion

Obtain Notes 4.0 upgrade licenses.

Modify training materials based on results of pilot projects.

Divide users into logical groups.

Schedule server upgrades.

Schedule user training sessions for each group.

Schedule user upgrades to Notes 4.0 for each group.

Schedule weekly feedback sessions throughout the implementation.

It's Done!

It will take a lot of work and a few long weekends, but the upgrade to Notes 4.0 will benefit the entire company. It may seem overwhelming during the conversion, but a rapid upgrade is less disruptive in the long run. Users will be able to get back to "normal" in a shorter period of time, and the company can concentrate on improving profits instead of absorbing technology.

B

Loading and Using the Software

A book on Notes wouldn't be complete without a CD full of databases, screencams, and software packages that show you what Notes can do. Of course, the 50 databases that were described in Chapter 9 are included on the CD, along with software supplied by Lotus Development and many other companies that work with Notes and were more than willing to supply Notes-related software. The result: a CD filled with over 170MB of information and programs.

The CD is organized so that you can simply copy its contents to your hard disk without disturbing your existing installation. Only one product, Common Ground, must be installed using a setup program supplied on the CD; all other software products have been preinstalled to eliminate some of the complexities in their installation.

The CD contains a separate Notes desktop with two user IDs that must be used when you try out the Notes databases. It also contains a copy of SmartSwitcher, the Lotus freeware program that allows you to store setup parameters for several users and launch Notes using them. In this way, you can launch Notes as one of the two sample users without affecting your "live" Notes settings.

The information in this appendix assumes that you have already installed Lotus Notes on your local hard drive and that all of the files from the CD will reside on the C: drive. *It is very important that you copy the files to a C: drive and that you do not change the directory structures as shown on the CD because all of the databases and demos are set up to use those structures!* Of course, once you have viewed the databases and understand how they work, you can adjust their locations to match your needs.

Both the installation and operation of the sample software have been tested to ensure that you will be able to use the contents of the CD. However, it is impossible to test for every possible configuration of Notes and Windows, and, unfortunately, no technical support is available if you do have a problem. If you have a problem with a product that sparks your interest, contact the vendor to determine if there is a dealer in your area who can also demonstrate the product or if you can obtain the demonstration software via a bulletin board, Notes, or the Internet.

The demonstration also requires that you load several files in your Windows and Windows Systems directories. In some cases, these files may overwrite versions of the same files that you may have loaded for other software; therefore, be sure to create a backup of your hard drive before copying the demonstration software to it. Should one of the files from the CD cause an application to fail, you can simply restore the previous version from your backup.

More about the CD

The CD contains three folders, Catalog, Dynamics, and Notesbk, as shown in Figure B.1. The Catalog directory holds an application developed by John Wiley & Sons as a complete catalog of Wiley book titles. The Dynamics folder holds a completely functional copy of the Great Plains Dynamics Accounting Software. The Notesbk directory contains the software listed in Table B.1.

Copying the Contents of the CD to Your Hard Drive

To move the contents of the CD to your hard drive, use one of the following methods. In the examples, I assume that your CD drive is D:, that your Windows directory is called \WINDOWS, and your Notes directory is called \NOTES.

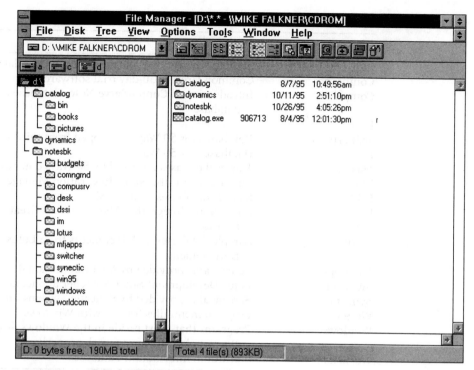

FIGURE B.1 Directory structure for the CD.

Using DOS

1. Move all folders to the C: drive by typing at the C: prompt:

```
XCOPY D:\Dynamics\*.* C:\/S/E
XCOPY D:\Notesbk\*.* C:\/S/E
```

2. Files copied from a CD are flagged by DOS as read-only, so you must use the ATTRIB utility to clear the read-only flag. Type:

```
ATTRIB -R C:\Dynamics\*.* /S
```

When the process is complete, type:

```
ATTRIB -R C:\Notesbk\*.* /S
```

3. Move the contents of the \Notesbk\Windows folder to the Windows directory by typing:

```
XCOPY C:\Notesbk\Windows\*.* C:\Windows /S
```

4. For Windows 95 users, move the contents of the \Notesbk\Win95 directory to the Windows directory by typing:

```
XCOPY C:\Notesbk\Win95\*.* C:\Windows\Start Menu\Programs /S
```

TABLE B.1 Notesbk Contents

Directory	Description
Budgets	Sample budgets used for the Notes Budget database
Comngrnd	Common Ground 30-day trial software
Compusrv	Introduction to CompuServe Notes database and WALNUT database
Desk	
3rdParty	Databases for 50 Ways developed from third-party templates
Detail	Databases for 50 Ways
Master	Master databases accessed by 50 Ways databases
Win	SmartIcons for the Notes Integration Manager
DSSI	Sample databases from DSSI
IM	Lotus Notes Integration Manager from Great Plains Software
Lotus	Sample databases and documents from Lotus Development
MFJApps	Screencams provided by MFJ International
Switcher	Lotus Development SmartSwitcher application
Synectic	Screencams provided by Synectic Systems Ltd.
Win95	Program menu files for use with Windows 95
Windows	Programs that must reside in the Windows directory for the sample software to work properly
Worldcom	WorldCom information database

Using the Windows File Manager

1. Display two windows in the File Manager, one showing the C: drive and one showing the CD (D:).
2. Select both the Dynamics and Notesbk folders in the window representing the CD, and drag them onto the folder that represents the C: drive.
3. Files copied from a CD are flagged by DOS as read-only so you must use the **ATTRIB** utility to clear the read-only flag. Select the File menu and select RUN. Type:

```
ATTRIB -R C:\Dynamics\*.* /S
```

   When the process is complete, select the File menu and select RUN. Type:

```
ATTRIB -R C:\Notesbk\*.* /S
```

4. Open the Notesbk folder on the C: drive and open the Windows folder.
5. Drag the contents of the Windows folder (including the System folder) onto the folder representing the Windows directory on the C: drive.

Using the Windows 95 Desktop

1. Open the icon that represents your computer (often called My Computer).
2. From the Start menu, select Programs, Windows Explorer.
3. In the Explorer, display the contents of the CD drive.
4. Select both the Dynamics and the Notesbk folders from the Explorer window and drag them onto the icon in the My Computer window that represents the C: drive.
5. Files copied from a CD are flagged as read-only so you must use the **ATTRIB** utility to clear the read-only flag. From the Start menu, select Programs, MS-DOS prompt. Type:

   ```
   ATTRIB -R C:\Dynamics\*.* /S
   ```

   When the process is complete, type:

   ```
   ATTRIB -R C:\Notesbk\*.* /S
   ```

   Exit the DOS prompt by typing EXIT.
6. In the My Computer window, open the icon that represents the C: drive to display the folder that represents the Windows 95 directory.
7. In the Explorer, open the Notesbk folder in the C: drive, then open the Windows folder.
8. From the Explorer menu, select View, Options, Show all files, and click OK.
9. Drag the contents of the Windows folder shown in the Explorer window into the folder representing the Windows 95 directory shown in the My Computer window.
10. In the Explorer window, open the Notesbk folder in the C: drive and open the Win95 folder.
11. In the My Computer Window, open the folder representing the Windows 95 files and open the Start Menu folder to display the Programs folder.
12. Drag the contents of the Notesbk folder shown under the Win95 folder in the Explorer window into the Programs folder shown in the My Computer window.

Installing the Windows Program Group or Windows 95 Menu

To help you more easily access the software on the CD, I have included a Program Group file (NOTESBK.GRP) in the \Notesbk\Windows directory for Windows 3.1 users (see Figure B.2), and a program menu directory with shortcuts in the \Notesbk\Win95 directory (Notes Book) for Windows 95 users (see Figure B.3). In both cases, the icons and shortcuts point to the software listed here.

Lotus Notes via Smart Switcher

Command Line:	C:\Notesbk\Switcher\SSWITCH.EXE
	C:\Notesbk\Switcher\SSWITCH.INI
Working Directory:	C:\Notesbk\Switcher

Install Common Ground

Command Line:	C:\Notesbk\Comngrnd\Cginstal\Disk1\SETUP.EXE
Working Directory:	C:\Notesbk\Comngrnd\Cginstal\Disk1

Install Win32S

Command Line:	C:\Dynamics\Win32s\Disk1\SETUP.EXE
Working Directory:	C:\Dynamics\Win32s\Disk1

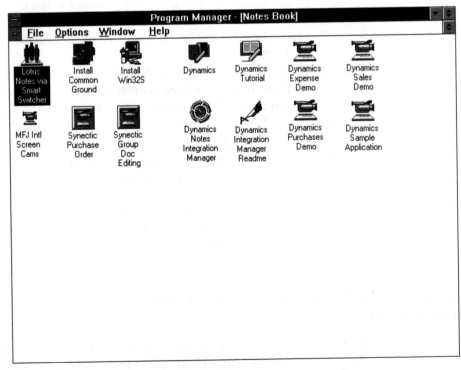

FIGURE B.2 Program group for CD software.

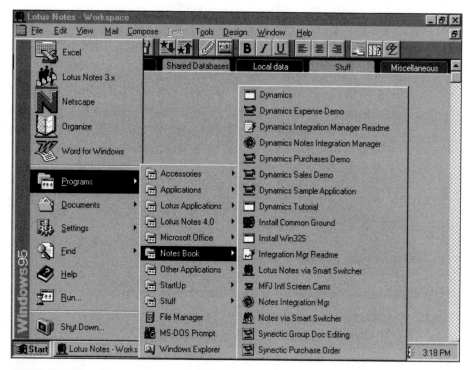

FIGURE B.3 Windows 95 program menu.

MFJ International Screen Cams

Command Line: C:\Notesbk\Mfjapps\SCRNMAN.EXE
Working Directory: C:\Notesbk\Mfjapps

Synectic Systems Ltd Purchase Order

Command Line: C:\Notesbk\Synectic\SSLPO-A1.EXE
Working Directory: C:\Notesbk\Synectic

Synectic Systems Ltd Group Doc Editing

Command Line: C:\Notesbk\Synectic\SSL-EL.EXE
Working Directory: C:\Notesbk\Synectic

Dynamics

Command Line: C:\Dynamics\DYNAMICS.EXE C:\Dynamics\
                     NOTEDEMO.SET
Working Directory: C:\Dynamics

Dynamics Tutorial

Command Line: C:\Dynamics\DYNAMICS.EXE C:\Dynamics\TUTO-RIAL.SET

Working Directory: C:\Dynamics

Dynamics Expense Demo

Command Line: C:\Notesbk\lm\Scr_cams\EXPENSE.EXE

Working Directory: C:\Notesbk\lm\Scr_cams

Dynamics Sales Demo

Command Line: C:\Notesbk\lm\Scr_cams\SALES.EXE

Working Directory: C:\Notesbk\lm\Scr_cams

Dynamics Notes Integration Manager

Command Line: C:\Notesbk\lm\DIMGR.EXE

Working Directory: C:\Notesbk\lm

Dynamics Integration Manager Readme

Command Line: WRITE.EXE C:\Notesbk\lm\README.WRI

Dynamics Purchases Demo

Command Line: C:\Notesbk\lm\Scr_cams\PURCHASE.EXE

Working Directory: C:\Notesbk\lm\Scr_cams

Dynamics Sample Application

Command Line: C:\Notesbk\lm\Scr_cams\SAMPLE.EXE

Working Directory: C:\Notesbk\lm\Scr_cams

To install the Windows 3.11 group file:

1. Display the Program Manager on the screen.
2. Select File, New, Program Group.
3. Enter Notes Book for the description.
4. Enter C:\Windows\NOTESBK.GRP for the group file.
5. Select OK to create the group.

Windows 95 users will find the Notes Book applications listed as part of the programs listed when they select the Start button and choose Programs. An entry called Notes Book will be displayed in the list of programs. Select it and Windows 95 will display a list of the applications that were copied from the CD.

Using Lotus SmartSwitcher

Lotus Development created SmartSwitcher to assist Notes users who must maintain multiple configurations for their Notes settings. When executed via the program icon or program menu choice, SmartSwitcher displays two IDs, Jennifer Johnson and Harry Harrison. Select the ID that you'd like to use and then select OK to continue. SmartSwitcher will load Lotus Notes using the IDs and the desktop provided on the CD. To change your Notes directory or file locations, press the Move button and SmartSwitcher will display a screen where you can make changes (see Figure B.4).

Using the Sample Notes Desktop

The Notes desktop provided on the CD uses tabs to organize its many databases. The first three tabs hold the icons that represent the 50 databases discussed in Chapter 9. The 3rd Party tab holds the icons that point to the databases provided by CompuServe, WorldCom, Common Ground, Great Plains, DSSI, Synectic, and WALNUT. The tab labeled Master represents

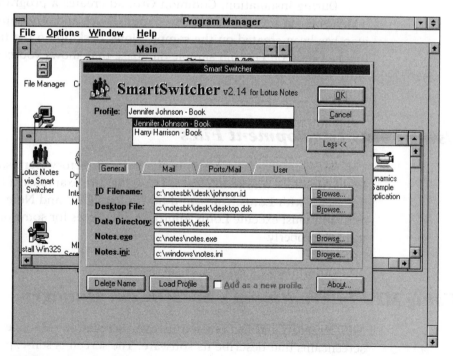

FIGURE B.4　Lotus SmartSwitcher.

master databases, name and address book, and other databases used by the "50 Ways" databases in the other tabs. The Lotus tab contains databases provided by the Approach team that demonstrates the integration of Approach and Lotus Notes. Simply double-click on an icon to open the Notes database. If you encounter a request for a password, use NOTES.

Installing and Using Common Ground

The 30-day trial copy of Common Ground must be installed before you can test the application. It also comes with a deinstaller so that you can remove it from your drive after you have tested it. To install Common Ground, use the Install Common Ground icon from the program group or program menu that you just installed; or you can move directly to the Setup program in the \Notesbk\Comngrnd\Cginstal\Disk1 folder.

In rare instances, the Common Ground trial software may become corrupted during installation and generate a General Protection Fault when executed. To remedy the situation, delete the CGMAKER.DRV file from your \Windows\System directory, use the Common Ground Deinstaller to remove the software, and then reinstall it.

During installation, Common Ground creates a program group from which you can access its full viewer, miniviewer, and other applications. An icon has been created on the sample Notes desktop on the third-party tab for the Common Ground sample database that shows you how it interacts with Notes.

Using Lotus Development Files

The Notes databases and files in the Lotus directory were supplied by the Lotus Approach marketing team. These files are examples of how Approach integrates with Lotus Notes, and how it uses OLE and Notes/FX technologies. You must execute Lotus Approach and Notes for some of the examples to work properly.

Using MFJ International's ScreenCam Manager

MFJ International has created its own ScreenCam Manager for all of the screencams that describe its software. The screen is self-explanatory. However, at the time the demos were provided, no screencams were provided for the first item listed on the opening screen (Introduction to OverQuota) or for the last item (Interprise OverQuota). Selecting these items will exit the program.

Using the Synectic Systems Ltd. ScreenCams

The screencams from Synectic Systems Ltd. require no installation or special instructions. More information about Synectic is contained in a database called About Synectic shown on the third-party tab on the sample Notes desktop supplied with the CD.

Installing and Using Great Plains Dynamics

Great Plains Dynamics version 2.10 has already been installed for you on the CD. However, since Dynamics is a 32-bit application, you must install Win32s if you are using Windows 3.11. Dynamics will work without Win32s if you are using Windows 95 or if you have already installed Win32s as a part of the Common Ground installation. By the time this book is published, Great Plains will have released version 2.11. This new version clears up some minor problems that users experienced with Windows 95. However, if you have Windows 95, version 2.10 of Dynamics on the CD will operate properly in most cases.

To install Win32s, use the Install Win32s icon from the program group or program menu that you just installed; or move directly to the Setup program in the \Dynamics\Win32S\Disk1 folder. Launch Dynamics using the Dynamics icon in the program group or program menu. It will display an opening screen that allows you to select a user. Select Lesson User 1 and click on the OK button. You can now use Dynamics with the sample data provided. I suggest that you first go through the Dynamics Tutorial before using Dynamics to familiarize yourself with its operation. If you encounter a request for a password, use ACCESS.

Using the Dynamics Notes Integration Manager

The Dynamics Notes Integration Manager moves information between Notes and Dynamics. Three components must be loaded in the following order for the integration to work properly: Dynamics first, the Integration Manager next, and Lotus Notes last. Dynamics and Notes will use as much memory as they can find, and therefore, machines with minimum memory configurations may run out of memory.

The Integration Manager also ships with an example of an expense form that integrates Notes, Dynamics, and Lotus 1-2-3 for Windows. To execute this example, load the three components as stated in the previous paragraph and then load 1-2-3 for Windows. Again, the loading of these packages may use up all of your memory and result in an out-of-memory condition. Experiment with loading the components in a different order if the condition persists.

Instructions for executing the demonstrations of the Integration Manager are included in a Notes database provided on the CD. An icon has been created on the sample Notes desktop (Dynamics Integration Demo Information) on the third-party tab to help you display the instructions.

Using the DSSI Databases

The DSSI sample databases were generated using the tools that they sell. More information about DSSI is contained in a database called About DSSI shown on the third-party tab on the sample Notes desktop supplied with the CD.

About the Contributors

It wasn't difficult to convince this book's contributors to send software for the accompanying CD. These companies are stalwart supporters of Lotus Notes and are anxious to see the market expand. Of course, as you become a regular user of Notes, they hope that these demos and screencams will influence you to consider their software for your organization. I found the representatives of each of these companies to be courteous and willing to help me with any problems that I encountered. I sincerely hope that you do consider them as potential vendors. Here's a little more information about them.

Common Ground Software

Formerly called No Hands Software, Common Ground Software is a pioneer in the development of software that creates fully formatted electronic documents that can be viewed without requiring the presence of the originating application. This technology enables Notes users to more easily mail and publish documents in a cross-platform workgroup environment. Common

Ground also incorporates document annotation, text searches, and document security with its software to make the product an even more valuable workgroup tool.

CompuServe Inc.

CompuServe Inc. has enabled Notes users to open up their databases to a larger audience than ever before. Instead of buying dedicated servers, Notes users can place their databases on the CompuServe network of Notes servers, allowing anyone within reach of a CompuServe connection to tap into the information. Companies can now reach thousands of vendors, customers, and potential customers without the huge investment required to purchase and support Notes servers.

CompuServe also provides a wealth of information services for the Notes user. These services bring together information from many Usenet forums and Internet Mailing Lists and publish them in Notes databases. You can take advantage of news services such as Comtex and Computergram International and browse information gathered from existing CompuServe forums and placed into Notes.

Distributed Systems Solutions, Inc.

Distributed Systems Solutions, Inc. (DSSI) is a Beacon award-winning developer of Notes management tools. DSSI also provides a wide range of Notes integration services, including software and training development and software implementation services. The DSSI tools help Notes administrators access control lists, manage design changes, replication logs, database usage, and a number of mail events such as vacations and timed events.

Great Plains Software

Great Plains Software is a leader in the development of multiuser accounting software for the DOS and Windows market. Dynamics, its flagship Windows product, is a full-featured, 32-bit application that operates on both PC and Macintosh platforms communicating to database servers running the Netware, Windows NT, and Unix operating systems. The product supports the Btrieve and Faircom database managers, with Microsoft SQL Server 6.0 support due to arrive early in 1996.

In creating the Beacon award-winning Dynamics Notes Integration Manager, Great Plains enabled Notes developers to automate the workgroup-intensive processes that surround accounting transactions and to integrate them into the Dynamics software. Used in conjunction with Dexterity, the Great Plains fourth G/L tool used to create and modify Dynamics, developers can move information between Notes and Dynamics and initiate activities in either product based on actions taken in both.

Lotus Development

After reading a few thousand words about Lotus Development, you probably don't need to know much more about them. But be aware that the databases provided by the Approach team are just a few of the many samples and helpful tools available from Lotus to help you make better use of Notes. For more information on Lotus, contact its Web site on the Internet or the Lotus Solution Provider in your area.

MFJ International

MFJ International is a Beacon award-winning information technology consulting firm with a long-standing presence in the Notes community. MFJ provides its clientele one-stop shopping for complete business solutions and offers its consulting services while working with hardware solution providers to develop an appropriate and complete Notes solution. MFJ also offers training and technical support after the sale.

The OverQuota Notes application demonstrated in the screencams is a sophisticated sales tool for managing the entire sales process. Salespeople can load and track leads, manage accounts, and query a knowledgebase of questions answered for prior sales activities. They can log activities against an account, and their managers can call up the sales "pipeline" to review the probability of sales occurring and to determine the value of pending sales. The sales team can use the Team Talk database to track discussions and the Market encyclopedia to store presentations, marketing materials, and other sales tools.

Synectic Systems Ltd.

Synectic Systems Ltd. is a systems integrator and software developer with a long history of active involvement with Lotus Notes. Synectic offers consulting services that cover the complete spectrum of a Notes installation from planning to follow-up support. As an offshoot of its development activities, Synectic has designed a wide range of development tools for end users, including an Applications Architecture and Development Methodology, Application Development Kits to help fledgling Notes development teams, and an Enterprise Development Kit that offers tools, software libraries, and applications to help build an internal Notes development team.

The Synectic Group Editing screencam demonstrates an application that supports the typical document editing process by a workgroup. The database is ideal for document-intensive departments such as developers of proposals who track document status, edit dates, editor comments, and disclosure information. The Purchase Order screencam demonstrates a sophisticated purchase requisition database that ultimately integrates with the Great Plains Dynamics accounting software using the Dynamics Notes Integration Manager. The product also shows how the integration takes place with Dynamics simply in the background.

Wolf Communications

Wolf Communications was the first company to offer global communications services that matched the needs of Notes users. Its service, called WorldCom, offers access points to its services throughout the world and will help you connect your users and servers through its network. WorldCom also offers electronic mail gateways to 100 electronic mail systems; access to news services and public discussions; integration with the Internet for electronic mail; Internet mailing lists and Usenet newsgroups; and services to help you create a Web presence from a Notes database.

I N D E X

Page references followed by lowercase Roman i represent illustrations. Page references followed by lowercase Roman t represent tables. Software titles are indexed **without** associated manufacturer. Thus Lotus Notes is indexed simply as Notes, Microsoft Exchange simply as Exchange, etc.

◆ *Notes* ◆

WILEY

Publishers Since 1807